DATE DUE

COMPENSATING FOR PSYCHOLOGICAL DEFICITS AND DECLINES

Managing Losses and Promoting Gains

COMPENSATING FOR PSYCHOLOGICAL DEFICITS AND DECLINES

Managing Losses and Promoting Gains

Edited by

ROGER A. DIXON
University of Victoria

LARS BÄCKMAN
University of Gothenburg and
Stockholm Gerontology Research Center

 LAWRENCE ERLBAUM ASSOCIATES, PUBLISHERS
1995   Mahwah, New Jersey

Lawrence Erlbaum Associates, Inc., Publishers
10 Industrial Avenue
Mahwah, New Jersey 07430

Library of Congress Cataloging-in-Publication Data

Compensating for psychological deficits and declines : managing
    losses and promoting gains / edited by Roger A. Dixon, Lars Bäckman.
        p.   cm.
    Includes bibliographical references and indexes.
    ISBN 0-8058-1559-7 (alk. paper)
    1. Compensation (Psychology). 2. Adjustment (Psychology).
    I. Dixon, Roger A., 1952–   . II. Bäckman, Lars.
    BF337.C65C66 1995
    155.2′4—dc20   95-15780
                                                      CIP

Books published by Lawrence Erlbaum Associates are printed on acid-free
paper, and their bindings are chosen for strength and durability.

Printed in the United States of America
10 9 8 7 6 5 4 3 2 1

Contents

Contributors

(Chapter numbers in parentheses.)

(1) **Lars Bäckman**
     Department of Psychology
     University of Gothenburg
     Haraldsgatan 1
     S-413 14 Gothenburg
     Sweden

     and

     Stockholm Gerontology Research Center
     Karolinska Institute
     Dalagatan 9-11
     S-113 82 Stockholm
     Sweden

(3) **Margret M. Baltes**
     Research Unit for Psychological Gerontology
     Department of Gerontopsychiatry
     Free University of Berlin
     Ulmenallee 32
     14050 Berlin
     Germany

(3) **Paul B. Baltes**
     Center for Psychology and Human Development
     Max Planck Institute for Human Development and Education
     Lentzeallee 94
     14195 Berlin
     Germany

(7) **Elizabeth A. Bosman**
Centre for Studies of Aging
University of Toronto
455 Spadina Ave., Suite 305
Toronto, ON M5S 2G8
Canada

(4) **Jochen Brandtstädter**
Department of Psychology
Trier University
Postfach 3825
D-5500 Trier
Germany

(5) **Laura L. Carstensen**
Department of Psychology
Stanford University
Stanford, CA 94305

(7) **Neil Charness**
Department of Psychology
Florida State University
Tallahassee, FL 32306-1051

(13) **Anne E. Cunningham**
Educational Psychology
College of Education
University of Washington
Seattle, WA 98195

(1) **Roger A. Dixon**
Department of Psychology
University of Victoria
Victoria, BC V8W 3P5
Canada

(6) **Melissa M. Farmer**
Department of Sociology
Purdue University
1365 Stone Hall
West Lafayette, IN 47907-1365

(6) **Kenneth F. Ferraro**
Department of Sociology
Purdue University
1365 Stone Hall
West Lafayette, IN 47907-1365

(5) **Alexandra M. Freund**
Department of Psychology
Stanford University
Stanford, CA 94305

(11) **Cheryl L. Grady**
Laboratory of Neuroscience
NIA/LNS, Bldg. 10, Room 6C414
9000 Rockville Pike
Bethesda, MD 20892

(9) **Catherine Hanson**
Department of Psychology
Temple University
Philadelphia, PA 19122

(5) **Kaaren A. Hanson**
Department of Psychology
Stanford University
Stanford, CA 94305

(14) **Albert Kozma**
Gerontology Center and Department of Psychology
Memorial University of Newfoundland
St. John's, Newfoundland A1B 3X9
Canada

(3) **Frieder R. Lang**
Research Unit for Psychological Gerontology
Department of Gerontopsychiatry
Free University of Berlin
Ulmenallee 32
14050 Berlin
Germany

(3) **Michael Marsiske**
Center for Psychology and Human Development
Max Planck Institute for Human Development and Education
Lentzeallee 94
14195 Berlin
Germany

(11) **Raja Parasuraman**
Department of Psychology
Cognitive Science Laboratory
Catholic University of America
Washington, DC 20064

(12) **Jerker Rönnberg**
Department of Education and Psychology
Linköping University
S-581 83 Linköping
Sweden

(10) **Leslie J. Gonzalez Rothi**
Department of Neurology
College of Medicine
University of Florida
Box J236
Gainesville, FL 32610

(2) **Timothy A. Salthouse**
School of Psychology
Georgia Institute of Technology
Altanta, GA 30332

(13) **Keith E. Stanovich**
Department of Applied Psychology
Ontario Institute for Studies in Education
252 Bloor St. West
Toronto, ON M5S 1V6
Canada

(14) **M. J. Stones**
Department of Health Studies and Gerontology
University of Waterloo
Waterloo, ON N2L 3G1
Canada

(4) **Dirk Wentura**
Department of Psychology
Trier University
Postfach 3825
D-5500 Trier
Germany

(13) **Richard F. West**
Department of Psychology
James Madison University
Harrisonburg, VA 22807

(8) **Barbara A. Wilson**
Medical Research Council
Applied Psychology Unit
15 Chaucer Rd.
Cambridge CB2 2EF
England

(9) **Diana S. Woodruff-Pak**
Department of Psychology
Temple University
Philadelphia, PA 19122

and

Laboratory of Cognitive Neuroscience
Philadelphia Geriatric Center
Philadelphia, PA 19141

Preface

The concept of *compensation* in psychology refers to processes through which a gap or mismatch between currently accessible skills and environmental demands is reduced or closed. These gaps can be principally the result of: (a) losses, such as those associated with aging or interpersonal role changes; (b) injuries, such as those that may occur to the neurological or sensory systems; (c) organic or functional diseases, such as the dementias or schizophrenia; and (d) congenital deficits, such as those apparent in autism or some learning disabilities. Whether the demand–skill gaps can be bridged completely, reduced only moderately, or are impossible to close, depends on a variety of factors. In every case, however, the guiding notions of compensation are that: (a) some such deficits may be amendable, (b) the continuation of the gap's effects may be avoidable, and (c) some functioning may be recoverable. In this sense, compensation is related to adaptation—it is about overcoming deficits, managing the effects of losses, and promoting improvement in psychological functioning.

Compensation is a concept that has a long and rich history in numerous domains of psychological research and practice. Remarkably, there are literally hundreds of published scholarly works employing notions of psychological compensation. To date, however, few of the relevant research domains have benefited explicitly or optimally from considering alternative perspectives on the concept of compensation. Although researchers and practitioners in several areas of psychology have actively pursued programs with compensation as a central concept, communication across disciplinary divides has been lacking. Comparing and contrasting the uses and implications of the concept across neighboring (and even not-so-adjacent) areas of psychology can promote advances in both theoretical and practical pursuits.

The goal of this book is to carry inchoate integrative efforts to a new level of clarity. To this end, we have recruited major authors from selected principal areas of research and practice in psychological compensation. We invited the authors to review the current state of compensation scholarship in their domains of specialization. State-of-the-art reviews of this rapidly expanding area of scholarship are, therefore, collected under one cover for the first time. In this way, a wide variety of readers—who might otherwise rarely cross professional paths with one another—can quickly learn about alternative preferences, agendas, and methods, as well as novel research results, interpretations, and practical applications.

This volume is designed to contain broad, deep, and current perspectives on compensation. However, we did not expect to uncover a single unifying and "pure" definition of *compensation*—a crystalline concept at the heart of all uses of the term in psychology, one that is unequivocally embraced or applied to all programs of research and practice. Instead, and arguably more important, this volume continues the processes of: (a) explicating the concept of compensation, (b) linking and distinguishing compensation from neighboring concepts, (c) describing the variety of compensatory mechanisms operating in a wide range of phenomena, and (d) illustrating how compensatory mechanisms can be harnessed or trained to manage losses or deficits and to promote gains or at least maintenance of functioning.

We owe a special gratitude to the chapter authors, each of whom accomplished his or her challenging review tasks admirably and efficiently. Several individuals helped us perform a variety of editorial duties: We thank especially Debra Hultsch, Oliver Jost, Maggie Knowlan, and David Meers. We would like to acknowledge the assistance of grants from the Natural Sciences and Engineering Research Council of Canada and the Canadian Aging Research Network (to editor R.D.), and from the Swedish Council for Research in the Humanities and the Social Sciences and the Swedish Council for Social Research (to editor L.B.). We would like to thank our spouses, Nancy Galambos and Agneta Herlitz, for the always crucial support they provide during extended commitments such as that involved in producing this book. Finally, we dedicate this book to our children, Gillian Dixon, Daniel Bäckman, Hannes Bäckman, and Elias Bäckman: May they easily compensate for any deficits or losses, especially those attributable to us.

—Roger Dixon
Lars Bäckman

COMPENSATING FOR PSYCHOLOGICAL DEFICITS AND DECLINES

Managing Losses and Promoting Gains

PART ONE

CONCEPTUAL ISSUES IN PSYCHOLOGICAL COMPENSATION

CHAPTER ONE

Concepts of Compensation: Integrated, Differentiated, and Janus-Faced

Roger A. Dixon
University of Victoria

Lars Bäckman
*University of Gothenburg and
Stockholm Gerontology Research Center*

Although the concept of *compensation* is an important and growing concern in numerous literatures in psychology, relatively few efforts have been made to explore the variety of definitions and uses of the term. Still fewer attempts have been aimed at differentiating or integrating the meanings of compensation appearing in these literatures. In this chapter, we explore questions such as the following: What degree of commonality exists in definitions and uses of compensation across literatures in psychology? Is there a core concept of compensation—are there even core features to a single concept—or is the concept, like so many in psychology, composed of fuzzy boundaries and fluid (but detectable) features? Is one universal feature of the concept its apparent Janus-like quality—of having immediate relevance to both psychological theory and practice? The concept of compensation in psychology, the possibility of multiple concepts of compensation, and the degree to which we can learn about the concept through consulting neighboring disciplines are the concerns at the heart of this chapter and this book.

VIEWS OF COMPENSATION

What is psychological compensation, and what do we know about it? Compensation has been referred to poetically as a "sublime law" of life, as a means of restoring balance: "Every excess causes a defect; every defect an excess. . . . For everything you have missed, you have gained something

3

else; and for everything you gain, you lose something" (Emerson, 1900, p. 85). With some differences in meaning, the term *compensation* has appeared in a variety of psychological and nonpsychological literatures, and even predating psychology (e.g., Brandtstädter & Wentura, chap. 4, this volume). In psychology, compensation has been operationally referred to as a behavior or action, the goal of which is "to make amends for some lack or loss in personal characteristics or status" (English & English, 1958, p. 101). As much as 40 years ago, it was believed that compensatory behavior could take any one of several different forms. For example, the mechanism for restoring balance or achieving satisfaction can include employing different (substitutable) activities, increasing the effort expended at achieving the original goal, modifying the degree to which the original goal is valued, and, perhaps, pursuing alternatives (English & English, 1958). Today, both the principle of compensation—overcoming an imbalance or deficit—and the range of mechanisms for achieving balance or satisfaction are cornerstones of a growing number of areas in psychology. In becoming more generally recognized and relevant in psychology, the concept of *compensation* may have become more adapted to particular domains, and perhaps more differentiated and specific.

Within particular literatures, especially, we know a great deal about compensatory mechanisms, and the chapters in this volume give explicit testimony to this. We know how it works or might work in some domains, and we know how it does not work in these and others. We know that it is one of those unique processes that has almost immediate contact with the two faces of psychology. For want of better terms, we refer to these two faces as *theoretical* and *practical.* In many literatures in psychology, compensation reaches deeply into fundamental theoretical concerns, and yet it always rapidly returns with practical implications for human lives. In theoretical aspects of psychology, compensation is sometimes associated with reversibility or plasticity—the extent and means through which acquired losses, normal declines, or congenital deficits may be less permanent, less debilitating, less global, more recoverable, and more reversible than might otherwise be indicated. In a wide variety of literatures, the issue of whether and how a decrement or deficit can be reversed or overcome has important theoretical implications. In the applied psychologies, research on compensatory processes can lead to the development and evaluation of effective means of managing losses, overcoming deficits, or even promoting gains. It can lead to knowledge of the possibilities for successful adjustment to a variety of challenges, and to programs and regimens designed to close the gap between the demands of the environment and the skills of the individual. More specific theoretical and practical implications are increasingly well articulated in the relevant literatures of psychology. The chapters in this book present the most recent information available.

SOME FOCI OF COMPENSATION RESEARCH

In fact, many, if not most, of the principal literatures with active interest in the concept of *compensation*—whether theoretical, practical, or both—are represented in this book. Conceptual issues of this evolving concept are discussed in this chapter, as well as chapters by Timothy A. Salthouse (chap. 2, this volume) and Michael Marsiske, Frieder R. Lang, Paul B. Baltes, and Margret M. Baltes (chap. 3, this volume). A variety of compensatory mechanisms employed by adults faced with challenges—such as planning the life course, shifting cultural expectations, and personal role changes or losses—are examined by Jochen Brandtstädter and Dirk Wentura (chap. 4, this volume), Laura L. Carstensen, Kaaren A. Hanson, and Alexandra M. Freund (chap. 5, this volume), and Kenneth F. Ferraro and Melissa M. Farmer (chap. 6, this volume). Compensation is linked to the promotion of successful life-span human development in the earlier chapter by Marsiske et al. (chap. 3). Compensating for decrements or deficits through psychological mechanisms is obviously quite important, but in chapter 7, Neil Charness and Elizabeth A. Bosman focus on compensation through modifying the environment.

Neurological changes—whether the result of aging, disease, or injury—may result in impairments for which compensation is possible. Clinical and neuropsychological research and practice have led to considerable advances in understanding memory rehabilitation (Barbara A. Wilson, chap. 8, this volume), biological compensation in Alzheimer's disease (Cheryl L. Grady and Raja Parasuraman, chap. 11, this volume), and compensation in language disorders (Leslie J. Gonzalez Rothi, chap. 10, this volume). Compensation as it relates to plasticity in the aging brain is addressed by Diana S. Woodruff-Pak and Catherine Hanson (chap. 9, this volume). In addition to the neurological system, other specific performance domains have been explored for compensation. Regarding cognitive skills, Richard F. West, Keith E. Stanovich, and Anne E. Cunningham (chap. 13, this volume) describe their program of research on compensation for reading deficits, and Timothy A. Salthouse (chap. 2, this volume) offers examples of his work on compensation in cognitive aging. The possibility of compensation in the sensory realm (for vision and hearing losses) is examined by Jerker Rönnberg (chap. 12, this volume). Examining exceptional athletic achievement and, especially, the challenges facing aging athletes, M. J. Stones and Albert Kozma (chap. 14, this volume) focus on an important frontier of compensation research.

In an earlier review (Bäckman & Dixon, 1992), we began a process of analyzing the concept of *compensation* in some of the previously cited (and several other) literatures. Although some literatures on psychological compensation could be dated as early as the 1920s and 1930s, most literatures seem to have emerged with some force in the 1960s and 1970s. Examples of the earlier literatures include the notion that a loss in one sensory system was balanced by a gain in sensitivity in another (e.g., Hayes, 1933) and

Adler's (1920/1927) initial view of compensation in personality as a crucial defense mechanism. Although the evidence for such early views is mixed, the use of the concept of *compensation* has spread in the intervening years.

Our analysis led us to offer a working definition and theory of *compensation* that cut across the main trends in these literatures. In our definition, *compensation* was presented as a process of overcoming losses or deficits through one of several recognizable mechanisms. These compensatory mechanisms included: (a) investing more time and effort in performing a task reflective of a loss or decline; (b) substituting a latent skill for a declining one; (c) developing a new skill to take over the performance of an absent, lost, or declining skill; (d) altering one's goals and expectations to be more concordant with the demands of the niche in which they are operating; or (e) selecting alternative niches or alternative goals (Bäckman & Dixon, 1992). One purpose of our analysis was to provoke integrative activities within and across psychological disciplines, such that innovative basic research and comprehensive intervention and evaluation practices could be promoted. It became clear to us as we reviewed the extensive literatures accumulating in many areas of psychological research that little cross-fertilization had occurred. Although the actual concept(s) of compensation in each of the areas shared a great deal, the pattern of referencing suggested neither a common origin to the concepts of compensation present in the literatures nor an immediate prospect for effective integration.

GOALS OF THE CHAPTER

Although the purpose of this book is to carry the integrative efforts of our earlier article much further—through the invaluable contributions of eminent scholars—the goals of the present chapter are more modest. We introduce the concept of psychological compensation in its broadest sense, foreshadowing its appearance, usually in more specific senses, in each of the following chapters. Of course we have our own perspective on the contours and details of the concept, and we describe the evolution of our perspective and its current state in the next section. Afterward, we briefly compare the concept(s) of compensation as represented in several chapters in this book. We hope to provide guidance both to the reader interested in the esoteria of conceptual issues in compensation and to the reader seeking further understanding of how psychological compensation occurs for a set of common life challenges, aging decrements, or physical deficits.

STRUCTURING THE CONCEPT OF COMPENSATION

We begin by briefly mentioning a fundamental issue in science with immediate repercussions for our discussion of compensation. The issue is where the definition of a scientific concept should be located on a continuum from a precise set of pure, explicit, and exclusive criteria, to a multifarious sense in which a range of meanings and uses of the concept are valued and incorporated. Should compensation theories be held to the criteria that the principal concept be unarguably specific, crystalline, and unwavering? Should the boundaries between compensation and neighboring concepts be firmly delineated and impenetrable? Overall, is the scientific value of a concept lessened proportionally to the degree it does not meet such strict and rigid standards? Although we embrace the goal of moving toward clarity of the concept of compensation—and we hope our work contributes to this end—we argue that the analysis and evaluation of this concept should be flavored with its actual use by psychologists, whether working in the armchair, lab, or field.

This position may imply that such concepts will be defined more functionally, and less unanimously, and have relatively fuzzy or overlapping boundaries. It may also imply that it is possible—in the life history of a concept—to too hastily foreclose its opportunities for change, or to too rigidly circumscribe its malleability. Without engaging in an immense digression into philosophy of science, we note only that we take some support for our approach by linking it with the views of the later Wittgenstein (1958; see also Toulmin, 1972), who maintained that relatively fuzzy or blurred concepts were, in fact, normal in philosophy and science, and no less a concept than those with specific and well-defined boundaries. The degree of precision should reflect the purpose or context in which the concept is being communicated. That compensation may have blurred boundaries may reflect not simply imprecision, but that it is in fact a multifarious, essentially contested, and still-evolving concept.

We certainly do not propose to abandon rigorous conceptual analysis and evaluation. If compensation is one of the (many?) dynamic, somewhat fuzzy concepts in psychology, there is still sufficient conceptual clarity associated with it to locate it at a safe distance from careless imprecision or bland amorphousness. Both of these conditions could indicate either that key conceptual features have yet to be examined or profitably linked, or even that the concept is not a fertile one. As it stands now, however, despite considerable scholarly attention, the concept of *compensation* is also at some distance from a universal and consummate definition. As we noted earlier, this condition may be a suitable goal, but it could also signal a premature finality or stagnation to the evolution of the concept. Our earlier work was designed both to reveal and construct some structure and integrity to the concept. To be sure, if this were not possible, one must face the possibility that one is not dealing (at least yet) with a scientific concept.

To this end, we reviewed a wide range of literature, from the prose of Emerson (1900) to biographies of famous highly achieving compensators (such as the Greek orator, Demosthenes, and the American figure skater, Scott

Hamilton); from the psychodynamic views of Alfred Adler to the sciences of the sensory and neurological systems; from the cognitive sciences to the social sciences. True to our expectations, we uncovered a set of commonalities, both principles and features, that cut across nearly all of the literatures in compensation. We hasten to note that we did not have many specific expectations about precisely what these principles and features would be. Rather, we had the general expectation that similarities undergirded the diversity, and that a more useful and better defined concept of compensation could emerge.

Features of an Inclusive Definition

Some examples of the diversity—and of the underlying commonality—in uses of the term *compensation* may clarify our own definition. First, consider our own definition, as it was formulated in 1992:

> Compensation can be inferred when an objective or perceived mismatch between accessible skills and environmental demands is counterbalanced (either automatically or deliberately) by investment of more time or effort (drawing on normal skills), utilization of latent (but normally inactive) skills, or acquisition of new skills, so that a change in the behavioral profile occurs, either in the direction of adaptive attainment, maintenance, or surpassing of normal levels of proficiency or of maladaptive outcome behaviors or consequences. (Bäckman & Dixon, 1992, p. 272)

We concede (then as now) that this is a complex definition. However, it was designed to reflect a complex phenomenon—one that is dynamic, fuzzy, and yet remarkably coherent. The definition was derived primarily from an extensive review of research and theory in psychological compensation. Although abstract and ideal principles informed our original perspective and the ways in which the term has been used in the literature we reviewed, the definition reflects our observations of its continuing appearance and evolving application in several domains of research, theory, and practice. The definition also reflects our comparison of the evolving concept across these domains and our goal of developing an integrated framework. In the original article, we unpacked the key elements of the definition, focusing on them individually and in combination. In subsequent writings, we continued this explicative process by examining compensation as it relates to reading comprehension skills and aging (Dixon & Bäckman, 1993a), intelligence (Dixon & Bäckman, in press), and general cognitive and methodological implications (Dixon & Bäckman, 1993b). However, we have not substantially altered the basic definition, although we have come to better understand some of its repercussions, qualifications, and limitations. Indeed, the authors of the chapters in this volume have clarified our own perspective on the concept of compensation. In addition, all of the chapters have contributed to the evolution of the concept in particular subsets of the literature, as well as the overall clarity of meaning of compensation. In the following subsections, we identify the paramount elements of our definition of *compensation*, and note some of the more important implications.

Origins. First, we noted that compensation must have its origins in a mismatch between the skills a person possesses and the demands of the environment. Whether objective or subjective, the mismatch can be the result of an individual's deficit (or decline) vis-à-vis the relatively constant environmental demands, or the result of an increase in environmental demands that is not matched by an increase in the individual's skills. Without a mismatch—with no deficit—there is no rationale for compensation. The rationale for compensation must be to close the gap between expected level of performance and actual level of performance. Inferences regarding compensation must be supported with a clear understanding of the behavior's origin. A mismatch is necessary, but not sufficient, for compensation. Indeed, there are several qualifications or reasons that compensation might not occur for any given mismatch. These include the following situations: (a) when there is a high degree of support in the individual's environment or context and thus no need for self-initiated compensation, and (b) when the deficit is so severe that compensation is impossible to effect (see Bäckman & Dixon, 1992).

Mechanisms. We have termed the second step *compensatory mechanisms*, or the means through which an alleviation or attenuation of the mismatch is pursued. According to the literature we have reviewed—and which is updated and expanded in this book—there are several classes of compensatory mechanisms. Whatever the origins of compensation, there are several mechanisms through which the actual compensatory behavior may occur. For example, an individual may: (a) increase the time or effort expended at the task or devoted to continuing to maintain the pertinent skill; (b) access a substitutable skill from the individual's present repertoire, the use of which results in a narrowing of the gap; (c) use or develop a new skill, conceding, as it were, the deficit or decline in the previously useful one; (d) modify expectations about performance, such that the gap is less troubling, thereby reducing one's criterion of success; (e) separate the personal expectation of performance from the environmental demand, such that the former resides closer to the actual level of performance or ability; and (f) select alternative tasks or goals—related or unrelated to the original skill—such that, although the original mismatch continues, it is reduced in its prominence and perhaps eventually forgotten.

Awareness. Third, in analyzing the process of compensation through any of the previous mechanisms, it may be useful to consider the notion of awareness. We view the awareness dimension as a continuum. On the one hand, compensation may be associated with awareness of a mismatch and with deliberate action intended to overcome the deficit. On the other hand, it may be associated with the absence of awareness of the mismatch, or even the compensatory behavior (e.g., compensation in some domains may be relatively automatic). Indeed, in some compensatory processes, both differences between phases in awareness and changes in awareness through time are possible. For example, it is possible that some compensatory behaviors may originate in an awareness of a mismatch, and perhaps even a desire to remediate the mismatch. However, the actual mechanism of compensation, and indeed the fact of compensation, may not be available to, much less planfully executed by, the individual. In addition, in these or similar situations the awareness of the mismatch or compensatory mechanism may fade (or grow) with time. Compensatory behaviors, like skills, may become relatively automatized and less effortful to execute (e.g., Ohlsson, 1986; Rothi & Horner, 1983). Thus far in research on psychological compensation, information on the awareness dimension is rarely collected. To characterize the compensatory behavior in terms of automaticity, we have argued that it is important to use creative means to collect information on awareness (Dixon & Bäckman, 1993b).

Consequences. In the process of preparing our 1992 article on compensation, we learned early that some observers were surprised that the fourth phase of compensation—that of consequences—was discussed at all. A common implicit theory of compensation included the reasonable assumption that compensatory processes have a necessarily positive or successful outcome. How could psychological compensation involve a loss or, even more perplexing, end in a loss? After all, in its nonpsychological meaning of legal, financial, or in-kind balancing of a debt, compensation typically means a gain to one individual. Because it is a perplexing wrinkle in compensation theory, we devote some extra space to discussing this issue.

As Emerson (1900) noted (see also Baltes, 1987), for every gain in life there is a loss. For nonpsychological compensation, Individual A may be compensated for (say) a service rendered to Individual B, or Individual X may be compensated for (say) a disservice caused by Individual Y. In the former financial case, B has gained a service (to which A has invested time, effort, or expertise—a loss of sorts), for which a balancing loss (e.g., of money) is to be transferred from A to B. In the latter legal case, the disservice (e.g., libel, damage, or personal harm) incurred by X has caused a loss (e.g., reputation, financial) to X. That is, a mismatch between what was and what is has been created, or a gap between ability to perform and the demands of the task has been opened. To balance this loss, Y may be compelled to compensate X. At this point, Y loses something and X gains. Thus, in the big picture, the consequences of compensation are not uniformly positive: Gains in one part of a system may imply losses in another.

In a simple analogous sense, this gains-losses balance also applies to psychological compensation. As noted in this volume by both Marsiske et al. (chap. 3) and Brandtstädter and Wentura (chap. 4), just as pursuing one skill avidly leads to inevitable losses (of at least potential) in other skills, pursuing one form of compensation for a given mismatch decreases the possibility that other forms, skills, or mismatches will be pursued or addressed. It may mean that fewer domains may be maintained because the demands on one's resources are, at least temporarily, increased. For example, if compensation for a psychological deficit is achieved through the investment of more time, there is a sense in which the loss of time is notable.

In general, compensatory efforts within one domain of functioning are carried out at the expense of functioning in another area. Suppose Individual A, who is managing Skills X, Y, and Z, detects a growing disparity between expectation and performance of Skill Y. Efforts to compensate may detract from the ability to continue successful management of skills X and Z. LeVere and LeVere (1982) noted that brain-injured patients' compensatory behavior may generate interference with residual capacities of the injured system. Gaillard (1983) noted that behaviors to compensate for brain injury may result in some improvement in a particular aspect of behavior, but stagnation or regression in another. Within-system negative consequences also may occur. For example, as noted by Eaves and Klonoff (1970), a visually challenged individual who concentrates all compensatory efforts on residual visual capacities hinders the enhancement and use of other possibly substitutable modalities. In the social realm, Carstensen et al. (chap. 5) note that a spouse investing continued energy in a failing (and doomed) marriage may be experiencing further losses with little prospect of realizing gains.

The consequences of compensation may involve gains and losses in even more fundamental respects. Compensation usually results in adaptation and, where awareness is involved, is certainly intended to promote success. Nevertheless, some, if not many, compensatory efforts—whether automatic or deliberate—may yield no success at all. This lack of success at closing the mismatch may, in turn, require some adaptive behavior. However, it establishes the possibility that compensatory behaviors may yield, in addition to adaptation and success, no basic result, no change in the mismatch, and no demonstrable consequence. Still another possible consequence to compensatory behavior—and this may be the most surprising of all—is a negative or maladaptive outcome. This possibility was documented in several literatures (see Bäckman & Dixon, 1992). For example, compensatory efforts may not have the intended beneficial consequences for the producer or for other people. Some parents' attempts to compensate for a child's deficit may hinder the child's development, in general, and his or her ability to compensate for the deficit, in particular (e.g., Wasserman, Allen, & Solomon, 1985). Some behaviors of autistic children have been viewed as compensatory in nature, but maladaptive in eventual consequence (e.g., reliance on proximal sensory input; Masterton & Biederman, 1983). Finally, in Adler's (1920/1927) psychodynamic theory, feelings of inferiority may be compensated for by aggressive power seeking, which may have eventual negative consequences for both the actor and some of those in the actor's social world.

Summary

We have summarized the key points in our framework for analyzing the process of compensation. Not all apply equally to all domains of compensation, and the theoretical and practical impact varies as well. Nevertheless, we argue that it is useful to unpack the process of compensation so that, whenever possible, information on these nodes can be collected and evaluated. A deeper understanding of compensation—both theoretically and practically—involves appreciation for the origins, mechanisms, consequences, and degree and role of awareness in the process. In the next section, we explore the conceptual space of compensation, particularly whether and how it shares some space with alternative concepts.

COMPENSATION AND NEIGHBORING CONCEPTS

A psychological concept may be said to occupy a certain "conceptual space." This space may be constrained and homogeneous, or it may be broader and more heterogeneous. That is, a concept may be less a word with a single universally unambiguous definition than a space with some variation in usages, emphases, meanings, and operational definitions. This space—its range of meaning and usage—may overlap (or not) with neighboring concepts to the extent that it shares principles, definitions, purposes, or theoretical and methodological implications. A fuzzier concept may have less distinct boundaries than a precisely circumscribed concept, and therefore it may share some principles with neighboring concepts. As noted earlier, from some perspectives—based on both research literature and pretheoretical assumptions—this sharing may be both advantageous and desirable; from others, it may be a sign of an underdeveloped concept.

The conceptual space of compensation may be represented graphically, as in Fig. 1.1. In the figure, the outer boundary of the concept is the bold circumference of the circle. The fuzziness of the conceptual space of compensation is indicated by broken lines separating it and the neighboring concepts. Whereas a broad, inclusive concept of compensation may incorporate or integrate all of the neighboring concepts in the circle, a more narrow concept would include only carefully selected terms, carving out some of the broader conceptual space. The other concepts may either be

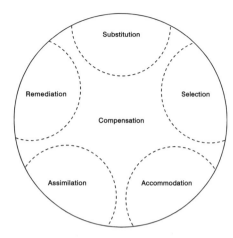

FIG. 1.1. Schematic representation of the conceptual space of compensation.

special cases or varieties of compensation, on the one hand, or alternative but related concepts, on the other hand. Although there could be others, we have selected five neighboring concepts, with representative definitions. *Accommodation* has been defined as involving adjustments in the goal structure (see Brandtstädter & Wentura, chap. 4; Salthouse, chap. 2). *Assimilation* involves overcoming losses by modifying behavior. *Selection* refers to the process of choosing from an array of possible directions or goals (see Carstensen et al., chap. 5; Marsiske et al., chap. 3). *Substitution* is perhaps a classic sense of compensation, and involves counterbalancing a specific loss with a specific gain (see Bäckman & Dixon, 1992; Rönnberg, chap. 12; Salthouse, chap. 2). *Remediation* refers to increasing the level of effort expended as a function of decline or impairment (see Bäckman & Dixon, 1992; Salthouse, chap. 2). The range of the compensation concept may be as small as that indicated by the exclusion of all other conceptual spaces, or as large as that included by the entire figure.

Relations Among Neighboring Concepts

Domains of psychological research and practice understandably vary in conceptual preferences and emphases, as well as in the extent of interest and progress in conceptual matters. The chapters in this book reflect this natural variation in the degree to which they explicitly address conceptual issues in compensation. The authors vary in the way they circumscribe or trace the borders of the concept of compensation. As the subject matter warrants the borders of neighboring concepts are identified, and the relationship between these concepts and compensation is explicated. Understandably, not all neighboring concepts receive attention in all of the chapters. Despite the notable differences among the chapters, it may be possible to characterize each of them in terms of the relationships among the constituent aspects of compensation. We immediately acknowledge that an effort to characterize all of the chapters along the same dimensions is necessarily delicate and inexact. To our knowledge, there are few previously articulated common dimensions, criteria, or definitions of compensation; the risk of overlooking nuances across domains of research is considerable. Our two main goals in making an initial explicit comparison of concepts' of compensation are: (a) to promote further conceptual discussion and eventually common understanding, and (b) to explore possible implications for the meaning of the concept.

As can be seen in Table 1.1, there is considerable agreement, but also some fascinating differences, in how the concept of compensation is represented in different fields. There are three main columns in the table. For the first column, we have included the five neighboring concepts or aspects of compensation: accommodation, assimilation, selection, substitution, and remediation. When our reading of a chapter suggests that a given concept is addressed or mentioned, we assign an X to indicate (at least) its presence in the conceptual vicinity of compensation. We adopted a fairly liberal criterion for assigning an X in a category. That is, it could be assigned to a concept that is distinguished from compensation and integrated with compensation, as well as to a process that may exist under a different name in a given literature, but which shares features with one in the table.

Still more complicated than this, in the second major column in the table, we attempt to represent telegraphically the possible hierarchical relationship between compensation and the neighboring concepts. This is more complicated because it involves both more guesswork and a correspondingly greater risk of error. With qualification, then, this column of the table illustrates: (a) the breadth of the concepts related to compensation by various scholars, and (b) the potential range of conceptual structures. There are several possible types of structures, representing a variety of possible relationships among the neighboring concepts. As we use the term in this table, a *horizontal structure* is one in which compensation is presented as one of several basically equivalent (in level) concepts, such as Salthouse's (chap. 2) firm distinction among compensation, accommodation, and elimination. Similar in structure, although not details, is Brandtstädter and Wentura's (chap. 4) scheme, in which accommodation and assimilation are distinguished, with compensation being an important aspect of the former. A hierarchical structure is one in which compensation is presented as either a relatively superordinate concept, including other concepts (e.g., Dixon & Bäckman, chap. 1), or a concept relatively subordinate to another related concept, that of selective optimization with compensation (e.g., Marsiske et al., chap. 3). In some research areas, compensation is the focus of research and no hierarchical structure is apparent.

Our own approach to the concept of compensation has focused on integrating the neighboring concepts. We have come to view them as closely

TABLE 1.1

Conceptual Relations Among Compensation and Neighboring Concepts

Chapter and Author[a]	Neighboring Concepts[b]					Possible Structure[c]	Other Concepts
	AC[d]	AS[d]	SE[d]	SU[d]	RE[d]		
Conceptual Chapters							
Dixon and Bäckman (1)	X	X	X	X	X	Hi C+	
Salthouse (2)	X	U	X	X	X	Ho C=	Elimination
Marsiske et al. (3)	X	X	X	X	X	Hi C−	Optimization, Plasticity
Life-Course Compensation Chapters							
Brandtstädter and Wentura (4)	X	X	X	U	X	Hi C−	Adjustment
Carstensen et al. (5)	U	U	X	X	X	Ho C=	
Ferraro and Farmer (6)	X	X	X	X	X	Hi C+	Social compensation
Charness and Bosman (7)	X	X	X	X	X	Hi C+	Environmental compensation
Neurological Impairment Chapters							
Wilson (8)	X	X	U	X	X	Hi C+	Rehabilitation
Woodruff-Pak and Hanson (9)	U	U	U	X	U	FC	Plasticity
Gonzales Rothi (10)	U	U	U	X	U	FC[e]	Physiological restitution / Physiological substitution via vicariation / Behavioral compensation
Grady and Parasuraman (11)	U	U	U	X	U	FC	Functional compensation / Synaptic plasticity / Network reorganization
Sensory- and Skill-Compensation Chapters							
Rönnberg (12)	U	U	U	X	U	FC	Cognitive compensation / Nonadaptive compensation
West et al. (13)	U	U	U	X	U	FC	Online compensation / Experiential compensation
Stones and Kozma (14)	X	X	X	X	X	Hi C+	Societal compensation / Expertise

[a]Chapter authors with chapter number in parentheses.

[b]X = The concept is noted; U = The concept is not noted.

[c]Structure of concept of compensation: Hi C+ = relatively hierarchical (compensation superordinate); Hi C− = relatively hierarchical (compensation subordinate); Ho C = relatively horizontal (compensation at equal level); FC = focus on compensation (usually as substitution).

[d]AC = Accommodation; AS = Assimilation; SE = Selection; SU = Substitution; RE = Remediation.

[e]Distinguishes forms of substitutive compensation.

15

related to—included in the same conceptual family or space as—compensation. The functions they represent are different in important ways, but they share family resemblance with one another and can be usefully collected under the umbrella of compensation. Thus, *compensation* is a superordinate term for a set of related processes, including accommodation, assimilation, selection, substitution, and remediation. At the most basic level, these processes are united in that they are directed at overcoming a deficit. In addition, they share in a pool of features or attributes of the origins, mechanisms, and consequences of compensation (Bäckman & Dixon, 1992). Despite our inclusive view, we recognize the importance of distinguishing among these neighboring concepts. Furthermore, we understand that, for some purposes, it may be useful to separate them conceptually. Indeed, as is evident in the table, in some literatures it may be unnecessary to attend to more than one alternative concept. A given neighboring concept may not appear in a particular literature for the convincing reason that it is not relevant to the deficit under consideration, or it is not typically a part of the conventional research priorities of the literature. For example, literature on compensation for neurological impairments rarely discusses the role of goal selection and adjustment—concepts that are prominent in social compensation research.

We did not include all possible neighboring concepts as column entries in the table. Therefore, in the third and final major column, we note some of the other concepts mentioned by compensation theorists. Overall, Table 1.1 is designed to be representative, but not exhaustive. The chapter authors present far more information—and, importantly, a more comprehensive and differentiated discussion of their perspectives—in their own chapters. Our purpose in this table is simply to offer an accessible overview of the fascinating theoretical puzzles and solutions presented by the concept of compensation.

Interpreting Alternative Relations

What inferences should be made from this table? The first inference we make has been alluded to already. It is apparent that there are some general, perhaps predictable, differences between clusters of domains of compensation research. Broader ranges of conceptual connections or explicit distinctions typify the chapters focusing on social and environmental compensation through the life course. Although not apparent in the table, the separations between concepts in this domain are often explicit. One aspect of compensation is explicitly defined in terms of another aspect (or separate concept). A hierarchical structure may be inferred from the writing in most of the cases. These observations do not hold for the chapters devoted to compensation in the brain and cognitive sciences. Typically, one aspect of compensation—often substitution, or a similar process—is identified and the other neighboring concepts are simply not noted. Therefore, the separate notation in the table in these chapters indicates an implicit conceptual distinction, rather than an explicit one.

Second, at a more global level, there are some differences among concepts of compensation employed by psychologists in different domains. However, the differences among these concepts are neither substantially definitional, nor do they reflect fundamental variations in the meaning, purpose, role, place, and impact of compensation. The modest differences may have evolved because of selection factors such as: (a) those presented by differing requirements, purposes, and usages of compensation in different domains; (b) those indexed simply by the varying approaches to the science of psychology and the nature of scientific concepts; or (c) a combination of the two. In the first case, different research areas may select for genuinely different emphases in compensation. For example, the notion of *selection*—an important element in social compensation—is less likely to be as emphasized in brain compensation (although in clinical practice it may play a role). In the second case, we already noted that there is a variety of legitimate approaches to conceptual analysis. Although we have followed one in which some fuzzy boundaries between concepts are allowed (and perhaps encouraged), other scholars may adhere to an approach in which a principal sign of scientific progress is to make such conceptual boundaries clear and distinct, even if the science is not yet to that point of clarity.

The third inference we take from the table is implied by our discussion of the first; namely, there is a considerable consensus on the concept of compensation in psychology. Despite some differences in (a) the range and specificity of the concept, (b) the emphasis on similarities or distinctions, and (c) the structure of the relationships among related concepts, there is considerable overlap in all. We reached a similar conclusion earlier (Bäckman & Dixon, 1992), and it was the basis, in fact, of our own conceptual framework. Indeed, a conceptual framework of compensation meant to apply to many areas of psychology makes little sense if the conceptual space is deeply and mutually impenetrably divided, or if the conceptual neighbors turn away orthogonally from one another. Our view of this book's chapters supports our optimism that we are all talking about the same thing when we say compensation, although it is still critical, as it is throughout psychology, to define our terms carefully.

The fourth inference we make from Table 1.1 is that it is crucial for scholars and practitioners to continue to examine the concept of compensation in their own specializations, as well as those in other areas of psychology. Borrowing perspectives, emphases, methods, and even concepts from one another may, in the long run, expand and strengthen the activity in one's own area. This, indeed, has been a result of our own reviews of literatures in compensation, and has been reinforced by our reading of the scholarly chapters in this book. By focusing on the distinctions as well as the similarities among the conceptual neighbors to compensation, we learn that many of the same issues arise in quite different contexts, and that different solutions have been tried. These different solutions to similar problems include varying terminology, distinctions, and emphases, as well as the clustering of concepts. We suspect that it is the rare area in the psychology of compensation that cannot benefit from the fertile ideas and accomplishments of another area.

CONCLUSION

Although compensation is a concept with a long history and a wide application—and although it has appeared in hundreds of scholarly works in psychology in the last several decades—it has not been the subject of concerted attention. In this chapter, we have continued our efforts to explore the concept of compensation—its origins, mechanisms, and consequences—as it applies to a wide range of psychological phenomena. Perhaps because of our method to understand compensation by examining a wide range of its application, our concept is broad and generally inclusive. To be sure, it excludes some well-researched psychological phenomena, such as learning and coping with daily stresses. Within the umbrella of compensation, however, we include some neighboring notions that other observers choose to separate. We approve of this difference because it reflects, we think, different goals. Whereas our goal is to construct a general theoretical framework of psychological compensation, it seems only natural that the goal of applying such a framework to specific areas of compensation research and practice would involve some selection.

Overall, the chapters in this book speak strongly of the extensiveness and relevance of the concept of psychological compensation. We are heartened that the concept continues to be vital to numerous areas of psychology. We are challenged by both the consistency and the variability represented in its evolving conceptual space. We are delighted that it continues to be a Janus-faced concept—with one face toward psychological practice and the goal of improving human lives, and the other face toward psychological theory and the goal of improving our scientific understanding of human behavior.

ACKNOWLEDGMENTS

The first author appreciates grant support from the Natural Sciences and Engineering Research Council of Canada and the Canadian Aging Research Network. The second author acknowledges grant support from the Swedish

Council for Research in the Humanities and the Social Sciences and the Swedish Council for Social Research.

REFERENCES

Adler, A. A. (1927). *Practice and theory of individual psychology* (P. Radin, Trans.). New York: Harcourt Brace. (Original work published 1920)

Bäckman, L., & Dixon, R. A. (1992). Psychological compensation: A theoretical framework. *Psychological Bulletin, 112*, 259–283.

Baltes, P. B. (1987). Theoretical propositions of life-span developmental psychology: On the dynamics between growth and decline. *Developmental Psychology, 23*, 611–626.

Dixon, R. A., & Bäckman, L. (1993a). Reading and memory for prose in adulthood: Issues of expertise and compensation. In S. R. Yussen & M. C. Smith (Eds.), *Reading across the life span* (pp. 193–213). New York: Springer-Verlag.

Dixon, R. A., & Bäckman, L. (1993b). The concept of compensation in cognitive aging: The case of prose processing in adulthood. *International Journal of Aging and Human Development, 36*, 199–217.

Dixon, R. A., & Bäckman, L. (in press). Compensatory mechanisms. In R. J. Sternberg (Ed.), *Encyclopedia of intelligence.* New York: Macmillan.

Eaves, L., & Klonoff, H. A. (1970). A comparison of blind and sighted children on a tactual and performance test. *Exceptional Children, 37*, 269–273.

Emerson, R. W. (1900). *Compensation.* New York: Caldwell.

English, H. B., & English, A. C. (1958). *A comprehensive dictionary of psychological and psychoanalytic terms.* New York: Longman Green.

Gaillard, F. (1983). Recovery as a mind-brain paradigm. *International Journal of Rehabilitation Research, 6*, 331–338.

Hayes, S. P. (1933). New experimental data on the old problems of sensory compensation. *Teachers Forum, 5*, 22–26.

LeVere, N. D., & LeVere, T. E. (1982). Recovery of function after brain damage: Support for the compensation theory of behavioral deficit. *Physiological Psychology, 10*, 165–174.

Masterton, B. A., & Biederman, G. B. (1983). Proprioceptive versus visual control in autistic children. *Journal of Autism and Developmental Disorders, 13*, 141–152.

Ohlsson, K. (1986). Compensation as skill. In E. Hjelmquist & L.-G. Nilsson (Eds.), *Communication and handicap: Aspects of psychological compensation and technical aids* (pp. 85–101). Amsterdam: North-Holland.

Rothi, L. J., & Horner, J. (1983). Restitution and substitution: Two theories of recovery with application to neurobehavioral treatment. *Journal of Clinical Neuropsychology, 5*, 73–81.

Toulmin, S. (1972). *Human understanding.* Princeton, NJ: Princeton University Press.

Wasserman, G. A., Allen, R., & Solomon, C. R. (1985). At-risk toddlers and their mothers: The special case of physical handicaps. *Child Development, 56*, 73–83.

Wittgenstein, L. (1958). *Philosophical investigations* (3rd ed.). New York: Macmillan.

CHAPTER TWO

Refining the Concept of Psychological Compensation

Timothy A. Salthouse
Georgia Institute of Technology

According to the *American Heritage Dictionary of the American Language* (1992), *compensation*, as the term is used in psychology, refers to behavior that develops either consciously or unconsciously to offset a real or imagined deficiency. A more specific definition is that compensation exists when the same, or a superior, level of proficiency on some criterion activity is achieved, despite deficiencies in one or more behavioral constituents of that activity.

The term *compensation* has been widely used in psychology, particularly in reference to individuals who have (or had) some type of deficit or impairment and yet still manage to perform at a competent level in a related activity. The idea that a limitation or impairment in one presumably relevant aspect of behavior does not necessarily preclude the attainment of a high level of functioning in a given domain is obviously very appealing. However, previous usages of the term *compensation* have been confusing and sometimes inconsistent. Thus, the concept runs the risk of becoming vacuous and devoid of meaning unless it can be clarified and unambiguously distinguished from alternative concepts.

The primary goal of this chapter is to discuss a number of issues relevant to the interpretation of the concept of compensation. My intention is not to redefine the concept, but instead to stimulate a closer examination of its meaning, and how it might be distinguished from related concepts. There are three major sections to this chapter. The first is concerned with distinguishing compensation from alternative concepts. The second raises a number of issues believed to be important in understanding the nature of compensation. Finally,

21

the third section consists of an examination of two research projects in terms of the questions and issues raised in the first two sections.

WHEN IS COMPENSATION COMPENSATION?

A recent comprehensive review of compensation by Bäckman and Dixon (1992) identified three types of compensation: (a) development or activation of substitutable skills, (b) investment of more time or effort, and (c) relaxation of the criteria (or standards or expectations) for successful performance, or adoption of different goals. This classification scheme is useful because it is much more explicit than earlier references to compensation, which sometimes implied that compensation could be inferred to exist whenever convergent group-by-task interactions were found, in which a poor-performing group improved more with variations in the task conditions than did a higher-performing group (e.g., Bäckman, 1989).

Nevertheless, questions can still be raised regarding whether each of the categories discussed by Bäckman and Dixon should be considered examples of compensation, as opposed to manifestations of alternative concepts. Consider the last category first. If the performance standards change, or if there is a shift in the nature of the criterion behavior, one can question whether it may be more accurate to state that the subject has adapted, or accommodated, to the deficit rather than compensated for it. That is, if there is a change in the nature of the goal, rather than in the means used to achieve the same goal, one can question if it might be more meaningful to classify the phenomenon as *accommodation* instead of compensation (Salthouse, 1987, 1990a, 1990b).

It seems reasonable that as deficits appear, changes may occur in the nature of the activities in which one engages, or in the level of expectation in the same activities, in order to minimize the consequences of those deficits. However, if the criterion behavior is no longer the same, it is not obvious that the concept of compensation is relevant.

Of course, if one views goals or criterion behavior in broad terms, such as ensuring adequate self-esteem, it could be argued that a change in the nature of the activities in which one engages is consistent with maintaining the same level of overall or global competence. This is a plausible perspective, although the assessment of competence is clearly much more difficult with such a broad interpretation of behavioral goals. Furthermore, the linkage between a deficit or a loss in one aspect of behavior and the level of functioning in a different type of activity is often tenuous when different behavioral domains are involved.

A similar objection to such a broad interpretation of compensation was raised by Bäckman and Dixon (1992) in their discussion of empirically evaluating Adler's views on compensation:

Because we all have defects, it is possible to take any behavior, relate it to some presumed feeling of inferiority, and classify the behavior as an example of compensation or overcompensation. However, a variety of behaviors that may be interpreted as a result of feelings of inferiority may instead be prompted by other causative factors. (p. 271)

Now consider the second category of compensation mentioned by Bäckman and Dixon. In this case, the same degree of criterion competence is achieved, but only after the individual has invested more time and effort than that typical of people without the deficit. Notice that the presumed compensatory activity is not at the level of constituents of the criterion behavior, but instead is at a higher level concerned with what is responsible for, or enables, the changes in the relevant mechanisms. The question therefore arises as to whether alterations at different levels should be considered examples of compensation.

One possible interpretation is that compensation necessarily involves changes at the same level as the behavioral deficit. For example, Bäckman and Dixon suggested that there is some consensus in the view of compensation as overcoming a behavioral deficit by an increase of some other behavioral component. The implication of this particular interpretation is that the deficit and the compensatory component are at the same level. Other levels, both higher (e.g., motivation) and lower (e.g., neurophysiological), are interesting and ultimately need to be understood—but, at least from this perspective, they may not be central to the question of how competence in a given criterion activity is achieved.

An alternative view of *compensation* is that the term is applicable whenever some type of deficit is not associated with expected limitations in relevant aspects of behavior. In other words, the level at which potential consequences of the deficit are overcome may not be germane to the classification of a phenomenon as compensation.

The issue of the level of analysis is particularly relevant in the present context because at least two different types of mechanisms could be affected by increased time or effort, and yet it is debatable whether either of them would be considered examples of compensation. To illustrate, one possibility is that the greater time and/or effort served to eliminate the initial deficit, and if the deficit has truly been remediated, there may be less need for compensation. That is, to the extent that the initial deficit no longer exists, the individual is not distinct from "normals" without the deficit, and hence the concept of compensation may be superfluous. The term *remediation* has been proposed to apply to situations in which an initial deficit has been eliminated by the investment of more time and/or effort, or by some other means (Salthouse, 1987, 1990a, 1990b).

A second possible outcome of the investment of greater time and effort is a different level of skill; in which the deficient component is no longer relevant to competence in the criterion activity. In research on skill acquisition, it has been suggested that the components shift in importance as a skill is acquired (e.g., Ackerman, 1989; Anderson, 1982). This could occur because the deficit is only relevant to the initial stage of learning, but not to later stages where other components become more important. Alternatively, the skill could have been compiled such that the efficiency of the component is no longer pertinent to the criterion behavior.

A key feature in both of these interpretations is that the critical component may not be important or relevant to the criterion behavior after the investment of time and/or effort has resulted in a higher level of learning. If this is the case, then at a functional level the deficit no longer exists, and hence there is no need for compensation. It has been proposed that the term *elimination*, or possibly *compilation*, should be used when the deficit still exists but is no longer relevant to the criterion behavior (Salthouse, 1987, 1989, 1990a, 1990b).

The first compensation category mentioned by Bäckman and Dixon (1992) appears consistent with the exchange, balance, or offset mentioned in most definitions of *compensation*. A fundamental aspect of this interpretation is that the same (or higher) level of criterion functioning is achieved by means of different processes or mechanisms. However, several additional issues still need to be considered before one can have confidence in the classification of a phenomenon as involving true compensation. Therefore it may be prudent to treat it as only possible compensation until the phenomenon has been subjected to further examination.

The distinctions discussed earlier are summarized in the flowchart illustrated in Fig. 2.1. It is important to realize that there is not yet any resolution to the issues and questions that have been raised in the preceding paragraphs. Nevertheless, representing potential alternatives in the form of a flowchart raises the possibility that the term *compensation* may be applicable to many fewer situations than is sometimes assumed. At the very least, consideration of how the concept of compensation is distinct from other concepts should serve to clarify the meaning—by increasing the discriminative validity, of this term.

FURTHER ISSUES

If the alternatives of accommodation, remediation, and elimination or compilation of the critical component are ruled out, what additional issues need to be considered before deciding that a phenomenon is true or genuine compensation? Six issues relevant to the interpretation of compensation are discussed in this section. The issues are framed in the form of questions about the nature of compensation. No particular resolutions will be advo-

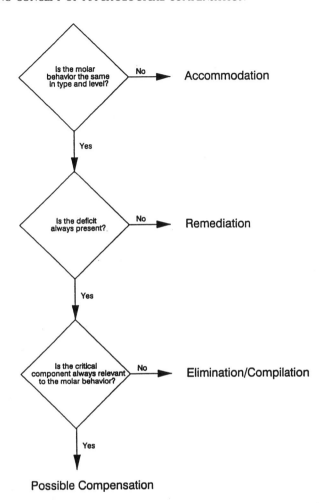

FIG. 2.1. Flowchart that might be used to distinguish compensation from other related concepts.

cated, but they are raised because of a belief that some consensus on all of them is necessary before the concept of compensation can be considered useful and meaningful.

Identification of the Compensatory Component

Must a behavioral component or aspect associated with increased proficiency be identified in order for a phenomenon to be classified as involving compensation? This question originates from a logical analysis of what presumably occurs when compensation exists. That is, if the same (or higher) level of criterion functioning is maintained and yet there is a deficit in a critical component, there is presumably a gain in some other component or aspect. Therefore, it seems reasonable to ask whether the phenomenon would still be considered an example of compensation if the compensating mechanism cannot be identified. In effect, the concern represented by this issue is whether we are justified in believing that compensation is involved if we cannot specify how the compensation is achieved.

On the one hand, it could be argued that some type of compensation must be operating if: (a) a deficit exists in a relevant behavioral component; (b) a high level of functioning is achieved in the criterion activity; and (c) the alternatives of accommodation, remediation, and elimination/compilation have been ruled out. On the other hand, it is not satisfying to invoke the concept of compensation when there is little understanding of what is actually doing the compensating.

Causal Ordering of Gains and Losses

Must the loss in the deficient component necessarily occur prior to the gain in the presumed compensatory component? This issue is of interest because several possibilities are inconsistent with the assumption of causality that seems to be implicit in the concept of compensation. For example, the gain could precede the loss, perhaps because the gain caused the loss through some type of suppression (Uttal & Perlmutter, 1989). Another possibility is that the gain occurred concurrent with the loss, but that the gains and losses are independent and unrelated phenomena and not involved in a causal relationship with one another (Uttal & Perlmutter, 1989). Finally, it is conceivable that some type of selective deterioration could have occurred such that the criterion competence and the efficiency of all components might previously have been at a high level, but a greater loss occurred in the critical or deficient component. In this case, it might be more accurate to refer to small and large losses rather than gains and losses (Salthouse, 1984).

Each of the cases mentioned previously could result in a configuration in which weaknesses or deficits in one or more behavioral components appear to be offset by strengths or gains in other behavioral components. However, in none of the these situations does the balancing or counteracting component of behavior develop in response to, or as a consequence of, the behavioral deficiencies. The question therefore arises as to whether a temporal and causal linkage must be established between the onset of the deficit and the emergence of compensatory behavior.

Although it may be preferable to reserve the term *compensation* for situations in which, by means of longitudinal research or other types of evidence, one is confident that the losses preceded, and likely contributed to, the gains, the possibility of functional compensation should also be considered

(Salthouse, 1990a). That is, if a high level of proficiency in one behavioral component allows for the maintenance of competency in a criterion activity despite a low level of proficiency in another component, would this not be considered effective or functional compensation regardless of the origin or temporal ordering of the strength relative to the weakness? Adoption of a functional definition of *compensation* such as this would greatly broaden the applicability of the concept, but in the process the implied causal ordering of a loss producing a gain would be abandoned. Further consideration of this issue is needed to determine whether it is meaningful to refer to compensation when the compensatory behavior has no causal relationship to the deficient behavior for which it is purportedly compensating.

Awareness of the Deficit

Must the individual be aware of the deficit and take deliberate action to compensate? In other words, is compensation a conscious and deliberate process, or could it occur relatively automatically and without the individual's awareness? Although the distinction between automatic and deliberate processes can be quite subtle, the question of whether compensation necessarily involves an awareness of a deficit and a choice to engage in potentially compensatory behavior is important for determining the nature of compensation.

Bäckman and Dixon (1992) suggested that compensation may be unlikely if the individual is not aware of the deficit and thus does not make a deliberate attempt to compensate. However, the justification for claiming that compensation could not occur unconsciously is not clear, and adoption of this criterion may severely limit application of the concept of compensation. As a rather mundane example, several years ago I was walking with a taller person who had a much longer stride than me. After several minutes of walking I realized that I was becoming tired because I had been taking many more steps than him in an attempt to keep up with his pace. Changing the manner in which the criterion behavior—in this case, walking at a given speed—is achieved seems to meet most of the criteria associated with compensation. However, in this case I was not immediately aware that I had altered my walking pattern, and therefore this example would presumably not qualify as compensation if a criterion of awareness and deliberate decision were to be employed.

Locus of the Compensatory Mechanism

Must the compensatory mechanisms be internal to the individual, or could reliance on external aids or prosthetics be considered compensation? Dixon and Bäckman (1992–1993) suggested that the use of external memory aids, such as notes or even other people, could be considered compensatory mechanisms. However, two questions immediately arise if an interpretation of this type is adopted: will the criterion behavior remain the same when an external aid or device is used? If so, is it the individual or the external aid that is doing the compensating?

As an example, consider a situation in which a business executive with a poor memory relies on a secretary to remember all of the former's appointments. The desired criterion behavior of not forgetting the appointments may be achieved by this strategy, but is it accurate to refer to this as compensation? It could be argued that the delegation of behavior to another person is not compensating for a deficit within the individual, but instead is an instance of accommodating to the deficit by shifting responsibility and essentially altering the nature of the criterion activity. That is, in this example, the behavioral deficit within the individual is not offset by an increase in some other aspect of her behavior. Instead, the goal of attempting to remember appointments herself is effectively abandoned, and thus responsibility for that particular type of competence is assigned to another individual.

One possibility is that the term *compensation* should be limited to situations in which the individual takes an active role in the compensatory process, and not to those in which a barrier is removed, such as providing eyeglasses to correct a visual deficiency (Salthouse, 1990a). The difficulty with this suggestion is that it is not always clear when an individual is taking an active role, nor what constitutes a barrier. Provision of corrective lenses may not require any action on the part of a mildly visually impaired individual, but the use of a visual-tactile substitution device almost certainly requires special action on the part of a blind individual. In both cases, individuals with deficits in a relevant component of reading behavior can accomplish the global activity of reading written materials because a sensory barrier is removed, but it is not obvious that compensation is involved in each instance.

Uniqueness of Mechanisms

Must the compensatory mechanisms be restricted, or unique, to individuals with a deficit, or can they also be evident in normal individuals? If they can occur in people without a deficit, what is the basis for identifying them as compensatory? Would the exact same behavior in a person without a deficit be considered compensation? If so, what deficiencies are being compensated? A key issue in this context is whether the behavior of the compensating person must be qualitatively or quantitatively distinct from that of a normal person.

Uniqueness of the compensatory mechanisms is clearly a complex issue. However, it is also a critical one for the concept of compensation because it concerns a fundamental aspect of what is meant by compensation. That is, if the compensatory mechanisms are effective, why are they not used by normal individuals who do not have a deficit? Are there substantial costs in the acquisition or utilization of the compensatory mechanisms that reduce their value to individuals without a deficit? Or are these mechanisms only possible when a deficit is present? If the latter is the case, what is there about the presence of a deficit that enables the use of mechanisms that apparently facilitate competence in a particular domain?

Composition of Competence

Is the same level of criterion competence achieved by an altered importance of the components, or by different levels of the components (Salthouse, 1989, 1993)? This distinction can be clarified by expressing the relationship between the criterion behavior and the components in the form of a regression equation.

$$(1) \quad Y = b_1 X_1 + b_2 X_2 + c$$

Assume that of the two components relevant to the criterion behavior Y, one group of individuals has a deficit in component X_1. It is logically possible for the same criterion level of functioning (Y) to be achieved with a deficit in X_1 either by altering the regression weights for the two components (i.e., decreasing b_1 and increasing b_2) or by increasing the level of X_2.

One characteristic often mentioned in connection with the concept of compensation is that the behavioral profile (Bäckman & Dixon, 1992) or the composition of the competence (Salthouse, 1990a) differs between normal and compensating individuals. The question of interest in this context is whether both of the alternatives mentioned earlier fit this criterion and should be considered instances of compensation. That is, is it compensation if the same mechanisms—in the sense of relative importance of the components—are used? Or should the term *compensation* be reserved for situations in which individuals with and without the critical deficit achieve similar levels of functioning with different mechanisms, perhaps as reflected by different coefficients in a regression equation?

TWO CASE STUDIES

The relevance of the preceding issues to research on compensation can be illustrated by considering their applicability to two research projects from my laboratory. Both projects involved adults of different ages as the research participants, and in each the primary behavioral deficit of interest was processing speed as measured by tests such as finger-tapping rate, choice reaction time, digit-symbol substitution time, or perceptual comparison time. Previous research has revealed that increased age is associated with lower levels of performance in a wide variety of speeded tasks (see Salthouse, 1985, for a review). It also was assumed that for many older adults, slower speed functioned as a behavioral deficit in certain criterion activities.

In the first project (Salthouse, 1984), the criterion activity was transcription typing. Processing speed was presumed to be relevant to this activity because the rate of typing is dependent on the speed with which the typist can execute appropriate keystrokes. Research participants in this project were deliberately selected so that there was no relationship between age and proficiency in the criterion behavior (i.e., speed of typing). This was an important feature of the design because it allowed a determination of how typists of different ages were able to achieve the same level of molar or criterion functioning, despite a deficit in a relevant component on the part of older typists. Obtaining a sample in which there was no relationship between age and typing speed typically requires a positive relationship between age and experience. However, this is not a problem in this type of design because the interest is not in the source of the compensatory mechanisms (e.g., experience or other factors related to age), but rather in their identity or nature.

The goal of the Salthouse project was to identify how older typists could perform at the same level as young typists despite a slower processing speed, as reflected by measures such as finger-tapping rate and choice reaction time. Several possible compensatory mechanisms were investigated in this project, including dependency on sequential constraints in language and efficiency of different types of keystrokes (e.g., those on the same hand vs. those on different hands). The only measure in which age-related increases were found was the eye-hand span, which represented how far ahead of the current keystroke the subject was processing the to-be-typed text. This span was measured by varying the amount of to-be-typed text while the individual was typing, and then determining the amount of visible text needed to maintain one's normal rate of typing. In both of the studies reported in Salthouse (1984), older typists were found to have larger eye-hand spans than younger typists. These results were recently replicated by Bosman (1993).

One of the interpretations originally proposed to account for the observed pattern of results was that the older typists might have been compensating for their slower perceptual-motor speed by expanding their span of anticipation. That is, older typists appear to begin their processing of to-be-typed characters farther in advance of younger typists, thereby minimizing the consequences of their slower processing speed.

Let us now reexamine this phenomenon in terms of the issues discussed in the preceding sections. It is convenient to begin by considering the issues portrayed in the flowchart in Fig. 2.1. Because the design of the study ensured that the average level of competence in the criterion activity was equivalent across the age range, we can rule out the possibility of accommodation as an interpretation of this phenomenon. Furthermore, because the age-related difference in the speed measures was present even among the most skilled typists, we can rule out that the deficit was remediated through extensive experience or some other means. Although no pertinent data were reported, it seems likely that measures of perceptual-motor speed were still relevant to typing performance even at high levels of typing proficiency, and thus the interpretation of elimination or compilation also seems improbable in this situation.

What about the other issues relating to the identification of a phenomenon as compensation? In the Salthouse (1984) project, the anticipation or eye-hand span was identified as a possible compensatory mechanism because it was found to be larger among older typists than younger typists of the same skill level. However, the causal ordering of the increased eye-hand span and slower perceptual-motor speed is not known because no longitudinal data were available. Therefore, it is possible that the increased span and decreased speed were independent and unrelated phenomena, or that selective deterioration occurred because of a decrease with increased age in perceptual-motor speed, but not in eye-hand span. No data were collected with regard to whether the older typists were aware of their deficit in perceptual-motor speed, and there was no evidence that any of the typists deliberately decided to expand their eye-hand span as a compensatory mechanism.

Because the increased eye-hand span is a mechanism within the individual, the presumed compensation is not attributable to a reliance on external aids. The hypothesized compensatory mechanism is not unique to individuals with a speed deficit because several fast younger typists in the studies also exhibited large eye-hand spans. Finally, no direct statistical tests were conducted to compare the regression equations of younger and older typists, but the pattern of an age-related decrease in perceptual-motor speed and an age-related increase in eye-hand span is consistent with the interpretation of a different composition of the competence for adults of different ages.

Does this phenomenon qualify as compensation on the basis of the information presented earlier? Although it does not appear to be accommodation, remediation, or elimination/compilation, there are several respects in which the phenomenon appears inconsistent with potential criteria for compensation. That is, the causal linkage between the deficit and the presumed compensatory behavior is unknown, as is the awareness of the individual of his or her deficit and of the compensatory behavior. Furthermore, similar levels of the hypothesized compensatory mechanism were observed in normal individuals, and hence it was not unique to those with a deficit.

In a second project (Salthouse, 1993), the criterion behavior consisted of performance in timed verbal activities, such as anagrams, creating words by placement of letters in specified spatial locations, switching from one word to another by altering one letter at a time, and various fluency tasks. The presumed deficient component was processing speed as measured by perceptual comparison tasks, and the component expected to play a compensatory role was word knowledge as measured by performance on two vocabulary tests. Samples of younger and older adults were therefore administered two perceptual comparison speed tests and two vocabulary tests, in addition to several timed verbal tasks.

Of primary interest in this project were the regression equations which related the speed and vocabulary measures to prediction of performance in the criterion verbal tasks in the younger and older age groups. The key question was whether younger and older adults differed with respect to the weightings of speed and knowledge, or only in terms of the average levels of each variable.

Similar results were obtained across eight criterion tasks and two independent samples. In each case younger and older adults were found to differ primarily in terms of the average levels of the components, and not with respect to the regression coefficients. That is, on the average, older adults were slower and had greater knowledge of word meanings than younger adults, but the two groups did not differ significantly in the coefficients relating either speed or knowledge to criterion performance.

Now consider the application of the issues discussed earlier to these results. Because younger and older adults were fairly similar in their average performance on most of the criterion tasks, there is no evidence that the older adults accommodated to their speed deficit by shifting the nature of the activity performed, or by altering the level of performance in that activity. The speed deficit was always present, and therefore the possibility of remediation can be ruled out. There was no direct examination of the relevance of speed to performance on the criterion tasks among the highest performing individuals, but there seems little reason to suspect that the critical components were no longer relevant because they had been eliminated or compiled. In terms of the flowchart in Fig. 2.1, therefore, it appears that this phenomenon would be classified as *possible compensation.*

The remaining issues can be examined to determine whether the phenomenon qualifies as true compensation. A greater quantity of relevant knowledge was identified as the probable compensatory component in this project, but no information was available about the causal ordering of the increase in knowledge and the decrease in speed. However, it seems highly improbable that the decrease in speed caused or contributed to the increase in word knowledge. Furthermore, although no information was available about the older adults' awareness of their slower perceptual comparison speed, it is unlikely that they would have decided to increase their vocabulary to be prepared to perform well in future tests requiring both speed and word knowledge. The locus of the hypothesized compensatory mechanism was internal because it is assumed to be increased knowledge of word meanings. Possession of high levels of knowledge about word meanings was not limited to older adults with a deficit in speed, however, and thus the hypothesized compensatory mechanism is not unique to individuals with a deficit. Finally, direct statistical comparisons revealed that younger and older adults did not differ in the coefficients or weightings of speed and knowledge in the prediction of performance in the criterion tasks, but instead differed in the average levels of those variables.

Again it is ambiguous whether the phenomenon should be considered an example of compensation. The small to nonexistent age differences in the criterion verbal tasks, despite large age-related differences in the measures of processing speed, do not seem attributable to related concepts such as accommodation, remediation, or elimination/compilation. However, there is no evidence of a causal connection between the deficit and the presumed compensatory behavior, nor of any awareness of the deficit or possible compensatory actions. The hypothesized compensatory mechanism was not restricted to individuals with a deficit in the critical component, and direct evaluation revealed that groups with and without the deficit did not differ in the relative importance, or weightings, of the relevant behavioral components.

The purpose of examining these two phenomena in terms of the issues discussed herein was to illustrate that classification of a phenomenon as involving compensation is neither straightforward nor unequivocal. In each of the cases described, arguments could be made both for and against invoking the concept of compensation. Until this ambiguity is eliminated by resolution of the issues mentioned, *compensation* may be a term with more popular appeal than scientific value.

CONCLUSION

It should be apparent by now, if it was not already, that compensation is a complex concept. Although it represents an intriguing and appealing idea, the term *compensation* has been used in an inconsistent, and often confusing, manner. I have suggested that a number of issues need to be carefully examined and resolved for the concept of compensation to be meaningful and useful in scientific discourse. This chapter does not exhaust the list of relevant issues, nor was any attempt made to provide a definitive resolution of any of the issues that were discussed. Nevertheless, my hope is that the process of raising some of these issues will eventually lead to the refinement of one of the most interesting, and potentially important, concepts in the field of psychology.

REFERENCES

Ackerman, P. L. (1989). Individual differences in skill acquisition. In P. L. Ackerman, R. J. Sternberg, & R. Glaser (Eds.), *Learning and individual differences: Advances in theory and research* (pp. 165–217). New York: Freeman.

American Heritage Dictionary of the English Language (3rd ed.). (1992). Boston: Houghton Mifflin.

Anderson, J. R. (1982). Acquisition of cognitive skill. *Psychological Review, 89,* 369–403.

Bäckman, L. (1989). Varieties of memory compensation by older adults in episodic remembering. In L. W. Poon, D. C. Rubin, & B. A. Wilson (Eds.), *Everyday cognition in adulthood and late life* (pp. 509–544). Cambridge, England: Cambridge University Press.

Bäckman, L., & Dixon, R. A. (1992). Psychological compensation: A theoretical framework. *Psychological Bulletin, 112,* 259–283.

Bosman, E. A. (1993). Age-related differences in the motoric aspects of transcription typing skill. *Psychology and Aging, 8,* 87–102.

Dixon, R. A., & Bäckman, L. (1992–1993). The concept of compensation in cognitive aging: The case of prose processing in adulthood. *International Journal of Aging and Human Development, 36,* 199–217.

Salthouse, T. A. (1984). Effects of age and skill in typing. *Journal of Experimental Psychology: General, 113,* 345–371.

Salthouse, T. A. (1985). Speed of behavior and its implications for cognition. In J. E. Birren & K. W. Schaie (Eds.), *Handbook of the psychology of aging* (2nd ed., pp. 400–426). New York: Van Nostrand Reinhold.

Salthouse, T. A. (1987). Age, experience, and compensation. In C. Schooler & K. W. Schaie (Eds.), *Cognitive functioning and social structure across the life course* (pp. 142–150). Norwood, N.J.: Ablex.

Salthouse, T. A. (1989). Aging and skilled performance. In A. Colley & J. Beech (Eds.), *The acquisition and performance of cognitive skills* (pp. 247–264). Chichester, England: Wiley.

Salthouse, T. A. (1990a). Cognitive competence and expertise in aging. In J. E. Birren & K. W. Schaie (Eds.), *Handbook of the psychology of aging* (3rd ed., pp. 310–319). San Diego, CA: Academic Press.

Salthouse, T. A. (1990b). Influence of experience on age differences in cognitive functioning. *Human Factors, 32,* 551–569.

Salthouse, T. A. (1993). Speed and knowledge as determinants of adult age differences in verbal tasks. *Journal of Gerontology: Psychological Sciences, 48,* P29–P36.

Uttal, D. H., & Perlmutter, M. (1989). Toward a broader conceptualization of development: The role of gains and losses across the life span. *Developmental Review, 9,* 101–132.

CHAPTER THREE

Selective Optimization
With Compensation:
Life-Span Perspectives on
Successful Human Development

Michael Marsiske
Max Planck Institute for Human Development and Education

Frieder R. Lang
Free University of Berlin

Paul B. Baltes
Max Planck Institute for Human Development and Education

Margret M. Baltes
Free University of Berlin

In this chapter, we embed the unifying concept of this volume, *psychological compensation,* within the framework of life-span developmental psychology. The model of *selective optimization with compensation,* as proposed by M. Baltes and P. Baltes (e.g., M. Baltes, 1987; M. Baltes & Carstensen, 1994; P. Baltes, 1987, 1991, 1993, 1994; P. Baltes & M. Baltes, 1980, 1990a; P. Baltes, Dittmann-Kohli, & Dixon, 1984), captures and applies many of the central propositions contained in life-span developmental psychology. In our view, the status of this model in the literature, to date, has been largely conceptual. It has attempted to represent scientific knowledge about the nature of psychological development and aging, with a particular emphasis on the consideration of "successful" or adaptive life-span development (P. Baltes & M. Baltes, 1990b). The model has remained less developed, however, with regard to its empirical operationalization and its hypothesis-guided evaluation. One emphasis of the current chapter, then, is to consider the empirical basis of the model in more detail, and to outline future directions for research.

Selective optimization with compensation can be understood as a *meta-model* for the study of successful adaptation and development across the life span. It is considered a metamodel because its scope can be extended beyond specific functions and domains to involve, more broadly, systemic properties of the developmental person-context matrix. Throughout this chapter, however, we generally refer to selective optimization with compensation as a *model*, but this is mainly a shorthand to simplify the presentation. Selective optimization with compensation always can be invoked at a metalevel of analysis; as we suggest in greater detail later, it is not specific to particular functional domains.

This chapter has three major aims. First, we describe the model of selective optimization with compensation and its three subcomponents as they evolve from theoretical propositions of life-span developmental psychology. Second, the chapter attempts to illustrate the usefulness of the selective optimization with compensation model as an integrative tool for bringing together research findings on successful adaptation across the life span in a variety of domains of functioning. Third, we will consider the implications of the model for development in general (not just successful development), and we will explore whether and how the model might be used to ask new questions and undergird new research in developmental psychology.

SELECTIVE OPTIMIZATION WITH COMPENSATION: A PERSPECTIVE BASED IN LIFE-SPAN DEVELOPMENTAL PSYCHOLOGY

The model of selective optimization with compensation is embedded in, and draws on, ideas from the life-span perspective on development and aging. What is life-span developmental psychology? As P. Baltes (1987) has noted, it does not exist as a formal theory with a fixed body of concepts and methods. Rather, scholars who work within this perspective seem to share a commitment to a common body of theoretical propositions and questions. Although none of these theoretical ideas is necessarily unique to life-span psychology, they function together to define the life-span approach. A key feature of the life-span orientation is its attempt to integrate a diversity of concepts into a *family of perspectives* characterizing life-span development. Because the life-span developmental perspective is associated with important metatheoretical assumptions, within which the model of selective optimization with compensation is grounded, we begin by summarizing some of the key propositions of the life-span developmental approach to human development (see P. Baltes, 1987; Staudinger, Marsiske, & P. Baltes, in press; see also Lerner, 1984, 1991, for discussions of these ideas).

From the perspective of life-span developmental psychology, development can be understood as the outcome of ongoing, *lifelong adaptive processes* (P. Baltes, 1987). Such adaptation (Lerner, 1991; Lerner & Busch-Rossnagel, 1981) occurs throughout life; no age period has superiority in regulating development. Moreover, adaptive processes are seen as being both proactive and reactive (Lawton, 1989). On the one hand, environmental or organismic changes, like new social roles or changes in the physical maturation associated with puberty, may initiate or require behavioral changes from individuals and their environments. On the other hand, it is important to remember that organisms are also active agents. They can actively select and change particular contexts as well. Evidence that these processes of adaptation include individualized features can be seen, for example, in the empirical suggestion that lifelong developmental trajectories are characterized by much heterogeneity, especially when it comes to the second half of life (P. Baltes & M. Baltes, 1990b; Dannefer, 1992; Maddox, 1987; Schaie, 1989).

A further characteristic of life-span theory is that, at any point in time and across ontogenetic time, life-span researchers conceive of development as *multidimensional* and *multidirectional.* Behavior occurs in many, varied domains—behavior is not just a homogeneous class of functions—and considerable diversity or pluralism is found in the directionality of changes that constitute ontogenesis, both within and between domains. The prototypical exemplar of such multidirectionality and multidimensionality comes from research on the adult development of intellectual functioning (e.g., P. Baltes, 1993; Cattell, 1971; Horn & Hofer, 1992; Salthouse, 1991; Schaie, 1994). Particularly, psychometric research has suggested that, especially in young and middle-aged adults, intelligence can be best understood as multiple abilities, rather than as a unitary construct. Moreover, different abilities show different developmental trajectories across adulthood. Abilities that are thought to represent the "mechanics of intelligence" (P. Baltes, 1993)—like speed, working memory, and fluid intelligence—typically show normative ("universal") declines beginning in middle to late adulthood. Conversely, abilities that represent the "pragmatics of intelligence" (i.e., domain-general and domain-specific knowledge that a person acquires through experience and through transactions with the surrounding culture) may show stability or even increase until late adulthood.

Another characteristic of life-span theory is that development is conceived of not as a monolithic process of progression and growth, but as an ongoing, changing, and interacting system of *gains and losses.* The process of development is not a simple movement toward higher levels of efficacy, such as incremental growth. There is no pure developmental gain. Rather, throughout life, development always consists of the joint occurrence of gains and losses, both within and across domains of functioning. There are several metaphors that illustrate this dynamic. Using an investment metaphor, any resource invested at a given point in development necessarily precludes investment of that resource in other options. This is because living systems possess finite, but not fixed, pools of developmental resources (Brent, 1978; Edelman, 1987; Ford, 1987). As investment in one option is elaborated and deepened, it may become increasingly difficult to have available resources for investment in new developmental options. Similarly, it is often the case that there may be negative transfer from the acquisition of one skill or resource to another (P. Baltes, 1987). Another metaphor for this gain-loss dynamic is the consumption metaphor. As we know from dynamic systems theory in physics and biology (e.g., Brent, 1978; Prigogine, 1980), as functions and systems are used and developed, their "operation" results in long-term costs (e.g., consumption and usage costs). In this view, the effective functioning of a system early in ontogenetic time may have long-term consequences for its functioning later in time. Of course, because humans are self-organizing systems capable of budgeting and managing their resources, and because humans are also able to acquire knowledge systems, one major idea in this chapter is that individuals may be able to overcome or postpone negative ("entropic") developments (P. Baltes & Graf, in press).

Another major emphasis of the life-span developmental perspective has been on the study of behavioral *plasticity* (P. Baltes, 1993; Kliegl & P. Baltes, 1987; Lerner, 1984). Much intraindividual plasticity (within-person modifiability) can be found in psychological development. One major focus of developmental research is the search for the range of plasticity and its limits. Although development has been characterized as a dynamic system of gains and losses, this dynamic is never "fixed" because individuals are capable of investing in new developmental outcomes as long as there is some plasticity (e.g., inactivated or underdeveloped resources).

Plasticity, however, is not of the same quality and quantity across the life span. One source for this age-related change in plasticity is associated with the very definition of *development* as selection, with its resultant restriction in the range of developmental options. Another source can be found in biology-based age-related changes. For instance, in old age, there are losses in plasticity due to reduced resources and increased illnesses. As a result, in the second half of life, there is an increasing shift from growth-related adaptations to maintenance and repair.

Figure 3.1 attempts to illustrate this notion of an age-related shift in resource investment. On the left, the figure suggests that there is a shifting balance between gains and losses across the adult life span (the data for this figure involved adults' view of the life course; see Heckhausen, Dixon, & Baltes, 1989). The right side of the figure suggests that with age—because of reduced resources and increased risks—there is increased demand for maintenance rather than growth (Staudinger, Marsiske, & Baltes, 1993). Of course, the specific pattern of selective investment into developmental gains will vary across individuals and contextual circumstances, an idea we revisit later. Furthermore, investment is used metaphorically here, and does not necessarily connote conscious or volitional strategies.

The idea of *contextualism* is another key concept from life-span theory. Developing individuals exist in contexts (internal and external conditions)

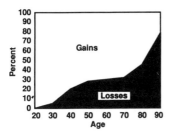 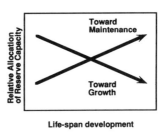

FIG. 3.1. Gains and losses across the life span. The left side of the figure shows subjective expectations based on work reported in Heckhausen, Dixon, and Baltes (1989). The right side shows the interplay between age changes in plasticity and the allocation of reserve capacity into two general goals of functioning: maintenance versus growth (adapted from Staudinger, Marsiske, and Baltes, 1993, with permission of Cambridge University Press). In addition, with age, the overall amount of reserve capacity is reduced.

that create opportunities for and limitations to individual developmental options. Delineation of these contexts in terms of macrostructural features, like social class, ethnicity, and roles, is a major agenda for the sociological analysis of the life course (e.g., Brim & Wheeler, 1966; Dannefer, 1984, 1989, 1992, Featherman, 1983; Kohli & Meyer, 1986; Mayer, 1986; Riley, 1987). Another approach is to organize the contexts by considering them in terms of dimensions like ontogenetic time, historical time, and contextual breadth and depth. In this vein, any particular course of individual development can be understood as the outcome of the interactions (dialectics) among three systems of developmental influences (P. Baltes, Reese, & Lipsitt, 1980): *Age-graded* influences are those organismic and environmental aspects that, because of their dominant age correlation, shape development in relatively normative ways for all individuals. *History-graded* influences are those organismic and environmental aspects that may make the experience of development different across individuals born in different historical periods, thereby creating historical cohorts and period effects. Finally, *non-normative* organismic and environmental influences on development reflect the individual, idiosyncratic events (such as winning in a lottery) that, although more unique, can have powerful influences in development (Bandura, 1982a). These three classes of developmental influences can also be conceptualized as sources for developmental tasks (see M. Baltes & Carstensen, 1994). In considering these systems of influences, it is important to underscore that none of them works monolithically. There are always individual differences in the experience of these influences and their consequences for individual behavior (Dannefer, 1984, 1991; Riley, 1987).

How must these life-span developmental propositions be applied to understand successful development (P. Baltes & M. Baltes, 1990b)? First, the idea of development as lifelong adaptation highlights that a model of successful development must not focus on any particular period of the life course alone. Successful development is possible, in principle, from birth until death. Second, the ideas of multidimensionality and multidirectionality emphasize the notion that an individual may develop in many domains simultaneously, but not necessarily always in the same direction. Moreover, resources may be withdrawn from some domains to support development in other domains. This is a key idea in our subsequent discussion of selective optimization with compensation.

Third, we argue that there is no pure developmental gain or loss. Rather, gains and losses coexist, both within and across domains of functioning. A model of successful development must provide some understanding of how individuals can minimize losses that impair effective functioning, while maximizing gains that promote growth and maintenance. A fourth issue deals with the existence of plasticity in development. This focus on plasticity highlights the utility of distinguishing between realized (phenotypic behavior) and unobserved, latent potential (genotypic potential). This distinction is similar to the norm of reaction in behavioral genetics (Dunn, 1965; Lerner, 1984). When plasticity is available, individuals can increase or decrease their behavioral output to meet changing organismic and environmental demands. With age, there are changes in plasticity due to both biological and environmental factors. The activation of latent plasticity and the management of resource limitations, then, is necessarily a key focus for a model of successful development.

Finally, an emphasis on developmental contextualism (Lerner, 1991; Magnusson, 1990, 1993) underscores that, in considering plasticity and the management of gains and losses, it is important not to focus exclusively on individuals. Successful development is not simply a matter of individual choices and volition, but also one of the particular contexts of an individual. Throughout this chapter, we emphasize individual embeddedness in a set of organismic and environmental conditions that can act as powerful moderators of developmental outcomes.

A MODEL OF SUCCESSFUL DEVELOPMENT

In the following section, we present the model of selective optimization with compensation as a metamodel of successful development across the life span (M. Baltes & Carstensen, 1994; P. Baltes, 1993, 1994; P. Baltes & M. Baltes, 1980, 1990a; P. Baltes et al., 1984). We begin this section with a consideration of the use of the term *success* from the perspective of life-span developmental psychology. In the second part of this section, we describe the model of selective optimization with compensation and its three subcomponents. The model is based on a view that human organisms have the capability to employ available resources in ways that produce desired developmental outcomes while minimizing undesired outcomes (e.g., Brandt-städter & Greve, 1994; Ford, 1987; Heckhausen & Schulz, 1993). We argue that the selective optimization with compensation model suggests processes by which individuals may adapt successfully to developmental changes in biological, psychological and socioeconomic conditions. Because the model can be applied to various domains and at different levels of analysis, it does not specify the particular micromechanisms and outcomes of successful development. Rather, specific theories are needed to understand individual manifestations of selective optimization with compensation, and to define criteria of success.

What are criteria of success? At a nomothetic level, these are difficult questions to answer because success means very different things to different people, as well as to researchers with differing theoretical commitments. The definitional emphases of success are also likely to change across the life span. Indeed, the definition of success needs to include variations between contexts—like sociocultural settings, social class, age, and gender—and between behavioral domains—such as health and financial achievement or social relationships (P. Baltes & M. Baltes, 1990a).

Broadly defined, and from a psychological and behavior-oriented perspective, success can be understood as goal attainment. *Goal attainment* here means the realization of desired outcomes and the avoidance of undesired outcomes. Without the invocation of social-philosophical theories of values, the concept of *successful development* has no objective, a priori end state. It is fundamentally an idiographic and a sociographic term; desirable goal states vary over individuals, time, and sociocultural contexts. Of course, in human societies, success is never completely individually defined. There is some social consensus, as well as socially induced homogeneity. M. Baltes and Carstensen (1994; see also Boesch, 1971) tried to distill this view by arguing that success can be defined by different criteria of assessment (objective or subjective), by different authorities (e.g., individual, family, clinical/medical, societal), and by different norms. Success-defining norms include functional (i.e., success as being able to function), statistical (i.e., success as being above the average), and ideal (i.e., success as reaching the thinkable best level of an outcome) criteria.

This perspective on variability and multidimensionality of success-relevant criteria helps to emphasize the status of selective optimization with compensation as a metamodel. To understand specific instantiations of successful development, the criteria of success must first be carefully delineated and identified within a matrix of alternatives, including the possibility of incompatibility between success criteria. Individual norms of success (e.g., the attainment of a drug-induced, alternate psychological state) may be in opposition to sociocultural norms (e.g., legal-moral arguments against drug use). Similarly, success in one domain of functioning (e.g., career) may come at the cost of success in another domain (e.g., sport or leisure). Consequently, it would be inappropriate to specify one single set of principles as a sole guiding orientation. Moreover, from a life-span perspective, one must also be aware that goals and goal-related criteria of success can change as individuals' life courses unfold (P. Baltes & M. Baltes, 1990a).

Beyond success criteria, a major point we try to make is that the model components labeled *selection, optimization,* and *compensation* are integrated to fulfill the two major goals of life-span development: growth (higher levels of functioning) and maintenance (avoidance of negative outcomes). Taken together, selection, optimization, and compensation describe how individuals may successfully adapt to changing biological (organismic) and contextual demands and opportunities. Our central position, then, is that the model of selective optimization with compensation is a life-span model of "successful" development that describes how individuals and their life environments can manage opportunities for, and limits on, resources at all ages. The model also suggests how individuals and their life environments might manage an age-related shift toward a less positive balance of gains and losses in later life. Thus, it is a general model of successful adaptation. Here, *adaptation* is taken to mean not just passive or reactive changes of the organism in response to changing contextual demands, but also proactive behavioral changes arising out of organism volition for mastery and challenge in particular domains.

Table 3.1 draws on life-span developmental ideas about the major influences on, and systems of, development. The table tries to illustrate the idea that selection, optimization, and compensation can originate from age-graded, history-graded, and non-normative sources, as well as that the model has evolved out of the underlying assumptions of life-span developmental psychology. The table also provides a concrete illustration of what is meant by the terms *selection, optimization,* and *compensation.*

The first component (*selection*) suggests that any process of development is inherently focused or specialized. There are two reasons. The first is that positive changes in any adaptive capacity require a cumulative process of resource development in a given direction (e.g., typically toward higher levels of functioning). The second is associated with the issue of finite resources. Organisms not only represent evolution-driven specializations, but some subset of the entire spectrum of potentials. It is not possible to engage the organism in all possible developmental domains. Thus, narrowing the range of domains through selection is necessary. Behavioral plasticity highlights the second component: Individuals and their biopsychosocial environments can modify behavioral output to meet specific and changing contextual demands. This facilitates the enhancement or maintenance of levels of performance efficacy through optimization. Finally, the third component contained in the table, *compensation,* refers to the notion that when

TABLE 3.1

Life-Span Developmental Influences on Selective Optimization with Compensation: Selected Examples

Developmental Influence	Selection	Optimization	Compensation
Age-graded			
Universal, normative, time-ordered biological or environmental influences on development	*Examples:* Age norms, developmental tasks, critical and maturational periods, processes of specialization	*Examples:* Maturation, experience accumulation, expertise	*Examples:* Availability of intergenerational solidarity or pragmatic knowledge about life
History-graded			
Influences on development that vary over era, epoch, generation, cohort, or culture	*Examples:* Changing rules and laws about school attendance or retirement age, changing social norms & restrictions	*Examples:* Improvements in health-care system or athletic training methods, introduction of lifelong learning	*Examples:* Improvement in medical technology (e.g., hearing aids, glasses) for dealing with specific conditions, retraining programs following war or unemployment cycles
Non-normative			
The idiosyncratic influence on development; includes differences in genome, life constellation, family configuration, personal volition	*Examples:* Individual skills & preferences, family norms, migration to another culture, physical disability	*Examples:* Personalized training and practice, multicultural experiences	*Examples:* Availability of specialized knowledge, support groups, prescription of assistive footwear for a walking problem

Note: Age-graded, history-graded, and non-normative influences condition the instantiations of selection, optimization, and compensation; they provide contextual "frames" for understanding successful development. These examples are meant to illustrate potential ways in which life-span influences on development might play a regulatory role in adaptation.

adequate performance in these selected domains is compromised (e.g., by new time constraints or by the onset of pathological or biological aging processes), individuals and their contexts are challenged to reassess their earlier means-end strategies, and/or to construct alternative strategies (compensation). When available resources are insufficient, or when resources cannot be modified to a sufficient level to meet particular challenges, new internal or external means can be sought to support adaptation (i.e., to reach desired goal states and avoid undesirable ones). One example from everyday life is the use of a hearing aid.

Although several earlier discussions of the model of selective optimization with compensation emphasized its utility in representing the development of intellectual functioning (P. Baltes et al., 1984; Staudinger, Cornelius & P. Baltes, 1989), it is important to emphasize that the model is applicable to all domains of development (P. Baltes & M. Baltes, 1990b). Moreover, as a life-span model, a key assumption is that even in childhood the components of selection, optimization, and compensation are fundamental themes. However, old age may be associated with an increased pressure for selection and compensation because of losses in plasticity (reserve capacity) and impending death. In other words, to manage age-associated losses and the finitude of life, strategies of selective optimization with compensation may need to be engaged in more actively or more frequently.

Table 3.1 is also meant to highlight that the implementation of selective optimization with compensation components will vary over persons, cultures, and domains. Thus, as was suggested earlier, specific theories are needed to understand particular manifestations of the model. Consequently, understanding the unfolding of selection, optimization, and compensation will hinge on the domain of interest, the persons studied, and the particular person-context matrix under investigation. Moreover, explication of the operation of selective optimization with compensation will also hinge on the theoretical process variables that a particular researcher is committed to using. A good example is work by Heckhausen and Schulz (1993, 1995). Their effort includes a specific use of the model within the context of a psychological theory of primary and secondary control. We will later offer additional examples that illustrate how the model might be applied to a variety of domains and processes and with differing theoretical perspectives.

THE THREE SUBCOMPONENTS OF THE MODEL: SELECTION, OPTIMIZATION, COMPENSATION

The model of selective optimization with compensation presents a coalition of components that operates dynamically as a unit or a package. Even when one particular component is in the foreground, the other components are necessarily operating, even if that operation is latent or indirect. Moreover, the logical status of a particular component can change over time. Take compensation as an example. Some means, such as those that were originally acquired or enhanced to serve some compensatory function in a particular domain, can later be used as part of the resources now available for use in reaching other goals. Consequently, although we offer definitions of the individual components, and we offer research to suggest their operation in several developmental domains, we do so for demonstration purposes. At the same time, it is important not to lose sight of the fact that the combined process is selective optimization with compensation—a set of interacting components whose logical status can change over time. In our consideration of these components, we draw on earlier discussions (especially M. Baltes, 1987; M. Baltes & Carstensen, 1994; P. Baltes, 1987, 1993, 1994; P. Baltes & M. Baltes, 1990a).

Selection

The component of *selection* refers to the (conscious or unconscious) choice of particular behavioral domains or goals for continued development (growth or maintenance). Selection can be understood as a fundamental component of any behavioral or developmental process (see Nesselroade, 1991; Siegler, 1989). Thus, selection was fundamental to behaviorist B. F. Skinner (e.g., 1966; see also Crow, 1985), who argued that phylogenetic and ontogenetic contingencies shaped complex behavior from relatively "undifferentiated material" (Skinner, 1966, p. 1206). Similarly, another concrete illustration comes from developmental biology, where development can be characterized as specialization, or canalization (Waddington, 1975). Indeed, an important concept we adapt from evolutionary science is that of *ontogenetic selection pressure*, which acknowledges the array of forces—like age-graded, history-graded, and non-normative factors—which give direction to development.

How can we better understand the sources of ontogenetic selection pressure? We have already argued that a first source of ontogenetic selection pressure stems from genome-based potentials, or norms of reaction. The behavioral genetic evidence increasingly suggests that genetic differences continue to control development throughout life (Plomin, Pedersen, Lichtenstein, & McClearn, 1994; Scarr, 1993). In addition to these basic selection pressures, selection over the life course seems to be guided by three general sets of influences. One is the cultural and individual pressure for specialization and adaptation into life trajectories (e.g., P. Baltes, 1993; Cole, in press; Lerner, 1984); such forces reflect what we have called *history-graded* and *age-graded* influences on development. Many of these influences can be understood under the rubric of developmental goals and tasks (e.g., Havighurst, 1948; Oerter, 1986), as well as general norms or expectations of development (Heckhausen & Krueger, 1993). A second, more individual-difference-oriented ontogenetic selection pressure is associated with social inequality and social differentiation (by gender, social class, ethnicity), a structural process in the center of sociological analyses of the life course (Elder, 1985; Kohli, 1986; Kruse, 1992; Mayer, 1986, 1990; Riley, 1987), and a process that Dannefer (1984, 1989) calls *sociogenic differentiation*. Finally (within the framework of ontogenetic selection pressure), a third set of influences that seems to modulate average trends and to be generative of interindividual differences is what P. Baltes, Reese, and Lipsitt (1980) labeled *non-normative* influences (see Table 3.1). As a whole, these influence patterns and opportunity structures also codetermine another requirement for the effectiveness of selection, namely, that of variability—both intra- and inter-individual (P. Baltes, 1994; Nesselroade, 1991; Nesselroade & Thompson, in press; Siegler, 1994).

Another condition for ontogenetic selection pressure is finite resources. Across the life span, one adaptive response to limited availability of resources may be the active narrowing of the range of domains in which efficacious functioning is expected. Time, biological, mental, and motivational resources are limited, therefore not all possible domains and trajectories can unfold in any one organism. Moreover, it is here that an added feature of human aging seems to enter the picture. There are age-related changes in plasticity and associated resources. The first decades of life witness major increments largely associated with physical maturation and cultural learning (Cole, 1990, 1991, in press), whereas in the second half of life, because of biological limitations and an age-related increase in morbidity and other vulnerabilities, the entire pool of resources (plasticity) is reduced. Such resource reduction is a hallmark of aging (P. Baltes, 1993; Salthouse, 1991). With age, then, the pressure for selection is increasingly magnified.

Thus far, we have highlighted selection as a general characteristic of life-span development. What is selection from a psychological point of view? In our view, selection implies goal or domain choice. However, the locus of choice is not always in the individual. For example, mandatory school attendance in industrialized nations, or genetic features like eye color represent selections that occur outside individual volition. Thus, selections are broadly defined and include multiple levels and categories of goals. Here, the behavioral distinction between proximal and distal goals is also relevant (Bandura, 1986). By emphasizing the goal-related nature of selection, we draw on the idea that goals have the properties of emergence and of a system. Thus, the choice of a particular behavioral domain (whether internally or externally) implies that a whole set of domain-relevant goals may be involved. For example, choosing the vocation of physician implies an embedded set of more proximal subgoals: One must receive certain kinds of schooling, pass certain kinds of examinations, receive a medical degree, and find an opportunity to practice. Indeed, from a psychological point of view, it is at this individual level that the theoretical connection between selection and goals becomes most explicit, and where successful development is highly dependent on reaching those goals that persons have identified for themselves.

What about selection in old age? As suggested earlier, and articulated by P. Baltes and M. Baltes (1990a), selection is a lifelong process. In old age, the ontogenetic selection pressure takes on a special characteristic. With aging, the normal state of limited resource availability becomes more pronounced, because advanced adulthood seems to be associated with increasing loss of resources and reserve capacity (Bäckman & Dixon, 1992; P. Baltes, 1993; Brandtstädter & Greve, 1994; Salthouse, 1991; Staudinger et al., 1993). Consequently, there is increased pressure for selection. The age-related increase in selection pressure can take a number of forms, including goal maintenance and transformation. The pressure for maintenance or growth in some domains, under conditions of shrinking resource availability, may imply some relinquishing of other domains or reassessment of goal hierarchies, either by individuals or their life environments, if continued successful adaptation is to be possible. One form of such goal-related transformation includes the resetting of aspiration levels in particular behavioral domains. Indeed, this may become particularly important in late life (e.g., Brandtstädter, Wentura, & Greve, 1993; Brim, 1992; Heckhausen & Krueger, 1993; Markus & Herzog, 1991; Markus & Wurf, 1987; Nurius & Markus, 1990; Ryff, 1989).

In summary, selection is the model component concerned with: (a) creating and giving direction to development, and (b) managing the fundamental resource limitations inherent in all living systems. Selection acts to focus developmental trajectories and to reduce and make manageable the number of challenges and demands impinging on individuals. It is important to note again that selection must not necessarily be under the control of individual volition. The pressure and direction for selection can have their origins within individuals' own motivational and cognitive constraints, or they can be directed by biological and social forces outside the individual.

Optimization

In the most fundamental sense, *optimization* reflects the view that development is the internally and externally regulated search for higher level, efficacious, and desirable levels of functioning (Harris, 1957; Lerner, 1986). Optimization can be seen as a fundamental component of developmental progression and maintenance (see also Brandtstädter & Schneewind, 1977). Although the gain-loss argument suggests that life-span development can actually be multidirectional and that no development is pure gain (P. Baltes,

1987), we argue here that optimization reflects the notion that—for the targeted domain(s) of functioning—the outcome is expected to be an increase in adaptive fitness. Thus, in general, our expectation is that people exploit organismic and environmental opportunities and engage in behaviors to enrich and augment their general reserves, and to maximize—within societal, subcultural, and personal norms—their chosen life courses with regard to quality and quantity (P. Baltes & M. Baltes, 1990b).

Generally speaking, *optimization* means that—within the framework provided by the genome and society—individual competencies, existing goal-directed means, and outcomes are acquired and maintained at levels as well as in directions desirable for a person. It encompasses those processes or mechanisms by which behavioral or developmental progress is achieved and maintained in select domains of functioning. It is important to note that optimization does not imply that individuals reach some absolute optimum of functioning. Rather, optimization is aimed at enhancing or maintaining the means or strategies for goal attainment.

It is also necessary to acknowledge that, as one considers the person in context as a whole, optimization can also occur at a broader, domain-general level. Optimization can also imply generalization and positive transfer. Two examples help demonstrate this point. First, the "canon" of educational objectives (i.e., the acquisition of such basic skills as reading and writing [literacy] and arithmetic [numeracy]) constitute skills which are fundamental to a variety of other desirable cognitive activities (e.g., Resnick, 1990; Smith & Marsiske, in press; Tuijnman, Kirsch, & Wagner, in press). Second, enhancement of children's level of optimism and sense of personal control also carries a general-purpose significance (e.g., Bandura, 1982b). In both cases, the optimization of general-purpose mechanisms can contribute to the optimization of functioning in a number of domains.

Of the three components in the selective optimization with compensation model, optimization—like the traditional concept of *development* as growth or progress (Nisbett, 1980)—is the only component with an a priori valence and direction: It always serves the purpose of enhancing or maintaining desired ends or levels of functioning. *Optimization*, by definition, implies a movement in the direction of increased adaptive fitness. Although selection and compensation may also contribute to successful adaptation, their definitions do not imply a predefined direction. Thus, it is possible to speak of "over-selection" (discussed later) or "over-compensation" (Bäckman & Dixon, 1992).

As with selection, and as we shall suggest later for compensation, we argue that optimization is directed by a broad range of forces, including epigenesis, sociohistorical changes (e.g., the fall of the Berlin Wall in Germany) and idiosyncratic influences. In the context of an investment metaphor, optimization reflects resource investment into a system of goals and behaviors. This investment is directed at efficacious and desirable functioning. Aside from environmental support factors, concepts like training, practice, and motivational enhancement represent the most direct psychological demonstrations of the optimization process (e.g., P. Baltes & Lindenberger, 1988; Bandura, 1986; Brandtstädter et al., 1993; Ericsson, Krampe, & Tesch-Römer, 1993; Willis, 1987).

Compensation

The final component of the model, *compensation*, results particularly from internal and external limits and losses in the range of plasticity, reserve capacity, and contextual opportunities. In other words, limits and losses that concern both the person and the context may be sources for compensation.

Generally speaking, compensation originates from two major sources. The first source of compensation is related to the special and finite amount of resources available to any living system. Aside from genetic and social constraints and opportunity structures, time and spatial factors set limits on what an individual can do. In other words, a given organism is limited in its potential for genetic reasons, and because not all possible domains and skills can be developed to the same degree. Thus, for some areas of functioning, the appropriate means may not be available to produce criterion-matched performance. Consider an American citizen taking a trip through France, but who is unable to speak French. Linguistic specialization carries the consequence of linguistic insufficiency in a different cultural environment. In such instances, compensatory behaviors or new means are required to satisfy the goal of communication; possible examples might include increased reliance on nonverbal communication strategies (such as pointing), dictionaries and phrase books, or translators and travel guides.

A second source of compensation emerges from the loss of criterion-relevant means, which is frequently age related. In this sense, compensation summarizes strategies of adjustment, such that the functional impact of losses and limits on resources are minimized by relying on other internal or external resources that are not part of a previously effective behavior system. In other words, when the internal or external means to attain particular selected goals have been lost, compensation comes to the foreground as a key adaptive process. A primary factor in the onset of conditions for compensation is age-associated losses in plasticity. As we discuss in greater detail later, however, individuals experience losses throughout the life span because development cannot occur without loss. Another important factor in the onset of compensation is changes in the opportunities and challenges confronting an individual. These changes can be both internally and externally directed; that is, while individuals can be passive recipients of increased levels of challenge (e.g., a supervisor adds new duties at work), they can also actively select higher aspiration levels (e.g., a faster time or higher score in an athletic pursuit). In all cases, however, when the current means (those active, and those that can be activated or developed) are insufficient to achieve particular goal states or meet particular performance expectations, compensatory efforts using other organismic or environmental means become necessary.

Conceptually, the logical status of compensatory behaviors is not fixed. What originally may have been compensatory (e.g., the use of nonverbal communication skills in a country whose language one does not speak) in a different context (such as becoming a pantomime) may turn out to be criterion-enhancing behavior. Another example of a change in the functional significance of compensatory behavior is its role in developmental transitions. In early childhood stages of locomotor development (i.e., as infants learn to walk), their parents may provide compensatory assistance such as handholding. Another example is the use of glasses to correct for vision deficits. However, such compensatory assistance is also in the interest of positive change in adaptive capacity (i.e., maintenance- or growth-directed). Although these supportive behaviors and devices may serve a compensatory function—"making up" for particular deficiencies or losses of competence— the same behaviors and devices may have different logical status from another frame of reference. Handholding may be an optimization strategy in the parent–child affectional relationship and wearing glasses may represent an attempt to optimize one's social presentation through fashion. In other words, as one evaluates whether a given behavior is compensatory, one needs to consider the location of behavior in its action and developmental context, as well as the multifunctionality of behavioral consequences (see M. Baltes, in press-b, for an illustration using dependent behavior in old age).

Indeed, the changing logical status of adaptive behaviors constitutes a major element of cultural evolution. A telling example comes from work in cultural anthropology and evolution. In those fields, a major school of thought views cultural progress (e.g., optimization of social structures and the emergence of knowledge and technology) as inherently compensatory; that is, cultural evolution is a response to human organisms' biological deficits (see P. Baltes, 1993, 1994; Gehlen, 1956). Of course, elements of cultural practice that were once compensatory may acquire new logical status. For example, the wearing of clothes may once have been truly compensatory (to help humans keep warm; to protect regions of the body), but clothing has now taken on sociocultural meanings that bear little relationship to compensation. The parent who dresses his or her infant in attractive clothes may not even be thinking of the compensatory function of the clothing.

The means required for compensation may already be available in a person's repertoire (for substitution), or they may need to be newly acquired. Together with, or as a part of, optimization, compensation increases the likelihood of goal attainment. This point deserves emphasis. Our view (selective optimization with compensation) is that compensation is always integrated with a general process of optimization. In the context of particular action sequences, however (i.e., behavioral repertoires aimed at particular goals or domains), compensation relates only to those processes and strategies whereby new means are acquired or old means are reconstructed and used to counterbalance functional limits or losses.

Another conceptual issue that deserves consideration (see P. Baltes, 1994), and that is a subject for continued conceptual work, concerns the role of compensation in the dynamics between contexts, goals, and action systems. Thus far, we have focused our discussion of compensation on a single action system, when new means are used for a particular goal. It may also be useful to invoke the principle of compensation when one domain (action system) is relinquished as a goal because the resources required for that goal are needed to achieve adequate performance in another, concurrently targeted goal domain. In other words, compensation can also occur when one restricts success in one domain to facilitate the optimization of another. Here, one can see the potential intertwining of selection and compensation: Selection can "free up" the means for compensation. Unfortunately, at a conceptual level, this reference to an "interdomain" compensatory process seemingly may lead to difficulties in separating compensation from selection. For example, consider a person who has been pursuing Goal A and Goal B. If this person enlists new motivational means (which were previously attached to Goal B) in pursuit of attaining Goal A (perhaps because of some recognized loss or insufficiency of means, or because of new levels of challenge regarding Goal A), this person is engaging in compensation (involving Goal A). At the same time, this person is also engaging in selection (by withdrawing from Goal B). Thus, the same behavioral unit involves both compensation and selection (i.e., multifunctionality).

Figure 3.2 (adapted from P. Baltes & M. Baltes, 1990a) summarizes the key features of selection, optimization, and compensation as they have been discussed thus far. In addition to summarizing the major ideas of the model, its antecedents, and its outcomes, the figure also illustrates the dynamic interrelationship among the components (or component processes, to emphasize that these components involve mechanisms and are time ordered). Feedback from the outcomes of adaptation may act as the antecedents for a new sequence of adaptation. Moreover, one needs to consider the model's systemic and interdomain features. The way in which selective optimization with compensation is constructed in one area may impact on another domain. Furthermore, over time and across contexts, and because of multifunctionality, the logical status of the components may change.

Although the foregoing discussion emphasizes individual model components, in practice the model of selective optimization with compensation argues that the components are interwoven. In other words, none of the

52   MARSISKE ET AL.

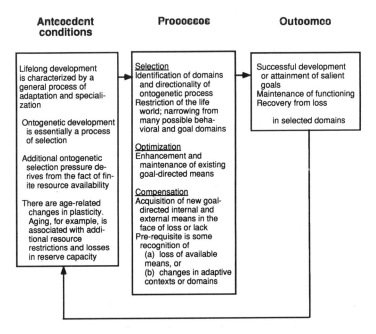

Antecedent   Processes   Outcomes
conditions

FIG. 3.2. The life-span model of selective optimization with compensation.
The essentials of the model are proposed to be universal, but specific
manifestations will vary by domain, individual, sociocultural context, and
theoretical perspective (adapted from P. Baltes & M. Baltes, 1990a, copyright
(1990). Adapted with the permission of Cambridge University Press).

three components is mutually exclusive. Moreover, because of development,
multifunctionality, and contextual embeddedness, the logical status of adaptive behaviors may vary (as suggested earlier, a behavior seen as compensatory from one perspective may be seen as optimizing or selective from
another). Rather than focus on single components, it may be most useful
to always consider the coalition of processes together.

How might the interweaving of model components work in practice? An
athlete, for example, has typically selected a particular behavioral domain
for optimization (e.g., soccer, basketball). In the course of deliberate practice
(Ericsson & Charness, 1994; Ericsson et al., 1993), typically seen as an optimization strategy, there can be aspects of compensation involved. For
instance, the athlete may realize that he or she has reached a performance
plateau beyond which he or she must move to reach a personal athletic
goal, like winning a specific competition. Thus, in addition to enhancing
existing performance means (such as additional weight training for leg muscles and/or additional hours of practice), new means may be introduced
into the performance repertoire because of a limit in a given behavior component, such as height. For example, shoes with specialized soles represent
a resource for performance enhancement (i.e., they contribute to optimiza-

tion). In such an instance, adding new shoes represents features of both optimization and compensation, because the added shoes serve as a resource for performance enhancement, but draw on new performance means as a response to existing means' insufficiency. In general, we would consider the acquisition of new shoes more compensatory if the shoes were of special origin and were acquired, for instance, due to the recognition of a deficit, such as a particular injury or pathological foot condition. This permits us to emphasize once more that the model is entitled *selective optimization with compensation*, implying that the analytic usefulness of the model components emerges only in examining them together and when recognizing the multicausality and multifunctionality of a given behavior.

SELECTION, OPTIMIZATION, AND COMPENSATION: THEORETICAL AND EMPIRICAL EXAMPLES

To illustrate selection, optimization, and compensation in more concrete and empirical ways, we have drawn on two broad domains of life-span developmental literature. Congruent with our areas of primary expertise, these represent the domains of cognitive/intellectual and social development. To clarify the concepts, we illustrate them separately, although we expect them to function together in everyday life.

Selection

Selection begins, of course, in embryonic development with features of the sensory systems, such as differential sensitivity to light wavelengths and pattern configurations. Neurophysiologically prepared modules of information processing (e.g., Barkow, Cosmides, & Tooby, 1992, Gigerenzer, in press; Karmiloff-Smith, 1992; Klix, 1993; Siegler, 1989) represent another fundamental example of selection and specialization. Subsequently, selection continues over ontogenetic time. Throughout development, selection reflects the coordinated interplay between genetic, environmental, and culture-based opportunities. At the same time, selection is not always cumulative and fixed. As we have attempted to show, ontogenetic selection pressure is also undergoing changes due to contextual demands, changes in plasticity, or the occurrence of health crises.

Cognitive and Intellectual Development. How might selection operate in the cognitive domain? On the surface, selected domains of cognitive development appear to have a high degree of congruence across individuals because they are selected by the culture. With regard to cognitive development in childhood and adolescence, for example, early cognitive development is characterized by the almost universal acquisition of language and basic problem-solving skills. Subsequently, the mastery of academic skills associated with reading, writing, and arithmetic seems to constitute the dominant domain of intellectual development in early life for most children (e.g., Sternberg & Wagner, 1986). Cognitive development continues into and beyond adolescence, with the ability to think logically being the traditional and normative "general" goal of mature reasoning in Western industrialized societies. This selection is regulated by social-legal entities, as well as by a high commonality of beliefs among socialization agents. The school system with its age-ordered curriculum, or the normative expectations of parents and their "canons" of social expectation, represent examples of this institutional- and culture-based selection. These familial, societal, and school-based systems seem to introduce substantial homogeneity of selection into human beings' early cognitive development.

Despite this apparent commonality in early intellectual socialization influences—for reasons of individual differences in genotypic constellation, variability in nurturing conditions, and individual embeddedness in particular social and economic groups—specialization and differentiation of intellectual competencies (e.g., in mathematical-spatial vs. verbal aptitudes) come to be characteristic of intellectual development in childhood and adolescence (Anastasi, 1983; Humphreys, Lubinsky, & Yao, 1993; Reinert, 1970). In fact, the pervasive findings of large interindividual differences and "types" of persons is the direct result of differential selection pressures (see also Nesselroade & Jones, 1991, Nesselroade & Thompson, in press, for additional methodological perspectives).

The specialization of intellectual tasks continues to be a dominant feature of adulthood and late life. In adulthood, much of the specialization seems to focus on work domains (e.g., Derr, 1980; Kohn & Schooler, 1982; Smelser & Erikson, 1980). Although professional work is commonly experienced by most adults, specific occupational experiences are a substantial source of heterogeneity among individuals. From the outset, different work settings select individuals for particular aptitude constellations. For example, air traffic controllers and pilots need to be selected and trained for high levels of spatial reasoning ability (Ackerman & Kanfer, 1993; Gordon & Leighty, 1988). Moreover, occupational choice and environments introduce substantial pressure for specialization over the work career. Different work settings seem to require, interfere with, or enhance different intellectual competencies (e.g., Carroll, 1986; Dowie & Elstein, 1988; Scribner, 1986; Wagner & Sternberg, 1986). For instance, Featherman, Smith, and Peterson (1990) showed that, among engineers, two distinct subtypes emerge over the work career. In their research, one engineer subtype specialized in "rational problem solving," while another subtype specialized in "reflective planning." The two groups did not differ in general ability profiles, leading the investigators to argue that engineering subtypes reflected the influences of social organization of work, career structures, and task sets.

In adulthood, the constellations of age-graded, history-graded, and non-normative "developmental tasks" (Havighurst, 1948, 1973) continue to be relevant for understanding task specialization. As suggested by Labouvie-Vief (e.g., 1982; see also Blanchard-Fields, 1986; Damon, in press; Staudinger & P. Baltes, 1994) adulthood and maturity seem to be associated with an increasing tendency to shift from predominantly cognitive/intellectual considerations in problem solving to increased considerations of emotional and social features of the problem-solving situation. This is an idea that is also consistent with research on the life-span ontogeny of wisdom (P. Baltes, Smith, & Staudinger, 1992).

The developmental tasks of late life, too, seem to introduce features of task specialization and selection. For example, Willis and colleagues (e.g., Marsiske & Willis, in press-a, in press-b; Willis, 1991) suggested that tasks of daily living—like self-care and home management—become increasingly important in late life because the goals of many post-retired individuals in advanced ages become focused on maintaining independence in the community. Moreover, as argued previously, because of age-related losses in plasticity, selection pressure may involve giving up cognitive goals and means (e.g., M. Baltes, in press-a; Brandtstädter & Greve, 1994; Brim, 1992, Heckhausen & Schulz, 1993, 1995).

Social Development. Throughout their lives, individuals shape and are shaped by their distal and proximal social contexts. Initial selection pressure, focused on the immediate context of nurturance, begins shortly after birth, if not prenatally, with the formation of a system of distinct behavioral contingencies between mother (or other primary caregiver) and infant. These contingencies result in increasingly discriminating behaviors on the part of infants toward mothers and other persons. Such capacity to discriminate social stimuli is already detectable in the first weeks after birth (Ainsworth, 1972; Bowlby, 1969; Rauh, 1990).

A closely related, yet more lifelong illustration of selection is the social convoy model, which emphasizes that close relationships created at earlier phases of the life course have a strong influence on structural and functional properties of the social network in later life phases (Antonucci, 1990; Field, Minkler, Falk, & Leino, 1993; Kahn & Antonucci, 1980). In other words, early selections concerning social partners have long-term adaptive consequences, which can be either functional or dysfunctional. For example, romantic love relationships and marriage are associated with substantial restructuring of the social network; that is, partners in intimate relationships tend to abandon relationships with other potential mates (e.g., previous dating relationships) and to homogenize their social networks (Bott, 1971; Gordon & Downing, 1978; Johnson & Leslie, 1982). This selection of particular kinds of relationships relatively early in adulthood exerts important influences throughout life. For example, early mate and peer selections will structure the kin and non-kin network available to individuals in adulthood in major ways. Such networks can contribute to, or interfere with, continued growth and resilience in the face of adverse events (e.g., Fisher, 1982; Staudinger et al., in press). We will consider this idea in greater detail in our later section on compensation.

Ontogenetic selection processes in the domain of social behavior are also governed by the particular social contexts in which individuals are actively or passively embedded. Educational settings, work environments, professional networks, family configurations, and living environments (including institutional and residential care settings) all represent environments that can facilitate and limit the opportunity structures to which individuals are exposed. On a macrosociological level, this is the essence of sociologically framed life-course theory, with its joint focus on commonality and individual differentiation (Dannefer, 1989, 1991; Mayer, 1986, 1990). Institutional contexts determine both the constraints and the options by which individuals can realize their social behaviors and preferences. Institutional membership, then, is an important selection mechanism through which all individuals pass, and institution-associated contexts are important determinants of subsequent development.

Long-term-care institutions in late life serve as an example. Selection of the institutionalization option (whether to institutionalize, and where) is governed by a variety of selection pressures, including the physical, social, and economic conditions in which individuals live. Individual factors are also important. If institutionalization occurs, it is not always, but definitely can be, successful (i.e., an individual can continue to pursue selected goals) when it is selected to match an individual's goal structure and sense of control, and the move or relocation is directed at a match between an individual's perceived competence and environmental demand characteristics (M. Baltes, Wahl, & Reichert, 1992; Lawton, 1989). Institutions can regulate still other selections: Specific social behaviors may be selectively reinforced (e.g., the initiation of dependency-support and independence- ignore scripts, as described by M. Baltes, in press-b, in the context of the learned dependency model).

In addition to general views on selection in social development, there are also more specific theoretical accounts. One conceptual framework of life-span social development advanced recently is *socioemotional selectivity theory*. This theory postulates that there are three basic functions in social interactions (i.e., information acquisition, identity development or maintenance, and emotional regulation) that motivate individuals to select specific social contacts, and that these basic functions operate in different constellations across the life span (Carstensen, 1993; see also Carstensen, Hanson, & Freund, chap. 5). Specifically, an increasing age-related shift to maximizing emotional regulation instead of the two other components (information acquisition and identity development) has been identified.

In our terminology, the changed saliency of motives in socioemotional selectivity theory would be akin to a changing ontogenetic selection pressure. In younger years, the future is perceived as largely open ended, and the choice of social partners is guided by long-term goals, such as factors conducive to identity formation and knowledge associated with career plans. Thus, social interactions in the first half of life are frequently sought for their informational potential (Carstensen, 1992, 1993). In the later years of life, or when individuals perceive close future endings, informational and identity-related functions of social contact are hypothesized to diminish. At the same time, emotional regulation assumes dominance, in part, because long-term future plans become less important and maintenance or preservation of well-being and resilience becomes more salient (Carstensen & Fredrickson, 1994; Fredrickson & Carstensen, 1990).

Optimization

Optimization is fundamental to any theory or model of development (Bandura, 1986; Brandtstädter & Schneewind, 1977; Lerner, 1986). It concerns the constellation of factors and processes that enhance plasticity and adaptive potential (P. Baltes, 1993; P. Baltes & M. Baltes, 1990b), and depends on the availability and adequacy of both elementary components (e.g., cognitive mechanics, prepared social behaviors) and organismically and environmentally based resources (e.g., cognitive pragmatics, learned social skills, accumulation of external resources). Thus, optimization also requires a mutually enhancing coalition of factors, including health, environmental, and psychological conditions.

Cognitive and Intellectual Development. In early childhood and adolescence, at least in industrialized societies, there is a universal and institutionalized intellectual optimization process reflected in parental nurturance and socialization, as well as the structures and functions provided by schools and mentors (Bloom, 1985). However, optimization seems to be a continued demand of the settings of adult intellectual functioning as well. For example, the avoidance of technological obsolescence (e.g., Willis & Dubin, 1990) and the pursuit of career advancement (e.g., Bailyn, 1980; Bray & Howard, 1980) place explicit selection pressures on individuals to enhance or maintain their job-related proficiency.

Indeed, the refinement of domain-specific expertise seems to be a central outcome of adults' engagement in professional or leisure pastimes (e.g., Brim, 1992; Ericsson & Charness, 1994; Ericsson & Smith, 1991; Glaser, 1984; Mandl & Spada, 1988; Weinert & Helmke, 1993; Weinert & Perner, in press). Achieving some profile, peak, or criterion-matched performance is the hallmark of professional development aimed at occupational advancement. To facilitate this optimization, cognitive, motivational, and goal-appropriate means need to be brought to convergence. The most explicit example of this type of selective optimization is perhaps "deliberate practice" (see Ericsson et al., 1993), or the engagement in intentional, effortful activities designed to yield improvement in a criterion task. Characteristics of deliberate practice include motivation to improve performance, repetitive performance of a similar set of tasks, and engagement in tasks that offer immediate feedback about performance efficacy. Such deliberate practice of personally salient intellectual tasks leads to higher levels of performance, as well as increased efficiency and automaticity in the cognitive process organization of task performance (Ackerman, 1992; Bandura, 1986, in press; Berg & Sternberg, 1985).

The degree of optimization achieved varies as a function of personal resources, social opportunities, and individual life histories. As a result, differential life-span trajectories arise, such as the different age curves found for fluid versus crystallized intelligence. Crystallized abilities like verbal skills, for example, are highly practical and show evidence of maintenance or even continued growth throughout most of adulthood (P. Baltes, 1993; Horn & Hofer, 1992; Schaie, 1994). Moreover, individuals who engage in relatively high levels of discretionary activity and health-maintaining behaviors, and who select intellectually superior mates, all seem to show benefits in terms of continued growth and maintenance in intellectual ability performance throughout adulthood (Schaie, 1994). Even after normative declines have occurred in the fluid mechanics, beginning in middle to late adulthood, training and practice research suggests that the potential or plasticity to remediate or enhance memory and intellectual functioning remains a feature of intellectual aging, albeit with increasing limits as people reach old age (P. Baltes & Lindenberger, 1988; P. Baltes & Willis, 1982; Kliegl, Smith, & P. Baltes, 1990; Lindenberger & P. Baltes, 1994; Willis, 1987).

Social Development. Theory is less well-developed when it comes to the optimization of social behavior and social functioning. Perhaps this is also because there is less cultural consensus in what defines optimal social behavior than is true for cognitive functioning (e.g., Little, 1994). Early in life, social games or cooperative play may be seen as the "deliberate practice" of social behaviors and social roles. Through such optimization, children can enhance their social skills and their social competence (Crawley et al., 1978; Ross, 1982). Social contexts such as friendships, peer relationships, and parent-child relationships promote and regulate these social experiences. Structured optimization of social skills and roles can be seen in the context-specific practice of gender identification and sex roles (cf. Maccoby, 1988, 1990), as well as the culture-specific encoding and socially encouraged practice of adaptive social behaviors (cf. Cole, 1988, 1991). Another illustration of the optimizing function of particular life contexts can be seen in the classic and replicated finding that children with older siblings, who presumably have had more social practice with older children than those children without older siblings, tend to be more socially responsive and are better able to elicit social responses from other children (e.g., Ross & Goldman, 1976; Shirley, 1933).

In adulthood, individuals can enhance their social connectedness and social integration when they act to increase feelings of belonging and intimacy in their personal relationships (Elbing, 1991; Weiss, 1982). Thus, individuals can actively influence the social provisions (i.e., relationship functions; e.g., Mancini & Blieszner, 1992; Weiss, 1974) emerging from their interpersonal relationships by acting to: (a) reciprocate benefits received, and/or (b) maintain and enhance feelings of equity in a relationship (Hatfield & Traupmann, 1981; Homans, 1961; Walster, Berscheid, & Walster, 1973). This enhancement of social integration can be seen in some long-term marriages, for instance, where spouses seem to regulate the climate of the relationships by actively avoiding specific conflict issues (Levenson, Carstensen, & Gottman, 1993). By demonstrating interest and care for another person, both the intimacy and the stability of a relationship can be enhanced (Clark & Reis, 1988).

Optimization in the social domain may be manifested not only at the dyadic level, but also at the aggregate level of social-network structure. For example, there is some suggestive evidence that old and very old adults seem to construct their networks to ensure fulfillment of a maximum of potential needs (e.g., instrumental and emotional support; Lang & Carstensen, 1994). Of course, such processes of social-network construction may occur at any point in the human life span. Further examples include the construction of new friendship networks in college students, or changes in network composition after critical life events such as becoming parents (e.g., Fisher, 1982). Similar social-optimization processes can be seen in work- and career-related networks. There is evidence that individuals construct their occupational networks to optimize group cohesion and organizational climate (Albrecht, 1991; Friedlander & Margulies, 1969; Lang & Hellpach, 1922; LaRocco & Jones, 1978), and to gain access to potential mentors and colleagues (e.g., Clawsen, 1980; Hill, Bahniuk, & Dobos, 1989).

Compensation

Earlier we defined *compensation* as an adjustment process, by which the functional impact of internal and external losses and limits are minimized by relying on other internal or external resources (means). We also emphasized that the logical status of a given compensatory behavior can change because of development, multifunctionality, and contextual embeddedness. We suggested that there are two major reasons or sources for compensation (see also Bäckman & Dixon, 1992).

A first source for compensation is related to the special and finite amount of resources (plasticity) available to any living system. This resource finitude is true across the life span. The second major reason for compensation, we have argued, emerges from loss of criterion-relevant resources or means, which may occur at any point in the life span, but which may become particularly salient in late life. In the following section, this loss-based subtype is the primary focus of our empirical consideration of compensation.

Cognitive and Intellectual Development. Although it is usually discussed with regard to old age, compensation is a lifelong feature of successful development. Internal or external losses occur throughout life and they involve both the individual as well as the context. For example, children may lose some of their ability for highly contextualized imagination and fantasy as they acquire the means of "decontextualized" formal logical reasoning (P. Baltes, 1987). With increasing age, and during late adulthood, such losses become more and more frequent. Several possible reasons for such cognitive losses include: (a) the loss of practice opportunities (e.g., loss of intellectual challenge with retirement), (b) negative transfer from specialization (e.g., domain-relevant knowledge interferes with performance in other domains), and (c) losses resulting from a reduction in the level of intellectual plasticity including age-related increases in morbidity (P. Baltes & Kliegl, 1992; Kliegl, Smith, & P. Baltes, 1990).

It is for this reason that P. Baltes and his colleagues originally argued that the potential for compensation resides in the "dual-face" nature of adult intellectual development. With advanced age, cognitive mechanics—including fluid intelligence—decline. For instance, older adults demonstrate lower cognitive speed and seem to be more likely to commit errors under some conditions (e.g., Cerella, 1985; Horn & Hofer, 1992; Salthouse, 1991). However, even after normative declines in the fluid mechanics of intelligence are noted, high levels of performance in personally salient domains may be maintained due to the compensatory power of accumulated domain-specific expertises, or the crystallized pragmatics of intelligence (e.g., P. Baltes, 1987, 1993; P. Baltes et al., 1984; Berg & Sternberg, 1985; Dixon & P. Baltes, 1986; Kliegl & Baltes, 1987; Knopf, Kolodziej, & Preussler, 1990; Staudinger et al., 1989; Uttal & Perlmutter, 1989).

As we suggest herein, this compensation may be a major feature of the age-related performance of adult workers (see Ericsson & Charness, 1994, for a review). The leisure and sport domains are also replete with examples of compensation. For example, Charness (1985) demonstrated that older expert chess players, despite losses in such cognitive mechanics as search speed, showed strategically superior (i.e., knowledge-based) performance in various components of chess performance (see also Knopf et al., 1990). Similarly, Krampe (1994) demonstrated that older expert pianists, despite mechanical losses in task components like tapping speed, evinced high levels of musical performance, in part because of enhanced use of strategic components like finger-movement preparation. Another example comes from the work of Salthouse (1984), who studied expert typists. Younger subjects demonstrated performance superiority on several measures of perceptual-motor speed, such as reaction time and rate of digit-symbol substitution, whereas older typists could evince comparable performance levels on typing tasks if given larger typing preview spans. Older adults seemed to use strategic knowledge about reading further ahead in to-be-typed text to compensate for performance disadvantages in response speed.

It is important to underscore that compensatory efforts need not always be based in the individual. Research by Bäckman and his colleagues is also relevant (Bäckman, 1991; Bäckman & Herlitz, 1990; Bäckman, Mäntylä, & Herlitz, 1990; Herlitz, Lipinska, & Bäckman, 1992). This research group demonstrated that, in patients with senile dementia of the Alzheimer's type, memory efficacy could be enhanced, under some conditions, with increased amounts of stimulus support (but type of support and severity of dementia seem to be important moderators of intervention efficacy; see Lipinska, Bäckman, & Herlitz, 1992). Similarly, Camp and his colleagues (Camp et al., 1993; McKitrick, Camp, & Black, 1992; see also M. Baltes & Barton, 1977) produced powerful memory-remediation results in demented older adults by enlisting a spaced retrieval procedure, which can be interpreted as the joint application of memory- and behavior-modification principles.

Throughout life, but especially in late life, the ability to compensate for deficits due to specialization and loss of functioning seems to be an important predictor of continued cognitive efficacy and the ability to live independently in the community (Wolinsky, Callahan, Fitzgerald, & Johnson, 1992). Whereas one strategy might involve "compensatory" selection, as in the increased restriction of discretionary task participation (see M. Baltes, Mayr, Borchelt, Maas, & Wilms, 1993), another strategy may be the increased reliance on other means of performance maintenance, including such noncognitive means as memory aids (e.g., Morrell, Park, & Poon, 1990), dependency in self and household care (M. Baltes, in press-a; Horgas, Wahl, & M. Baltes, in press), or social and caregiving support from others (Antonucci, 1990; MaloneBeach & Zarit, 1991).

Social Development. Two major types of social compensation are considered as examples in this section. One, the use of social support, serves as an example of a compensatory resource that can contribute to either the maintenance or the enhancement of functioning across the life span, not only after the onset of age-associated losses. A second example of compensation in the social domain, which is more prototypical of loss-initiated compensatory responses (both actual and threatened losses), concerns the use of social strategies or means to adjust or resolve conflict or distress within close relationships (i.e., "relational repair"; Duck, 1986, 1988).

In the "purest" sense, relationships that rely on the formal exchange of money, goods, and services (e.g., paid labor, formal caregivers) represent compensatory relationships that may arise to fulfill a compensatory function. Such relationships may represent relatively pure compensatory relationships because they are "added on" to the social network of the individual, and exist solely to address a loss or deficit in a particular individual. If the deficit or loss is remediated (i.e., the mechanic fixes the car, the health problem for which a patient is treated is cured), the relationship may cease to exist (although the relationship could also be transformed into another, less explicitly compensatory form, like friendship). This can be contrasted with the kinds of compensatory assistance that one's existing social networks provide. Here, although the assistance that network members provide may serve a compensatory function, the relationships may serve many functions beside compensation.

In other words, socially supportive relationships should not be interpreted as serving a purely compensatory function. At the same time, social support provides a powerful example of a compensatory resource that is available to facilitate adaptation to a variety of life challenges. Supportive relationships can imply trustworthiness, reassurance, caring, and instrumental aid. In all phases of life, having close relationships can contribute significantly to how well an individual succeeds in mastering developmental tasks, life transitions, or life events (Bosse, Aldwin, Levenson, & Workman-Daniels, 1991; Caldwell, Pearson, & Chin, 1987; Connell & D'Augelli, 1990; Krause, 1987; Schwarzer & Leppin, 1991).

The emotional and instrumental support of others, then, can act as a resource that facilitates individuals' ability to pursue selected goals and maintain or even enhance levels of functioning, regardless of whether they have explicitly experienced losses. Typical everyday examples help to illustrate the point. The supportive spouse may assume the disproportionate share of household or childrearing responsibilities to permit the marriage partner to concentrate on career advancement. The family caregiver may offer both physical support and emotional reassurance to an ailing elderly relative. Parental encouragement may help a child or adolescent to achieve higher levels of academic and athletic performance, and to develop higher levels of self-efficacy. Social resources may, of course, serve particularly important compensatory functions after the experience of losses, including social losses (e.g., widowhood; Lopata, 1978; Rice, 1989) and health-related losses (Cobb, 1992; Cohen & Wills, 1985).

Compensation in the domain of social behavior may also operate through the use of passive or proxy control (M. Baltes & Carstensen, 1994; Bandura, 1982b). When active behaviors are no longer effective for achieving mastery, individuals may compensate by modifying their social environment through passive behaviors. Some of the clearest evidence for such compensation stems from research on nursing home residents (M. Baltes, Neumann, & Zank, 1994; M. Baltes & Reisenzein, 1986; M. Baltes & Silverberg, 1994; M. Baltes et al., 1992; Horgas, Wahl, & M. Baltes, in press). M. Baltes and her colleagues found that dependent self-care behaviors of nursing home residents were often reinforced with dependency-supportive behaviors from social partners (e.g., staff). In other words, nursing home residents received the most social attention from staff members when the former displayed dependent behaviors. M. Baltes (in press-b) has suggested that this research on dependency can be taken as an instantiation of selective optimization with compensation via the learned dependency model. From this perspective, the mechanisms of compensation can be either instrumental (albeit passive) control or self-elected proxy control—both are compensation strategies by which social contact is optimized.

Compensation is also needed when intimate or significant relationships are in danger of disintegration because criterion-relevant motivation and skills are lost. In this case, individuals may try to counteract such disruptions by using strategies summarized by Duck (1986, 1988) as "relational repair." Here, the interwoven nature of social compensation and optimization can be seen again. For example, relationship partners can evaluate and modify the balance of exchanges in their relationship to promote increased reciprocity and equity. To the extent that the restructuring of exchange patterns corrects for deficits in the relationship, this may be compensation. Similarly, an individual may maintain a sense of intimacy in a relationship by changing negative beliefs and reinterpreting the partner's behavior, expectations or motives (Miller & Parks, 1982). Finally, compensation can be seen in reliance on the help of third parties (e.g., marriage counselors, clergy, family members) to deal with distress in close relationships (e.g., LaGaipa, 1982; Pilisuk & Minkler, 1980). The use of outside consultants to deal with a threatened relationship clearly constitutes drawing on "new means" for achieving relationship goals (i.e., compensation). But to the extent that the relationship is improved by such consultation (akin to consulting a trainer or coach in the cognitive or athletic domains), third-party counsellors may also constitute an optimizing influence.

Taken together, then, our illustrations from the empirical literature converge to suggest that selective optimization with compensation may offer a useful way to structure and understand the kinds of adaptive strategies that individuals use in the pursuit of particular goals and life pathways. Although the specific instantiations of the model components may vary substantially from example to example (with some examples emphasizing particular strategies more than others), the general features of the adaptive processes contained in these literatures seem to have much in common. In our final section, we attempt to consider once more the metatheoretical implications of the selective optimization with compensation model.

OUTLOOK AND REFLECTIONS

In this chapter, a major goal has been to describe the model of selective optimization with compensation, drawing heavily on conceptual and empirical examples to illustrate how the model components might operate within the cognitive, intellectual, and social domains. In this final section, we tie these ideas into the broader thrust of the present volume by considering two major issues. First, we consider the conditions under which selective optimization with compensation may lead to successful development, asking whether use of these adaptive strategies could also lead to maladaptive outcomes. Second, we offer preliminary suggestions to guide future research.

Successful Development

A defining feature of the model of selective optimization with compensation is that it offers a view of how individuals can develop "successfully." In our approach, *success* is defined contextually and involves variations of goal attainment. Goals vary over particular temporal, sociocultural, individual, and lifetime contexts. They can also have multiple meanings within different behavior domains, given the multifunctionality of particular behaviors. Aside from questions of theoretical precision and empirical operationalization, two issues are worth commenting on here. First, what is the relationship of the model and its components to unsuccessful development? Second, does pursuit of selective optimization with compensation strategies guarantee successful development?

Our understanding of unsuccessful development shifts according to level of analysis and it is quite dependent on what criteria of adaptive fitness are considered (P. Baltes & M. Baltes, 1990a; Brandtstädter & Schneewind, 1977). In general, we treat unsuccessful development as polar to successful development. In other words, for a particular individual within a particular domain, unsuccessful development occurs whenever (a) there are no goals to guide development, and/or (b) goal attainment cannot be achieved. Thus, when individuals and their contexts fail to arrange for directionality and goals, and when a desired end state in a given domain of functioning is not and cannot be reached, a lack of developmental success has occurred. Furthermore, unsuccessful development may also be seen in those instances where the movement in the direction of optimal development in particular domains (e.g., expertise) is associated with negative outcomes in other domains of functioning. For example, the cellist Pablo Casals claimed that his finger movements were so highly specialized for his musical profession that he could no longer even open a package of cheese (Casals, 1970). In other words, the possibility of negative transfer resulting from specialization means that some negative outcomes can also result from the selective optimization process. For example, consider the potentially negative outcomes associated with such selective optimizations as being a professional wrestler or boxer. Such examples highlight again that the meaning of success cannot be made clear independent of a specific frame of reference, as well as that any developmental progression is never pure gain.

These observations on systems of functioning, and ontogenetic changes in the criteria of adaptive fitness, draw attention to the role of cross-domain relationships in the delineation of selective optimization with compensation. Lack of success in one domain can be compensated for by detaching from a particular goal hierarchy and selecting alternative goal domains. Lack of goal attainment in a particular domain, then, does not necessarily imply a general lack of success. The opposite may be true. Research conducted from the perspective of the learned dependency model by M. Baltes and her colleagues (M. Baltes, in press-b; M. Baltes & Silverberg, 1994; M. Baltes et al., 1992; Horgas et al., in press) is again a prototypical example. In the domain of self-care, individuals who engage in dependent behaviors could, at first glance, be seen as failing to manage basic tasks of daily living. This is the typical view of research on everyday competence in the study of aging. At the same time, however, the evidence suggests that some individuals may turn this seemingly maladaptive outcome into an adaptive outcome as they shift to compensatory and selective strategies and make use of the multifunctional consequences of a given behavior in context (M. Baltes, in press-a; M. Baltes & Silverberg, 1994), although the process is not necessarily active nor conscious. Specifically, dependency in self-care can serve as a vehicle to ensure that (a) others meet basic personal care needs, and (b) one experiences success in other domains (social contact, leisure time). Thus, although a lack of functioning can be experienced in a particular domain, the model highlights—drawing on a systemic, multifunctional view of human living systems (Chapman, 1988)—that, on a broader, interdomain level of analysis, successful development is still possible if individuals and their biopsychosocial contexts can achieve desired ends in particular domains with high salience.

Consideration of the positive and negative consequences of selective optimization with compensation within a systems view of development is consistent, however, with one of the major tenets of life-span developmental psychology: There is no gain without loss, and no loss without gain (P. Baltes, 1987). Therefore, it is important to emphasize that engagement in processes associated with selective optimization with compensation does not, in itself, constitute a guarantee of successful development. Rather, it is a necessary, but not a sufficient, condition. There may be too much optimization in one area at the expense of another. Furthermore, motivational systems may change with ontogeny, as may the criterion demands associated with external circumstances.

In a similar vein, compensation cannot unequivocally be associated with successful development. Compensation implies maintenance of functioning in selected domains via alternative means. Alternative means, in turn, imply the availability of resources. However, aging has been described as a process of increasing resource restriction, such that resources (and alternative means) are increasingly less available. There must be some "letting go" of less central goal domains, a process that is consistent with Brandtstädter's (Brandtstädter & Greve, 1994) concept of *accommodative* (vs. assimilative) *coping.* Hence, compensation which is not attenuated by selective optimization could lead to negative system outcomes—a lack of success in many domains because of general resource depletion. However, when individuals and their life environments restrict life domains and goals more than even their finite resource profiles necessitate ("over-selection"), the result can be reduced and impoverished lives (e.g., "excess disability"; Teri, 1991; "foreclosure"; Slugoski, Marcia, & Koopman, 1984; "stagnation"; Erikson, Erikson, & Kivnick, 1986). With this, we wish to underscore that it is the joint use of selection, optimization, and compensation, adjusted to the current status of a particular biopsychosocial system, that can move the organism in the direction of developmental success. Moreover, a given constellation of selection, optimization, and compensation is not fixed, and it is likely to undergo changes with time and with contextual constraints and opportunities. In this sense, it is consistent with Lerner's metatheory of probabilistic dynamic contextualism (Lerner, 1991).

Toward Further Empirical Evaluations

What research approaches would strengthen the empirical basis of selective optimization with compensation? Although we have argued that there is research that supports the positive developmental outcomes associated with elements of selection, optimization, and compensation, the status of the model as a methatheoretical and multilevel analysis conception allows its empirical operationalization only by invoking specific theories. For this reason, we have argued that process- and domain-specific instantiations of the model are necessary to maximize testability. In addition to Bäckman and Dixon's (1992) work on compensation, other exemplars of specific theories consistent with the selective optimization with compensation model include Heckhausen and Schulz's (1993, 1995) model of motivational optimization via primary and secondary control. Other examples of process- and domain-specific explications include Carstensen's (1993; see also Carstensen, Hansen, & Freund, chap. 5) theory of socioemotional selectivity, Brandtstädter's model of assimilative and accommodative coping (e.g., Brandtstädter & Greve, 1994; Brandtstädter, Wentura, & Greve, 1993), and the model of learned dependency (M. Baltes, in press-b).

The implication of the metamodel status of selective optimization with compensation means that research informed by this perspective would ideally follow a broad, three-stage sequence. First, researchers would identify a particular domain of interest. Second, researchers would examine existing theories about functioning and adaptation within the domain, to identify whether conceptualizations and operationalizations that are congruent with selection, optimization, and compensation already exist within the literature. Third, the model can then be used to: (a) integrate existing theoretical conceptions or favor particular perspectives, and/or (b) propose alternative conceptions. In other words, selective optimization with compensation ideally informs and guides theoretical work within particular domains, and does not directly lead to research. Rather, the resultant theoretical work, which is now embedded within a particular literature and substantive domain, is used to derive testable propositions and operationalizations.

Beyond this general sequence, our position is that future developmental research on selective optimization with compensation needs to consider the sequence of research goals labeled as *description, explanation,* and *modification* (after M. Baltes, 1988; P. Baltes, 1993). Descriptive work needs to identify the presence of the selective, compensatory, and optimizing processes in life-span development, and to describe their fundamental features. Autobiographical data suggest one possible avenue: Personal histories and observations used by persons who have targeted different domains for development provide naturally structured examples of individual approaches to adaptation. Inspection of such anecdotal material permits investigators to see (a) whether selection-, optimization-, and compensation-like strategies are mentioned spontaneously as individuals describe the organization of their life courses, and their functioning within particular performance domains; and (b) how the selective optimization with compensation components might be tailored to specific personal and environmental contexts.

Table 3.2 offers three examples (music, basketball, physics) that illustrate this individualized, biographic approach. A related approach is life-review research (e.g., Staudinger, 1989), which has the benefit of examining the life courses of relatively less eminent individuals. In this approach, individuals retrospectively recount the challenges faced at different periods in their lives, and the adaptive strategies they used to manage these challenges. Of course, such research suffers from the cognitive and self-perception biases inherent in any retrospective research, but biographical data from individuals may provide a rich source of information for how the components might be applied in everyday life. Another potentially fruitful approach, drawing on strategies common in cognitive research with problem solving (e.g., Cornelius & Caspi, 1987; Denney, 1984), would be to present individuals with vignettes and then would ask subjects how they would manage presented problems. Response coding could provide information about the

TABLE 3.2
Selective Optimization with Compensation: Biographical Examples

Source	Selection	Optimization	Compensation
Concert pianist Rubinstein (Baltes & Baltes, 1990a)	Played smaller repertoire of pieces in late life	Practiced more hours with age	Slowed performance before fast movements (*ritardando*) to heighten contrast
Athlete Michael Jordan (Greene, 1993)	Focused only on basketball in youth, excluding swimming and skating	Daily line drills and upper body training	Reliance on special footwear to deal with chronic foot injury
Scientist Marie Curie (Curie, 1937)	Excluded political and cultural activities from her life	Spent a fixed number of hours daily in isolation in her laboratory	Turned to the advice of specific colleagues when encountering scientific problems that were beyond her expertise

prevalence of both selective optimization with compensation responses, and of other types of strategies used (see Marsiske & Willis, in press-b)

An operationalizable set of behavioral manifestations of selection, optimization, and compensation—within and across biopsychosocial contexts—must be delineated (either from new descriptive research or from the existing research literature; see M. Baltes & Carstensen, 1994, for a literature overview) before *explanatory* research can proceed. One quasi-experimental approach that has yielded success in the domain of self-care behaviors in elderly adults is the research we have cited from M. Baltes and her colleagues (e.g., M. Baltes, in press-b; M. Baltes, Wahl, & Reichert, 1992; Horgas et al., in press). Such microgenetic research incorporates a real-time longitudinal approach (Kruse, Lindenberger, & P. Baltes, 1993), with a careful examination of the antecedent and consequent conditions surrounding the particular adaptive strategies used by individuals. Such microgenetic research allows the study of adaptation as it unfolds, and could be incorporated with studies of short-term variability (Nesselroade, 1991) and temporally lagged causation (Schmitz & Skinner, 1993; Tesch-Römer, 1993). Explanation, in the experimental sense, may also be possible by simulating resource restriction and age-related losses, and by studying behavioral adaptations (M. Baltes & Carstensen, 1994; Kruse et al., 1993).

Modification research offers a long-term possibility of most stringently testing the adaptive outcomes associated with selective optimization with compensation. For example, Staudinger et al. (in press) suggested that one resilience-enhancing intervention for older adults might be instruction in general adaptive strategies; this would imply the necessity of individualized feedback as trained subjects work out person-specific applications of selective optimization with compensation in their own lives. Experimentally, these intervention and simulated resource-restriction conditions could be combined; pre-post comparisons of "trained" and "untrained" individuals following simulated losses on selected outcome variables could constitute one potential direction for evaluating the adaptive benefits, if any, conferred by selective optimization with compensation.

In summary, our goal has been to delineate the model of selective optimization with compensation, striving for empirical and theoretical illustrations of the heuristic utility of the model components for structuring discourse about successful developmental outcomes. We have argued that, across the life span, selective optimization with compensation is a process that, on a metalevel of analysis and coordination, is a necessary condition for successful development. We have also emphasized the contextual and person-specific variations of goals and criteria of evaluation involved in defining success. As the model is tested, more specific operationalizations will be necessary, which, depending on the theoretical framework chosen and the domain under consideration, are likely to reflect the unique concepts and methods, the preferred substantive content, and the theoretical predilections of individual researchers.

ACKNOWLEDGMENTS

The authors wish to thank John R. Nesselroade for helpful comments on an earlier version of this chapter. We are thankful to our colleagues from the Berlin Aging Study, the Max Planck Institute for Human Development and Education, the Research Unit of Psychological Gerontology of the Free University of Berlin, and the Network on Successful Midlife Development of the MacArthur Foundation (G. Brim, Director) for valuable discussions of many of the issues considered in this chapter. Frieder R. Lang and Michael Marsiske were both supported by Postdoctoral Research Fellowships from the Max Planck Institute for Human Development and Education during the writing of this chapter.

REFERENCES

Ackerman, P. L. (1992). Predicting individual differences in complex skill acquisition: Dynamics of ability determinants. *Journal of Applied Psychology, 77,* 598–614.
Ackerman, P. L., & Kanfer, R. (1993). Integrating laboratory and field study for improving selection: Development of a battery for predicting air traffic controller success. *Journal of Applied Psychology, 78,* 413–432.
Ainsworth, M. D. S. (1972). Attachment and dependency: A comparison. In J. L. Gewirtz (Ed.), *Attachment and dependency* (pp. 97–137). New York: Wiley.
Albrecht, T. L. (1991). Facilitating talk about new ideas: The role of personal relationships in organizational innovation. *Communication Monographs, 58,* 273–288.

Anastasi, A. (1983). Evolving trait concepts. *American Psychologist, 38*, 175–184.

Antonucci, T. C. (1990). Social support and social relationships. In R. H. Binstock & E. Shanas (Eds.), *Handbook of aging and the social sciences* (pp. 205–227). New York: Academic Press.

Bäckman, L. (1991). Recognition memory across the adult life span: The role of prior knowledge. *Memory and Cognition, 19*, 63–71.

Bäckman, L., & Dixon, R. A. (1992). Psychological compensation: A theoretical framework. *Psychological Bulletin, 112*, 259–283.

Bäckman, L., & Herlitz, A. (1990). The relationship between prior knowledge and face recognition memory in normal aging and Alzheimer's disease. *Journal of Gerontology: Psychological Sciences, 45*, P94–P100.

Bäckman, L., Mäntylä, T., & Herlitz, A. (1990). The optimization of episodic remembering in old age. In P. B. Baltes & M. M. Baltes (Eds.), *Successful aging: Perspectives from the behavioral sciences* (pp. 118–163). New York: Cambridge University Press.

Bailyn, L. (1980). The slow-burn way to the top: Some thoughts on the early years of organizational careers. In C. B. Derr (Ed.), *Work, family and the career* (pp. 94–108). New York: Praeger.

Baltes, M. M. (1987). Erfolgreiches Altern als Ausdruck von Verhaltenskompetenz und Umweltqualität [Successful aging as an expression of behavioral competence and environmental quality]. In C. Niemitz (Ed.), *Der Mensch in Zusammenspiel von Anlage und Umwelt* (pp. 353–377). Frankfurt: Suhrkamp.

Baltes, M. M. (1988). The etiology and maintenance of dependency in the elderly: Three phases of operant research. *Behavior Therapy, 19*, 301–319.

Baltes, M. M. (in press-a). Dependencies in old age: Gains and losses. *Current Directions in Psychological Science.*

Baltes, M. M. (in press-b). *The many faces of dependency in old age.* New York: Cambridge University Press.

Baltes, M. M., & Barton, E. M. (1977). New approaches toward aging: A case for the operant model. *Educational Gerontology, 2*, 383–405.

Baltes, M. M., & Carstensen, L. L. (1994). *The process of successful aging.* Unpublished manuscript, Free University of Berlin.

Baltes, M. M., Mayr, U., Borchelt, M., Maas, I., & Wilms, H.-U. (1993). Everyday competence in old and very old age: An interdisciplinary perspective. *Ageing and Society, 13*, 657–680.

Baltes, M. M., Neumann, E. M., & Zank, S. (1994). Maintenance and rehabilitation of independence in old age: An intervention program for staff. *Psychology and Aging, 9*, 179–188.

Baltes, M. M., & Reisenzein, R. (1986). The social world in long-term care institutions: Psychosocial control toward dependency? In M. M. Baltes & P. B. Baltes (Eds.), *The psychology of control and aging* (pp. 315–343). Hillsdale, NJ: Lawrence Erlbaum Associates.

Baltes, M. M., & Silverberg, S. B. (1994). The dynamics between dependency and autonomy: Illustrations across the life span. In D. L. Featherman, R. M. Lerner, & M. Perlmutter (Eds.), *Life-span development and behavior* (Vol. 12, pp. 42–91). Hillsdale, NJ: Lawrence Erlbaum Associates.

Baltes, M. M., Wahl, H. W., & Reichert, M. (1992). Successful aging in long-term care institutions. In K. W. Schaie & M. Powell Lawton (Eds.), *Annual review of gerontology and geriatrics* (Vol. 11, pp. 311–337). New York: Springer.

Baltes, P. B. (1987). Theoretical propositions of life-span developmental psychology: On the dynamics between growth and decline. *Developmental Psychology, 23*, 611–626.

Baltes, P. B. (1991). The many faces of human aging: Toward a psychological culture of old age. *Psychological Medicine, 21*, 837–854.

Baltes, P. B. (1993). The aging mind: Potentials and limits. *Gerontologist, 33*, 580–594.

Baltes, P. B. (1994, August). *Life-span developmental psychology: On the overall landscape of human development.* Invited address, American Psychological Association Annual Convention, Los Angeles, CA.

Baltes, P. B., & Baltes, M. M. (1980). Plasticity and variability in psychological aging: Methodological and theoretical issues. In G. E. Gurski (Ed.), *Determining the effects of aging on the central nervous system* (pp. 41–66). Berlin: Schering.

Baltes, P. B., & Baltes, M. M. (1990a). Psychological perspectives on successful aging: The model of selective optimization with compensation. In P. B. Baltes & M. M. Baltes (Eds.), *Successful aging: Perspectives from the behavioral sciences* (pp. 1–34). New York: Cambridge University Press.

Baltes, P. B., & Baltes, M. M. (Eds.). (1990b). *Successful aging: Perspectives from the behavioral sciences.* New York: Cambridge University Press.

Baltes, P. B., Dittmann-Kohli, F., & Dixon, R. A. (1984). New perspectives on the development of intelligence in adulthood: Toward a dual process conception and a model of selective optimization with compensation. In P. B. Baltes & O. G. Brim (Eds.), *Life-span development and behavior* (Vol. 6, pp. 33–76). New York: Academic Press.

Baltes, P. B., & Graf, P. (in press). Psychological and social aspects of aging: Facts and frontiers. In D. Magnusson (Ed.), *Nobel symposium on life-span development of individuals: A synthesis of biological and psychological perspectives.* New York: Cambridge University Press.

Baltes, P. B., & Kliegl, R. (1992). Further testing of limits in cognitive plasticity in old age: Negative age differences in a mnemonic skill are robust. *Developmental Psychology, 28,* 121–125.

Baltes, P. B., & Lindenberger, U. (1988). On the range of cognitive plasticity in old age as a function of experience: Fifteen years of intervention research. *Behavior Therapy, 19,* 283–300.

Baltes, P. B., Reese, H. W., & Lipsitt, L. P. (1980). Life-span developmental psychology. *Annual Review of Psychology, 31,* 65–110.

Baltes, P. B., Smith, J., & Staudinger, U. M. (1992). Wisdom and successful aging. In T. Sonderegger (Ed.), *Nebraska symposium on motivation* (Vol. 39, pp. 123–167). Lincoln, NE: University of Nebraska Press.

Baltes, P. B., & Willis, S. L. (1982). Plasticity and enhancement of intellectual functioning in old age: Penn State's Adult Development and Enrichment Project (ADEPT). In F. I. M. Craik & S. E. Trehub (Eds.), *Aging and cognitive processes* (pp. 353–389). New York: Plenum.

Bandura, A. (1982a). The psychology of chance encounters and life paths. *American Psychologist, 37,* 747–755.

Bandura, A. (1982b). Self-efficacy mechanism in human agency. *American Psychologist, 37,* 122–147.

Bandura, A. (1986). *Social foundations of thought and action: A social cognitive theory.* Englewood Cliffs, NJ: Prentice-Hall.

Bandura, A. (Ed.). (in press). *Self-efficacy in a changing society.* New York: Cambridge University Press.

Barkow, J. H., Cosmides, L., & Tooby, J. (Eds.). (1992). *The adapted mind: Evolutionary psychology and the generation of culture.* New York: Oxford University Press.

Berg, C. A., & Sternberg, R. J. (1985). A triarchic theory of intellectual development during adulthood. *Developmental Review, 5,* 334–370.

Blanchard-Fields, F. (1986). Reasoning in adolescents and adults on social dilemmas varying in emotional saliency: An adult developmental perspective. *Psychology and Aging, 1,* 325–333.

Bloom, B. (1985). *Developing talent in young people.* New York: Ballantine.

Boesch, E. E. (1971). Die diagnostische Systematisierung [The process of diagnostic systemization]. In R. Heiss (Ed.), *Psychologische Diagnostik* (pp. 930–959). Göttingen: Hogrefe.

Bosse, R., Aldwin, C. M., Levenson, M. R., & Workman-Daniels, K. (1991). How stressful is retirement? Findings from the Normative Aging Study. *Journal of Gerontology: Psychological Sciences, 46,* P9–P14.

Bott, E. (1971). *Family and social network: Roles, norms, and external relationships in ordinary urban families* (2nd ed.). London: Tavistock.

Bowlby, J. (1969). *Attachment: Attachment and loss* (Vol. 1). New York: Basic Books.

Brandtstädter, J., & Greve, W. (1994). The aging self: Stabilizing and protective processes. *Developmental Review, 14,* 52–80.

Brandtstädter, J., & Schneewind, K. A. (1977). Optimal human development: Some implications for psychology. *Human Development, 20,* 48–64.

Brandtstädter, J., Wentura, D., & Greve, W. (1993). Adaptive resources of the aging self: Outlines of an emergent perspective. *International Journal of Behavioral Development, 16,* 323–349.

Bray, D. W., & Howard, A. (1980). Career success and life satisfaction of middle-aged managers. In L. A. Bond & J. C. Rosen (Eds.), *Competence and coping during adulthood* (pp. 258–287). Hanover, NH: University Press of New England.

Brent, S. B. (1978). Prigogine's model for self-organization in nonequilibrium systems: Its relevance for developmental psychology. *Human Development, 21,* 374–387.

Brim, O. G. (1992). *Ambition: How we manage success and failure throughout our lives.* New York: Basic Books.

Brim, O. G., & Wheeler, S. (1966). *Socialization after childhood: Two essays.* New York: Wiley.

Caldwell, R. A., Pearson, J. L., & Chin, R. J. (1987). Stress-moderating effects: Social support in the context of gender and locus of control. *Personality and Social Psychology Bulletin, 13,* 5–17.

Camp, C. J., Foss, J. W., Stevens, A. B., Reichard, C. C., McKitrick, L. A., & O'Hanlon, A. M. (1993). Memory training in normal and demented elderly populations: The E-I-E-I-O model. *Experimental Aging Research, 19,* 277–290.

Carroll, J. S. (1986). Causal theories of crime and their effect upon expert parole decisions. In H. R. Arkes & K. R. Hammond (Eds.), *Judgment and decision making: An interdisciplinary reader* (pp. 243–254). Cambridge, England: Cambridge University Press.

Carstensen, L. L. (1992). Social and emotional patterns in adulthood: Support for socioemotional selectivity theory. *Psychology and Aging, 7,* 331–338.

Carstensen, L. L. (1993). Motivation for social contact across the life span. A theory of socioemotional selectivity. In J. Jacobs (Ed.), *Nebraska symposium on motivation: Developmental perspectives on motivation* (Vol. 40, pp. 209–254). Lincoln, NE: University of Nebraska Press.

Carstensen, L. L., & Fredrickson, B. (1994). *Social partner preference as a function of place in the life cycle.* Unpublished manuscript, Department of Psychology, Stanford University, Stanford, CA.

Casals, P. (1970). *Joys and sorrows: Reflections as told to Albert E. Kahn.* New York: Simon & Schuster.

Cattell, R. B. (1971). *Abilities: Their structure, growth, and action.* Boston: Houghton Mifflin.

Cerella, J. (1985). Information processing rates in the elderly. *Psychological Bulletin, 98,* 67–83.

Chapman, M. (1988). Contextuality and directionality of cognitive development. *Human Development, 31,* 92–106.

Charness, N. (Ed.). (1985). *Aging and human performance.* Chichester, England: Wiley.

Clark, M. S., & Reis, H. T. (1988). Interpersonal processes in close relationships. *Annual Review of Psychology, 39,* 609–672.

Clawsen, J. G. (1980). Mentoring in managerial careers. In C. B. Derr (Ed.), *Work, family, and the career: New frontiers in theory and research* (pp. 144–165). New York: Praeger.

Cobb, S. (1992). Social support and health through the life course. In H. I. McCubbin, E. A. Cauble, & J. M. Patterson (Eds.), *Family stress, coping and social support* (pp. 189–199). Springfield, IL: Thomas.

Cohen, S., & Wills, T. A. (1985). Stress, social support, and the buffering hypothesis. *Psychological Bulletin, 98,* 310–357.

Cole, M. (1988). Cross-cultural research in the sociohistorical tradition. *Human Development, 31,* 137–152.

Cole, M. (1990). Cultural psychology: A once and future discipline? In J. J. Berman (Ed.), *Nebraska Symposium on Motivation 1989: Cross-cultural perspectives* (pp. 279–335). Lincoln, NE: University of Nebraska Press.

Cole, M. (1991). A cultural theory of development: What does it imply about the application of scientific research? *Learning and Instruction, 1,* 187–200.

Cole, M. (in press). Interacting minds in a lifespan perspective: A cultural-historical approach to culture and cognitive development. In P. B. Baltes & U. M. Staudinger (Eds.), *Interactive minds: Life-span perspectives on the social foundation of cognition.* New York: Cambridge University Press.

Connell, C. M., & D'Augelli, A. R. (1990). The contribution of personality characteristics to the relationship between social support and perceived physical health. *Health Psychology, 9,* 192–207.

Cornelius, S. W., & Caspi, A. (1987). Everyday problem solving in adulthood and old age. *Psychology and Aging, 2,* 144–153.

Crawley, S. B., Rogers, P. P., Friedman, S., Criticos, A., Richardson, L., & Thompson, M. A. (1978). Developmental changes in the structure of mother-infant play. *Developmental Psychology, 14,* 30–36.

Crow, L. T. (1985). More on variability as a behavioral concept. *Psychological Record, 35,* 293–300.

Curie, E. (1937). *Madame Curie.* Vienna: Baumann-Fischer Verlag.

Damon, W. (in press). The lifelong transformation of moral goals through social influence. In P. B. Baltes & U. M. Staudinger (Eds.), *Interactive minds: Life-span perspectives on the social foundation of cognition.* New York: Cambridge University Press.

Dannefer, D. (1984). Adult development and social theory: A paradigmatic reappraisal. *American Sociological Review, 49,* 100–116.

Dannefer, D. (1989). Human action and its place in theories of aging. *Journal of Aging Studies, 3,* 1–20.

Dannefer, D. (1991). The race is to the swift: Images of collective aging. In G. M. Kenyon, J. E. Birren, & J. J. F. Schroots (Eds.), *Emergent theories of aging* (pp. 356–384). New York: Springer.

Dannefer, D. (1992). On the conceptualization of context in developmental discourse: Four meanings of context and their implications. In D. L. Featherman, R. M. Lerner, & M. Perlmutter (Eds.), *Life-span development and behavior* (Vol. 11, pp. 84–111). Hillsdale, NJ: Lawrence Erlbaum Associates.

Denney, N. W. (1984). A model of cognitive development across the life span. *Developmental Review, 4,* 171–191.

Derr, C. B. (Ed.). (1980). *Work, family, and the career.* New York: Praeger.

Dixon, R. A., & Baltes, P. B. (1986). Toward life-span research on the functions and pragmatics of intelligence. In R. J. Sternberg & R. K. Wagner (Eds.), *Practical intelligence: Nature and origins of competence in the everyday world* (pp. 203–235). New York: Cambridge University Press.

Dowie, J., & Elstein, A. (Eds.). (1988). *Professional judgment: A reader in clinical decision making.* Cambridge, England: Cambridge University Press.

Duck, S. (1986). *Human relationships.* London: Sage.

Duck, S. (1988). *Relating to others.* New York: Dorsey.

Dunn, L. L. (1965). *A short history of genetics.* New York: McGraw-Hill.

Edelman, G. M. (1987). *Neural Darwinism: The theory of neuronal group selection.* New York: Basic Books.

Elbing, E. (1991). *Einsamkeit* [Loneliness]. Göttingen: Hogrefe.

Elder, G. H. (1985). *Life course dynamics: Trajectories and transitions 1968–1980.* Ithaca, NY: Cornell University Press.

Ericsson, K. A., & Charness, N. (1994). Expert performance: Its structure and acquisition. *American Psychologist, 49,* 725–747.

Ericsson, K. A., Krampe, R. Th., & Tesch-Römer, C. (1993). The role of deliberate practice in the acquisition of expert performance. *Psychological Review, 100*, 363–406.

Ericsson, K. A., & Smith, J. (Eds.). (1991). *Towards a general theory of expertise: Prospects and limits.* New York: Cambridge University Press.

Erikson, E., Erikson, J. M., & Kivnick, H. (1986). *Vital involvement in old age: The experience of old age in our time.* London: Norton.

Featherman, D. L. (1983). The life-span perspective in social science research. In P. B. Baltes & O. G. Brim (Eds.), *Life-span development and behavior* (Vol. 5, pp. 1–59). New York: Academic Press.

Featherman, D. L., Smith, J., & Peterson, J. G. (1990). Successful aging in a "post-retired" society. In P. B. Baltes & M. M. Baltes (Eds.), *Successful aging: Perspectives from the behavioral sciences* (pp. 50–93). New York: Cambridge University Press.

Field, D., Minkler, M., Falk, R. F., & Leino, E. V. (1993). The influence of health on family contacts and family feelings in advanced old age: A longitudinal study. *Journal of Gerontology: Psychological Sciences, 48*, P18–P28.

Fisher, C. S. (1982). *To dwell among friends.* Chicago: The University of Chicago Press.

Ford, D. H. (1987). *Humans as self-constructing living systems: A developmental perspective on behavior and personality.* Hillsdale, NJ: Lawrence Erlbaum Associates.

Fredrickson, B., & Carstensen, L. L. (1990). Choosing social partners: How old age and anticipated endings make people more selective. *Psychology and Aging, 5*, 163–171.

Friedlander, F., & Margulies, N. (1969). Multiple impacts of organizational climate and individual value systems upon job satisfaction. *Personnel Psychology, 22*, 171–183.

Gehlen, A. (1956). *Urmensch und Spätkultur* [Primitive man and late culture]. Bonn: Athenäum.

Gigerenzer, G. (in press). Rationality: Why social context matters. In P. B. Baltes & U. M. Staudinger (Eds.), *Interactive minds: Life-span perspectives on the social foundation of cognition.* New York: Cambridge University Press.

Glaser, R. (1984). Education and thinking: The role of knowledge. *American Psychologist, 39*, 93–104.

Gordon, H. W., & Leighty, R. (1988). Importance of specialized cognitive functioning in the selection of military pilots. *Journal of Applied Psychology, 73*, 38–45.

Gordon, M., & Downing, H. (1978). A multivariate test of the Bott hypothesis in an urban Irish setting. *Journal of Marriage and the Family, 40*, 585–593.

Greene, B. (1993). *Hang time: Days and dreams with Michael Jordan.* New York: St. Martin's Press.

Harris, D. B. (Ed.). (1957). *The concept of development.* Minneapolis, MN: University of Minnesota Press.

Hatfield, E., & Traupmann, J. (1981). Intimate relationships: A perspective from equity theory. In S. W. Duck & R. Gilmour (Eds.), *Personal relationships: Studying personal relationships* (Vol. 1, pp. 165–178). London: Academic Press.

Havighurst, R. J. (1948). *Developmental tasks and education.* New York: McKay.

Havighurst, R. J. (1973). History of developmental psychology: Socialization and personality development through the life span. In P. B. Baltes & K. W. Schaie (Eds.), *Life-span developmental psychology: Personality and socialization* (pp. 3–24). New York: Academic Press.

Heckhausen, J., Dixon, R. A., & Baltes, P. B. (1989). Gains and losses in development throught adulthood as perceived by different adult age groups. *Developmental Psychology, 25*, 109–121.

Heckhausen, J., & Krueger, J. (1993). Developmental expectations for the self and most other people: Age grading in three functions of social comparison. *Developmental Psychology, 29*, 539–548.

Heckhausen, J., & Schulz, R. (1993). Optimization by selection and compensation: Balancing primary and secondary control in life-span development. *International Journal of Behavioral Development, 16*, 287–303.

Heckhausen, J., & Schulz, R. (1995). A life-span theory of control. *Psychological Review, 102*.

Herlitz, A., Lipinska, B., & Bäckman, L. (1992). Utilization of cognitive support for episodic remembering in Alzheimer's disease. In L. Bäckman (Ed.), *Memory functioning in dementia* (pp. 73–96). Amsterdam: Elsevier.

Hill, S. K., Bahniuk, M. H., & Dobos, J. (1989). The impact of mentoring and collegial support on faculty success: An analysis of support behavior, information adequacy, and communication apprehension. *Communication Education, 38,* 15–33.

Homans, G. C. (1961). *Social behavior. Its elementary forms.* New York: Harcourt Brace.

Horgas, A. L., Wahl, H.-W., & Baltes, M. M. (in press). Dependency in late life. In L. L. Carstensen, B. A. Edelstein, & L. Dornbrand (Eds.), *The practical handbook of clinical gerontology.* Newbury Park, CA: Sage.

Horn, J. L., & Hofer, S. M. (1992). Major abilities and development in the adult period. In R. J. Sternberg & C. A. Berg (Eds.), *Intellectual development* (pp. 44–59). New York: Cambridge University Press.

Humphreys, L. G., Lubinsky, D., & Yao, G. (1993). Utility of predicting group membership and the role of spatial visualization in becoming an engineer, physical scientist, or artist. *Journal of Applied Psychology, 78,* 250–261.

Johnson, M. P., & Leslie, L. (1982). Couple involvement and network structure: A test of the dyadic withdrawal hypothesis. *Social Psychological Quarterly, 45,* 34–43.

Kahn, R. L., & Antonucci, T. C. (1980). Convoys over the life course: Attachment, roles, and social support. In P. B. Baltes & O. G. Brim (Eds.), *Life-span development and behavior* (Vol. 3, pp. 254–283). San Diego, CA: Academic Press.

Karmiloff-Smith, A. (1992). *Beyond modularity: A developmental perspective on cognitive science.* Cambridge, MA: MIT Press.

Kliegl, R., & Baltes, P. B. (1987). Theory-guided analysis of mechanisms of development and aging mechanisms through testing-the-limits and research on expertise. In C. Schooler & K. W. Schaie (Eds.), *Cognitive functioning and social structure over the life course* (pp. 95–119). Norwood, NJ: Ablex.

Kliegl, R., Smith, J., & Baltes, P. B. (1990). On the locus and process of magnification of age differences during mnemonic training. *Developmental Psychology, 26,* 894–904.

Klix, F. (1993). *Erwachendes Denken: Eine Entwicklungsgeschichte der menschlichen Intelligenz* [Awakening thought: A developmental and evolutionary history of human intelligence]. Berlin: VEB Deutscher Verlag der Wissenschaften.

Knopf, M., Kolodziej, P., & Preussler, W. (1990). Der ältere Mensch als Experte: Literaturübersicht über die Rolle von Expertenwissen für die kognitive Leistungfähigkeit im höheren Alter [The older person as expert: A review of the role of expert knowledge in the cognitive performance of older adults]. *Zeitschrift für Gerontopsychologie und -psychiatrie, 1,* 117–126.

Kohli, M. (1986). Social organization and subjective construction of the life course. In A. B. Sörensen, F. Weinert, & L. R. Sherrod (Eds.), *Human development and the life course: Multidisciplinary perspectives* (pp. 271–292). Hillsdale, NJ: Lawrence Erlbaum Associates.

Kohli, M., & Meyer, J. W. (1986). Social structure and social construction of life stages. *Human Development, 29,* 145–180.

Kohn, M. L., & Schooler, C. (1982). Job conditions and personality: A longitudinal assessment of their reciprocal effects. *American Journal of Sociology, 87,* 1257–1286.

Krampe, R. Th. (1994). *Maintaining excellence: Cognitive-motor performance in pianists differing in age and skill level.* Berlin: Edition Sigma.

Krause, N. (1987). Life stress, social support, and self esteem in an elderly population. *Psychology and Aging, 2,* 349–356.

Kruse, A. (1992). Alter im Lebenslauf [Age in the life course]. In P. B. Baltes & J. Mittelstraß (Eds.), *Zukunft des Alterns und gesellschaftliche Entwicklung* (pp. 331–355). Berlin: DeGruyter.

Kruse, A., Lindenberger, U., & Baltes, P. B. (1993). Longitudinal research on human aging: The power of combining real-time, microgenetic, and simulation approaches. In D. Magnusson & P. Casaer (Eds.), *Longitudinal research on individual development* (pp. 153–193). New York: Cambridge University Press.

76

MARSISKE ET AL.

Labouvie-Vief, G. (1982). Dynamic development and mature autonomy: A theoretical prologue. *Human Development, 25*, 161–191.

LaGaipa, J. J. (1982). Rules and rituals in disengaging from relationships. In S. W. Duck (Ed.), *Personal relationships: Dissolving personal relationships* (Vol. 4, pp. 189–210). New York: Academic Press.

Lang, F. R., & Carstensen, L. L. (1994). Close emotional relationships in late life: Further support for proactive aging in the social domain. *Psychology and Aging, 9*, 315–324.

Lang, R., & Hellpach, W. (1922). *Gruppenfabrikation* [The construction of groups]. Berlin: Springer.

LaRocco, J. M., & Jones, A. P. (1978). Co-worker and leader support as moderators of stress-strain relationships in work situations. *Journal of Applied Psychology, 63*, 629–634.

Lawton, M. P. (1989). Environmental proactivity in older people. In V. L. Bengtson & K. W. Schaie (Eds.), *The course of later life: Research and reflections* (pp. 15–23). New York: Springer.

Lerner, R. M. (1984). *On the nature of human plasticity.* New York: Cambridge University Press.

Lerner, R. M. (1986). *Concepts and theories of human development* (2nd ed.). New York: Random House.

Lerner, R. M. (1991). Changing organism-context relations as the basic process of development: A developmental contextual perspective. *Developmental Psychology, 27*, 27–32.

Lerner, R. M., & Busch-Rossnagel, N. A. (1981). Individuals as producers of their development: Conceptual and empirical bases. In R. M. Lerner & N. A. Busch-Rossnagel (Eds.), *Individuals as producers of their development: A life-span perspective* (pp. 1–36). New York: Academic Press.

Levenson, R. W., Carstensen, L. L., & Gottman, J. M. (1993). Longterm marriage: Age, gender, and satisfaction. *Psychology and Aging, 6*, 28–35.

Lindenberger, U., & Baltes, P. B. (1994). Sensory functioning and intelligence in old age: A strong connection. *Psychology and Aging, 9*, 339–355.

Lipinska, B., Bäckman, L., & Herlitz, A. (1992). When Greta Garbo is easier to remember than Stefan Edberg: Influences of prior knowledge on recognition memory in Alzheimer's disease. *Psychology and Aging, 7*, 214–220.

Little, T. D. (1994). *Multi-CAM, A multi-dimensional instrument to assess children's action-related beliefs: Conceptual versions (English and German) for the domains of friendships and academic performance* (ACCD Tech. Rep. No. 2). Berlin: Max Planck Institute for Human Development and Education.

Lopata, H. (1978). Contributions of extended families to the support system of metropolitan widows: Limitations of the modified kin network. *Journal of Marriage and the Family, 40*, 355–364.

Maccoby, E. (1988). Gender as a social category. *Developmental Psychology, 24*, 755–765.

Maccoby, E. (1990). Gender and relationships: A developmental account. *American Psychologist, 45*, 513–520.

Maddox, G. L. (Ed.). (1987). *The encyclopedia of aging.* New York: Springer.

Magnusson, D. (1990). Personality development from an interactional perspective. In L. A. Pervin (Ed.), *Handbook of personality: Theory and research* (pp. 193–222). New York: Guilford Press.

Magnusson, D. (1993). Human ontogeny: A longitudinal perspective. In D. Magnusson & P. Caesar (Eds.), *Longitudinal research on individual development* (pp. 1–25). New York: Cambridge University Press.

MaloneBeach, E. E., & Zarit, S. H. (1991). Current research issues in caregiving to the elderly. *International Journal of Aging and Human Development, 32*, 103–114.

Mancini, J. A., & Blieszner, R. (1992). Social provisions in adulthood: Concept and measurement in close relationships. *Journal of Gerontology: Psychological Sciences, 47*, P14–P20.

Mandl, H., & Spada, H. (Eds.). (1988)., *Wissenpsychologie* [Psychology of knowledge]. Munich-Weinheim: Psychologie Verlags Union.

Markus, H., & Herzog, A. R. (1991). The role of the self-concept in aging. In K. W. Schaie (Ed.), *Annual review of gerontology and geriatrics* (Vol. 11, pp. 111–143). New York: Springer.

Markus, H., & Wurf, E. (1987). The dynamic self-concept: A social psychological perspective. *Annual Review of Psychology, 38*, 299–337.

Marsiske, M., & Willis, S. L. (in press-a). Dimensionality of everyday problem solving in older adults. *Psychology and Aging.*

Marsiske, M., & Willis, S. L. (in press-b). Practical creativity in older adults' everyday problem solving: Life-span perspectives. In C. E. Adams-Price (Ed.), *Creativity and aging: Theoretical and empirical approaches.* New York: Springer.

Mayer, K. U. (1986). Structural constraints on the life course. *Human Development, 29*, 163–170.

Mayer, K. U. (1990). Lebensverläufe und sozialer Wandel: Anmerkungen zu einem Forschungsprogramm [Life courses and social change: Notes on a research program]. *Kölner Zeitschrift für Soziologie und Sozialpsychologie, 42*(31), 7–21.

McKitrick, L. A., Camp, C. J., & Black, F. W. (1992). Prospective memory intervention in Alzheimer's disease. *Journal of Gerontology: Psychological Sciences, 47*, P337–P343.

Miller, G. R., & Parks, M. R. (1982). Communication in dissolving relationships. In S. W. Duck (Ed.), *Personal relationships: Dissolving personal relationships* (Vol. 4, pp. 127–154). London: Academic Press.

Morrell, R. W., Park, D. C., & Poon, L. W. (1990). Effects of labelling techniques on memory and comprehension of prescription information in young and older adults. *Journal of Gerontology: Psychological Sciences, 45*, P166–P172.

Nesselroade, J. R. (1991). Interindividual differences in intraindividual change. In L. M. Collins & J. L. Horn (Eds.), *Best methods for the analysis of change* (pp. 92–105). Washington, DC: American Psychological Association.

Nesselroade, J. R., & Jones, C. J. (1991). Multi-modal selection effects in the study of adult development: A perspective on multivariate, replicated, single-subject, repeated measures designs. *Experimental Aging Research, 17*, 21–27.

Nesselroade, J. R., & Thompson, W. (in press). Selection and related threats to group comparisons: An example comparing factorial structures of higher and lower ability groups of adult twins. *Psychological Bulletin.*

Nisbett, R. E. (1980). *History of the idea of progress.* New York: Basic Books.

Nurius, P., & Markus, H. (1990). Situational variability in the self-concept: Appraisal, expectancies, and asymmetry. *Journal of Social and Clinical Psychology, 9*, 316–333.

Oerter, R. (1986). Developmental tasks through the life span: A new approach to an old concept. In P. B. Baltes, D. L. Featherman, & R. M. Lerner (Eds.), *Life-span development and behavior* (Vol. 7, pp. 233–269). Hillsdale, NJ: Lawrence Erlbaum Associates.

Pilisuk, M., & Minkler, M. (1980). Supportive networks: Life ties for the elderly. *Journal of Social Issues, 36*, 95–116.

Plomin, R., Pedersen, N. L., Lichtenstein, P., & McClearn, G. E. (1994). Variability and stability in cognitive abilities are largely genetic in later life. *Behavior Genetics, 24*, 207–216.

Prigogine, L. (1980). *Being to becoming.* San Francisco, CA: Freeman.

Rauh, H. (1990). Die Rolle der Mutter in der Sozialisation des kleinen Kindes: Reprise eines kontroversen Themas [The role of the mother in the socialization of the little child: Reprise of a controversial topic]. In R. Schmitz-Scherzer, A. Kruse, & E. Olbrich (Eds.), *Ein lebenslanger Prozess der sozialen Interaktion. Festschrift zum 60. Geburtstag von Frau Professor Ursula Maria Lehr* (pp. 411–423). Berlin: Steinkopff.

Reinert, G. (1970). Comparative factor analytic studies of intelligence throughout the human life span. In L. R. Goulet & P. B. Baltes (Eds.), *Life-span developmental psychology: Research and theory* (pp. 467–486). New York: Academic Press.

Resnick, L. B. (1990). Literacy in school and out. *Daedalus, 119*, 169–185.

Rice, S. (1989). Single, older childless women. Differences between never-married and widowed women in life-satisfaction and social support. *Journal of Gerontological Social Work, 13,* 35–47.

Riley, M. W. (1987). On the significance of age in sociology. *American Sociological Review, 52,* 1–14.

Ross, H. S. (1982). Establishment of social games among toddlers. *Developmental Psychology, 18,* 509–518.

Ross, H. S., & Goldman, B. D. (1976). Establishing new social relations in infancy. In T. Alloway, P. Pliner, & L. Krames (Eds.), *Advances in the study of communication and affect: Attachment behavior* (Vol. 3, pp. 61–79). New York: Plenum.

Ryff, C. D. (1989). In the eye of the beholder: Views of psychological well-being among middle-aged and older adults. *Psychology and Aging, 4,* 195–210.

Salthouse, T. A. (1984). Effects of age and skill in typing. *Journal of Experimental Psychology: General, 113,* 345–371.

Salthouse, T. A. (1991). *Theoretical perspectives on cognitive aging.* Hillsdale, NJ: Lawrence Erlbaum Associates.

Scarr, S. (1993). Genes, experience, and development. In D. Magnusson & P. Caesar (Eds.), *Longitudinal research on individual development: Present status and future perspectives* (pp. 26–50). Cambridge, England: Cambridge University Press.

Schaie, K. W. (1989). The hazards of cognitive aging. *Gerontologist, 29,* 484–493.

Schaie, K. W. (1994). The course of adult intellectual development. *American Psychologist, 49,* 304–313.

Schmitz, B., & Skinner, E. (1993). Perceived control, effort, and academic performance: Interindividual, intraindividual, and multivariate time series analysis. *Journal of Personality and Social Psychology, 64,* 1010–1028.

Schwarzer, R., & Leppin, A. (1991). Social support and health: A theoretical and empirical overview. *Journal of Social and Personal Relationships, 8,* 99–127.

Scribner, S. (1986). Thinking in action: Some characteristics of practical thought. In R. J. Sternberg & R. K. Wagner (Eds.), *Practical intelligence: Nature and origins of competence in the everyday world* (pp. 13–30). Cambridge, England: Cambridge University Press.

Shirley, M. (1933). *The first two years: A study of twenty-five babies.* Minneapolis, MN: University of Minneapolis Press.

Siegler, R. S. (1989). Mechanisms of cognitive development. *Annual Review of Psychology, 40,* 353–379.

Siegler, R. S. (1994). Cognitive variability: A key to understanding cognitive development. *Current Directions in Psychological Science, 3,* 1–5.

Skinner, B. F. (1966). The phylogeny and ontogeny of behavior. *Science, 153,* 1205–1213.

Slugoski, B. R., Marcia, J. R., & Koopman, R. F. (1984). Cognitive and social-interactive characteristics of ego identity structures in college males. *Journal of Personality and Social Psychology, 47,* 646–661.

Smelser, N. J., & Erikson, E. H. (Eds.). (1980). *Themes of work and love in adulthood.* Cambridge, MA: Harvard University Press.

Smith, J., & Marsiske, M. (in press). Definitions and taxonomies of foundation skills and adult competencies. In A. Tuijnman, I. Kirsch, & D. A. Wagner (Eds.), *Adult basic skills: Innovations in measurement and policy analysis.* Cresskill, NJ: Hampton Press.

Staudinger, U. M. (1989). *The study of life review: An approach to the investigation of intellectual development across the life span.* Berlin: Edition Sigma.

Staudinger, U. M., & Baltes, P. B. (1994). Gedächtnis, Weisheit, und Lebenserfahrung: Zur Ontogenese als Zusammenwirken von Biologie und Kultur [Memory, wisdom, and life experience: Ontogenesis as interaction between biology and culture]. In D. Dörner & E. Van der Meer (Eds.), *Gedächtnis (Festschrift zum 65. Geburtstag von Friedhart Klix)* (pp. 431–484). Göttingen, Germany: Hogrefe.

Staudinger, U. M., Cornelius, S. W., & Baltes, P. B. (1989). The aging of intelligence: Potentials and limits. *The Annals of the American Academy of Political and Social Science, 503*, 43–59.

Staudinger, U. M., Marsiske, M., & Baltes, P. B. (1993). Resilience and levels of reserve capacity in later adulthood: Perspectives from life-span theory. *Development and Psychopathology, 5*, 541–566.

Staudinger, U. M., Marsiske, M., & Baltes, P. B. (in press). Resilience and reserve capacity in later adulthood: Potentials and limits of development across the life span. In D. Cicchetti & D. Cohen (Eds.), *Manual of developmental psychopathology.* New York: Wiley.

Sternberg, R. J., & Wagner, R. K. (Eds.). (1986). *Practical intelligence: Nature and origins of competence in the everyday world.* New York: Cambridge University Press.

Teri, L. (1991). Reducing excess disability in dementia patients: Training caregivers to manage patient depression. *Clinical Gerontologist, 10*, 49–63.

Tesch-Römer, C. (1993, November). *Coping with hearing loss in old age.* Paper presented at the 46th Annual Scientific Meeting of the Gerontological Society of America, New Orleans, LA.

Tuijnman, A., Kirsch, I., & Wagner, D. A. (Eds.). (in press). *Adult basic skills: Innovations in measurement and policy analysis.* Cresskill, NJ: Hampton Press.

Uttal, D. H., & Perlmutter, M. (1989). Toward a broader conceptualization of development: The role of gains and losses across the life span. *Developmental Review, 9*, 101–132.

Waddington, C. H. (1975). *The evolution of an evolutionist.* Edinburgh, Scotland: Edinburgh University Press.

Wagner, R. K., & Sternberg, R. J. (1986). Tacit knowledge and intelligence in the everyday world. In R. J. Sternberg & R. K. Wagner (Eds.), *Practical intelligence: Nature and origins of competence in the everyday world* (pp. 51–83). Cambridge, England: Cambridge University Press.

Walster, E., Berscheid, E., & Walster, G. W. (1973). New directions in equity research. *Journal of Personality and Social Psychology, 6*, 435–441.

Weinert, F. E., & Helmke, A. (1993). Wie bereichsspezifisch verläuft die kognitive Entwicklung? [How domain-specific is cognitive development?]. In R. Duit & W. Gräber (Eds.), *Kognitive Entwicklung und Lernen der Naturwissenschaften* (pp. 27–45). Kiel: Institut für Pädagogik der Naturwissenschaften.

Weinert, F. E., & Perner, J. (in press). Cognitive development. In D. Magnusson (Ed.), *Nobel symposium on life-span development of individuals: A synthesis of biological and psychological perspectives.* New York: Cambridge University Press.

Weiss, R. S. (1974). The provisions of social relationships. In Z. Rubin (Ed.), *Doing unto others* (pp. 17–26). Englewood Cliffs, NJ: Prentice-Hall.

Weiss, R. S. (1982). Issues in the study of loneliness. In L. Peplau & D. Perlman (Eds.), *Loneliness: A sourcebook of current theory, research, and therapy* (pp. 71–80). New York: Wiley.

Willis, S. L. (1987). Cognitive training and everyday competence. In K. W. Schaie (Ed.), *Annual review of gerontology and geriatrics* (Vol. 7, pp. 159–188). New York: Springer.

Willis, S. L. (1991). Cognition and everyday competence. In K. W. Schaie (Ed.), *Annual review of gerontology and geriatrics* (Vol. 11, pp. 80–109). New York: Springer.

Willis, S. L., & Dubin, S. S. (Eds.). (1990). *Maintaining professional competence.* San Francisco, CA: Jossey-Bass.

Wolinsky, F. D., Callahan, C. M., Fitzgerald, J. F., & Johnson, R. J. (1992). The risk of nursing home placement and subsequent death among older adults. *Journal of Gerontology: Social Sciences, 47*, S173–S182.

PART TWO

COMPENSATION IN THE LIFE COURSE

Adjustment to Shifting Possibility Frontiers in Later Life: Complementary Adaptive Modes

Jochen Brandtstädter
Dirk Wentura
University of Trier

"For man, there is never gain without loss, and no loss without gain . . . Compensation everywhere"—this proposition, advanced by Formey in 1759 (p. 381), already anticipates what Emerson (1900), more than a century later, came to denote as the "sublime law" of life: the compensatory balance of give and take, of winning and losing, of excesses and defects. Before we turn to the recent resurgence of this idea in developmental psychology, a brief historical sidestep seems appropriate. Etymologically, the concept of compensation refers to the activity of counterbalancing weights to achieve an equilibrium. In the 18th century, the concept of compensation became associated with notions of harmony, perfection, justice, and stability, and it was used as an explanatory principle in such diverse fields as economics, biology, physics, mechanics, law, military science, ethics, aesthetics, and theology (cf. Svagelski, 1981). Leibniz (1710) referred to a principle of compensation in his attempt to prove that our world, despite all obvious evils, is the best of all possible worlds. Buffon's (1760) comprehensive system of natural history largely centered on the notion of compensation as an organizing principle of animate and inanimate nature. In his famous essay on the roots of language, Herder (1772) speculated that language originates from the necessity to compensate for the adaptive deficiencies that characterize humans in comparison to animals.

Compensation has also become a key notion in contemporary anthropology. In the anthropological system of Gehlen (1940/1988), humans are defined as "deficient beings," characterized by a peculiar lack of those adaptive automatisms and specialized morphological structures by which animals are securely embedded to their special milieu. Human agents, however, overcome these constitutional handicaps by selecting and shaping the environment in accordance with their needs—by accumulating knowledge and transmitting it to following generations, and by institutionalizing their own life and development. To Gehlen, humans perforce are "acting beings," vitally dependent on culture as a self-created external means of adaptation, which thus becomes their "second nature" (Gehlen, 1988, p. 29). The notion of man as a "deficient being"—which Gehlen partly adopts from Herder— may be misleading because it equates lack of specialization with adaptive deficit. However, it brings to the fore that human development is simultaneously driven by nature, culture, and self-regulative action (cf. Brandtstädter, 1984; Lewontin, 1982), and that cultures characteristically devise prosthetic means that permit the human individual—as "homo compensator" (Marquard, 1983)—to transcend "natural" limitations (cf. Bruner, 1990; Geertz, 1973).

The present chapter centers on the process of adaptation to age and on the role that compensatory activities and related mechanisms play in that regard (see also Bäckman & Dixon, 1992; Baltes & Baltes, 1990; Salthouse, 1987). In fact, the characterization of humans as "deficient beings," in the sense given previously, seems to apply particularly well to the elderly person. Later life is commonly seen as a period during which the balance of developmental gains and losses gradually tips toward the negative (Baltes, 1987; Heckhausen, Dixon, & Baltes, 1989). This picture also emerges when elderly people are asked to evaluate their personal development in retrospect and prospect (Brandtstädter, Wentura, & Greve, 1993). One would assume that such gloomy prospects, although perhaps biased to some extent by social stereotypes and implicit theories about the aging process (see McFarland, Ross, & Giltrow, 1992), should undermine a sense of personal worth, continuity, and efficacy in later life. This widespread assumption, however, has received surprisingly little empirical support. Instead, a growing number of findings gives testimony to the astonishing resilience and adaptive flexibility of the aging self (cf. Brandtstädter & Greve, 1994). Contrary to what many researchers in the field of developmental psychology and gerontology have expected, there is no consistent evidence of a general or dramatic decline in perceived control (cf. Brandtstädter et al., 1993; Lachman, 1986) or in parameters of subjective well-being (e.g., Stock, Okun, Haring, & Witter, 1983), and there are no indications of an elevated risk of depression in later life (cf. Blazer, 1989; Bolla-Wilson & Bleecker, 1989).

It seems plausible to account for the phenomenal stability and resilience of the aging self by assuming that "gains in old age emerge to compensate for loss" (Uttal & Perlmutter, 1989, p. 102). Developmental gains that may counterbalance losses in later life, however, do not simply emerge in a fortuitous fashion. In our view, the personal balance of gains and losses primarily depends on the relationship between desired and actual courses of development, and on the ways in which the aging person constructs and adjusts this relationship.

In the following, we elaborate this argument. Expanding on theoretical concepts that evolved in conjunction with our research on perceived control and intentional self-development across adulthood (e.g., Brandtstädter, 1984, 1989, 1992; Brandtstädter & Greve, 1994; Brandtstädter & Renner, 1990; Brandtstädter et al., 1993), we consider two different, but complementary, modes of coping with the adaptive challenges of aging: (a) instrumental activities that aim to maintain desired levels of functioning in the transition to old age, and (b) processes that involve an adjustment of personal goals and frames of self-evaluation to changing developmental prospects.

ADJUSTING TO AGE-RELATED CHANGE IN RESOURCES AND POSSIBILITY FRONTIERS

What makes aging a taxing experience for many individuals is, above all, the fading of resources and adaptive reserves in many areas of life and functioning: Decrements in physiological and psychological domains, health problems, and role losses are implications of aging that, sooner or later, confront most of us as we grow older. Time, as time yet to be lived, is another valuable resource that dissipates with advancing age. Although the processes of aging are by no means uniform, and although specific competences (such as skills and expertise in particular professional domains; cf. Sternberg & Wagner, 1986) may even accrue with age, it is apparent that the efficient use and allocation of scarce physical and temporal resources are critical issues of life management for most elderly people. In other words, questions of how, when, why, and into which personal goals physical or temporal resources should be invested become increasingly urgent in later life. Unfortunately, efforts to alleviate or compensate for functional losses, too, are bounded by limited resources, so that eventually the person is forced to drop certain ambitions or disengage from goals that have become unfeasible (Brandtstädter & Renner, 1990; Brim, 1992).

These points are further elucidated in Fig. 4.1. Assume that an individual disposes of a certain limited amount of productive resources (e.g., time, money, physical effort), which can be allotted in various proportions to two different tasks or achievement domains (A and B). Because resources invested into one particular domain are not available for alternative uses, increasing levels of performance in A must eventually result in decreases in B, and vice versa.

The upper curve (function 1) in Fig. 4.1 defines those possible combinations of levels in A and B that can be attained under maximal or optimal use of

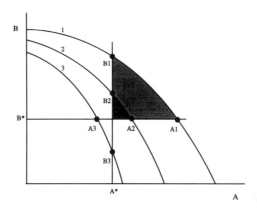

FIG. 4.1. Performance-possibility frontiers at changing resource levels. Shaded areas define those possible combinations of performance levels in two domains (A, B) that satisfy desired standards of performance (A*, B*). With decreasing resources, the range of possible combinations satisfying both standards becomes progressively constrained (cf. Functions 1, 2, and 3). Eventually, prior performance standards become incompatible and have to be adjusted to avoid prolonged strain and frustration. See text for further explanation.

resources. With decreasing resources, these boundaries become progressively narrower (curves 2 and 3). The limiting functions correspond to what economists call a *production-possibility frontier*; the curved shape of the functions reflects a law of diminishing returns (e.g., Samuelson & Nordhaus, 1985). For example, consider athletic performances (cf. Ericsson, 1990): As a performance approaches a maximal level, additional equal amounts of training yield smaller and smaller improvements, and thus involve more and more relative costs.

Now let us further assume that in performance domains A and B, certain personally or socially desired levels of functioning must be met (indicated in Fig. 4.1 by cutoff lines A* and B*). With progressively decreasing resources, maintaining a given normative standard in domain A will force the individual to accept decreasing levels in B, and vice versa (see points B1, B2, and B3 corresponding to A*, or points A1, A2, and A3 corresponding to B* on resource levels 1, 2, and 3, respectively). Note that all values of A and B within the shaded segments conform to the normative standards A* and B*. On higher resource levels, A* and B* obviously can be attained even with suboptimal use of available resources; there is even scope to exceed these normative margins, or to invest free resources into other domains. As possibility frontiers become narrower, attempts to maintain performance standards A* and B* involve a rising pressure to optimize the use and allocation of resources (see the dark-shaded area below curve 2). To maintain particular standards, individuals may employ a variety of strategies. They may try to boost their performance by increased training, concentrate their efforts on particular tasks, or deliberately use external aids to compensate for functional losses (cf. the model of selective optimization with compensation; Baltes & Baltes, 1980, 1990). By focusing on the most urgent concerns and reducing the expenditure of effort in other domains to a tolerable minimum, multiple task demands may be kept within manageable proportions. However, such compensatory efforts, too, are subject to a principle of diminishing returns. Even with the optimal use of resources, eventually it may become impossible to maintain desired standards or levels of aspiration (see Fig. 4.1: B3 < B*, A3 < A*). Under such conditions, the accommodation of personal goals and ambitions to given constraints will be the only way to alleviate prolonged strain or frustration.

These considerations illustrate our thesis that adaptation to age involves two distinct types of processes. Elsewhere, we have denoted these two adaptive modes as assimilative and accommodative, respectively (Brandt-städter, 1989; Brandtstädter & Renner, 1990). The core idea underlying this distinction is that to achieve congruence between actual and desired courses of development and aging, individuals may either try to alter or modify the course of personal development in accordance with personal goals and aspirations (assimilative mode), or adjust personal goals and standards to factual outcomes and constraints of development (accommodative mode). As we conceptualize it, the assimilative mode comprises all kinds of intentional activities that aim to maintain desired levels of functioning or a desired course of personal development; such activities may take the form of preventive, corrective, or optimizing efforts, depending on whether the intentional focus is on avoiding undesired developmental outcomes, alleviating losses, or enriching prospects of personal development. By contrast, the accommodative mode comprises processes that involve or enhance an adjustment of aspirations and goals to factual outcomes and constraints of development.

In the following, we consider these two complementary modes and their functional relationship in greater detail. To preview, we basically posit that assimilative and accommodative processes operate antagonistically: To the extent that assimilative tendencies prevail, accommodative tendencies will be inhibited, and vice versa. All else being equal, individuals will engage in assimilative activities as long as they see a reasonable chance that such efforts will pay off in terms of preventing or avoiding developmental losses; there should be no need to rescale or adjust personal goals and aspirations as long as they do not exceed the possibility frontiers that, in the sense given earlier, restrict the range of feasible options. By the same token, accommodative shifts in goals and preferences will become operative when assimilative tendencies begin to fade, as may be the case when assimilative efforts turn out to be futile or begin to overtax personal resources. This should not be read to imply that accommodation of goals and aspirations terminates any further assimilative activity. Rather, rescaling of goals often sets the stage for new commitments and establishes new reference points for assimilative efforts.

Before elaborating on these points, let us briefly reflect on how the concept of compensation relates to these distinctions. To obviate misunderstandings, it should first be noted that the concepts of assimilation and accommodation, as we have introduced them, differ in scope from the ways in which these terms are used in other contexts. For example, in Piagetian theorizing, the notions of assimilation and accommodation refer to the ways in which cognitive schemata influence and are influenced by the individual's transaction with the environment (cf. Flavell, 1964; see also Whitbourne, 1987). Salthouse (1987, 1990) uses the term accommodation to designate the process of adapting to real or perceived declines in performance by concentrating on performance domains in which relevant abilities have been preserved; accommodation, remediation, and compensation are considered different modes of buffering age-related performance decrements that may account for Age × Skill interactions.[1] In the dual-process model suggested here, by contrast, assimilation and accommodation are used in a more specific sense to designate complementary modes of eliminating discrepancies between achievements and aspirations. Our focus is on the interplay between these processes and their function in preserving a sense of well-being and self-esteem in the transition to old age. Obviously, intentional efforts or activities to compensate for functional losses are prototypical cases of assimilative activities, as defined earlier. The affective neutralization of losses and constraints that characterizes accommodative processes, too, seems to involve an element of compensation. Considering the balance as a root metaphor of compensation, it is obvious that a favorable ratio of gains and losses in personal development and aging may be attained not only by intentional actions, which are geared toward realizing positive or avoiding negative developmental outcomes, but likewise by shifts in the system of preferences and criteria that individuals apply in evaluating developmental outcomes as gain or loss. However, these formal commonalities should not detract from functional differences between assimilative and accommodative processes. Whereas the former typically involve a decision that is based on a consideration and evaluation of possible action-outcome contingencies (e.g., a "decision to compensate" that results from the "awareness of a mismatch" between environmental demands and actual skill levels; Bäckman & Dixon, 1992, p. 273), the latter apparently cannot be cast in such intentionalistic or rationalistic terms. Although basic to the regulation of action, accommodative shifts in goals and self-evaluative standards need not be

---

[1]To point to an interesting parallel, similar models have been suggested to account for Aptitude × Treatment interactions in the domain of learning and instruction (see Brandtstädter, 1982; Salomon, 1972).

actuated by intentional decisions and may even run counter to the individual's prior intent. Fortunately or not, we cannot choose our beliefs according to payoffs, and we are not able to disengage from goals or drop ambitions merely because it seems advantageous to do so (for a broader discussion of this point, see Brandtstädter et al., 1993; Gilbert, 1993; Lanz, 1987; Lazarus & DeLongis, 1983).[2] To understand the mechanisms that help aging persons preserve a positive view of themselves and their personal development even under progressively constrained action resources, it seems important to pay heed to the interplay of intentional and automatic processes.

MAINTAINING GOALS AND STANDARDS DESPITE DIMINISHING RESOURCES: ASSIMILATIVE ACTIVITIES

As purposeful agents, adult individuals shape their development and try to keep it in stride with personally and socially desired standards. Through activities of intentional self-development, an individual's developmental history becomes, as it were, an extension of the self. This action-theoretical perspective (Brandtstädter, 1984) affords an orienting framework for understanding activities designed to prevent or compensate for anticipated developmental losses. From an action-theoretical viewpoint, such assimilative efforts are basically related to the individual's cognitive representation of personal past and future development over the life span. These representations form the basis for the individual's evaluation of personal developmental prospects. To the extent that expected trajectories of personal development deviate from "desired possible selves" (Markus & Nurius, 1986), individuals will engage in instrumental behaviors that they consider effective to counteract undesirable changes, as long as such efforts do not exceed their resources and capabilities.

Assimilative activities are, in a double sense, self-related: They are targeted to the subject's own behavior or development, and they depend on the individual's construction of past, current, and future selves. For example, with advancing age, staying physically and mentally in good shape becomes an increasingly salient concern. Individuals may try to accomplish this aim by dieting, exercising, shifting daily routines and patterns of living, or whatever else their means-end beliefs suggest. Such self-corrective tendencies seem to increase during middle adulthood (Brandtstädter, 1989). As functional losses loom larger, the intentional focus of assimilative activities should shift toward more explicitly compensatory objectives. Mental or physical

---

[2]To obviate misunderstandings, it should be added that we may be able to intentionally manipulate conditions that result in a rescaling of goals or aspirations. According to our distinctions, however, this would be a variant of assimilative activity.

skills, for example, are multiply determined so that a deterioration of specific skill-relevant functional components may be offset by the strengthening or selective use of other components, or by employing prosthetic means that counterbalance internal functional losses (Bäckman & Dixon, 1992; Baltes & Baltes, 1980, 1990; Salthouse, 1985). In contexts of intervention, efficient compensatory strategies may be derived from systematic task analyses, combined with a task-oriented diagnosis of relevant skills analogous to procedures designed for remedial instruction (Brandtstädter, 1982).

Besides the instrumental activities mentioned previously, assimilative modes of coping with loss, as we conceive them, also include activities of symbolic self-confirmation (Brandtstädter & Greve, 1994). People generally prefer self-confirmatory feedback, and they actively strive to acquire such feedback; to secure personal continuity, people tend to select situations and contexts that support their self-views, and that eventually make developmental losses less salient. To achieve such aims, people may even change their physical appearance; there is a whole industry that makes a profit on—and, to that aim, also fosters—the reluctance of elderly persons to accommodate their desired bodily self to their aging bodies (Swann, 1983).

As already intimated, assimilative activities should prevail as long as they remain within the individual's span of control. With decreasing resources, however, goals and performance standards of earlier adulthood may drift beyond the feasible range. Although in many areas of mental or physical performance this process may be delayed, e.g., by designing appropriate training procedures, it is equally true that such compensatory interventions often yield diminishing gains with increasing age (for pertinent evidence, see Kliegl, Smith, & Baltes, 1989). Under such conditions, accommodative processes involving a readjustment of goals and aspirations become operative.

WHEN GOALS BECOME UNFEASIBLE: ACCOMMODATING PREFERENCES AND PRIORITIES

Corrective and compensatory activities of the assimilative type basically involve an adherence to established developmental goals and ambitions. We assume that there is an ordered sequence of processes that ensue when goals become unattainable and ambitions begin to exceed a level of "just manageable difficulty" (Brim, 1992). Initially, there may be a reactant increase of efforts to squeeze or boost resources. When such ultimate efforts become too taxing or turn out to be futile, feelings of hopelessness and helplessness may arise. These aversive emotional states will endure as long as the blocked options retain their positive valences for the subject; in fact, being unable to let go of unattainable developmental options seems to be a key feature of reactive depression (Brandtstädter & Renner, 1990; Carver & Scheier,

1990). So far, the postulated sequence of events largely converges with theoretical notions of perceived control, reactance, and learned helplessness (see, e.g., Peterson & Seligman, 1984; Wortman & Brehm, 1975). However, these theoretical perspectives do not afford a deeper understanding of why and how people recover from states of hopelessness and depression even in situations involving uncontrollable and irrevocable loss (e.g., Coyne, 1992; Needles & Abramson, 1990; Teasdale, 1988), which are typical for later adulthood and old age.

In our view, feelings of helplessness mark the critical point where accommodative processes become activated that set the individual free to turn to new and satisfying commitments. Helplessness experiences may even promote such accommodative shifts (see also Klinger, 1975). As outlined earlier, the accommodative process adjusts the individual's normative construction of self and personal future to the subjectively feasible range. Re-scaling of aspirations, adoption of less demanding performance standards, positive reappraisal of initially aversive developmental outcomes, devaluation of blocked goals, and upgrading of alternative options are prototypical features of the accommodative mode. We assume that the cognitive and evaluative changes underlying the accommodative process are subject to constraints of consistency and self-enhancement. When facing the biological, psychological, and social implications of aging, individuals will most strongly defend those elements of their self-definition that are most important for their self-esteem, and that are most firmly entrenched by prior experience (Brandtstädter & Renner, 1992; Brandtstädter et al., 1993). For example, consider the elderly person who harbors a self-image of intellectual competence, but is confronted with increasingly potent self-discrepant feedback. Such discrepancies may be warded off by accommodating the personal concept of intelligence so that competences that have remained intact (e.g., expertise, adroit use of skills) are more strongly emphasized, whereas aspects of functioning that tend to deteriorate with age (e.g., mnemonic skills, perceptual speed, performance in decontextualized intellectual tasks) are devalued. Self-descriptions can also be stabilized by shifting the criteria or anchoring points of relevant attributes. Even in everyday language, the standards that are used in ascribing attributes such as health or physical competence to some extent depend on the age of the target person. In a similar vein, the salience of perceived functional losses crucially depends on comparative standards; for elderly people, positive self-comparisons may be enhanced when same-aged persons rather than younger people (or oneself at a younger age) are taken as a reference group. Related to this point, Brandtstädter and Greve (1994) demonstrated that when elderly adults compare themselves favorably to individuals of their age group (which the majority of participants did), perceived losses have a less negative emotional impact. Processes such as disengagement from blocked goals or lowering of aspirations have usually been looked upon in the psychological

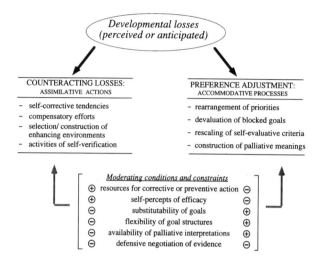

FIG. 4.2. Assimilative and accommodative processes as antagonistic, but complementary, modes of neutralizing developmental loss (conditions that differentially enhance or inhibit assimilative and accommodative processes are marked by "+" and "–," respectively).

literature with slight contempt, and have often been associated with notions of resignation and loss of control. The theoretical stance taken here suggests on the contrary that in the transition toward old age, such processes gain importance for maintaining a positive self-view and a sense of personal continuity.

Figure 4.2 summarizes these considerations. In addition, it outlines some moderating conditions that differentially influence the strength or duration of assimilative and accommodative processes. In the following, we discuss these constraints in greater detail.

CONSTRAINTS AND MODERATING CONDITIONS

Most of the conditions that enhance assimilative efforts to offset or compensate developmental losses tend to suppress accommodative tendencies, and vice versa. This reflects the antagonistic, but complementary, character of these processes mentioned earlier. Logically, adherence to goals and disengagement from them are mutually exclusive states. As indicated in Fig. 4.2, assimilative and accommodative processes depend, in opposed ways, on available resources or means for corrective actions, on generalized or specific self-beliefs of efficacy, on the substitutability of goals, as well as on the adaptive flexibility of goal structures and personal projects. In addition, Fig. 4.2 depicts conditions that may dampen both assimilative and accommodative tendencies. In particular, a tendency to ignore or deny self-discrepant data should inhibit both self-corrective activities and the readiness to adjust personal ambitions.

Availability of Means for Corrective and Compensatory Action: Self-Percepts of Control

As intimated, the motivation to counteract perceived or expected developmental losses critically hinges on the individual's confidence to achieve the desired outcome. All else being equal, assimilative tendencies should be suppressed in individuals who harbor self-percepts of low control over personal development, or who consider developmental losses as inevitable or irreversible.

The impact of perceived control and self-efficacy on the strength and perseverance of coping efforts has been amply documented in the literature (e.g., Bandura, 1982), with a general tendency to extol the salutary effects of high control. From the theoretical position taken here, however, it becomes apparent that, under specified circumstances, self-percepts of high control may have dysfunctional implications. By impeding an adjustment of goals and delaying the shift toward accommodative modes, strong efficacy beliefs may put the individual at a disadvantage particularly in situations involving factually irreversible changes or losses, and under such circumstances may even contribute to prolonging or aggravating states of frustration, disorientation, and despair (cf. Janoff-Bulman & Brickman, 1982; Wolk, 1976). Presumably, such dysfunctional side effects could partly account for the inconsistency of findings concerning the alleged negative relationship between measures of perceived control and depression (see also Barnett & Gotlib, 1988; Coyne, 1992).

In action-theoretical terms, the subjectively expected utility of assimilative activities—be they corrective, preventive, or compensatory—should depend on both outcome expectancies and the personal value or importance attributed to the respective outcomes. Accordingly, compensatory or corrective efforts may endure even under conditions of low subjective control, given that the importance of the expected outcome is sufficiently high. However, desired outcomes tend to lose their attractiveness when the costs to attain them become exceedingly high. Somewhat paradoxically, this accommodative devaluation even serves to stabilize a sense of control over personal development in later life. We consider this implication in a later section.

Flexibility of Goal Structures and Self-Complexity

An individual's system of goals and preferences is structured by semantical and assumed instrumental linkages. Although in principle processes of disengagement and devaluation can involve any level of this system, parts of it may be less amenable to such accommodative changes. The scope for substitution or replacement may become increasingly narrow when moving toward superordinate goals, or toward goals that are central in the sense that they serve a multitude of other goals. When such goals are blocked or threatened, finding a new or satisfactory arrangement may be impossible without destroying larger parts of the person's cognitive architecture of self and life, and even amount to a radical transformation of identity. But even lower-level instrumental goals can be so closely tied to superordinate goals that they cannot be relinquished without increasing losses at higher levels (cf. Carver & Scheier, 1990). For example, for a person who holds a belief that earning lots of money is the only way to gain social recognition, a reduced income would be tantamount to a serious status loss. There are presumably large individual differences regarding complexity and adaptive flexibility of goal systems. Generally, a thematically diversified or multifocal structure of goals will provide more scope to neutralize losses through accommodating priorities; self-complexity, by enhancing a flexible adjustment of priorities, may help to deemphasize losses and act as a buffer against depression (cf. Linville, 1987). Parenthetically, the sequential arrangement of developmental tasks across the life cycle, which is common in age-graded societies, may foster disengagement from goals that have drifted outside the individually feasible range. Social norms and stereotypes of aging may have a similar enhancing effect—a possible boon that may be set off against the potentially limiting functions of such normative expectations that have been emphasized within cognitive or phenomenological theories of aging (e.g., Banziger, 1987; Kuypers & Bengtson, 1973; Rodin & Langer, 1980).

Availability of Palliative Cognitions

Whether and to what extent a given developmental outcome—from the individual's point of view—constitutes a loss critically hinges on the meanings and effects that are associated with the outcome. Acceptance of an initially aversive situation, or even its reappraisal as a gain, may be enhanced by selectively focusing on desired consequences, or by giving a greater weight to beliefs that support positive outcome-related expectancies. Within the limits of rationality, there is usually scope to attribute positive meanings even to serious losses (for vivid examples from studies with cancer patients, see Taylor, 1983). The degree to which palliative cognitions are available varies across individuals and situations. Constructs such as *optimism* (Scheier & Carver, 1985) or *accommodative flexibility* (Brandtstädter & Renner, 1990) tap dispositional differences in the readiness to focus on positive implications in situations of crisis and loss. As regards situational constraints, it is known that emotional states are backed by an increased accessibility of mood-congruent information (Blaney, 1986). Although there is some discussion in the literature about whether such effects operate symmetrically for positive and negative emotional states (Taylor, 1991), it is obvious that for individuals in a depressed and despondent mood congruency effects may inhibit positive reappraisals. Presumably, accommodative processes engage "override mechanisms" (Carver & Scheier, 1990) that are able to break through this vicious cycle. Accessibility of positive meanings may be enhanced by a tendency to withdraw attentional resources from negative events or losses as soon as they appear irreversible, or as soon as perceived costs of assimilative efforts exceed expected benefits by a critical margin. Furthermore, any process that reduces aversive emotional states will probably be strengthened by a mechanism of negative reinforcement. We assume that this mechanism does not only apply to overt behavior, but to mental processes such as the production of palliative cognitions or downgrading of blocked goals as well (for fuller discussion of these points, see Brandtstädter et al., 1993). Such processes are largely automatic and nonintentional; thus, models of reasoned action and personal control may be too narrow to capture the full range of processes by which the aging self defends itself against discontinuity and experiences of loss.

Defensive Negotiation of Self-Discrepant Evidence

A person's self-concept is a dynamic system that tends to secure integrity and continuity by protecting itself against self-discrepant and self-derogatory evidence (Greenwald, 1980; Markus & Wurf, 1987; Swann, 1983). For example, discrepant or threatening feedback may be warded off or neutralized by doubting the credibility of the information, by twisting the interpretation of data in ways that lessen their apparent linkage to desired self-attributes, or even by altering the semantic structure of self-descriptive concepts (Brandtstädter & Greve, 1994). For example, consider the elderly person who has difficulty in remembering items on a shopping list. This failure may be accounted for by shifting the causal linkage to external disturbances (such as the noisy surroundings in the shopping mall) so that attributes of forgetfulness no longer apply, or by doubting whether the particular skill has anything to do with mnemonic competence (e.g., the individual may consider skills such as remembering biographical episodes as more pertinent to judge that competence). When the feedback is so potent that exonerating ways of "reality negotiation" (cf. Snyder, Irving, Sigmon, & Holleran, 1992) are not available, the person may downscale the negative valence of the event by assuming that other competences are more important than having a good memory (such a move, however, would already verge on accommodative processes as defined earlier). It is obvious that self-protective biases in the processing of self-related information, even if they do not involve a blatant denial of aversive evidence, may suppress both self-corrective or compensatory efforts and accommodative tendencies. With advancing age, people accumulate a large stock of data about themselves; this, too, may render the elderly person's self-view more resistant to discrepant evidence (cf. Atchley, 1989). However, we would not go so far as to assume that the phenomenal resilience of the aging self results primarily from a general tendency to ignore or misconstrue the implications of aging (Lazarus & Golden, 1981). As noted already, elderly people are quite perceptive of losses and do not seem particularly prone to illusory distortions in their processing of self-relevant evidence (see also Brandtstädter et al., 1993).

EMPIRICAL ILLUSTRATIONS[3]

Some implications of the theoretical model outlined have been tested on samples in middle and later adulthood. In connection with this research, a questionnaire has been designed to assess dispositional differences in assimilative and accommodative tendencies. This instrument is composed of two scales: Flexible Goal Adjustment (FGA) and Tenacious Goal Pursuit (TGP). The FGA scale measures the readiness to easily disengage from blocked goals and to focus on positive aspects of aversive situations. The TGP scale assesses the tendency to cling to goals even in the face of setbacks and obstacles. The two scales seem to define largely independent facets of adaptive competence. Both FGA and TGP are positively related to parameters of optimal development and successful aging, such as low depression, optimism, resilience in stressful situations, and life satisfaction (Brandtstädter & Renner, 1990). Despite such similarities, the scales exhibit clearly opposite regressions on age. Our findings indicate that, in later adulthood, an accommodative style of coping with losses and constraints (as measured by FGA) becomes increasingly predominant, whereas assimilative tendencies (as measured by TGP) tend to decrease. Given that irreversible losses cumulate in the second half of life, such a shift seems functional to maintain a sense of well-being. In line with our theoretical assumptions, subjects scoring high in FGA revealed a stronger tendency to rescale the importance of developmental goals in ways that mitigate or neutralize perceived losses or deficits. Furthermore, there is evidence that accommodative tendencies as measured by the FGA scale buffer the negative impact of perceived developmental losses and deficits on subjective well-being. This buffering effect also emerges when age-typical adaptive tasks such as adjustment to health problems or situational constraints are considered (Brandtstädter, 1989, 1992; Brandtstädter & Baltes-Götz, 1990; Brandtstädter & Renner, 1990, 1992; Brandtstädter et al., 1993).

---

[3]The research reported in this section was supported by grants from the German Minister for Research and Technology and the German Research Foundation to the senior author.

In the following, we present three illustrations that further exemplify ways in which accommodative processes may help the aging person to preserve a sense of self-esteem, control, and well-being. The first research example takes issue with a phenomenon that has spurred our theoretical interest in the processes by which the aging self construes personal continuity in the transition to later adulthood (viz., the puzzling stability of self-percepts of control in middle and later adulthood). A second example focuses on the adaptive challenges that arise from the gradual narrowing of future perspectives in later life. Our third illustration describes an experimental attempt to trace accommodative changes in the associative meaning of the concept *old*.

Stabilizing a Sense of Control in Later Life

As noted already, research on the age-control relationship has not supported widespread assumptions of a decline in perceived control in late adulthood (see also Gatz & Karel, 1993). Although there is a wealth of theoretical arguments that suggests an age-related decrement in perceived control (e.g., Rodin, 1987; Schulz, 1980), the fact that such predictions have not been successful still begs for a satisfying explanation.

The model of assimilative and accommodative processes affords an improved understanding of the mechanisms that buffer a person's sense of control against the limitations of physical and temporal resources, which are intrinsic to the aging processes. Our theoretical account departs from the premise that the extent to which losses of control in specific domains of life and functioning affect an individual's general sense of control critically depends on the personal importance of that domain. Thus, accommodative shifts in the importance of the corresponding domains should serve to maintain a general sense of control. Specifically, we posit that when the individual's subjective potential to attain particular goals is reduced, a general sense of efficacy may be preserved by downgrading the importance of these goals. However, feelings of hopelessness and depression should be more pronounced when the individual maintains his or her commitment to the barren goal.

Brandtstädter and Rothermund (1994) have investigated these assumptions by drawing on data from a cross-sequential panel study involving a core sample of 735 participants between 30 and 60 years of age. With respect to 17 different developmental goals, participants were asked to rate the personal importance of each goal, as well as the degree to which they believed they had personal control over their development within that particular goal domain (internal and external control beliefs were separately assessed for each goal). Global control beliefs were measured by a factorial composite involving the Levenson scales (German version; Krampen, 1981), as well as an aggregate of goal-specific ratings of perceived control. Mod-

erated multiple regressions were performed to check whether the relationship between domain-specific and global self-percepts of control was buff-
ered by the personal importance of the respective goals in the predicted
way. Consistent with the predictions, results showed that, with decreasing
personal importance of the goal, perceived deficits of control within that
goal domain have a less negative impact on the individual's global sense of
control. Figure 4.3 exemplifies this moderating effect for the goal domain
of *social recognition*. The plotted functions give the regression of perceived
control (global measure) on goal-specific control for high (+2 *SD*) and low
(−2 *SD*) levels of the moderating variable (rated importance of goal; the
interaction effect is significant with $p < .01$). This type of moderating effect
was obtained for the majority of goals (viz., emotional stability, wisdom,
self-esteem, occupational efficiency, assertiveness, personal independence,
prosperity, intellectual efficiency, self-development, physical fitness, satisfying friendship, and commitment to ideals). Similar buffering effects emerged
when longitudinal change scores in perceived control, as well as in goal
importance, were taken as the basis for moderation analyses (longitudinal
change was assessed over a 4-year interval). Supplementary analyses revealed that, although losses of control in a particular goal domain generally
were accompanied by rising depression, this effect was mitigated by down-
scaling the importance of the respective goal.

Adjusting to Narrowing Future Perspectives

Recognizing that some valued goals and ambitions may be left forever un-
achieved is a common experience for elderly people. Whereas younger
individuals can resolve conflicts between goals by postponing some projects,
older persons who foresee a limited future may find themselves forced to

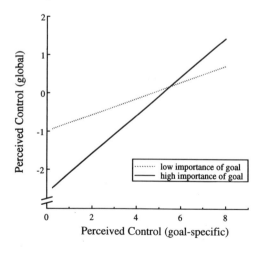

FIG. 4.3. Regression of self-percepts of control (global measure)
on perceived control within a particular goal domain (sample case:
social recognition): Moderating effect of goal importance. With decreasing personal importance of a
goal, perceived deficits of control
within that goal domain have a less
negative impact on the individual's
general sense of control.

concentrate on a reduced set of goals that can be attained with their remaining physical and temporal resources, and to abandon other, perhaps equally attractive options. Thus, the rearrangement of priorities and flexible adjustment of preferences, as well as dispositional differences in the readiness or capability to relinquish barren commitments, should be of great importance in coping with these adaptive challenges.

Departing from these theoretical premises, Brandtstädter and Wentura (1994) analyzed attitudes related to the personal future. This study involved over 1,200 participants in the age range of 57 to 78 years. As part of the assessment procedure, a six-item scale was used to measure the affective valence of personal future (AVF; sample items: "For me, the future is full of hopes," "I'm looking toward my future with confidence"). Furthermore, participants were asked to give an estimate of their personal life expectancy; by subtracting the respondents' chronological age from this estimate, an index of residual life expectancy (RLE) was obtained. As expected, AVF tended to deteriorate with decreasing RLE ($r = .30$, $p < .001$); the correlation of AVF with chronological age was less clear-cut ($r = -.09$, $p < .05$), although subjective estimates of RLE were of course strongly related to the age of respondents ($r = -.67$, $p < .001$).

Together with the mentioned variables, the FGA scale was administered to assess individual differences in accommodative tendencies. It was expected that, for subjects scoring high in FGA, the affective valence of future perspectives should be less negatively affected by a decrease in residual life expectancy. Results of moderated multiple regression analyses involving AVF as target variable, RLE as predictor, and FGA as moderator variable were consistent with this prediction. Figure 4.4 depicts this moderating effect ($p < .05$); conditional regressions are given for high (+2 SD) and low (−2

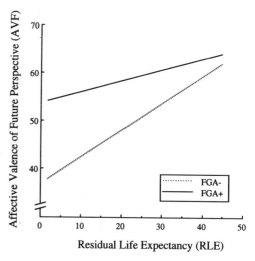

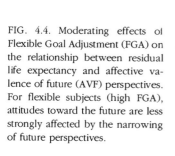

FIG. 4.4. Moderating effects of Flexible Goal Adjustment (FGA) on the relationship between residual life expectancy and affective valence of future (AVF) perspectives. For flexible subjects (high FGA), attitudes toward the future are less strongly affected by the narrowing of future perspectives.

SD) levels of accommodative flexibility (FGA). The moderating effect for the TGP scale was found to tend in the opposite direction; this effect fell short of significance, however. These findings hint that the capability to adjust priorities and preferences to the feasible range dampens the emotional distress that may arise from the gradual fade-out of temporal resources in later life.

Accommodative Shifts in the Meaning of "Being Old"

Social stereotypes of aging are commonly loaded with negative and self-deprecating implications. Elderly persons may evade these implications by describing themselves as being (or feeling) younger than they are chronologically; it is a common observation that such self-enhancing discrepancies between subjective and objective age tend to increase in later life (e.g., Bultena & Powers, 1978; Filipp, Ferring, & Klauer, 1989). Another, more subtle self-protective process that has received less attention would be to enrich the personal notion of "being old" with positive meanings that may replace or neutralize negative connotations to a lesser or greater extent. With advancing age, it presumably becomes increasingly difficult to display the signs of a youthful self; to the same extent, a tendency to tinge the personal concept of "being old" with positive and self-enhancing meanings should be induced. According to our theory, this accommodative process should be further enhanced by a dispositional readiness to adjust personal goals and preferences to the feasible range.

In an ongoing series of experiments, we investigate these assumptions on a microanalytic level. Our experimental approach is based on a semantic priming paradigm (cf. Neely, 1991). In the typical priming procedure, a word stimulus (the prime) is briefly presented; following the prime, a second stimulus word (the target) is presented. Exposure to the prime facilitates the processing of the target word to the extent that prime and target are semantically or associatively connected (such as *metal* and *iron*). This facilitating effect is reflected in a quicker lexical decision (decision whether the target stimulus is a word or a non-word, i.e., a meaningless sequence of letters or syllables). Applied to our research objectives, we assume that when the word *old* is presented as a prime, positive or palliative shifts in the connotational profile of this attribute should be reflected in an enhanced processing of positively valued target words. One might further speculate at this juncture that, for the concept *young*, an opposite, age-related shift toward negative— or away from positive—connotations might emerge. To preview, our findings do not reveal such a trend, thus indicating that the assumed accommodative shifts in meaning are specific to the attribute *old*.

The assumed accommodative shifts in the meaning of being old were investigated on a sample of 120 participants aged 56 to 80 years ($M = 67.6$

years). The attributes *old* and *young* were presented on a monitor as primes; under a control condition, neutral attributes (*male, female*; *poor, rich*) were presented in the priming position. On word trials, the primes were followed either by a positively connoted target word (such as *balanced, active, happy, optimistic, calm*) or by a negatively connoted target (such as *confused, dependent, unsuccessful, incapable*). Each prime was presented for 500 ms; the target stimuli were presented 1,000 ms after the onset of the prime. Reaction time was automatically registered (in ms; for further procedural details, see Rothermund, Wentura, & Brandtstädter, in press).

As expected, the results hint that with advancing age, the subjective concept of "being old" is enriched with positive meanings. If the mean lexical decision time for positive targets primed by *old* is subtracted from the corresponding mean obtained under control conditions for each subject, this difference (D^{pos}) tends to increase with age ($r = .18$, $p < .05$). The analogous difference for negative targets (D^{neg}) does not exhibit a significant correlation with the age variable ($r = .06$, ns). This pattern of findings suggests that if there is an age-related increase in negative connotations for the concept of "being old," it seems to be neutralized or compensated for by an increase in positive meanings. Obviously, this effect may mitigate the self-deprecating implications of considering oneself as old. In line with our assumptions, the strength of this compensatory effect was found to depend on accommodative flexibility as measured by the FGA scale. For participants scoring high in FGA (median split), the correlation of D^{pos} with age rises to $r = .28$ ($p < .05$), whereas the correlation of D^{neg} with age vanishes ($r = .00$, ns). By contrast, for participants scoring below the median in FGA, the correlation of D^{pos} with age is lower than for the total sample, whereas it tends to be higher for D^{neg} ($r = .04$, ns; and $r = .13$, ns, respectively). The corresponding moderation effect (i.e., the FGA × age interaction effect on the difference between D^{pos} and D^{neg}) is significant ($p < .05$).

SUMMARY

In recent years, evidence has accumulated that gives testimony to the intriguing stability and resilience of the aging self. A focal concern of the present contribution was to account for this phenomenon within a theoretical framework which, while recognizing age-related losses and constraints in physical and temporal resources, spells out different but complementary ways in which elderly people come to terms with these adaptive challenges.

When analyzing the processes and mechanisms that serve to maintain a favorable balance of gains and losses in later life, it is important to recognize that developmental outcomes can be evaluated as a gain or a loss only with reference to certain values or normative standards. Such evaluations depend, in particular, on the goals and normative standards that individuals adopt for their own development and aging. These frames of self-evaluation are, of course, not static. As developmental options and resources for goal attainment change over the life course, personal goals are permanently revised and redefined. It follows that losses can be alleviated by intentional efforts to change the course of personal development, as well as by accommodative shifts in preferences and priorities.

We have outlined a theoretical model that integrates these different aspects of coping with loss in later life, and that specifies situational and personal conditions that determine whether and when assimilative or accommodative modes will predominate. As long as the individual considers perceived or anticipated losses as reversible—which depends on the type of loss, as well as on dispositional factors such as self-percepts of control— active, instrumental (preventive, corrective, or compensatory) efforts will prevail. In domains of performance and functioning, which involve rigid norms and behavioral expectations, such intentional activities will presumably be the preferred mode of coping with loss. With diminishing resources, however, goals may gradually drift outside the feasible range, and additional efforts to maintain desired levels of performance may yield diminishing returns. Such conditions give rise to a second adaptive mode that involves a readjustment of priorities and preferences to situational constraints. We have posited that accommodative processes are enhanced by conditions such as flexibility of goal structures and availability of palliative cognitions. Our model predicts that with advancing age, accommodative processes become increasingly important in managing personal aging.

REFERENCES

Atchley, R. C. (1989). A continuity theory of normal aging. *The Gerontologist, 29*, 183–190.

Bäckman, L., & Dixon, R. A. (1992). Psychological compensation: A theoretical framework. *Psychological Bulletin, 112*, 259–283.

Baltes, P. B. (1987). Theoretical propositions of life-span developmental psychology: On the dynamics between growth and decline. *Developmental Psychology, 23*, 611–626.

Baltes, P. B., & Baltes, M. M. (1980). Plasticity and variability in psychological aging: Methodological and theoretical issues. In G. Gurski (Ed.), *The effects of aging on the central nervous system* (pp. 41–66). Berlin: Schering.

Baltes, P. B., & Baltes, M. M. (1990). Psychological perspectives on successful aging: The model of selective optimization with compensation. In P. B. Baltes & M. M. Baltes (Eds.), *Successful aging: Perspectives from the behavioral sciences* (pp. 1–34). New York: Cambridge University Press.

Bandura, A. (1982). Self-efficacy in human agency. *American Psychologist, 37*, 122–147.

Banziger, G. (1987). Contemporary social psychology and aging: Issues of attribution in a life-span perspective. In R. P. Abeles (Ed.), *Life-span perspectives and social psychology* (pp. 85–102). Hillsdale, NJ: Lawrence Erlbaum Associates.

Barnett, P., & Gotlib, I. H. (1988). Psychosocial functioning and depression: Distinguishing among antecedents, concomitants, and consequences. *Psychological Bulletin, 104*, 97–126.

Blaney, P. H. (1986). Affect and memory: A review. *Psychological Bulletin, 99*, 229–246.

Blazer, D. (1989). Depression in late life: An update. *Annual Review of Gerontology & Geriatrics, 9*, 197–215.

Bolla-Wilson, K., & Bleecker, M. L. (1989). Absence of depression in elderly adults. *Journal of Gerontology: Psychological Sciences, 44*, P53–P55.

Brandtstädter, J. (1982). Prävention von Lern- und Entwicklungsproblemen im schulischen Bereich. In J. Brandtstädter & A. von Eye (Eds.), *Psychologische Prävention. Grundlagen, Programme, Methoden* [Prevention of learning disorders and developmental problems in schools] (pp. 207–304). Bern: Huber.

Brandtstädter, J. (1984). Personal and social control over development: Some implications of an action perspective in life-span developmental psychology. In P. B. Baltes & O. G. Brim Jr. (Eds.), *Life-span development and behavior* (Vol. 6, pp. 1–32). New York: Academic Press.

Brandtstädter, J. (1989). Personal self-regulation of development: Cross-sequential analyses of development-related control beliefs and emotions. *Developmental Psychology, 25*, 96–108.

Brandtstädter, J. (1992). Personal control over development: Some developmental implications of self-efficacy. In R. Schwarzer (Ed.), *Self-efficacy: Thought control of action* (pp. 127–145). Washington, DC: Hemisphere.

Brandtstädter, J., & Baltes-Götz, B. (1990). Personal control over development and quality of life perspectives in adulthood. In P. B. Baltes & M. M. Baltes (Eds.), *Successful aging: Perspectives from the behavioral sciences* (pp. 197–224). New York: Cambridge University Press.

Brandtstädter, J., & Greve, W. (1994). The aging self: Stabilizing and protective processes. *Developmental Review, 14*, 52–80.

Brandtstädter, J., & Renner, G. (1990). Tenacious goal pursuit and flexible goal adjustment: Explication and age-related analysis of assimilative and accommodative strategies of coping. *Psychology and Aging, 5*, 58–67.

Brandtstädter, J., & Renner, G. (1992). Coping with discrepancies between aspirations and achievements in adult development: A dual-process model. In L. Montada, S.-H. Filipp, & M. Lerner (Eds.), *Crises and experiences of loss in adulthood* (pp. 301–319). Hillsdale, NJ: Lawrence Erlbaum Associates.

Brandtstädter, J., & Rothermund, K. (1994). Self-percepts of control in middle and later adulthood: Buffering losses by rescaling goals. *Psychology and Aging, 9*, 265–273.

Brandtstädter, J., & Wentura, D. (1994). Veränderungen der Zeit- und Zukunftsperspektive im Übergang zum höheren Erwachsenenalter: Entwicklungspsychologische und differentielle Aspekte [Future perspectives in later life: Developmental and differential aspects]. *Zeitschrift für Entwicklungspsychologie und Pädagogische Psychologie, 26*, 2–21.

Brandtstädter, J., Wentura, D., & Greve, W. (1993). Adaptive resources of the aging self: Outlines of an emergent perspective. *International Journal of Behavioral Development, 16*, 323–349.

Brim, G. (1992). *Ambition: How we manage success and failure throughout our lives.* New York: Basic Books.

Bruner, J. (1990). *Acts of meaning.* Cambridge, MA: Harvard University Press.

Buffon, G. L. L. (1760). *Histoire naturelle, générale et particulière* [Natural history] (Vol. 8). Paris: Librairie de l'Encyclopédie.

Bultena, G. L., & Powers, E. A. (1978). Denial of aging: Age identification and reference group orientations. *Journal of Gerontology, 33*, 748–754.

Carver, C. S., & Scheier, M. F. (1990). Origins and functions of positive and negative affect: A control-process view. *Psychological Review, 97*, 19–25.

Coyne, J. C. (1992). Cognition on depression: A paradigm in crisis. *Psychological Inquiry, 3*, 232–235.

Emerson, R. W. (1900). *Compensation.* New York: Caldwell.

Ericsson, K. A. (1990). Peak performance and age: An examination of peak performance in sports. In P. B. Baltes & M. M. Baltes (Eds.), *Successful aging: Perspectives from the behavioral sciences* (pp. 164–196). New York: Cambridge University Press.

Filipp, S.-H., Ferring, D., & Klauer, T. (1989). Subjektives Alterserleben - ein Merkmal erfolgreichen Alterns? [Subjective age: An indicator of successful aging?] In M. M. Baltes, M. Kohli, & K. Sames (Eds.), *Erfolgreiches Altern: Bedingungen und Variationen* (pp. 296–300). Bern: Huber.

Flavell, J. H. (1964). *The developmental psychology of Jean Piaget.* Princeton, NJ: Van Nostrand.

Formey, S. (1759). Ébauche du système de la compensation [Sketch of the system of compensation]. In Académie Royale des Sciences et Belles-Lettres à Berlin (Ed.), *Histoire de l'Académie Royale des Sciences et Belles-Lettres à Berlin* (Vol. 25, pp. 378–389). Berlin: Haude & Spener.

Gatz, M., & Karel, M. J. (1993). Individual change in perceived control over 20 years. *International Journal of Behavioral Development, 16,* 305–322.

Geertz, C. (1973). *The interpretation of cultures: Selected essays.* New York: Basic Books.

Gehlen, A. (1988). *Man: His nature and place in the world.* New York: Columbia University Press. (Original work published 1940)

Gilbert, D. T. (1993). The assent of man: Mental representation and the control of belief. In D. M. Wegner & J. W. Pennebaker (Eds.), *Handbook of mental control* (pp. 57–87). Englewood Cliffs, NJ: Prentice-Hall.

Greenwald, A. G. (1980). The totalitarian ego. *American Psychologist, 35,* 603–618.

Heckhausen, J., Dixon, R. A., & Baltes, P. B. (1989). Gains and losses in development throughout adulthood as perceived by different adult age groups. *Developmental Psychology, 25,* 109–121.

Herder, J. G. (1772). *Abhandlung über den Ursprung der Sprache* [The origin of language]. Berlin: Voß.

Janoff-Bulman, R., & Brickman, P. (1982). Expectations and what people learn from failure. In N. T. Feather (Ed.), *Expectations and actions* (pp. 207–237). Hillsdale, NJ: Lawrence Erlbaum Associates.

Kliegl, R., Smith, J., & Baltes, P. B. (1989). Testing-the-limits and the study of adult age differences in cognitive plasticity and mnemonic skill. *Developmental Psychology, 25,* 247–256.

Klinger, E. (1975). Consequences of commitment to and disengagement from incentives. *Psychological Review, 82,* 1–25.

Krampen, G. (1981). *IPC-Fragebogen zu Kontrollüberzeugungen* [IPC-Questionnaire of control beliefs]. Göttingen: Hogrefe.

Kuypers, J. A., & Bengtson, V. L. (1973). Social breakdown and competence. *Human Development, 16,* 181–201.

Lachman, M. E. (1986). Locus of control in aging research: A case for multidimensional and domain-specific assessment. *Psychology and Aging, 1,* 34–40.

Lanz, P. (1987). *Menschliches Handeln zwischen Kausalität und Rationalität* [Human action between causality and rationality]. Frankfurt: Athenäum.

Lazarus, R. S., & DeLongis, A. (1983). Psychological stress and coping in aging. *American Psychologist, 38,* 245–254.

Lazarus, R. S., & Golden, G. Y. (1981). The function of denial in stress, coping, and aging. In J. L. McGaugh & S. B. Kiesler (Eds.), *Aging, biology and behavior* (pp. 283–307). New York: Academic Press.

Leibniz, G. W. (1710). *Essais de theodicée sur la bonté de Dieu, la liberté de l'homme et l'origine du mal* [Essays of theodicy]. Amsterdam: Isaac Troyel.

Lewontin, R. C. (1982). Organism and environment. In H. C. Plotkin (Ed.), *Learning, development and culture* (pp. 151–170). Chichester, England: Wiley.

Linville, P. W. (1987). Self-complexity as a cognitive buffer against stress-related illness and depression. *Journal of Personality and Social Psychology, 52,* 663–676.

Markus, H., & Nurius, P. (1986). Possible selves. *American Psychologist, 41,* 954–969.

Markus, H., & Wurf, E. (1987). The dynamic self: A social psychological perspective. *Annual Review of Psychology, 38,* 299–337.

Marquard, O. (1983). Entlastungen. Theodizeemotive in der neuzeitlichen Philosophie [Motives of theodicy in modern philosophy]. In P. Wapnewski (Ed.), *Wissenschaftskolleg. Jahrbuch 1982* (pp. 245–258). Berlin: Siedler.

McFarland, C., Ross, M., & Giltrow, M. (1992). Biased recollections in older adults: The role of implicit theories of aging. *Journal of Personality and Social Psychology, 62,* 837–850.

Needles, D. J., & Abramson, L. Y. (1990). Positive life events, attributional style, and hopefulness: Testing a model of recovery from depression. *Journal of Abnormal Psychology, 99,* 156–165.

Neely, J. J. (1991). Semantic priming effects in visual word recognition: A selective review of current findings and theories. In D. Besner & G. W. Humphreys (Eds.), *Basic processes in reading: Visual word recognition* (pp. 264–336). Hillsdale, NJ: Lawrence Erlbaum Associates.

Peterson, C., & Seligman, M. E. P. (1984). Causal explanations as a risk factor for depression: Theory and evidence. *Psychological Review, 91,* 347–374.

Rodin, J. (1987). Personal control through the life course. In R. P. Abeles (Ed.), *Life-span perspective and social psychology* (pp. 103–119). Hillsdale, NJ: Lawrence Erlbaum Associates.

Rodin, J., & Langer, E. (1980). Aging labels: The decline of control and the fall of self-esteem. *Journal of Social Issues, 36,* 12–29.

Rothermund, K., Wentura, D., & Brandtstädter, J. (in press). Selbstwertschützende Verschiebungen in der Semantik des Begriffs "alt" im höheren Erwachsenenalter [Self-protective shifts in the associative structure of the concept "old" in later adulthood]. *Sprache & Kognition.*

Salomon, H. (1972). Heuristic models for the generation of ATI-hypothesis. *Review of Educational Research, 42,* 327–343.

Salthouse, T. A. (1985). *A theory of cognitive aging.* Amsterdam: North-Holland.

Salthouse, T. A. (1987). Age, experience, and compensation. In K. Schooler & K. W. Schaie (Eds.), *Cognitive functioning and social structure over the life course* (pp. 142–150). Norwood, NJ: Ablex.

Salthouse, T. A. (1990). Cognitive competence and expertise in aging. In J. E. Birren & K. W. Schaie (Eds.), *Handbook of the psychology of aging* (3rd ed., pp. 310–319). San Diego, CA: Academic Press.

Samuelson, P. A., & Nordhaus, W. D. (1985). *Economics* (12th ed.). New York: McGraw-Hill.

Scheier, M. F., & Carver, C. S. (1985). Optimism, coping, and health: Assessment and implications of generalized outcome expectancies. *Health Psychology, 4,* 219–247.

Schulz, R. (1980). Aging and control. In J. Garber & M. E. P. Seligman (Eds.), *Human helplessness: Theory and applications* (pp. 261–277). New York: Academic Press.

Snyder, C. R., Irving, L. M., Sigmon, S. T., & Holleran, S. (1992). Reality negotiation and valence/linkage self-theories: Psychic showdown at the "I'm ok" corral and beyond. In L. Montada, S. H. Filipp, & M. J. Lerner (Eds.), *Life crises and experiences of loss in adulthood* (pp. 275–297). Hillsdale, NJ: Lawrence Erlbaum Associates.

Sternberg, R. J., & Wagner, R. K. (Eds.). (1986). *Practical intelligence: Nature and origins of competence in the everyday world.* New York: Cambridge University Press.

Stock, W. A., Okun, M. A., Haring, M. J., & Witter, R. A. (1983). Age and subjective well-being: A meta-analysis. In R. J. Light (Ed.), *Evaluation studies: Review annual* (Vol. 8, pp. 279–302). Beverly Hills, CA: Sage.

Svagelski, J. (1981). *L'idée de compensation en France 1750–1850* [The idea of compensation in France 1750–1850]. Lyon: Editions L'Hermès.

Swann, W. B. (1983). Self-verification: Bringing the social reality in harmony with the self. In J. Suls & A. G. Greenwald (Eds.), *Psychological perspectives on the self* (Vol. 2, pp. 33–66). Hillsdale, NJ: Lawrence Erlbaum Associates.

Taylor, S. E. (1983). Adjustment to threatening events. *American Psychologist, 38,* 1161–1173.

Taylor, S. E. (1991). Asymmetrical effects of positive and negative events: The mobilization-minimization hypothesis. *Psychological Bulletin, 110,* 67–85.

Teasdale, J. D. (1988). Cognitive vulnerability to persistent depression. *Cognition and Emotion, 2,* 247–274.

Uttal, D. H., & Perlmutter, M. (1989). Toward a broader conceptualization of development: The role of gains and losses across the life span. *Developmental Review, 9,* 101–132.

Whitbourne, S. K. (1987). Personality development in adulthood and old age: Relationships among identity style, health, and well-being. *Annual Review of Gerontology and Geriatrics, 7,* 189–216.

Wolk, S. (1976). Situational constraint as a moderator of the locus of control-adjustment relationship. *Journal of Consulting and Clinical Psychology, 44,* 420–427.

Wortman, C. B., & Brehm, J. W. (1975). Responses to uncontrollable outcomes: An integration of reactance theory and the learned helplessness model. In L. Berkowitz (Ed.), *Advances in experimental social psychology* (Vol. 8, pp. 278–336). New York: Academic Press.

CHAPTER FIVE

Selection and Compensation in Adulthood

Laura L. Carstensen
Kaaren A. Hanson
Alexandra M. Freund
Stanford University

Normatively, adulthood is the time in life when people establish independence from their families of origin, pursue careers, identify life partners, and raise children of their own. During this period, expertise in specialized domains is attained and social networks are created and solidified. In many ways, adulthood is characterized as a time of acquisition, as well as a process of differentiation (Whitbourne, 1986).

Although adulthood is filled with advances and gains, it is also marked by challenges and losses. Career goals are sometimes foiled. Intimate relationships fail. Inevitably, loved ones die. Toward the end of life, physical losses are nearly always encountered. Moreover, even under the best of circumstances, decisions to pursue certain life paths require not pursuing alternate life paths. For example, selection of a career enhances exposure to certain opportunities, but inevitably limits exposure to others. Such choices have cumulative effects that exert considerable influence over a lifetime (Dannefer, 1987). Potentials in some environments are foreshortened by the selection of alternate environments.

We contend that, unlike childhood and adolescence, when parents and other caregivers provide considerable guidance and structure, adulthood represents the time in life when individuals, more than any other time, actively construct their own lives. As they do, they face both risks and opportunities and experience associated gains and losses. In this chapter, we explore the utility of applying the constructs of selection and compensation to behavioral and psychological changes typically evinced during

107

adulthood transitions. Although most of the empirical research we review was not designed with this theoretical framework in mind, we attempt to show that selection and compensation represent common themes that weave throughout diverse arenas. We contend that selection and compensation may well represent core psychological and behavioral processes that permit adaptation, adjustment, and differentiation in adulthood, and that allow people to optimize life's potentials and manage life's obstacles.

THE CONSTRUCTS OF SELECTION AND COMPENSATION

Many phenomena described in the literature on life-span development are suggestive of selection and compensation. Yet only recently have attempts been made to operationalize the theoretical constructs in a way that promises to generate empirical investigation. P. Baltes and M. Baltes (1990) proposed the model of selective optimization with compensation to account for successful adaptation in the face of an increasingly negative ratio between gains and losses in old age. Although the model focuses on old age, it speaks to adaptation throughout adulthood.

The P. Baltes and M. Baltes model specifies three processes—selection, optimization, and compensation—that enable people to master goals despite or even because of vulnerabilities. According to the model, selection involves the restriction of life domains in the face of aging loss such that the highest priority domains are maintained. Selection is not limited to established domains; people sometimes select new domains in the face of loss.

Optimization involves the enrichment and augmentation of skills and general reserves toward the aim of maximizing performance in selected domains. In some ways, optimization reflects what Lawton called "person-environment fit" (Lawton, 1987; Lawton & Nahemow, 1973), in which environments challenge, but do not defeat, individual competencies. Thus, optimization refers to the refinement of expertise (e.g., work) or enhanced emotional closeness (e.g., intimate relationships). It is facilitated by the increased investment of resources in selected domains.

In this model, compensation refers to behavioral and psychological efforts to maintain adequate functioning in the face of loss. Compensation draws frequently on existing, but previously unused, reserves and skills, but also can be accomplished by developing new skills or competencies.

In a recent theoretical review, Bäckman and Dixon (1992) elaborated on a theoretical framework for compensation that incorporates what P. Baltes and M. Baltes (1990) refer to as optimization. They wrote:

> Compensation can be inferred when an objective or perceived mismatch between accessible skills and environmental demands is counterbalanced (either

automatically or deliberately) by investment of more time or effort (drawing on normal skills), utilization of latent (but normally inactive) skills or acquisition of new skills, so that a change in behavioral profile occurs, either in the direction of adaptive attainment, maintenance, or surpassing of normal levels of proficiency or of maladaptive outcome behaviors or consequences. (p. 272)

Accordingly, compensation emerges from a skill–demand mismatch and involves an increase in one or more behavioral domains to compensate for a targeted deficit. Bäckman and Dixon argued that not all skill–demand mismatches result in compensation. Contextual support and deficit severity influence the emergence of compensatory behaviors. If the level of contextual support is high, compensatory activities on the part of the individual may not be needed to achieve a desired level of performance. For example, a man who is hearing impaired, but who is surrounded by social partners who enunciate their words very clearly, may not actively compensate for the deficit. Alternatively, if the environmental demand–skill mismatch is small (e.g., if a woman is unable to discern high-frequency sounds that are rarely produced in spoken language), compensation may not be needed. At the other extreme, if a deficit is large, behavioral compensation may be impossible, but psychological compensation such as changing goals may be pursued (Brandtstädter & Greve, 1994). No amount of behavioral compensation will allow a marathon runner who loses both legs to run, for example, yet by adjusting goals to include other sports such as wheelchair racing, the person can continue to compete athletically.

Although the constructs of *selection* and *compensation* provide reasonable heuristics for the discussion of fundamental human processes, there are also limitations to their utility. First, they can be fully understood only in context. For example, at first glance, choosing from an array of goals is consistent with selection, and recovery from goal obstruction is consistent with compensation. However, a person with a substantial hearing loss who selects social partners who speak loudly or who are familiar with the hearing problem is engaging in selection as a compensatory mechanism (Tesch-Römer, 1993). We argue that selection and compensation are best distinguished when judged according to functional standards. When selection is evoked in response to a mismatch between skills and demands, selections represent functional compensation, and thus should be considered a special case of compensation (viz., compensatory selection). This is true even if the topography of the behavior suggests selection. We contend that selection is best reserved for proactive or anticipatory limitations that can, but do not necessarily, relate to loss. *Selection* refers to restrictions in domains that result from cultural or temporal constraints (e.g., in most Western societies, you cannot have more than one spouse on legal grounds, and you cannot have numerous careers due to temporal restraints) *or* the anticipation of loss (e.g., approaching the end of life). When selection occurs in *response* to a circumscribed loss toward the aim of maintaining an exisiting goal, it is best considered *compensation.*

Second, in most cases, the link between the skill–demand mismatch and subsequent compensatory behavior is weak (Uttal & Perlmutter, 1989). To be considered compensatory, causality must be established between the skill–demand mismatch and the subsequent behavior (Bäckman & Dixon, 1992). Yet studies demonstrating the dynamics of selection or compensation are notable lacking. At present, most of the relevant literature, including the work we review herein, is correlational, and thus fails to discriminate between compensatory and noncompensatory behavior (e.g., Avis, Brambilla, Vass, & McKinlay, 1991; Kessler, Turner, & House, 1987, 1988; Zisook & Schuchter, 1991). Although such findings can suggest possibilities, experimentation is necessary for firm conclusions about compensation. However, in light of the unlikely and unethical experimental manipulation of events like job loss and illness, researchers are left with more indirect means to disentangle relationships between loss and compensation. Quasi-experimental methods may be useful. For example, researchers could monitor individuals' goals and behaviors over time, and consider behaviors compensatory only if they are (a) temporally contingent on loss, and (b) not observed in persons who share similar goals but have not experienced a similar loss over the same time period. By documenting specific goals, recording events that block the goals, and observing behavioral changes that enable people to reach blocked goals, researchers could better specify instances of compensation when they occur. Analogue studies, in which hypothetical situations are presented to subjects who voice anticipated responses, also may be useful.

Unless evidence of causal relationships is demanded, virtually any behavior can be viewed as compensatory. For example, if widows have larger social networks than nonwidows, this could reflect compensatory efforts stemming from the loss of a primary relationship, or, alternatively, it could reflect the pursuit of long-standing friendship goals previously thwarted by a primary commitment to a life partner. Only in the former would development of a broad friendship base be considered compensatory. For compensation to be a useful construct, scientists must be able to say when it occurs *and* when it does not occur. If all behavior subsequent to goal obstruction is, by definition, compensation, it serves little predictive or explanatory utility. The tendency to interpret behavior change of any kind as compensatory is especially strong in gerontology. All too often, evidence of mastery or growth in old age, whatever the domain, tends to be viewed as compensation. We (Carstensen & Freund, 1994) feel this reflects the tacit belief that aging per se is a threat to the organism and steers scientists away from consideration of growth hypotheses. Subsequently, a false dichotomy between early life and later life is reinforced, with the former representing gains and the latter representing loss (P. Baltes, 1987).

The Life Course of Selection

With age, people become increasingly different from one another in physical, social, and psychological domains (Dannefer, 1987; Nelson & Dannefer, 1992). This differentiation occurs largely through two forms of selection: structural and behavioral. Although in this chapter we focus on the latter, it is essential to acknowledge the former. People do not choose freely and evenly among all of life's possibilities. *Structural selection* refers to societal practices that limit or open opportunities depending on factors such as gender, race, class, and age (Carstensen & Pasupathi, 1993; Dannefer, 1992). By limiting or expanding people's options according to such characteristics, structural selections channel people into a subset of developmental trajectories.

Differences in resource accessibility early in life greatly influence available options throughout the life span (Dannefer, 1987). Over time, differences between "advantaged" and "disadvantaged" people loom ever larger. Merton (1968) labeled this phenomenon the "Matthew effect" after the biblical quotation in the Gospel of Matthew:

> For unto every one that hath shall be given and he shall have abundance; but from him that hath not shall be taken away even that which he hath not. (Matthew 25:29)

In contrast to the way that structural selections are imposed on people, behavioral selection involves actively choosing one or more life paths from among many. Unlike structural selection, in which external circumstances act upon individuals, behavioral selections allow people to actively influence their own life trajectories. For example, once people identify global educational and career paths, they continue to make choices about acquiring specialized knowledge that subsequently leads to greater expertise in work domains (Featherman, 1980; Featherman, Smith, & Peterson, 1990). Performance in selected domains profits from the increasing allocation of resources. Thus, despite that career is influenced by structural selections independent of individual competencies or desires, behavioral selections also play an important role.

Social network building provides another example of behavioral selection. It appears that people engage in less social interaction in later life than in early life (Field & Minkler, 1988; Lawton, Moss, & Fulcomer, 1987; Palmore, 1981). Because social relationships are clearly central to physical and mental well-being, predicting even longevity (Berkman & Syme, 1979), this finding has raised considerable concern in gerontology. Yet analyses of change patterns suggest that selections are not arbitrary. Rather, it appears that reductions in peripheral contacts are discarded, whereas close emotional relationships are maintained into old age (Carstensen, 1992; Lang & Carstensen, 1994). That is, while interaction rates with acquaintances are decreasing, interaction rates with close social partners are maintained (i.e., selected) or even increased, and appear to become increasingly satisfying over time (Carstensen, 1992). Socioemotional selectivity theory explains reduced rates of social contact by changes in goal hierarchies that occur when people perceive approaching endings (Carstensen, 1993). Because behavioral changes occur *in anticipation* of constraints, rather than in response to loss, social reductions meet our criterion for classification as selection, not compensation.

Antonucci and her colleagues (Antonucci, 1991; Antonucci & Akiyama, 1987, 1991) documented a life-span process in which people actively create social environments that match personal needs. She contended that individuals construct a relatively stable "convoy" of social partners, which accompanies the individuals through life. By selecting out of the social network people who do not fulfill social needs, and by investing more time and energy in social partners who do, social potentials may be most effectively realized.

Social selection also has costs. Although the life-course pattern described previously may be largely adaptive, selections inevitably result in false negatives as well. That is, the failure to pursue some relationships, no doubt, foreshortens some social possibilities. At the same time, by allocating emotional and social resources to a select few, meaningful relationships develop.

THE ROLE OF COMPENSATION IN ADULTHOOD

Negative Life Events as Losses in Adulthood

Frequently referred to as "negative life events," experiences such as divorce, chronic illness, loss of loved ones, or loss of employment typically lead to blocked goals. People often compensate for blocked goals by engaging in alternate behaviors that achieve a similarly desirable feeling or state. For example, if a woman values emotional closeness but loses her best friend, she may compensate by investing more time and energy into another friendship.

It is important to appreciate individual differences in the experience of negative life events (e.g., separation from a spouse may not necessarily be a negative life event). In fact, if the marriage has been turbulent, it may have quite the opposite effect. Even if a divorce is indeed experienced as a loss, researchers should be cautious about interpreting an increase in activities or behaviors after such an event as compensatory. It could be that marriage represses certain activities or behaviors that are simply not possible until after divorce (Chiriboga & Catron, 1991; Weiss, 1975). Finally, compensatory behaviors are not necessarily successful in obtaining the desired goal. Indeed, compensatory behaviors may lead to negative consequences.

For example, if the woman noted earlier invests her time and energy in a bad relationship, she may ultimately feel even more emotionally isolated than she did before making compensatory efforts.

Nevertheless, we report evidence herein that divorce, widowhood, chronic illness, and unemployment are associated with significant distress for *most* people, and thus can be viewed reliably as losses. We also present evidence that the vast majority of people who experience the associated distress return to previous levels of well-being. This literature underscores the impressive resilience of human beings even faced with substantial insults to physical or social well-being. More important for our purposes, behavior change surrounding such events may point to instantiations of compensation in adulthood. First, we review the events and the associated distress. Second, we discuss evidence for compensatory behavior that the events appear to elicit.

Specific Losses in Adulthood

Divorce and *widowhood* represent two of the most stressful life events (Holmes & Rahe, 1967). Divorce encompasses a broad array of life changes (Chiriboga, 1991) and is associated with many health-related and psychological problems, such as alcoholism (Hallberg & Mattsson, 1989), suicide (Stack, 1989), and relatively high rates of morbidity and mortality (United Nations, 1987). Similarly, widowhood is associated with increased morbidity (Thompson, Breckenridge, Gallagher, & Peterson, 1984), mortality (Stroebe, Stroebe, & Hansson, 1988), mental distress (Avis et al., 1991), and depression (Avis et al., 1991; Gallagher, Breckenridge, Thompson, & Peterson, 1983).

Interestingly, as stressful as they are, negative symptoms associated with widowhood and divorce are rarely permanent. Stress-related symptoms generally begin to decrease two years post-divorce. Adjustment to widowhood occurs even more rapidly; depressive symptoms and mental distress decrease significantly over a one-year period (Avis et al., 1991; Zisook & Schuchter, 1991). In addition, widowhood per se is not associated with poor health, increased mortality, or poor psychological functioning (McCrae & Costa, 1988). Thus, psychological distress immediately following divorce or widowhood appears to dissipate over a relatively short time period.

Chronic diseases (e.g., diabetes, cancer) and *permanent disabilities* (e.g., spinal cord injuries) both represent permanent losses that carry long-term consequences. Managing illness demands adjustment to limited mobility and painful medical procedures. Not surprisingly, depression and anxiety are common initial responses to the diagnosis of a chronic illness or permanent disability (Taylor & Aspinwall, 1990; Wortman & Silver, 1987).

Nevertheless, with time most people return to previous levels of psychological functioning. Although people recently diagnosed with a chronic illness suffer relatively high rates of depression, after three months they are neither more anxious nor more depressed than healthier comparisons (Cassileth et al., 1984). Additional evidence for adjustment to physical loss has been found in the area of spinal cord injury. Although people who suffer from spinal cord injury are frequently depressed and anxious over the initial 2-month period post-trauma, levels of distress decrease significantly thereafter (Wortman & Silver, 1987).

Job loss has been associated with depression (Dew, Bromet, & Penkower, 1992; Kessler, Turner, & House, 1987, 1988), anxiety, somatization, and physical illness (Kessler, et al., 1987, 1988) as well as a lowered sense of well-being (Brenner & Starrin, 1988). Retirement has been found to carry similarly negative consequences for a significant minority of individuals (Antonovsky, 1992; Bosse, Aldwin, Levenson, & Workman-Daniels, 1991; Hardy, 1991; Thompson, Strieb, & Kosa 1960), particularly those who feel pressured into retirement (Floyd et al., 1992; Swan, Dame, & Carmelli, 1991). In this way, forced retirement functions as unemployment for older workers (Hardy, 1991). Yet, most people adjust with time (Brenner & Starrin, 1988).

Although it is possible that the distress simply "lifts," changes in behavior post spousal loss, discussed in subsequent sections on strategies and resources, suggest compensatory efforts. The core losses associated with divorce, widowhood, poor health, unemployment, and mandatory retirement are often long lasting, yet negative symptoms associated with these transitions rarely persist. How do adults compensate for the loss of their spouse, their job, or their health? On what resources do they draw? What strategies do they employ? In the next section, we discuss the external resources (e.g., financial solvency, friends) and the internal resources (e.g., self-efficacy beliefs, control beliefs) that appear to be critical in guiding selection and activating compensation.

EXTERNAL RESOURCES

Compensation is influenced by access to resources, which is intimately tied to selections made earlier in life. Again, social and physical characteristics such as race, class, education, and gender play a prominent role in access to resources, affecting people's school choices, career options, income, and financial security. Resource access influences the degree of control people are able to exert over their environments. In Western societies, it is widely accepted that White, male, highly educated, wealthy individuals have greatest access to societally valued resources and, consequently, to a greater selection of options from which to choose when compensation is required. Of course there are exceptions: Oprah Winfrey wields more power and status than the vast majority of White men in America. Moreover, access to certain resources, such as extended social networks, are sometimes even more available to less advantaged than advantaged subgroups. Thus, structurally advantaged people do not necessarily have greater resource access across domains. We focus next on financial and social resources to illustrate the relationship between resources and compensation.

Financial Resources

Financial resources influence the decision to divorce and the decision to retire (viz., selections), and the compensatory strategies people employ. Divorce is likely to occur when the relative appeal of marriage is low and resources, such as income and social support, exist outside of the marriage (Dixon & Weitzman, 1982; Levinger, 1976). The decision to retire seems to be made on similar grounds. When personal costs of employment do not justify rewards, retirement is likely to be initiated as long as adequate financial resources are available.

Swan, Dame, and Carmelli (1991) found that the most frequently reported reasons for voluntary retirement were financial feasibility and the desire to increase enjoyment in life. Adequate financial resources are also associated with faster adaptation post-retirement, suggesting considerable collinearity between resources and compensation. People without adequate financial resources suffer longer and to a greater degree from job loss (Bosse, Aldwin, Levenson, & Workman-Daniels, 1991; Dew et al., 1992; Kessler et al., 1987, 1988; Mallinckrodt & Bennett, 1992) and marital dissolution (Booth & Amato, 1991; Clarke-Stewart & Bailey, 1989; Stroebe & Stroebe, 1987) than their financially stable counterparts. Because money is a necessary prerequisite for many activities (e.g., sports-related activities, movies, social outings), the financial resources at one's disposal can have important implications for the range of possibilities from which one can select compensatory behaviors.

Social Resources

Social Support. The size and composition of social networks influence compensation (and compensatory selection) in the face of loss. Simply, social network size relates to the probability that functions previously served but lost can be replaced by other network members. The more diversified the social network, the more likely specific functions can be replaced.

Gander and Jorgensen (1990) found that the best predictors of well-being in divorced persons (ages 50 years and older) are emotional closeness to children, number of people perceived to be in the social support network during an emergency, and frequency of contact with a close friend. In some ways counterintuitive, greater frequency of contact is related to lower well-being. Very likely, the frequency of contact with a supportive friend reflects the extent of distress people are experiencing and subsequently seeking social support. The availability of a confidant alone does not predict well-being post divorce. Chiriboga and Catron (1991) reported that no single indicator of social support (e.g., network size, presence of a confidant, perceived social support, and support seeking) significantly predicts level of distress in divorced men, whereas aggregated they explain significant variance. The picture that emerges for women is very similar.

Young, childless couples seem to suffer from fewer post-divorce problems than divorcing parents (Daniels-Mohring & Berger, 1984; Smith & Barnet, 1990). However, children also function as resources (Brown, Felton, Whiteman, & Manela, 1980), especially for couples that divorce relatively late in life (Gander & Jorgensen, 1990). We expect that children who are still young—and thus dependent on parents—demand time, energy, and emotional and financial support from caregiving parents (which could generate additional stress). Non-caregiving parents separated from their children may suffer from the loss of contact with children, or feelings of guilt. When children are adults, they may actively provide divorcing parents with emotional and instrumental support.

Job loss is another domain in which social support may function as a compensatory resource. When people become unemployed, they not only lose the experience of work and financial solvency, but also the social contact facilitated by the work environment. Several investigators report that decreased levels of social interaction negatively influence the physical and psychological well-being of the unemployed. For example, Kessler et al. (1988) found that having a confidant and being integrated into affiliative social networks are negatively correlated with physical illness, anxiety, and depression following job loss. Unemployed men and women who have infrequent social contacts report greater depression after job loss than their more socially integrated counterparts (Bolton & Oatley, 1987). Taken together, the reported findings suggest that social networks and social support are recruited to compensate for both losses associated with divorce and losses related to unemployment.

Social Activities. One way to compensate for losses due to unemployment or divorce is to invest more time in social activities. Warr and Payne (1983) asked a large sample of men who had been unemployed for 6–11 months to compare time expenditure when they were employed versus unemployed. Unemployment was associated with domestic work (e.g., household chores), domestic pastimes (e.g., sleeping, listening to the radio), and outdoor chores (e.g., gardening). In addition, the unemployed men reported socializing with friends and neighbors more when they were unemployed than when they had been employed. Spending more time socializing and spending less time in solitary activities (e.g., sleeping) were associated with greater satisfaction (see also Feather, 1989). Jones' (1991) study led to similar conclusions. As the length of unemployment increases, so does time spent interacting with family members and friends. It appears that unemployed men may compensate for losses related to unemployment by spending more time with friends, family members, or neighbors.

A similar point can be made with respect to divorce. An important factor in adjustment seems to be time since divorce (Chiriboga & Catron, 1991; Clarke-Stewart & Bailey, 1989). Because time is a poor explanatory variable, one must ask what happens after divorce that helps individuals to recover from the losses associated with divorce. For example, after divorce, men are more likely to participate in social activities (Raschke, 1977). But establishing new activity patterns requires time. Accordingly, people who already have established a large repertoire of social activities prior to experiencing a loss are better off because they have immediate access to a wide array of alternative activities from which to select. Chiriboga and Turnher (1980) found that women who have independent hobbies, interests, and leisure activities prior to divorce experience a higher level of happiness post divorce than women who do not. Taken together, the findings of these studies suggest that establishing social support and engaging in social activities help people compensate for losses associated with negative life events.

PSYCHOLOGICAL PROCESSES INVOLVED IN SELECTION AND COMPENSATION

The presence of resources alone is insufficient to facilitate adaptation. Resource utilization is mediated by beliefs about resources, behavioral competence and controllability of the environment. In this way, psychological processes are centrally involved in selection and compensation. For example, if a woman is confident in her teaching ability, but not confident about her ability to secure employment, she may select life paths that fail to utilize her expertise. A man who has a heart attack and believes that his recovery is beyond his control may fail to engage in behaviors that might otherwise compensate for his loss of physical capacity. In the following sections, we discuss self-efficacy, control beliefs, and goal adjustment as central psychological processes in selection and compensation.

Self-Efficacy

Self-efficacy refers to the belief in one's own capabilities to organize and engage in particular actions to deal with specific situations. Self-efficacy influences the initiation of action, as well as the time and effort committed to behaviors that may overcome obstacles (Bandura, 1977, 1986). Furthermore, self-efficacy influences the choice (or selection) of goals and environments (Bandura, 1993).

How is self-efficacy related to compensation? As noted previously, one form of compensation is the use of existing resources (whether internal or external), or the generation of new resources to minimize a loss-induced mismatch between a goal and current status. We argue that whether and which compensatory resources are selected are determined, in part, by self-efficacy beliefs. In the following discussion, we focus briefly on the health domain in illustrating this contention.

A substantial literature suggests that self-efficacy beliefs play a major role in the adoption of health-related behaviors and the planning and maintaining of actual performance (Schwarzer, 1992). For example, self-efficacy is related to rehabilitation efforts (e.g., engagement in physical exercise) of myocardial infarction patients and mediated training gains (Ewart, Stewart, Gillilan, & Kelemen, 1986). In chronic diseases, such as chronic arthritis, efficacy predicts pain level above and beyond physical disability (Holman, Mazonson, & Lorig, 1989). Interestingly, even the self-efficacy beliefs of close social partners influence compensatory behavior. A study by Taylor, Bandura, Ewart, Miller, and DeBusk (1985) demonstrated that wives' confidence in their husbands' capabilities after a myocardial infarction is significantly related to performance measures recorded in husbands (e.g., treadmill heart rate, workload). As these examples illustrate, self-efficacy is an important psychological factor that contributes to compensation.

Control Beliefs

As is the case for self-efficacy, the degree to which a person perceives him or herself as having control over the environment can mediate the experience of loss and subsequent compensation. A strong sense of internal control is positively related to adjustment to negative events. This is true for a number of illnesses, including cancer (Taylor, 1983), arthritis (Affleck, Tennen, Pfeiffer, & Fifield, 1987), and myocardial infarction (Michela, 1982).

There is some suggestion in the literature that control beliefs of the frail elderly are particularly important. Studies of nursing home residents provide provocative evidence that control beliefs may influence longevity. Although nursing home placement can threaten independence, autonomy, and control, it represents a structural or behavioral selection that more than 40% of people will experience at some time during their lives. Although nursing home placement can lower competence and well-being (e.g., Baltes & Wahl, 1987; Baltes, Wahl, & Reichert, 1991), the effects of relocation appear to be moderated powerfully by perceived control. Following a classic intervention study—in which nursing home residents were afforded increased personal responsibility for their environments—Rodin and Langer (1977) concluded that enhancing a sense of control not only influences well-being, but relates positively to health and mortality. More recently, Carstensen and Pasupathi (in preparation) conducted a longitudinal study of nursing home placement, in which frail, older people were followed from the community into a nursing home and compared with a group of frail, community elderly. Over a 1-year period, nursing home residents were significantly more likely to die than community residents. More important, perceived control predicted death even after controlling for age, health, depression, and other forms of psychological distress.

Control beliefs are strongly related to the timing of life-course events. Whether an event occurs "on time" and thus is anticipated, or "off-time" and thus unexpected, appears to influence the consequences. A good example is the timing of widowhood. Compared with younger widows, older widows are at lower risk for psychological and health-related problems (e.g., Stroebe & Stroebe, 1987). This result can be explained in at least two ways. First, it may be that older widows often care for their ill spouses, and widowhood relieves them of the burden of caregiving. Second, death in old age is expected (Wortman & Silver, 1990). Knowing about the impending death of a spouse beforehand implies that the many changes in one's life can be anticipated and, to a certain degree, controlled. For example, Bryant and Morgan (1989) found that financial preparation during the year before the death of the spouse had a significant effect on well-being. Moreover, widows who had neither financial experience prior to widowhood nor preparation for handling finances after the death of the spouse were more likely to report economic distress.

Goal Adjustment

An interesting approach to conceptualizing control was proposed by Heckhausen and Schulz (1993) who distinguished primary from secondary control and related these concepts to selection and compensation. In the case of primary control, selection denotes the investment of internal resources, whereas compensation is conceived of as the implementation of external resources. However, selection in terms of secondary control is conceptualized as meta-volitional, involving, for example, increased commitment to a given goal. Changing goals is seen as compensation. Similarly, Brandtstädter and his colleagues (e.g., Brandtstädter & Greve, 1994) viewed the lowering of aspiration level, or shifting of goals (when initial goals are blocked), as a form of compensation called accommodative coping. As Bäckman and Dixon (1992) pointed out, shifting goals can be a form of compensation for a perceived mismatch between an initial goal and a current state.

The use of accommodative processes, operationalized as flexible goal adjustment, appears to increase with age, whereas tenacious goal pursuit decreases with age (Brandtstädter & Renner, 1990). Moreover, flexible goal adjustment moderates the negative relationship between perceived developmental deficits and life satisfaction. People do appear to change their goals and criteria for psychological functioning over the life span. When asked to indicate their relevance for well-being and psychological functioning, middle aged and older adults placed less emphasis on personal growth and more emphasis on environmental mastery and autonomy compared with younger adults (Ryff, 1989). Furthermore, younger and middle-aged adults expect future gains in their development, whereas older adults expect decline in various domains (e.g., Heckhausen, Dixon, & Baltes, 1989). Yet older people also rate themselves as being better off than most of their peers (Heckhausen & Krueger, 1993), and they achieve a closer match between their actual and ideal self-perceptions than younger adults (Cross & Markus, 1991; Ryff, 1991). These results can be interpreted as indicators of shifting goals, lowering of the level of aspiration by changing the criteria for achievement, or psychological functioning to compensate for age-related losses and decline. For example, Taylor and colleagues (Taylor, 1983; Taylor & Brown, 1988), claimed that people who experience serious physical illness use downward social comparison to feel relatively well off, even if they are operating at a relatively low level of functioning.

In summary, psychological processes such as self-efficacy beliefs, control beliefs, and goal adjustment serve to guide selection and act as resources for compensation. When people shift goals or lower aspiration levels, they can reduce discomfort generated by a demand-skill mismatch. Self-efficacy and control beliefs seem to play powerful roles in initiating and maintaining behavior. Thus, it is not sufficient to focus on the mere presence of resources, such as finances or education. Instead, the psychological strategies that actually activate utilization must be considered in understanding selection and compensation.

CONCLUSION

Throughout this chapter, we have attempted to illustrate how the constructs of selection and compensation provide an overarching theoretical framework that helps coalesce findings from a number of divergent areas. The literatures we explored (e.g., divorce, widowhood, chronic illness), although not designed toward this end, easily conformed to postulates consistent with selection and compensation. Selection may account for the systematic increase in within-age group heterogeneity over time; and compensation may explain why certain psychological dimensions, such as life satisfaction, remain stable throughout adulthood, even for persons who experience significant loss.

Of course the empirical findings examined herein were, for the most part, correlational. Moreover, in our review, we presumed that certain behavioral changes are chosen and experienced as gains (e.g., career paths), whereas other behavioral changes are imposed upon individuals and thus experienced as losses (e.g., unemployment). In the absence of experimental studies, however, we cannot be certain if behaviors that appear to represent selection and compensation truly do so.

Although the constructs may be useful in organizing the existing literature and generating hypotheses, we urge researchers to precisely define and judiciously apply them to behavior. Defined too broadly, all behavior can be classified as selection or compensation, and subsequently the functional significance of the processes can become quickly diluted. For example, although we agree that the conscious adoption of a new goal *can* represent compensation, goal changes do not *always* represent compensation. As Carstensen and Freund (1994) pointed out, it is extremely important to demonstrate that changes in behavior and cognition result from blocked goals before they are to be considered compensatory. Goals can change for reasons other than age-related loss; when they do, they are more appropriately considered selections. It is also important to keep in mind that selections and compensatory efforts sometimes fail. They can be misdirected (e.g., increasing activity level as a superficial or short-term distracter from a problem) or insufficient to successfully adapt to loss. Thus, simply documenting behavioral responses to losses is insufficient. Rather, we must move beyond this initial step to document the conditions under which people select and compensate, which forms of compensation appear most adaptive, and which forms are least adaptive. We underscore assertions—previously voiced by Uttal and Perlmutter (1989) and Bäckman and Dixon (1992)—that the establishment of causal relationships is essential to conclude that behaviors or psychological processes are compensatory.

Nevertheless, we feel that, as heuristics, the constructs of selection and compensation have a great deal to offer students of life-span development. By sharpening theoretical definitions—showing when and how selection and compensation processes occur, as well as when they do not—we may gain new insights into adulthood transitions, particularly concerning the remarkable resiliency of human beings to persevere in the face of significant loss.

REFERENCES

Affleck, G., Tennen, H., Pfeiffer, C., & Fifield, J. (1987). Appraisals of control and predictability in adapting to a chronic disease. *Journal of Personality and Social Psychology, 53,* 273–279.

Antonovsky, A. (1992). Can attitudes contribute to health? *Advances, The Journal of Mind-Body Health, 8,* 33–49.

Antonucci, T. (1991). Attachment, social support, and coping with negative life events in mature adulthood. In E. M. Cumming, A. L. Greene, & K. H. Karraker (Eds.), *Life-span developmental psychology: Perspectives on stress and coping* (pp. 261–276). Hillsdale, NJ: Lawrence Erlbaum Associates.

Antonucci, T., & Akiyama, H. (1987). Social networks in adult life and a preliminary examination of the convoy model. *Journal of Gerontology, 42*, 519–527.

Antonucci, T., & Akiyama, H. (1991). Social relationships and aging well. *Generations, 15*, 39–44.

Avis, N. E., Brambilla, D. J., Vass, K., & McKinlay, J. B. (1991). The effect of widowhood on health: A prospective analysis from the Massachusetts Women's Health Study. *Social Science & Medicine, 33*, 1063–1070.

Bäckman, L., & Dixon, R. A. (1992). Psychological compensation: A theoretical framework. *Psychological Bulletin, 112*, 259–283.

Baltes, M. M., & Wahl, H. W. (1987). Dependence in aging. In L. L. Carstensen & B. A. Edelstein (Eds.), *Handbook of clinical gerontology* (pp. 204–221). New York: Pergamon.

Baltes, M. M., Wahl, H. W., & Reichert, M. (1991). Successful aging in long-term care institutions. *Annual Review of Gerontology and Geriatrics, 11*, 311–337.

Baltes, P. B. (1987). Theoretical propositions of life-span developmental psychology: On the dynamics between growth and decline. *Developmental Psychology, 23*, 611–626.

Baltes, P. B., & Baltes, M. M. (1990). Psychological perspectives on successful aging: The model of selective optimization with compensation. In P. B. Baltes & M. M. Baltes (Eds.), *Successful aging: Perspectives from the behavioral sciences* (pp. 1–34). New York: Cambridge University Press.

Bandura, A. (1977). Self-efficacy: Toward a unifying theory of behavior change. *Psychological Review, 84*, 191–215.

Bandura, A. (1986). *Social foundations of thought and action: A social cognitive theory.* Englewood Cliffs, NJ: Prentice-Hall.

Bandura, A. (1993). Perceived self-efficacy in cognitive development and functioning. *Educational Psychologist, 28*, 117–148.

Berkman, L. F., & Syme, S. L. (1979). Social networks, host resistance, and mortality: A nine-year follow up study of Alondra county results. *American Journal of Epidemiology, 109*, 186–204.

Bolton, W., & Oatley, K. (1987). A longitudinal study of social support and depression in unemployed men. *Psychological Medicine, 17*, 453–460.

Booth, A., & Amato, P. (1991). Divorce and psychological stress. *Journal of Health and Social Behavior, 32*, 396–407.

Bosse, R., Aldwin, C. M., Levenson, M. R., & Workman-Daniels, K. (1991). How stressful is retirement? Findings from the normative aging study. *Journal of Gerontology: Psychological Sciences, 46*, P9–P14.

Brandtstädter, J., & Greve, W. (1994). The aging self: Stabilizing and protective processes. *Developmental Review, 14*, 52–80.

Brandtstädter, J., & Renner, G. (1990). Tenacious goal pursuit and flexible goal adjustment: Explication and age-related analysis of assimilative and accommodative strategies of coping. *Psychology and Aging, 5*, 58–67

Brenner, S., & Starrin, B. (1988). Unemployment and health in Sweden: Public issues and private troubles. *Journal of Social Issues, 44*, 125–140.

Brown, P., Felton, B. J., Whiteman, V., & Manela, R. (1980). Attachment and distress following marital separation. *Journal of Divorce, 3*, 303–317.

Bryant, S. L., & Morgan, L. A. (1989). Financial experience and well-being among mature widowed women. *Gerontologist, 29*, 245–251.

Carstensen, L. L. (1992). Social and emotional patterns in adulthood: Support for socioemotional selectivity theory. *Psychology and Aging, 7*, 331–338.

Carstensen, L. L. (1993). Motivation for social contact across the life span: A theory of socioemotional selectivity. In J. Jacobs (Ed.), *Nebraska symposium on motivation: 1992, Developmental Perspectives on Motivation, Vol. 40* (pp. 209–254). Lincoln: University of Nebraska Press.

Carstensen, L. L., & Freund, A. (1994). The resilience of the self. *Developmental Review, 14,* 81–92.

Carstensen, L. L., & Pasupathi, M. (1993). Women of a certain age. In S. Matteo (Ed.), *Critical issues facing women in the '90s* (pp. 66–78). Boston: Northeastern University Press.

Carstensen, L. L., & Pasupathi, M. *Psychological control as a predictor of mortality in the transition to nursing home living.* Unpublished manuscript. Stanford University, Stanford, CA.

Cassileth, B. R., Lusk, E. J., Strouse, T. B., Miller, D. S., Brown, L. L., Cross, P. A., & Tenaglia, A. (1984). Psychosocial status in chronic illness. A comparative analysis of six diagnostic groups. *The New England Journal of Medicine, 311,* 506–511.

Chiriboga, D. A. (1991). Risk factors in divorce: A life course perspective. In D. A. Chiriboga & L. S. Catron (Eds.), *Divorce. Crisis, challenge or relief?* (pp. 280–292). New York: New York University Press.

Chiriboga, D. A., & Catron, L. S. (1991). Divorce stress and adaptation. In D. A. Chiriboga & L. S. Catron (Eds.), *Divorce. Crisis, challenge or relief?* (pp. 38–73). New York: New York University Press.

Chiriboga, D. A., & Turnher, M. (1980). Marital life styles and adjustment to separation. *Journal of Divorce, 4,* 379–380.

Clarke-Stewart, K. A., & Bailey, B. L. (1989). Adjusting to divorce: Why do men have it easier? *Journal of Divorce, 13,* 75–94.

Cross, S., & Markus, H. (1991). Possible selves across the lifespan. *Human Development, 34,* 230–255.

Daniels-Mohring, D., & Berger, M. (1984). Social network changes and the adjustment to divorce. *Journal of Divorce, 8,* 17–32.

Dannefer, D. (1987). Aging as intracohort differentiation: Accentuation, the Matthew effect and the life course. *Sociological Forum, 2,* 211–236.

Dannefer, D. (1992). On the conceptualization of context in developmental discourse: Four meanings of context and their implications. In D. L. Featherman, R. M. Lerner, & M. Perlmutter (Eds.), *Life-span development and behavior* (pp. 83–110). Hillsdale, NJ: Lawrence Erlbaum Associates.

Dew, M. A., Bromet, E. J., & Penkower, L. (1992). Mental health effects of job loss in women. *Psychological Medicine, 22,* 751–764.

Dixon, R. B., & Weitzman, L. J. (1982). When husbands file for divorce. *Journal of Marriage and the Family, 44,* 103–115.

Ewart, C. K., Stewart, K. J., Gillilan, R. E., & Kelemen, M. H. (1986). Self-efficacy mediates strength gains during circuit weight training in men with coronary artery disease. *Medicine and Science in Sports and Exercise, 18,* 531–540.

Feather, N. T. (1989). Reported changes in behavior after job loss in a sample of older unemployed men. *Australian Journal of Psychology, 41,* 175–185.

Featherman, D. L. (1980). Schooling and occupational careers: Constancy and change in worldly success. In O. G. Brim & J. Kagan (Eds.), *Constancy and change in human development* (pp. 675–738). Cambridge, MA: Harvard University Press.

Featherman, D. L., Smith, J., & Peterson, J. G. (1990). Successful aging in a post retired society. In P. B. Baltes & M. M. Baltes (Eds.), *Successful aging: Perspectives from the behavioral sciences* (pp. 50–87). New York: Cambridge University Press.

Field, D., & Minkler, M. (1988). Continuity and change in social support between young-old, old-old, and very-old adults. *Journal of Gerontology: Psychological Sciences, 43,* P100–P106.

Floyd, F. J., Haynes, S. N., Doll, R. E., Winemiller, D., Lemsky, C., Burgy, T. M., Werle, M., & Heilman, N. (1992). Assessing retirement satisfaction and perceptions of retirement experiences. *Psychology and Aging, 7,* 609–621.

Gallagher, D. E., Breckenridge, J. N., Thompson, L. W., & Peterson, J. A. (1983). Effects of bereavement on indicators of mental health in elderly widows and widowers. *Journal of Gerontology, 38,* 565–571.

Gander, A. M., & Jorgensen, L. A. B. (1990). Post-divorce adjustment: Social supports among older divorced persons. *Journal of Divorce, 13*, 37–52.

Hallberg, H., & Mattsson, B. (1989). Life after divorce: A study of newly divorced middle aged men in Sweden. *Family Practice, 6*, 9–15.

Hardy, M. A. (1991). Employment after retirement. Who gets back in? *Research On Aging, 13*, 267–288.

Heckhausen, J., Dixon, R. A., & Baltes, P. B. (1989). Gains and losses in development throughout adulthood as perceived by different adult age groups. *Developmental Psychology, 25*, 109–121.

Heckhausen, J., & Krueger, J. (1993). Developmental expectations for the self and most other people: Age grading in three functions of social comparison. *Developmental Psychology, 29*, 539–548.

Heckhausen, J., & Schulz, R. (1993). Optimization by selection and compensation: Balancing primary and secondary control in life-span development. *International Journal of Behavioral Development, 16*, 287–303.

Holman, H. R., Mazonson, P., & Lorig, K. (1989). Health education for self-management has significant early and sustained benefits in chronic arthritis. *Transactions Association of American Physicians, 102*, 204–208.

Holmes, T., & Rahe, R. (1967). The social readjustment rating scale. *Journal of Psychosomatic Research, 11*, 213–218.

Jones, L. P. (1991). Unemployment: The effect on social networks, depression, and reemployment opportunities. *Journal of Social Service Research, 15*, 1–22.

Kessler, R. C., Turner, J. B., & House, J. S. (1987). Intervening processes in the relationship between unemployment and health. *Psychological Medicine, 17*, 949–961.

Kessler, R. C., Turner, J. B., & House, J. S. (1988). Effects of unemployment on health in a community survey: Main, modifying and mediating effects. *Journal of Social Issues, 44*, 69–85.

Lang, F. R., & Carstensen, L. L. (1994). Close emotional relationships in late life: Further support for proactive aging in the social domain. *Psychology and Aging, 9*, 315–324.

Lawton, M. P. (1987). Environment and the need satisfaction of the aging. In L. L. Carstensen & B. A. Edelstein (Eds.), *Handbook of clinical gerontology* (pp. 33–40). New York: Pergamon.

Lawton, M. P., Moss, M., & Fulcomer, M. (1987). Objective and subjective uses of time by older people. *International Journal of Aging and Human Development, 24*, 171–188.

Lawton, M. P., & Nahemow, L. (1973). Ecology and the aging process. In C. Eisdorfer & M. P. Lawton (Eds.), *Psychology of adult development and aging* (pp. 619–674). Washington, DC: American Psychological Association.

Levinger, G. (1976). A social psychological perspective on marital dissolution. *Journal of Social Issues, 32*, 21–47.

Mallinckrodt, B., & Bennett, J. (1992). Social support and the impact of job loss in dislocated blue-collar workers. *Journal of Counseling Psychology, 39*, 482–489.

McCrae, R. R., & Costa, P. T. (1988). Psychological resilience among widowed men and women: A 10-year follow-up of a national sample. *Journal of Social Issues, 44*, 129–142.

Merton, R. (1968). The Matthew effect in science: The reward and communications systems of science. *Science, 159*, 55–63.

Michela, J. (1982). Perceived changes in marital relationships following myocardial infarction. *Dissertation Abstracts International, 48*, 4245-B.

Nelson, E. A., & Dannefer, D. (1992). Aged heterogeneity: Fact or fiction? The fate of diversity in gerontological research. *The Gerontologist, 32*, 17–23.

Palmore, E. (1981). *Social patterns in normal aging: Findings from the Duke Longitudinal Study*. Durham, NC: Duke University Press.

Raschke, H. J. (1977). The role of social participation in post-separation and post-divorce adjustment. *Journal of Divorce, 1*, 129–140.

Rodin, J., & Langer, E. J. (1977). Long-term effects of a control-relevant intervention with the institutionalized aged. *Journal of Personality and Social Psychology, 12*, 897–902.

Ryff, C. D. (1989). Happiness is everything, or is it? Explorations on the meaning of psychological well-being. *Journal of Personality and Social Psychology, 57*, 1069–1081.

Ryff, C. D. (1991). Possible selves in adulthood and old age: A tale of shifting horizons. *Psychology and Aging, 6*, 286–295.

Schwarzer, R. (1992). Self-efficacy in the adoption and maintenance of health behaviors: Theoretical approaches and a new model. In R. Schwarzer (Ed.), *Self-efficacy: Thought control of action* (pp. 218–243). Washington, DC: Hemisphere.

Smith, M., & Barnet, H. (1990). Divorce stress and adjustment model: Locus of control and demographic predictors. *Journal of Divorce, 13*, 93–109.

Stack, S. (1989). The impact of divorce on suicide in Norway, 1951–1980. *Journal of Marriage and the Family, 51*, 229–238.

Stroebe, M. S., & Stroebe, W. (1987). *Bereavement and health: The psychological and physical consequences of partner loss.* Cambridge, England: Cambridge University Press.

Stroebe, M. S., Stroebe, W., & Hansson, R. O. (1988). Bereavement research: An historical introduction. *Journal of Social Issues, 44*, 1–18.

Swan, G. E., Dame, A., & Carmelli, D. (1991). Involuntary retirement, type A behavior, and current functioning in elderly men: 27-year follow-up of the western collaborative group study. *Psychology and Aging, 6*, 384–391.

Taylor, C. B., Bandura. A., Ewart, C. Miller, N. H., & DeBusk, R. F. (1985). Exercise testing to enhance wives confidence in their husband's cardiac capability soon after clinically uncomplicated acute myocardial infarction. *American Journal of Cardiology, 55*, 635–638.

Taylor, S. E. (1983). Adjustment to threatening events: A theory of cognitive adaptation. *American Psychologist, 38*, 1161–1173.

Taylor, S. E., & Aspinwall, L. G., (1990). Psychosocial aspects of chronic illness. In P. T. Costa & G. R. Vandenbos (Eds.), *Psychological aspects of serious illness: Chronic conditions, fatal diseases and clinical care* (pp. 3–60). Washington, DC: American Psychological Association.

Taylor, S. E., & Brown, J. D. (1988). Illusion and well-being: A social psychological perspective on mental health. *Psychological Bulletin, 103*, 193–210.

Tesch-Römer, C. (1993, November). *Coping with hearing loss in old age.* Paper presented at the meetings of the Gerontological Society of America, New Orleans, LA.

Thompson, L. W., Breckenridge, J. N., Gallagher, D., & Peterson, J. (1984). Effects of bereavement on self-perceptions of physical health in elderly widows and widowers. *Journal of Gerontology, 39*, 309–314.

Thompson, W. E., Streib, G. F., & Kosa, J. (1960). The effect of retirement on personal adjustment: A panel analysis. *Journal of Gerontology, 15*, 165–169.

United Nations. (1987). *Demographic yearbook.* New York: Author.

Uttal, D. H., & Perlmutter, M. (1989). Toward a broader conceptualization of development: The role of gains and losses across the life span. *Developmental Review, 9*, 101–132.

Warr, P., & Payne, R. (1983). Social class and reported changes in behavior after job loss. *Journal of Applied Social Psychology, 13*, 206–222.

Weiss, R. S. (1975). *Marital separation.* New York: Basic Books.

Whitbourne, S. K. (1986). *Adult development* (2nd ed.). New York: Pergamon.

Wortman, C. B., & Silver, R. C. (1987). Coping with irrevocable loss. In G. VandenBos & B. Bryant (Eds.), *Cataclysms, crises, and catastrophes. Psychology in action* (pp. 189–235). Washington, DC: American Psychological Association.

Wortman, C. B., & Silver, R. C. (1990). Successful mastery of bereavement and widowhood: A life-course perspective. In P. B. Baltes & M. M. Baltes (Eds.), *Successful aging: Perspectives from behavioral sciences* (pp. 225–264). Cambridge, England: Cambridge University Press.

Zisook, S., & Schuchter, S. R. (1991a). Depression through the first year after the death of a spouse. *American Journal of Psychiatry, 148,* 1346–1352.

Zisook, S., & Schuchter, S. R. (1991b). Early psychological reaction to the stress of widowhood. *Psychiatry, 54,* 320–332.

CHAPTER SIX

Social Compensation in Adulthood and Later Life

Kenneth F. Ferraro
Melissa M. Farmer
Purdue University

Many sociological theories and empirical research studies examine the losses that people experience during adulthood and later life. Health and physical functioning, income, and role activity are just a few of the salient domains of life that are often challenged in the later years. Although it is true that many losses occur during late middle age and later life, it is an oversimplification to characterize later life as simply, or primarily, a period of loss. Increasing evidence shows that adults, especially older adults, experience loss, but adapt to such events and processes with a variety of coping methods. One such adaptive response is compensation (Bäckman & Dixon, 1992). The purpose of this chapter is to examine the theoretical perspectives and previous research relevant to social compensation in later life. As is shown, the concept of *compensation* is implicit in many sociological theories of action and gerontological theories of social functioning. Evidence is accumulating that compensation is a widespread adaptive response, although its form varies by situational contexts and available resources.

SOCIAL THEORY AND COMPENSATION

The idea of compensation is implicit in most classical sociological theories of action. Whether it is structural-functionalism, symbolic interactionism, or exchange theory, actors are viewed as continually involved in evaluating lines of action and attempting to adjust their behavior to reach desired goals. When loss is experienced or inequity perceived, actors often attempt to make up for or counterbalance such an experience. In short, actors compensate. For functionalists, the emphasis is on the maintenance of social systems as actors attempt to strike a functional balance in social relations (Parsons, 1951; Parsons, Bales, & Shils, 1953). Interactionists see actors as adjusting their behavior in light of role expectations and the definition of the situation (Mead, 1934). Exchange theorists emphasize optimizing rewards during social transactions, which may require actors to alter their actions to achieve valued outcomes (Homans, 1961). In all of these and several other theories, compensation is viewed as a possible adaptive response either to benefit the actors or the social entity around which the actors are oriented. Because social life is replete with uncertainty and change—sometimes due to conflict—people adjust their actions to create favorable levels of social participation. When loss or inequity is experienced, revised goals or strategies for reaching the original ones may be substituted.

When it comes to sociological theories of aging, two conceptual models have dominated the discussion of adaptation and social functioning. In some cases, these models have been explicit in the theoretical discourse; in other cases, the models are implicit in the writings of scholars attempting to explain adaptation from a given theoretical perspective. The first one, the *decremental model*, emphasizes the stressful nature of losses in roles, income, and physical functioning (it was almost always implicit in the writings of social and behavioral gerontologists). In its most simple form, the decremental model is seen as leading to an identity breakdown (Kuypers & Bengtson, 1973; Miller, 1965; Rosow, 1967, 1973). Based on the assumption that the effects of stressors are additive or cumulative (Holmes & Rahe, 1967), the decremental model posits that the effects of loss are most serious in middle and later life for at least two reasons. First, later life typically entails several undesirable life events, as one's cohort shrinks and chronic illness affects human functioning. Second, adaptation to undesirable events experienced earlier in life may not have been adequately resolved—the problems experienced earlier may have shaped personality in ways that make successful adaptation more difficult in later life. Consider Rosow's (1973) treatment of the social rules that influence the aging self:

> The most crucial single rule by far involves the progressive loss of roles and functions of the aged, for this change represents a critical introduction of stress. Role loss generates the pressures and sets the conditions for the emerging crisis, and taken together, these delineate the social context of the aging self. What does this involve? First, the loss of roles excludes the aged from significant social participation and devalues them. . . . In a word, they are depreciated and become marginal, alienated from the larger society. (p. 82)

The decremental model of aging and social activity dominated scholarship in the 1950s and 1960s, as researchers focused on the problems of older people experiencing multiple losses (see Ferraro, 1990, for a review). For instance, disengagement theory stressed the decrease in social participation attendant with growing older. However, there was widespread dissatisfaction with the idea that aging results in an inevitable mutual withdrawal or dis-engagement from social life, as advanced by Cumming and her associates (Cumming, Dean, Newell, & McCaffrey, 1960; Cumming & Henry, 1961). But the idea that elders' social lives show an overall trend toward decreasing social participation is still popular. Even activity theory, which explicitly incorporates the idea of compensation, anticipates the decrement in social activity. As Dowd (1975) asserted, activity theory "actually assumes much the same behavioral phenomena in old age as disengagement theory. Neither theory argues that old age is characterized by anything but a generalized decrease in social interaction" (p. 585). The difference is this: Activity theory views older adults who compensate for losses as successful, whereas dis-engagement theory views such compensation as a sign of unsuccessful ag-ing—older people with high levels of social engagement are "off time" (Hochschild, 1975). Other theories, such as the social-breakdown syndrome, stress the decremental nature of social activity as most people grow older, but also allow for the possibility of compensation through a social-recon-struction syndrome (Kuypers & Bengtson, 1973).

The second model of aging and social participation acknowledges the impact of multiple losses in later life, but considers a much wider range of adaptive responses (Ferraro, Mutran, & Barresi, 1984). For some people, atrophy of social relationships is the norm. For others, social relationships are consolidated, shifted, or reconstituted. This model may be referred to as one based on compensation. Empirical research by Palmore (1968), pub-lished while disengagement theory was being strongly criticized, indicated that, although older people reduce their social participation in some net-works, they may compensate by increasing their social participation in other networks. *Social compensation* may be defined as changes in social rela-tionships when individuals and/or groups seek to substitute, modify, or rearrange existing patterns of association. Compensation is often prompted by the need to meet social exigencies or better manage experiences of loss, environmental demands, and/or perceived problems in social or individual functioning.

The compensation model of role loss and social participation bears con-siderable resemblance to Atchley's (1971) continuity perspective. Atchley (1989) stated that a central premise of "Continuity Theory is that, in making adaptive choices, middle-aged and older adults attempt to preserve and maintain existing internal and external structures and that they prefer to accomplish this objective by using continuity" (p. 183). Although the preservation and maintenance of internal and external structures may not always be a plausible objective in confronting some changes, such as loss of a spouse, continuity in strategies and values seems endemic to adaptation. Both Palmore and Atchley emphasized that personal change is continuous, and that there is an overall persistence of lifestyle in social activities and attitudes.

The idea of compensating for either loss or certain disadvantages is not new to the social sciences, but it can be seen to exist in the writings of researchers interested in a variety of topics. For instance, Klobus-Edwards, Edwards, and Klemmack (1978) pointed out that a compensation thesis has been used to explain the high involvement of African Americans in certain types of social participation (see also Ellison & London, 1992). In addition to Palmore's (1968) application of the conceptual model of compensation by social participation in social gerontology, others have noted its utility in lifecourse investigations (Knoke & Thomson, 1977). Pihlblad and Adams (1972) discussed the importance of maintaining a sense of personal equilibrium in social relationships (see also Wan & Odell, 1983). Similarly, Bock and Webber (1972) alluded to the act of substituting one type of social participation for another when discussing adaptation to widowhood. The theme of compensation in social activity has arisen in the writings of many researchers.

Theoretical perspectives that came to dominate social gerontology in the 1970s and 1980s were generally much more attuned to the possibility of compensation. Again, just as disengagement is not universal or inevitable, neither is compensation. Rather, most theories attempted to incorporate the possibility of compensation as a normal adaptive response. Although activity theory anticipated a reduction in social activity—role loss leads to a decrease in social activity—Lemon, Bengtson, and Peterson (1972) clearly anticipated compensation. They stated that the individual undergoing a role loss may be involved in a process of reestablishing a personal equilibrium in his or her role supports. Dowd's (1975) exchange theory of aging also permits the possibility of compensation as a normal adaptive response, although he sees the contingencies of reinforcement for compensation as unlikely for many older adults.

Age stratification theory combines much of the convergence of classical functionalism and interactionism (i.e., that people are influenced by age norms and cohort experiences and choose between alternative lines of action over the life course; Riley, 1985, 1987). Age stratification theory does not specify the likelihood of compensation in social life, but accounts for such actions in the process of relinquishing certain roles and assuming others. In short, social scientists have come to accept and expect the possibility of compensation in social functioning as a frequently occurring adaptive response in later life (Antonucci, 1990).

EVIDENCE FOR COMPENSATION:
REVIEW OF LITERATURE

The general movement in sociological theories of aging from decremental to compensational frameworks of analysis was propelled by a large number of findings regarding compensation in social life. Beyond the early and selective publications noted earlier, we now turn to a consideration of the evidence for social compensation in later life. Our review is not intended to be exhaustive, but to highlight the streams of research that provide evidence that older adults compensate in social relations for various losses or inequities. Social compensation can be intitiated by the individual or the social structures in which he or she is embedded. Indeed, it is probably a "negotiated" process due to the dialectical process of influence between the individual and social structure. There may also be exogenous sources of change due to forces outside the immediate social system that lead to social compensation.

Most of the empirical research on compensatory processes has come from studies of three general topics: life events, religion, and voluntarism. Indeed, the first two have accounted for the bulk of the evidence. Within the life events discussion presented next, we examine three specific events that are common in the literature: widowhood, retirement, and illness episodes.

Life Events

Research on life events in recent decades has moved from expectations that events simply cause negative outcomes to the expectation that events trigger a variety of adaptive responses. Central to this discussion are the distinctions between (a) positive and negative events, and (b) normative and non-normative events, as well as the recognition that adjustment does not necessarily mean linear change on the outcomes under consideration (George, 1980; Thoits, 1981). Although it is wholly expected that life events initiate change in the social life of older people, there is not agreement on the precise mechanisms of such change. By and large, longitudinal research is proving to be the most beneficial for advancing our knowledge of how and why people respond the way they do to such events. This is because adaptation is a process and events can be identified in time, thereby providing for the possibility of "before and after" measurements of social functioning. We briefly review findings on three life events here: widowhood, retirement, and illness episodes. However, the first two have garnered the most empirical evidence for social compensation in later life. Research on other events, such as relocation, also provide evidence of social compensation. Several previous studies show that many moves by older adults are intended to enhance social participation, especially with kin (Henretta, 1986; Litwak & Longino, 1987).

Widowbood. The loss of a spouse has long been identified as the event requiring the most social readjustment (Holmes & Rahe, 1967). Lopata's (1973) research on "compensations in widowhood" opened a new vista of research on the subject. She pointed out that the quality of married life was critical to the adjustment process, and that many widows, despite intense feelings of grief, found some benefits, such as free time or perhaps seeing a loved one relieved of suffering (see also Bass & Bowman, 1990; Bass, Bowman, & Noelker, 1991; Ferraro, 1989; Gerber, Rusalem, Hannon, Battin, & Arkin, 1975; Mullan, 1992; Wortman & Silver, 1989).

Lopata also observed compensation in social relationships, such as friendships among older widowed women. To date, there have been a number of studies, including several longitudinal ones, showing compensation in the social networks of widows, particularly for older widows. Many of these studies point to the importance of neighbor, and especially friendship, networks in aiding the adjustment of widows and, to a lesser extent, widowers (Adams, 1987; Berardo, 1970; Blau, 1961; Ferraro & Barresi, 1982; Ferraro et al., 1984; Kohen, 1983; Petrowsky, 1976; Pihlblad & Adams, 1972; Wan & Odell, 1983). It is now clear that the loss of a spouse does not simply lead to a linear decline in social participation. Widows appear to undergo a process of compensating for the loss of a spouse by seeking out fellow widows for interaction and establishing fairly intensive social ties about 2–3 years after the death of a spouse (Ferraro et al., 1984; Gallagher & Gerstel, 1993; Lowenthal & Haven, 1968; Waite & Harrison, 1992). A "society of widows" can offer more time and practical help than is often the case for kin relations, therefore engagement in them is highly predictive of widows' morale (Gallagher & Gerstel, 1993; Harvey & Bahr, 1974; Kohen, 1983).

Retirement. Considerable early research characterized retirement as a period of loss leading to identity disruption and an atrophy of social relations (Miller, 1965). Again, the more recent findings, especially those derived from longitudinal studies, reveal that the retirement adjustment process is far more complex and usually involves a shifting of social obligations and activities. If adequate pensions are available, a significant proportion of workers in modern societies opt for "early retirement," at which time they can engage in other activities. The time pressures attendant with modern societies often make retirement an attractive option for flexibility in scheduling activities. In addition, Ekerdt (1986) identified a "busy ethic," which legitimizes leisure and often leads to organizing an active lifestyle. Retirement does not necessarily imply a reduction in social activity, just a shifting of social relations.

In summarizing his research on retirement and continuity, Atchley (1991) claimed that "people who are involved in several roles and a variety of activities may not need to find *new* roles or activities to substitute for those they lose. They may find it easier to redistribute their time, energy, and emotional commitments among their remaining roles and activities" (p. 264, italics in original). Atchley referred to this as the consolidation of activities during adaptation to life changes; Mutran and Reitzes (1981) referred to it as a "realignment of role relationships." In other words, compensation does not necessitate engagement in new social networks, as found to be common with widows, but a reordering of time obligations, instrumentality, and affectivity in existing social networks. In other cases, it may well involve initiatory behavior as new networks are established (e.g, participation in a local chapter of the American Association of Retired Persons).

Recent findings from the longitudinal Normative Aging Study in Boston generally show that retirement does not significantly affect quantitative or qualitative measures of social support (Bosse, Aldwin, Levenson, Spiro, & Mroczek, 1993). Although social ties and activities change with retirement, overall social engagement does not. Most people compensate for the reduced interaction with co-workers by strengthening existing relations with other people, or adding social ties with "retired people" (Atchley, 1971, 1987; Mutran & Reitzes, 1981; Streib & Schneider, 1971). These findings are consistent with the "convoy model" of social adjustment which specifies that the inner circle of intimates remains quite stable but that the intermediate and outer circles are often replaced by interactions with nonwork-related associates (Antonucci, 1990; Kahn & Antonucci, 1980).

Illness Episodes.   Another life event that merits attention in a discussion of adaptation in later life is confronting an illness episode, especially a chronic illness episode. Because of the prevalence of chronic illness in later life and the amount of time spent coping with chronic illness, medical sociologists, gerontologists, and behavioral epidemiologists have tried to identify the social context of how people respond to such episodes. The research shows that social relations affect the coping process, and are affected by the management of chronic disease.

In some cases—such as a stroke, where the illness greatly limits the functional ability of the person—social participation is often transformed and reduced (Shirk, 1991). Yet the bulk of research on caregiving to disabled elders shows that social networks respond to illness (Miller & McFall, 1991; Stone, 1991). It may not always be the case that the person with the illness initiates the compensation. Rather, the network members could compensate to meet the needs of the ill person to keep order (and respect) and to honor past contributions.

In other cases, where functional ability may be reduced somewhat, social functioning may still proceed with considerable vibrancy—where the person with the chronic illness initiates social compensatory activities or at least cooperates with others in attempting to improve his or her health status. As has long been known, the legitimacy of the sick role is contingent on the sick person recognizing the undesirability of being sick and making an attempt to get well (Parsons, 1951; Wolinsky, 1988). Recognizing the nature of chronic illness, total recovery or disease remission may not be a feasible goal, but the individual is expected to optimize functioning via medical or self-care. Geertsen, Klauber, Rindflesh, Kane, and Gray (1975) attempted to replicate Suchman's (1965) work on sociomedical orientations and the sick role; they eventually developed the "Utah model" of social factors and health behavior. The researchers found that a health condition often activates an interpretative process that moves the actor toward appropriate responses, such as seeking treatment (see also Geertsen, 1988). In summary, illness episodes can spur compensatory social activities.

The vast literature on health promotion among adults, especially older adults, also points to the importance of illness episodes for spurring change in health practices and the critical role of social engagement in maintaining such practices (Danielson, Hamel-Bissell, & Winstead-Fry, 1993; Walker, 1990). For example, some health-promoting elders (e.g., walkers at malls) may be lifelong exercisers, but a significant proportion launched such an exercise program after an illness episode and maintain it with a group. From weight loss and smoking cessation programs to exercise and nutritional regimens, evidence is accumulating that social support plays a vital role in the initiation and maintenance of such behaviors to reach healthy goals. Illness episodes can spur compensatory social behavior immediately or after a season of renegotiating the definition of the situation with significant others.

Religious Involvement

Beyond specific life events, research on religious involvement shows evidence of social compensation. Numerous studies show that older adults generally have higher levels of participation in religious activities than younger adults (Ainlay & Smith, 1984; Moberg, 1990). Considerable debate has ensued as to why this is so; the debates have centered on the operation of selective survival, cohort succession, and awareness of finitude (e.g., Levin & Vanderpool, 1987; Moberg, 1990). An important finding from the literature is that it is essential to differentiate among the types of religious activity.

Mindel and Vaughn (1978) argued that aging and religious involvement is best understood in light of the meaning of *religiosity*; that is, religiosity is best conceived as a multidimensional phenomenon. When studied in this fashion, several studies (but not all) show that organizational participation in religious activities decreases in later life as older people find it increasingly difficult to travel to services at churches, synagogues, or temples (Ainlay & Smith, 1984; Blazer & Palmore, 1976; Levin, 1988; Mindel & Vaughn, 1978). By contrast, if one considers nonorganizational religiosity—such as participating in prayer, reading religious materials, "telephone fellowship," and observing religious programming on television or radio—then older adults do not generally show declines in religiosity. Often older adults maintain or increase their nonorganizational religious involvement (i.e., they compensate; Levin, 1988).

Two other streams of research are relevant to compensation in religious activities. First, despite the grand tendency to separate religion from public policy in many modern nations, there is an increase in the integration of religious and secular helping organizations designed to benefit older adults. Often such programs are designed to "enhance service provision to elderly persons" by churches and temples via educational and technical assistance with mental health professionals (Filinson, 1988). Other times the basic structure of the church may be oriented to practical service to older people. In both cases, a "pull" may exist toward religious activity for needy elders.

Second, research on the religious participation of African Americans clearly shows the tangible and meaningful assistance offered by churches and religious groups (Taylor & Chatters, 1986). There has been substantial debate about the generally higher religious participation of Black persons being due to socioeconomic and political deprivation—what is often called the *deprivation compensation hypothesis* (e.g., Taylor, 1986). Regardless of why it occurs, however, there is a large and growing body of evidence that African-American persons receive more church-based support than do White religious persons (Chaves & Higgins, 1992; Taylor & Chatters, 1986; Walls & Zarit, 1991). Taylor and Chatters (1988) showed that Black churches not only provide information and advice to their members, but also "are extremely involved in the provision of . . . material, emotional, and spiritual assistance" (p. 194). Thus, when considering compensation in religious involvement among older people, it should be recognized that some religious groups—especially Black churches—are purposefully developing ministries to aid needy elders.

Voluntarism

It has long been known from research on voluntary action that certain types of people are more apt to be volunteers. One such willing category is older people. Whether it is working the polls on election day or carrying flowers to hospital patients, older adults are actively engaged in voluntarism. According to Ekerdt (1986), the "busy ethic" is "at once a statement of value as well as an expectation of retired people—shared by retirees and nonretirees alike—that their lives should be active and earnest" (p. 240). Thus, one form of the compensation noted earlier from research on retirement is engagement in voluntary activity. Many older adults shift from work roles to volunteer roles. Middle-aged and older adults often play important roles in voluntary fraternal organizations (e.g., Shriners, Moose, and Daughters of the American Revolution).

Recent research by Herzog and Morgan (1992) examined the personal "productivity" of Americans based on paid and unpaid work. Using several approaches to estimate productivity—both economic and noneconomic—the authors found widespread evidence of older adults' engagement in productive activities (see also Herzog, Kahn, Morgan, Jackson, & Antonucci, 1989). Such activities include, but are not limited to, child care, housework, formal volunteer work, and informal help. Also consider the voluminous literature on caregiving for older adults; often older people are caring for their elders. The authors concluded that "many older people contribute to society by helping each other as well as by helping members of younger generations" (Herzog & Morgan, 1992, p. 197). Indeed, the literature on intergenerational helping also indicates that older adults make use of free time to aid the well-being of younger persons in a variety of ways.

MODELING SOCIAL COMPENSATION IN LATER LIFE

In many theoretical perspectives on aging, there is an implicit recognition that people often shift social relations when triggered by life events or perceived inequities. There is also considerable empirical evidence that adults and older adults compensate in social functioning. Growing older often entails loss of social roles and diminished functional capabilities. Yet evidence abounds that normal adaptive responses to such experiences are not simply permutations of an overall decremental drift. Rather, many older adults appear to compensate for loss by realigning social roles, consolidating obligations, and/or substituting social relations. We do not assume that all older adults compensate in social functioning for every loss experienced. Thus, our final goal for this chapter is to identify when social compensation is likely or unlikely. We articulate a model of social compensation in later life that transcends the specific research findings reviewed earlier and we suggest ways in which the research literature may be propitiously extended.

Expanding on the work by Ferraro et al. (1984), we articulate five propositions for a compensation model of life events and social functioning. Although the research on social compensation certainly includes more than just reactions to life events, these propositions, especially the first two, should serve as a useful point of departure. The first two propositions focus on inter- and intra-individual differences.

First, the authors stated that "individuals have varying propensities to participate in social life and therefore generally seek stability in the rate and variety of social functioning" (Ferraro et al., 1984, p. 254). The first proposition is grounded in continuity theory and social-psychological evidence on personality stability over the life course. Although people expect to change, the search for continuity tends toward maintaining or reestablishing a personal equilibrium in the social context.

Second, "when conditions arise in certain types of social activities that inhibit social interaction, e.g., role loss, individuals will tend to seek out other activities to maintain their propensity to social participation" (Ferraro et al., 1984, p. 254). People vary in the degree to which they are socially active. Among those who are less socially active, we expect that the magnitude of their compensations will generally be smaller—perhaps only meager attempts at compensation without actually transforming social relations over time. This proposition extends the inter-individual differences over time by anticipating changes aimed to foster stability over time. This is what is usually referred to as *continuous change* over the life course. People are constantly changing, but the adaptive strategies are often similar; therefore, outcomes manifest substantial similarity in the midst of change. Compensation is one of the adaptive strategies.

Third, drawing from the convoy model of social relations, adjustment typically entails considerable stability in the inner circle of intimates, but more change at the intermediate and outer circles of interaction (Antonucci, 1990; Kahn & Antonucci, 1980). Yet even the intimates are more likely to change when one considers older adults—because of higher mortality. It should also be stressed that, just because the friend and outer circles of interaction are more likely to change, it does not mean that they are less consequential to instrumental or affective benefit. Indeed, as noted earlier, it is often the voluntary social relations that have the largest impact on affective wellbeing.

Fourth, and closely related to the third proposition, social compensation may involve instrumental and/or affective dimensions. Instrumental support is usually some type of tangible or material aid. Often when a person loses a spouse, the person is then responsible for all the duties and errands the couple once shared. A neighbor who runs errands and/or helps with the housework would be providing instrumental support. Affectual support focuses on the emotional level, such as talking through problems with a friend. Depending on extant social resources, people may feel a sharper need for either instrumental or affective engagement, or they may desire to augment both domains.

Fifth, the capacity to compensate in social relations is dependent on the health, socioeconomic, and environmental resources of the individual (Ferraro et al., 1984). Social strata based on health, socioeconomic, and environmental resources predispose certain people to be more apt to initiate and succeed in substituting social relations over the life course. Of course age is correlated with such resources and not always in a linear fashion, but even among older people compensation is more or less likely based on such resources.

There are related models of adaptation based on person/environment relations and ecological states. One that may be particularly helpful to extend the social compensation model is Lawton and Nahemow's (1973) ecological model of adaptation and aging (Lawton, 1985; Nahemow & Lawton, 1973). If one applies the authors' use of the term *competence* to the specific case of social compensation, one may see the capacity for social compensation as dependent on environmental press. Given what we have said about the integral links between social life and adaptation, it may be useful to see compensation as a function of environmental press as well as social press. Their definition of *environmental press* covers the social domain, but greater discussion of the relationship between the physical environment and the social environment may be beneficial to modeling adaptation over the life course. Conceptually, it may be useful to extend their model of the relationship between environmental press and competence to a three-dimensional model as shown in Fig. 6.1.

As seen in the figure, a person's adaptation level—or the capacity for social compensation—is a function of three components: individual competence, environmental press, and social press. *Competence* refers to individual qualitites, such as cognitive aptitude and mental and physical health. *Social press* encompasses the impact of social structure and social functioning on adaptation. The physical environment, represented by *environmental press*, can have a positive or negative effect on adaptation, or no effect at all. It is important to note that social structures are related to physical structures, but that the relation is sometimes strong and other times quite weak. Despite fluctuations within each component, interaction among the parts is continuous.

To illustrate the joint effects of the competence and social and environmental press, consider relocation. Imagine that a person is forced to move from his or her home because of a natural disaster—a situation with high environmental press. The amount of social support available would have a major impact on how the person would compensate for the environmental disaster. High levels of social support may well reduce or buffer the effects of forced relocation. The absence of social support would decrease the likelihood of successful adaptation. If the person had become functionally

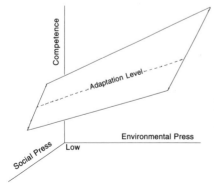

FIG. 6.1. A socioenvironmental model of adaptive competence. Adapted with permission from Lawton and Nahemow, 1973, Ecology and the aging process. In C. Eisdorfer and M. P. Lawton (Eds.) *The psychology of adult development and aging* (p. 661). Washington, DC: American Psychological Association.

disabled at some point, this would be an added impact on the person's adaptive capacity.

Another related illustration is the dilemma of an older couple struggling to remain in their two-story home after an illness episode that has compromised functioning. If one member of the couple cannot traverse stairs because of growing physical limitations, there are several ways for him or her to cope. First, the housing unit could be modified to maintain independence, but minimize the effects of impairment. Second, the other member of the couple may simply take on more responsibilities, but this will eventually become fairly taxing on a person. Third, helpers who assist with household tasks may become involved. Fourth, the couple may simply move to secure housing better suited to their needs. Even if they choose the last option, the social involvement associated with new housing is critical to the couple's adaptation. As stated earlier, compensation is dependent on the joint effects of individual competence, environmental press, and social press.

Social Status and Compensation

When modeling compensation and the aging process, it is also important to consider how social status may affect outcomes. Gender, ethnicity, and inequality are important in structuring social processes—including compensation—because differences in resources related to social status will probably affect adaptation, and not always in a manner that is intuitively obvious. Consider the cases of women and minority persons who may have access to more resources to facilitate compensation for their losses experienced during the aging process. Past research on social-life involvement has found that gender differences may affect the frequency and intensity of social contacts. Elderly women have been found to have more contacts with close friends and relatives than elderly men (Berardo, 1970; Kohen, 1983). Kohen explained that the difference in social contact could be attributed to patterns of social contact in earlier life. Women tend to maintain contact with larger kin and friend networks during the life course (Antonucci, 1990). Therefore, these networks provide women with more social resources with which to compensate in later life, despite that they may be disadvantaged in other resource domains.

Variance in compensation can also be attributed to ethnicity because ethnicity allows for differing channels of resources. There is considerable evidence to show that, despite higher rates of marital dissolution, African-American adults have a different and more extensive family organization involving supportive relationships (Cicirelli, 1983; Dowd & Bengtson, 1978; George, 1988; Mutran, 1985). Despite, and perhaps because of, the struggle against structural disadvantages, Black adults have drawn on family resources and assistance for daily living, especially in the southern region of the United

States (Chatters, Taylor, & Jackson, 1985; Scott, 1991). These exchanges and assistance patterns clearly include African-American older adults, as evidenced by the higher prevalence of three-generation households and reports of helping relationships (Chatters et al., 1985). Also, as explained earlier in the chapter, Black persons have been found to receive more church-based support than White religious persons (Chaves & Higgins, 1992; Taylor & Chatters, 1986; Walls & Zarit, 1991). Because the church is a resource for social interaction and social support, it allows for compensation.

Along with gender and ethnicity, socioeconomic status (SES) can also have an impact on compensation practices. Compensation has been found to vary by social class, particularly when related to self-esteem maintenance (Gecas & Seff, 1990). In addition, Adams (1987) found that changes in network patterns in later life vary by social class. For example, women of higher SES tend to contract but intensify their network relationships, whereas women of lower SES tend to expand their networks while decreasing the intensity of emotional involvement. Therefore, SES can have an important impact on the resources available for social interaction in later life. It is not just a simple matter of higher or lower social class correlated with levels of social activity; the types of social activity often vary by social class (Wan & Odell, 1983).

FUTURE RESEARCH AND SUMMARY

In conclusion, it may be useful to articulate the types of research that may be most beneficial for advancing our understanding of social compensation. Most of the qualities of such research are probably fairly evident, but we emphasize a few characteristics. First, research on social compensation in later life will benefit from incorporating advances in sociometry and the study of social support and social networks. Numerous studies over the past two decades have advanced our conceptualization and measurement of social support and structure (e.g., McFarlane, Norman, Streiner, & Roy, 1983; Sarason, Levine, Basham, & Sarason, 1983; Weinert, 1987). Differentiating between the structure and content of social relations is critical for understanding compensation. The structure of social networks includes concepts such as size, strength of ties, density, and the homogeneity and dispersion of membership (Perrucci & Targ, 1982; Walker, MacBride, & Vachon, 1977). Content includes instrumentality, affectivity, and commodities exchanged. Much of the available evidence only alludes to such concepts, or measures them indirectly.

Second, a compensation model of social functioning should be able to detect what Lowenthal and Robinson (1976) referred to as the "personal patterns of oscillation between social involvement and withdrawal" (p. 432).

Social compensation may not be a trait that is observable at any one point in time. Therefore, the type of research needed to further develop and test such processes is that which can follow subjects over time. Cross-sectional research may still be helpful, but studying processes such as social compensation will be greatly assisted by longitudinal research—especially on random community samples. Indeed, the most solid evidence on social compensation to date comes from the longitudinal investigations.

In summary, social compensation is a normal adaptive response throughout the life course (including later life). Growing older often entails a loss of social roles and diminished functional capabilities, but evidence abounds that normal adaptive responses to such experiences include compensation. It should not be assumed that all older adults compensate in social functioning for every loss experienced. Rather, the capacity for the individual to compensate in social relations is dependent on his or her health and the socioeconomic and environmental resources on which the person may draw.

REFERENCES

Adams, R. G. (1987). Patterns of network change: A longitudinal study of friendships of elderly women. *The Gerontologist, 27*, 222–227.

Ainlay, S. C., & Smith, R. (1984). Aging and religious participation. *Journal of Gerontology, 39*, 357–363.

Antonucci, T. C. (1990). Social support and social relationships. In R. H. Binstock & L. K. George (Eds.), *Handbook of aging and the social sciences* (pp. 205–226). San Diego, CA: Academic Press.

Atchley, R. C. (1971). Retirement and leisure participation: Continuity or crises? *Gerontologist, 11*, 13–17.

Atchley, R. C. (1987). *Aging: Continuity and change* (2nd ed.). Belmont, CA: Wadsworth.

Atchley, R. C. (1989). A continuity theory of normal aging. *The Gerontologist, 29*, 183–190.

Atchley, R. C. (1991). *Social forces and aging* (6th ed.). Belmont, CA: Wadsworth.

Bäckman, L., & Dixon, R. A. (1992). Psychological compensation: A theoretical framework. *Psychological Bulletin, 112*, 259–283.

Bass, D. M., & Bowman, K. (1990). The transition from caregiving to bereavement: The relationship of care-related strain and adjustment to death. *The Gerontologist, 30*, 35–44.

Bass, D. M., Bowman, K., & Noelker, L. S. (1991). The influence of caregiving and bereavement support on adjusting to an older relative's death. *The Gerontologist, 31*, 32–42.

Berardo, F. M. (1970). Survivorship and social isolation: The case of the aged widower. *The Family Coordinator, 19*, 11–25.

Blau, Z. S. (1961). Structural constraints on friendships in old age. *American Sociological Review, 26*, 429–439.

Blazer, D., & Palmore, E. (1976). Religion and aging in a longitudinal panel. *The Gerontologist, 16*, 82–85.

Bock, E. W., & Webber, I. L. (1972). Suicide among the elderly: Isolating widowhood and mitigating alternatives. *Journal of Marriage and the Family, 34*, 24–31.

Bosse, R., Aldwin, C. M., Levenson, M. R., Spiro III, A., & Mroczek, D. K. (1993). Change in social support after retirement: Longitudinal findings from the normative aging study. *Journal of Gerontology: Psychological Sciences, 48*, P210–P217.

Chatters, L. M., Taylor, R. J., & Jackson, J. S. (1985). Size and composition of the informal helper networks of elderly blacks. *Journal of Gerontology, 40*, 605–614.

Chaves, M., & Higgins, L. M. (1992). Comparing the community involvement of black and white congregations. *Journal for the Scientific Study of Religion, 31*, 425–440.

Cicirelli, V. G. (1983). Adult children's attachment and helping behavior to elderly parents: A path model. *Journal of Marriage and the Family, 45*, 815–826.

Cumming, E., Dean, L. R., Newell, D. S., & McCaffrey I. (1960). Disengagement—A tentative theory of aging. *Sociometry, 23*, 23–35.

Cumming, E., & Henry, W. E. (1961). *Growing old.* New York: Basic Books.

Danielson, C. B., Hamel-Bissell, B., & Winstead-Fry, P. (1993). *Families, health, and illness.* St. Louis, MO: Mosby.

Dowd, J. J. (1975). Aging as exchange: A preface to theory. *Journal of Gerontology, 30*, 584–594.

Dowd, J. J., & Bengtson, V. L. (1978). Aging in minority populations: An examination of the double jeopardy hypothesis. *Journal of Gerontology, 33*, 427–436.

Ekerdt, D. J. (1986). The busy ethic: Moral continuity between work and retirement. *The Gerontologist, 26*, 239–244.

Ellison, C. G., & London, B. (1992). The social and political participation of black Americans: Compensatory and ethnic community theories revisited. *Social Forces, 70*, 681–701.

Ferraro, K. F. (1989). Widowhood and health. In K. S. Markides & C. L. Cooper (Eds.), *Aging, stress, and health* (pp. 69–83). Chichester, England: Wiley.

Ferraro, K. F. (1990). The gerontological imagination. In K. F. Ferraro (Ed.), *Gerontology: Perspectives and issues* (pp. 3–18). New York: Springer.

Ferraro, K. F., & Barresi, C. M. (1982). The impact of widowhood on the social relations of older people. *Research on Aging, 4*, 227–247.

Ferraro, K. F., Mutran, E., & Barresi, C. M. (1984). Widowhood, health, and friendship support in later life. *Journal of Health and Social Behavior, 25*, 245–254.

Filinson, R. (1988). A model for church-based services for frail elderly persons and their families. *The Gerontologist, 28*, 483–485.

Gallagher, S. K., & Gerstel, N. (1993). Kinkeeping and friend keeping among older women: The effect of marriage. *The Gerontologist, 33*, 675–681.

Gecas, V., & Seff, M. A. (1990). Social class and self-esteem: Psychological centrality, compensation, and the relative effects of work and home. *Social Psychology Quarterly, 53*, 165–173.

Geertsen, R. (1988). Social group characteristics and health behavior. In D. S. Gochman (Ed.), *Health behavior: Emerging research perspectives* (pp. 131–148). New York: Plenum.

Geertsen, R., Klauber, M. R., Rindflesh, M., Kane, R. L., & Gray, R. (1975). A re-examination of Suchman's views on social factors in health care utilization. *Journal of Health and Social Behavior, 16*, 226–237.

George, L. K. (1980). *Role transitions in later life.* Belmont, CA: Wadsworth.

George, L. K. (1988). Social participation in later life: Black-white differences. In J. S. Jackson (Ed.), *The black American elderly: Research on physical and psychosocial health* (pp. 99–126). New York: Springer.

Gerber, I., Rusalem, R., Hannon, N., Battin, D., & Arkin, A. (1975). Anticipatory grief and aged widows and widowers. *Journal of Gerontology, 30*, 225–229.

Harvey, C. D., & Bahr, H. M. (1974). Widowhood, morale, and affiliation. *Journal of Marriage and the Family, 36*, 97–106.

Henretta, J. C. (1986). Retirement and residential moves by elderly households. *Research on Aging, 8*, 23–37.

Herzog, A. R., Kahn, R. L., Morgan, J. N., Jackson, J. S., & Antonucci, T. C. (1989). Age differences in productive activities. *Journal of Gerontology: Social Sciences, 44*, S129–S138.

Herzog, A. R., & Morgan, J. N. (1992). Age and gender differences in the value of productive activities. *Research on Aging, 14*, 169–198.

Hochschild, A. (1975). Disengagement theory: A critique and proposal. *American Sociological Review, 40*, 553–569.

Holmes, T. H., & Rahe, R. H. (1967). The social readjustment rating scale. *Journal of Psychosomatic Research, 11*, 213–218.

Homans, G. C. (1961). *Social behavior: Its elementary forms.* New York: Harcourt Brace Jovanovich.

Kahn, R. L., & Antonucci, T. C. (1980). Conveys over the life course: Attachment, roles, and social support. In P. B. Baltes & O. G. Brim, Jr. (Eds.), *Life-span development and behavior* (pp. 253–286). New York: Academic Press.

Klobus-Edwards, P., Edwards, J. N., & Klemmack D. L. (1978). Differences in social participation: Blacks and Whites. *Social Forces, 56*, 1035–1052.

Knoke, D., & Thomson, R. (1977). Voluntary association membership trends and the family life cycle. *Social Forces, 56*, 48–65.

Kohen, J. A. (1983). Old but not alone: Informal social supports among the elderly by marital status and sex. *The Gerontologist, 23*, 57–63.

Kuypers, J. A., & Bengtson, V. L. (1973). Social breakdown and competence: A model of normal aging. *Human Development, 16*, 181–201.

Lawton, M. P. (1985). The elderly in context: Perspectives from environmental psychology and gerontology. *Environment and Behavior, 17*, 501–519.

Lawton, M. P., & Nahemow, L. (1973). Ecology and the aging process. In C. Eisdorfer & M. P. Lawton (Eds.), *The psychology of adult development and aging* (pp. 619–674). Washington, DC: American Psychological Association.

Lemon, B. W., Bengtson, V. L., & Peterson, J. A. (1972). An exploration of the activity theory of aging: Activity types and life satisfaction among inmovers to a retirement community. *Journal of Gerontology, 27*, 511–523.

Levin, J. S. (1988). Religious factors in aging, adjustment, and health: A theoretical overview. *Journal of Religion and Aging, 4*, 133–146.

Levin, J. S., & Vanderpool, H. Y. (1987). Is frequent religious attendance really conducive to better health? Toward an epidemiology of religion. *Social Science and Medicine, 24*, 589–600.

Litwak, E., & Longino, Jr., C. F. (1987). Migration patterns among the elderly: A development perspective. *The Gerontologist, 27*, 266–272.

Lopata, H. Z. (1973). *Widowhood in an American city.* Cambridge, MA: Schenkman.

Lowenthal, M. F., & Haven, C. (1968). Interaction and adaptation: Intimacy as a critical variable. *American Sociological Review, 33*, 20–30.

Lowenthal, M. F., & Robinson, B. (1976). Social networks and isolation. In R. Binstock & E. Shanas (Eds.), *Handbook of aging and the social sciences* (pp. 432–456). New York: Van Nostrand Reinhold.

McFarlane, A. H., Norman, G. R., Streiner, D. L., & Roy, R. G. (1983). The process of social stress: Stable, reciprocal, and mediating relationships. *Journal of Health and Social Behavior, 24*, 160–173.

Mead, G. H. (1934). *Mind, self, and society.* Chicago, IL: University of Chicago Press.

Miller, B., & McFall, S. (1991). Stability and change in the informal task support network of frail older persons. *The Gerontologist, 31*, 735–745.

Miller, S. J. (1965). The social dilemma of the aging leisure participant. In A. M. Rose & W. Peterson (Eds.), *Older people and their social world* (pp. 77–92). Philadelphia: Davis.

Mindel, C. H., & Vaughn, C. E. (1978). A multidimensional approach to religiosity and disengagement. *Journal of Gerontology, 33*, 103–108.

Moberg, D. O. (1990). Religion and aging. In K. F. Ferraro (Ed.), *Gerontology: Perspectives and issues* (pp. 179–205). New York: Springer.

Mullan, J. T. (1992). The bereaved caregiver: A prospective study of changes in well-being. *The Gerontologist, 32*, 673–683.

Mutran, E. (1985). Intergenerational family support among Blacks and Whites: Response to culture or to socioeconomic differences. *Journal of Gerontology, 40,* 382–389.

Mutran, E., & Reitzes, D. C. (1981). Retirement, identity, and well-being: Realignment of role relationships. *Journal of Gerontology, 36,* 733–740.

Nahemow, L., & Lawton, M. P. (1973). Toward an ecological theory of adaptation and aging. In W. F. E. Preiser (Ed.), *Environmental design research* (pp. 24–32). Stroudsburg, PA: Dowden, Hutchinson & Ross.

Palmore, E. B. (1968). The effects of aging on activities and attitudes. *The Gerontologist, 8,* 259–263.

Parsons, T. (1951). *The social system.* New York: The Free Press.

Parsons, T., Bales, R. F., & Shils, E. A. (1953). *Working papers in the theory of action.* Glencoe, IL: The Free Press.

Perrucci, R., & Targ, D. B. (1982). Network structure and reactions to primary deviance of mental patients. *Journal of Health and Social Behavior, 23,* 2–17.

Petrowsky, M. (1976). Marital status, sex, and the social networks of the elderly. *Journal of Marriage and the Family, 38,* 749–756.

Pihlblad, C. T., & Adams D. L. (1972). Widowhood, social participation, and life satisfaction. *International Journal of Aging and Human Development, 3,* 323–330.

Riley, M. W. (1985). Age strata in social systems. In R. H. Binstock & E. Shanas (Eds.), *Handbook of aging and the social sciences* (pp. 369–411). New York: Van Nostrand Reinhold.

Riley, M. W. (1987). On the significance of age in sociology. *American Sociological Review, 52,* 1–14.

Rosow, I. (1967). *Social integration of the aged.* New York: The Free Press.

Rosow, I. (1973). The social context of the aging self. *The Gerontologist, 13,* 82–87.

Sarason, I. G., Levine, H. M., Basham, R. B., & Sarason, B. B. (1983). Assessing social support: The Social Support Questionnaire. *Journal of Personality and Social Psychology, 44,* 127–139.

Scott, K. Y. (1991). *The habit of surviving: Black women's strategies for life.* New Brunswick, NJ: Rutgers University Press.

Shirk, E. (1991). *After the stroke: Coping with America's third leading cause of death.* Buffalo, NY: Prometheus Books.

Stone, R. (1991). Defining family caregivers of the elderly: Implications for research and public policy. *The Gerontologist, 31,* 724–725.

Streib, G. F., & Schneider, C. J. (1971). *Retirement in American society: Impact and process.* Ithaca, NY: Cornell University Press.

Suchman, E. A. (1965). Social patterns of illness and medical care. *Journal of Health and Human Behavior, 6,* 2–16.

Taylor, R. J. (1986). Religious participation among elderly blacks. *The Gerontologist, 26,* 630–636.

Taylor, R. J., & Chatters, L. M. (1986). Church-based informal support networks among elderly blacks. *The Gerontologist, 26,* 637–642.

Taylor, R. J., & Chatters, L. M. (1988). Church members as a source of informal social support. *Review of Religious Research, 30,* 93–203.

Thoits, P. A. (1981). Undesirable life events and psychophysiological distress: A problem of operational confounding. *American Sociological Review, 46,* 97–109.

Waite, L. J., & Harrison, S. C. (1992). Keeping in touch: How women in mid-life allocate social contacts among kith and kin. *Social Forces, 70,* 637–655.

Walker, K. N., MacBride, A., & Vachon, M. L. S. (1977). Social support networks and the crisis of bereavement. *Social Science and Medicine, 11,* 35–41.

Walker, S. N. (1990). Promoting healthy aging. In K. F. Ferraro (Ed.), *Gerontology: Perspectives and issues* (pp. 266–282). New York: Springer.

Walls, C. T., & Zarit, S. H. (1991). Informal support from black churches and the well-being of elderly blacks. *The Gerontologist, 31,* 490–495.

Wan, T. T. H., & Odell, B. G. (1983). Major role losses and social participation of older males. *Research on Aging, 5,* 173–196.

Weinert, C. (1987). A social support measure: PRQ85. *Nursing Research, 36,* 273–277.

Wolinsky, F. D. (1988). Sick-role legitimization. In D. S. Gochman (Ed.), *Health behaviors: Emerging research perspectives* (pp. 181–192). New York: Plenum.

Wortman, C. B., & Silver, R. C. (1989). The myths of coping with loss. *Journal of Consulting and Clinical Psychology, 57,* 349–357.

CHAPTER SEVEN

Compensation Through Environmental Modification

Neil Charness
Florida State University

Elizabeth A. Bosman
University of Toronto

Humans are adaptive organisms with respect to the usual range of environments because they can reach their goals by many diverse routes. This flexibility complicates the life of the behavioral scientist intent on predicting behavior, given the difficulty in predicting the choice of method. However, this same flexibility is the reason for the success of the species on this planet. Yet there are limits to adaptability, given the physical and mental makeup of Homo sapiens. As people age, these limits become more evident. Lawton (1977) was one of the first to portray, in schematic form, the delicate balance between environmental demands ("press") and human capabilities, outlining the need for person–environment congruency.

Such distinctions fit nicely with the World Health Organization's (WHO) definitions of *impairment* and *disability* (World Health Organization, 1980). *Impairment* is defined as "any loss or abnormality of psychological, physiological, or anatomical structure or function" (World Health Organization, 1980, 47). Impairments are placed within the person. *Disability* is defined as "any restriction or lack (resulting from an impairment) of ability to perform an activity in the manner or within the range considered normal for a human being" (World Health Organization, 1980, 143). Thus, disability is the joint function of impairment and an unsupportive environment. Disability is the end state we wish to avoid, even when we suffer from impairments. As usual, we can attack this problem from both directions: working on the person to alleviate impairment, and working on modifying the environment to reduce disability. Our chapter focuses primarily on the latter. The main purpose is to provide examples of how environmental modification can alleviate the negative effects associated with age-related declines. Because design is still more an art than a science, we also wish to caution that the design process should not create more problems than it solves.

The topics of compensation, age, and human factors are too broad to permit comprehensive coverage in a single chapter. We attempt instead to provide an example-based chapter to illustrate the potential for compensation via environmental modification. We first define what we mean by compensation and the environment, illustrate a human–factors approach to design, and then provide a series of environmental modification examples to alleviate potentially disabling conditions.

COMPENSATION

The term *compensation* is used in both narrow (e.g., Salthouse, 1990) and broad (e.g., Bäckman & Dixon, 1992; Dixon & Bäckman, 1992–93) senses. Salthouse argued that compensation (in the cognitive domain) must involve some active, although not necessarily conscious, role in the compensatory process by the person with the impairment. Such compensatory processes are believed to take considerable time to develop. Compensation is seen as offsetting the negative impact of an age-related change so that it does not influence performance. The increase in older typists reliance on advance preparation of keystrokes (Bosman, 1993; Salthouse, 1984) is seen to compensate for age-related slowing in information processing, permitting older typists to equal the performance of their younger counterparts. When the opportunity to prepare keystrokes in advance is not available (by restricting preview for text), the typing speed of older adults slows. By this definition, *compensation* requires the use of different mechanisms to achieve the same outcome (e.g., typing 80 words per minute).

Thus, using Salthouse's sense of the term *compensation*, providing eyeglasses to a visually impaired person would not count as compensation, but as accommodation. Bäckman and Dixon (1992) used a broad set of principles to classify behavior as compensatory. For them, compensation encompasses the development and use (automatic or deliberate) of existing or latent skills to maintain or surpass normal levels of proficiency. Their framework also appears to include goal change as a form of compensation, so that if someone were to suffer age-related declines in say, chess-playing ability, and the person decided not to compete in tournaments, but became satisfied with club play, that change in level of aspiration would be considered a form of compensation.

We would like to consider a middle ground that anchors the term *compensation* to goals. We view this goal-centered approach to identifying compensation as a way to sharpen the distinctions implied by terms such as *skills–environmental demands mismatch* (e.g., Bäckman & Dixon, 1992; Dixon & Bäckman, 1992–93), or *capability–demand* deficits (e.g., Czaja, Weber, & Nair, 1993). We believe that one can only have a mismatch or a deficit with respect to a goal or a goal hierarchy.

By this sleight of hand, we can recast compensation within the well-worn theoretical framework of problem solving (e.g., Newell & Simon, 1972). Persons are said to have a problem when they have a goal, but do not immediately know how to reach it. Thus, they are forced to traverse a maze of possible actions on the way from the initial state to the goal state. When one method fails to achieve progress toward the goal it may be abandoned and another method tried. Substitution of methods or operators lies at the heart of such impasse resolution. For instance, if a "lightning calculator" (someone highly skilled at mental calculation) found that he or she was slowing down to an unacceptable extent with increasing age while calculating cubes for numbers in the range of 1–99, he or she might decide to invest effort into memorizing the values and gain speed by retrieving the answer rather than calculating it. The goal of obtaining the cube has not changed, but the method will have switched from mental multiplication to recognition. If the lightning calculator were to substitute a hand calculator for mental calculation, the goal will have changed (from mental calculation to calculation), and we would not classify this as a case of compensation.

Hence, we view compensation as a process adopted by the person, *behavioral modification* (used in the broad sense of this term, rather than in the narrower operant–conditioning sense), or a change to the environment, *tool* or *environmental modification*, that permits the individual to achieve an otherwise blocked goal. (Hence, if the goal is not achieved when a new method is attempted, we would not judge there to be compensation.) This intermediate definition permits classifying the use of eyeglasses as a form of compensation that enables visually–impaired (e.g., myopic, presbyopic) people to read the newspaper. But having someone else read the paper to the visually–impaired person represents a change in goal (from reading to listening to the news). Hence, this is not compensation, but goal change. However, if the visually impaired person's goal was merely to learn about the news, the latter case would become a form of compensation (by substitution).

We assume that people can articulate their goals well enough to allow us to judge whether there has been compensation or a change in the goal. We do not wish to gloss over the interpretive problems associated with relying on people to articulate their goals and interpret their own behavior (e.g., see Ericsson & Simon, 1993, for a summary of strengths and weaknesses of verbal reports). Nonetheless, we view approaches such as the use of verbal protocols and compensation questionnaires (e.g., Dixon & Bäckman, 1992–93) as promising techniques to identify personal goals. A combination of observational and experimental techniques will be required to infer when compensation is occurring.

As Baltes (1993) emphasized, a life-span developmental perspective stresses that there are both gains and losses associated with increasing age. We highlight how the age-associated losses that occur in human capabilities (impairments) can be compensated by designing more flexible environments and tools. Such design holds the promise of promoting gains in the ability to pursue important personal goals. Nonetheless, it is also evident within this framework that not all impairments can be alleviated, nor can all disability be avoided. In those cases, people may have to accommodate to the situation by changing their goals. Our thesis is that many of the impairments that normally accompany aging need not lead to disabilities if the environment can be made to be sufficiently supportive.

Redesign can be reactive or anticipatory. By *reactive*, we mean that an age–related impairment prompts compensatory redesign, usually at the level of the immediate personal environment, such as a home or apartment. Problem solving and associated solution costs occur at the level of the individual. A case in point would be adding a ramp to enable someone who is newly confined to a wheelchair to enter a dwelling. Anticipatory design usually represents problem solving and the assumption of costs at a societal level in anticipation of significant increases in impairment in the population. An example might be changing print size standards for road signs in the hope of making the highway environment safer for future cohorts of older drivers, or changing building codes to widen room entrances to accommodate future wheelchair users. Whether these and other types of environmental modifications practiced by industrialized countries really do compensate completely for physical impairments remains a question for program evaluation studies.

ENVIRONMENT

The term *environment* is often taken in a restrictive sense, referring to physical characteristics of the world outside the person. Others use a more inclusive framework that permits consideration of aspects of interpersonal relations: the social or organizational environment (e.g., Moos & Lemke, 1984). We consider environmental modification primarily as it pertains to the physical environment. Nonetheless, it must be remembered that social interaction is one of the hallmarks of the human species. Despite the early developmental trend of moving from complete dependence as an infant to independence as a young adult, even mature adults habitually rely on other people to help meet their needs. At the end of the lifespan, particularly with respect to nursing care for the frail elderly person, complete reliance on others may become the only alternative to helplessness.

There is usually a complex relationship between human abilities and the environments in which these abilities are exercised. Some environments provide maximal support for certain activities (picture water-filled swimming pools and swimming) whereas others do not (consider water-filled swimming pools and ice hockey).

Another important facet of an environment is its familiarity to the user. Some people move gracefully through an environment by virtue of their expertise with it. An older driver may have no difficulty navigating the streets in the immediate neighborhood but experience considerable difficulty navigating an unfamiliar part of a city at night. Expertise enables people both to sample more efficiently from the environment, matching information in memory via larger chunks, and to predict events accurately enabling them to prepare future actions. Expertise is a potentially important mediator between goals, environmental demands, and personal competence.

Part of the challenge facing our society as it ages is to design environments that will be maximally supportive for aging adults who are increasingly likely to suffer from physical and mental impairments. To do this successfully, as the field of human factors stresses, one must first know the user.

DEFINING HUMAN FACTORS: KNOW THE USER

Human factors is the field that seeks to maximize the functionality of everyday living and working environments. There are two approaches: changing the user and changing the environment. Changing the user, a process better known as *behavioral modification*, usually takes place through training in proper techniques for carrying out activities. Examples would be instruction on how to lift heavy items without straining ones back, or instruction on how to safely operate a motor vehicle. We deal minimally with this side of human factors in the chapter, although it is an often-neglected approach.

The successful use of behavioral modification as a means to compensate for age-related declines requires that the individual can be taught by some knowledgeable agent how to compensate for age-related declines, and that the individual will implement this new behavior. The other possibility is that the individual spontaneously modifies his or her behavior in response to the realization that he or she cannot do things the way that he or she used to do them. The latter change requires a certain amount of metacognitive awareness on the part of the individual—something that probably varies from individual to individual.

Changing the environment, *environmental modification*, or the tools in the environment, *tool modification*, are the two main approaches in human–factors research. We differentiate the environment from tools in that modifications to the environment provide their benefit without any effort by the individual. For example, the older adult presumably benefits from a room in which there is more light, but he or she does not have to exert any effort to derive this benefit. Conversely, a tool such as an illuminating stand magnifier must be deployed by the individual whenever there is a need to read small print. In this sense, our relationship with tools is more active than our relationship with the environment.

The apparent simple dichotomy between the user and the environment tends to break down in an important respect when considering the category of *assistive devices*. Are you changing the user or the environment when you provide a mobility-impaired person with a cane, or a hearing-impaired person with a hearing aid? Devices or tools that straddle the boundary between the user and the environment are particularly important for older adults. Eyeglasses are an excellent example of a *transparent* assistive device. The notion of *transparency* between the tool and the user is a highly prized goal of computer software design.

To design or redesign a tool or an environment, one must first know the capabilities of the user. This can often be accomplished through reference handbooks, such as that by Salvendy (1987). Typical sources for this information range from lab-based experimental research with small, unrepresentative samples, to field studies with larger, although still unrepresentative, samples, to survey and epidemiological studies with large, representative samples. The "cookbook" approach to human factors—in the form of tables of guidelines for furniture design based on human anthropometry, or equations for prediction of optimal conditions for lighting—is often a cost-effective approach. When it comes to design for older adults, however, there are often serious gaps in empirical research, resulting in inadequate information for guidelines and tables (e.g., Charness & Bosman, 1990, 1992, 1994).

An example might be deciding on how long to maintain a green light condition at an intersection to allow a person to walk across safely. One needs to know typical ranges of walking speed to set this parameter. Usual North–American assumptions are that pedestrians can walk at a rate of about 1.2 m/sec, although data on older adult walking speeds suggest that setting a crossing time interval on this basis will seriously inconvenience adults in their 80s (Charness & Bosman, 1990). Some cities, such as Graz, Austria, are now changing vehicle speed limits to 30 km/h to accommodate ". . . concern for urban quality of life especially for 'weaker traffic participants' such as children and older persons" ("Transportation," 1993, p. 31).

Most parameters that would assist design are based on samples of the population that are predominantly young or middle-aged, e.g., tables of anthropometric measurements that contain values for typical body dimensions and movement ranges (Stoudt, Damon, McFarland, & Roberts, 1965, 1973). Obviously to design for older adults, such tables need to be expanded and updated (see Kelly & Kroemer, 1990).

However, it would be unfortunate to do nothing but wait for more epidemiological and field research. Laboratory-based research on aging has provided some useful first approximation parameters, which we have discussed elsewhere (Charness & Bosman, 1990, 1992). In the following sections, we discuss general age-related changes and possible or attempted environmental modifications.

MODIFYING THE ENVIRONMENT

We take it as a given that environments can be changed to accommodate the normal aging process. Discussion of ways to improve environments at the macro– and the microlevels is a fairly new phenomenon (e.g., design of nursing homes, Koncelik, 1976; design of consumer products, Koncelik, 1982). Whether the environment should be changed is a matter for cost–benefit analysis within the relevant societal niche.

Physical Impairments

Agility and Dexterity. The chance that a person will suffer from an arthritic condition by age 65 is between 40% and 50% (Verbrugge, Lepkowski, & Konkol, 1991). Women are more prone to arthritic conditions than men, as Fig. 7.1 indicates. As a result, many adults can expect that activities that were effortless in earlier years will become increasingly effortful in later years. Reaching and grasping are two actions that are called for in many everyday activities (Clark, Czaja, & Weber, 1990; Czaja et al., 1993; Faletti, 1984).

There are two environmental modification approaches to dealing with this problem: minimizing reaching and grasping, and providing tools that facilitate these processes. Both types of solutions have been offered. A classic approach to kitchen activities has been to change the heights of counters, sometimes by using expensive motorized wall units, and to provide better designed units with drawers or baskets that pull out. A good example is in refrigerator design (e.g., Koppa, Jurmain, & Congleton, 1989), through the use of flexible shelving that either pulls out, or that pulls out and pops up.

Another type of solution is to use special grasping devices (grip manipulators mounted on long extensions). Reaching is eliminated, but a new skill must be acquired: using the tool. Each approach to compensation has its strengths and weaknesses. Kitchen cabinet or refrigerator redesign is expensive. Extension tools may require a significant learning period, and they may not solve all reaching problems because the grasper is often not effective for large objects. Another approach being advocated in some quarters is robotics (e.g., as early as Koncelik, 1982), although this introduces even more expense and learning.

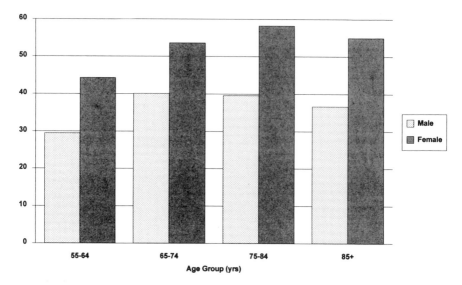

FIG. 7.1. Percent arthritis prevalence rates, United States 1984, derived from data presented in Verbrugge et al. (1991). The risk ratio for difficulty using fingers to grasp is 4:1 for arthritis versus nonarthritis.

Mobility. Sometimes mobility in older adults is so impaired—often because of disease processes such as arthritis—that canes, walkers, and even wheelchair use is necessary. All these devices are examples of tools to augment impaired mobility. Each has its pros and cons (Glendenning, Slavniek, & Forbes, 1992a, 1992b). Here again, however, it is necessary to examine the environment to select the best device and to maximize its usefulness. There are numerous suggestions for how to create barrier-free designs, particularly ones intended to minimize disability for wheelchair users (e.g., Carstens, 1985; Costa & Sweet, 1976; Government of Canada, 1987; Regnier & Pynoos, 1987). They range from retrofitting staircases with motorized lifts, to installing ramps to circumvent steps. Such redesign is often expensive and usually beyond the reach of financially impaired older occupants, even with government subsidies. As many have pointed out (e.g., Newman, Zais, & Struyk, 1984), today's older cohorts tend to live in old homes and spend a disproportionate amount of their income on housing.

When major architectural features are fixed, which is often the case for older adults in their own homes, careful consideration of the physical environment is necessary to choose from among alternative assistive devices. For instance, when considering a cane for a mobility-impaired senior who must navigate stairs, a multilegged cane bottom (e.g., a "quad-cane") is preferred over the standard single-foot cane bottom, even though there may be more problems with normal gait with a multilegged cane (Glendenning et al., 1992a). The reverse would be true for a one-level dwelling. Evaluation research is still needed to determine if these devices are cost-effective.

Visual Impairments

Older adults are likely to suffer from poorer accommodative (focusing) capacity, less transmission of light to the retina, greater susceptibility to glare, and slower adaptation to changes in light levels than their younger counterparts (Fozard, 1990; Verrillo & Verrillo, 1985). As a result, people are much more likely to report visual impairments with increasing age (Forbes, Hayward, & Agwani, 1993), such as the inability to read a newspaper or to see clearly a face across a room.

Text Legibility. Poor layout of text can handicap older adults, for instance, as seen in the small fonts used in telephone directories (e.g., Morrison & Rayner, 1985). Better illumination can improve the contrast ratio (dark print to white paper) for text. But, as those of us entering our bifocal years are well aware, size of visual detail can be the limiting factor in legibility. Larger print can make the difference between reading and not reading the instructional label on medication or food containers. There are significant short- and long-term costs associated with environmental modifications, such as installing new lights or using larger print (e.g., direct and indirect energy-related expenses). Assistive devices such as illuminating hand and stand magnifiers can enable visually impaired adults to modify the reading environment themselves. But once the proximity to the stimulus is not under control—as in the case of road signs—society will have to provide the modifications. There are promising techniques for sign design that appear to aid young and old alike (Kline & Fuchs, 1993).

Hearing Impairments

Laboratory studies of threshold hearing functions show that older adults, particularly men, suffer from hearing loss—first in the upper frequencies (high-pitched sounds) and later in the middle and lower frequencies (see Fozard, 1990). When sensitivity to the part of the spectrum that covers speech declines, communication impairments can arise. Further, hearing in noisy environments can be particularly difficult, because the ability to disembed signal from noise is also an age-sensitive process. Other characteristics such as sound reverberation (Davidson, Schonfield, & Winkelaar, 1982) or too rapid speech (Stine, Wingfield, & Poon, 1986) are particularly handicapping. Social interaction may become increasingly difficult given this double impairment of lower sensitivity to sound and increased sensitivity to background noise. Large-scale national surveys, such as the General Social Survey

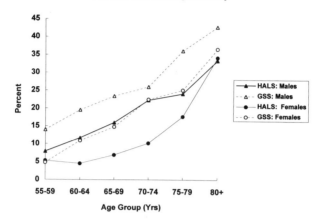

FIG. 7.2. Percent prevalence of reported hearing impairments by age and gender, derived from the Health and Activity Limitation Survey, Canada, 1986, and the General Social Survey, Canada, 1985 (Forbes et al., 1993).

(GSS) and Health and Activity Limitations Survey (HALS) in Canada (e.g., Forbes et al., 1993), show that pure-tone laboratory findings translate well to life. A significant percent of the older population reports having difficulty hearing, particularly males, as seen in Fig. 7.2.

Adverse Noise Levels. There are many ways to redesign the aural environment to cut down on background noise, or reverberation. One approach is to use sound-absorbing materials such as drapes, carpets, and other wall and floor-coverings. Use of quieter mechanical units for heating and cooling can also cut back on general noise pollution, as can the elimination of background music. Design of conversation corners away from noise sources may also help. Still, human speakers, particularly when they gather in large social groups, can also cause serious problems for older listeners. There are no simple solutions to the latter problem (aside from having smaller gatherings). When it comes to age-related difficulties in understanding speech, sensitivity of speakers to age-related changes in hearing ability (a case of modifying the social environment) is likely to be just as important as modifying the physical environment.

Severe Hearing Loss. For those with serious hearing impairment, hearing aids offer one avenue to compensation. Given the relatively low acceptability of such devices for those reporting impairment (e.g., Forbes et al., 1993), it appears that hearing aids may need redesign. Such devices typically boost all sounds, including background noise, and thus address only the threshold intensity problem, not the signal-to-noise ratio problem. The development of so-called "smart" hearing aids, which selectively dampen ambient noise, may provide a partial solution, although the frequency overlap of noise with signal makes intelligent filtering a difficult task. One option for public lecture situations is the provision of dedicated headphone sets that transmit a broadcast of the speaker's voice. Many older adults are heavy consumers of television programs (e.g., Moss & Lawton, 1982), so increased use of close-captioned television broadcasts (print substituting for voice) might be of significant help.

Cognitive Impairments

Memory. A major concern for many aging people is memory decline. The link between memory complaints and laboratory memory performance is usually weak or nonexistent (Hultsch, Hertzog, & Dixon, 1987; Zelinski, Gilewski, & Thompson, 1980). Nonetheless, episodic memory performance (memory for personally experienced events, such as recently seen word lists) does indeed show age–cohort decline (Craik & Jennings, 1992). Although there are good examples of behavioral modification as a means to support memory functioning, such as training mnemonics (e.g., Kliegl, Smith, & Baltes, 1989; Yesavage, Sheikh, Friedman, & Tanke, 1990), we focus on environmental modification.

Craik (1986) argued that the degree of memory impairment seen in aging adults is related to the extent to which there is "environmental support" for memory retrieval. Minimal age differences are observed for a recognition task, where the subject must choose which one of a set of items was previously presented. Maximal age differences are often observed when the task is free recall, where the subject must cue him or herself about previously presented items. (Who benefits most from supportive conditions for episodic memory is not always clear. A review by Bäckman, Mäntylä, & Herlitz, 1990, has shown all possible patterns: young with most benefit, old with most benefit and equal benefit.)

Environmental support for memory makes excellent sense for the young and old. External memory devices are frequently used by older adults, as research with metamemory questionnaires has shown (e.g., Hultsch et al., 1987). Older adults tend to rely on effective aids such as calendars, date books, and diaries to remember appointments, whereas younger adults— usually college students—tend to rely on less reliable internal (prospective) memory. It is not that surprising, then, to find older adults sometimes outperforming younger ones on prospective memory tasks, such as phoning the experimenter at a fixed time or sending in a postcard at a specific time

(West, 1988), given their greater use of such effective aids. Such age-related increased reliance on external memory aids may be a cohort effect (successive generations may value punctuality and external aids differently), or a response to different demands at different life stages, or a form of compensation for negative changes in memory (see Dixon, 1992, for a discussion). However, without longitudinal studies, it will be difficult to disentangle these explanations.

A failing memory can be alleviated, in part, with external support. A good example of external support is the practice—at conventions—of having delegates wear name tags. It is to be expected that human memory is not capable of remembering all the face–name combinations of dozens of new people that one meets in a short period of time. (Memory systems are likely to have evolved during a period where humans were clustered in relatively small groups.) In fact, remembering face–name pairings is viewed as one of the most difficult memory tasks faced by young and old alike, and is thus a likely candidate for training with mnemonics (e.g., Yesavage et al., 1990). A reasonable idea would be to provide this type of environmental support universally, by adopting the practice of wearing name tags daily.

Attention. Laboratory research has consistently shown that older adults have difficulty dividing attention between two competing sources of information, such as different spatial locations (e.g., Plude & Doussard-Roosevelt, 1989; Plude & Hoyer, 1985). A common example might be monitoring one's speed in an automobile by looking at the speedometer and monitoring the road ahead by looking through the windshield. Monitoring instrument gauges and a path through space is a common enough problem in other locomotion situations, such as piloting aircraft. One redesign proposal is to use a head-up display (HUD). Such displays project instrument readings in front of the viewer in virtual space at the perceived distance of the windshield. Previous research with young adults viewing superimposed television pictures (Neisser & Becklen, 1975) showed that a combined display still allowed effective selection of either task. Nonetheless, there is still controversy over the safety of such displays, as recent debates about fighter aircraft crashes make clear (e.g., Roscoe, 1993). There is talk of using HUDs in automobiles (Yanik, 1990). A problem for older drivers using bifocal lenses is that instrument panels are often at a distance for which neither part of the lens provides sharp focus. In theory, at least, HUDs should be particularly helpful for seniors. Nonetheless, before implementing this proposed solution to the problem of switching attention and maintaining good acuity across different spatial locations, considerable research is needed to determine whether switching attention effectively within such a complex superimposed display is at all age-sensitive. The cure should not turn out to be worse than the disease.

OLDER DRIVER SAFETY

Driving is one area where there is considerable evidence for changes in behavior with age, although it is unclear whether this represents goal change or compensation. Older drivers report less driving at night, in rush hour, and in poor weather conditions (Rothe, 1990). Apparently older drivers minimize their exposure to driving conditions that demand high levels of attention and effort (sometimes termed mental workload). The most extreme response to declining driving ability may be to give up driving entirely. The absolute mileage reported per year decreases drastically with age, as seen in Fig. 7.3. As is the case with all cross-sectional studies, such age-related reductions may not provide an accurate representation of longitudinal changes in driving habits, but may reflect persistent cohort differences in driving patterns. Further, it is difficult to predict future patterns for today's younger cohorts. There is also solid evidence that time of measurement is a critical predictor of driving patterns. Evans (1991) provided data indicating a sharp dip in fatality rates when the 55 mile/hr speed limits were instituted in the United States during the oil crisis of the early 1970s. Average annual driving distances also tend to drop sharply during economic recessions.

Why do older drivers reduce their driving mileage? Some of it stems from changes in lifestyle associated with retiring from paid employment (the drop around age 65). Much of the decline in annual mileage in peoples 70s and 80s probably represents a conscious attempt to avoid the increasing difficulties associated with changes in vision, hearing, attention, and other capabilities that impact driving ability.

Although minimizing the number of trips and reducing the driving distance are ways to compensate—actuarially-speaking—for the age-related increased risk of crashes, it has the side effect of reducing mobility in those countries

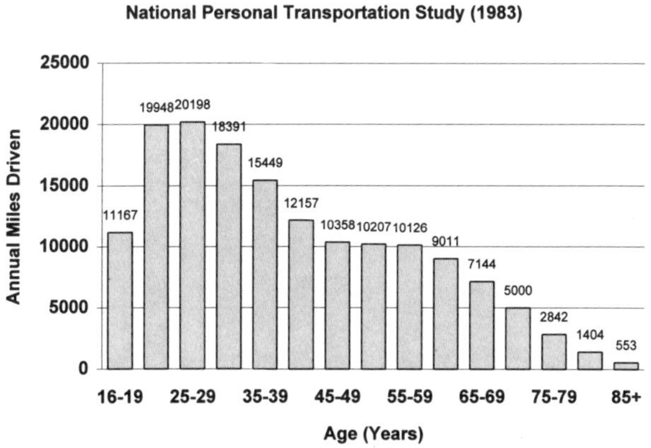

National Personal Transportation Study (1983)

FIG. 7.3. Annual mileage by driver age, derived from data in Cerrelli (1989).

that rely heavily on the private automobile (e.g., Canada, United States). Evans (1991) commented rather aptly that the older driver problem may be less one of stricter licensing to reduce crash rates and more one of concern for mobility restriction.

It is perhaps inaccurate to portray the problem as one solely of driving. Rather, the problem is better framed as one of transportation access and mobility for seniors. Older adults, particularly those dwelling in rural rather than urban settings, need to have access to physically distant shopping, medical care, and banking. Often friends and family members can drive in place of the senior—the case of substituting a social resource for independent mobility. Several other solutions have been proposed: better public transportation, taxi vouchers, special vehicles for wheelchair users ("wheeltrans"), community carpools, house calls by physicians or public health nurses, meals on wheels, wheels to meals, and home-computer networks for banking.

Some have argued that manufacturers should make modifications to automobiles to make them safer (tool modification), such as providing collision alert systems that warn that vehicles may be approaching a car from behind and the side. (It is assumed that collisions involving lane changes might be avoided this way.) Others have argued that traffic guidance systems should be embedded in the roadway and cars to aid navigation decisions, and—perhaps in their ultimate form—automating the driving task in much the same way that current large-passenger aircraft use computer-controlled autopilot systems.

Such technological and social modifications to the driving task may solve the transportation problem. However, they are unlikely to replace the pleasurable feelings of mastery that arise during the skillful exercise of driving, or the celebration of personal freedom by taking a Sunday drive to visit friends and family. The driver's lost sense of personal control over mobility may not be adequately compensated by these substitutions.

TRADE-OFFS IN REDESIGN

Redesign of automobiles should take into account the special needs of older adults so that the latter are not inadvertently handicapped or disabled. For instance, many new cars have tinted windshields. Tinting helps reduce glare and heat during the day, but may also reduce visibility at night. The suggested standard for tinting is 70% transmittance, but some jurisdictions in the United States allow tinting to 35% transmittance (Freedman, Zador, & Staplin, 1993).

Freedman et al. (1993) showed that accompanying reductions in visibility disproportionately affect older drivers (ages 56–75, 76 plus). In a study where drivers were required to detect targets through the rear window of the mock vehicle (e.g., slides of road debris, children, bicyclists, pedestrians, other cars), low–transmittance glass (22%, 36%) resulted in low detection probabilities for some targets with low contrast. At recommended tinting levels (69% transmittance), there were no real age differences, and performance was at ceiling. The worst case was a low–contrast slide of a pedestrian (.72 contrast) via 22% transmittance glass, with detection probability being .54 for 18 to 55-year-olds, .42 for 56 to 75-year-olds, and .17 for 76-year-olds and above.

Although there are clear benefits from increased tinting during the day (energy–consumption reduction for air conditioning, less glare), the corollary costs at night may be too great for older drivers. Technological advances in windshield glass could probably deliver the best of both worlds, although the initial costs may be high. Ideally, much as is the case for some types of sunglasses, the degree of the windshield tint would be automatically adjusted to suit ambient light levels.

Intelligent Vehicle–Highway Systems

Pilot studies are now being conducted on the use of within–vehicle navigation aids, such as "Travtek" (Andre, Hancock, & Smith, 1993). These devices use satellite global–positioning systems in conjunction with stored geographic information to display maps on display screens (e.g., alternate route information to avoid congested areas, as well as maps for route planning in unfamiliar areas). One of the potential design challenges for such devices is how route information is to be portrayed in reference to vehicle position (often shown superimposed on the map).

Spatial processes, such as mental rotation, are known to decline with age, even in highly trained and practiced adults (Salthouse, 1992). Hence, maps and other navigational aids should not force the viewer to rotate a frame of reference. Unfortunately, as Aubrey, Li, and Dobbs (1994) noted, even the commonplace "You Are Here" maps found in public buildings and shopping malls occasionally have the direction arrow misaligned with the viewer's frame of reference. These researchers have shown that such misalignment is much more likely to mislead older viewers. If the alignment is consistent, however, there are no age differences in ability to make correct directional choices, although older adults are still slower.

Such research suggests that navigation aids use a dynamically changing map scheme that reorients the map as the driver turns to keep the car–location marker constant. (An alternate scheme would keep the map grid constant and have the car marker change orientation.) Much experimental and fieldwork is needed to find a scheme (or a customizable design) that does not selectively disadvantage older drivers (e.g., Lerner, 1994). As we argued elsewhere, older adults may be the ideal group to use for testing the design of such systems, because they are usually more sensitive to flaws than younger adults.

RETRAINING OLDER WORKERS

Although our primary focus has been on environmental modification, we cannot overlook behavioral modification. As those in the field of rehabilitation have pointed out, vigorous exercise can change the capabilities of even severely physically disabled older adults—those for whom tool or environmental modifications would have been the a priori most likely candidates for promoting compensation (Khalil, Abdel-Moty, Diaz, Steele-Rosomoff, Rosomoff, 1994). We are more concerned with cognitive modification: training (learning a totally new task) and retraining (transferring skills to a similar task).

In a quickly changing economy, as is the case in most countries today, there is considerable stress on innovation. Innovation usually requires top-flight equipment and training support. In the rapidly growing service sector of the economy, computers have become essential for efficient operation. Further, software development has accelerated as the base of installed computers has grown. Unfortunately, training techniques for computer use have not advanced as quickly as computer hardware technology. Older computer users are generally a neglected subgroup, from the perspectives of hardware and software design. We focus on the issue of training for software (e.g., programs such as word processors and spreadsheets).

Barriers to training and retraining fall into three broad categories: attitudinal (e.g., Belbin & Belbin, 1972), organizational (Sterns & Dorsett, 1991), and technological (e.g., Kelley & Charness, in press). As the Belbins pointed out two decades ago, older workers may be reluctant to seek out retraining opportunities. Part of the problem may be that older workers do not think that they will be successful in their efforts. As Sterns and Dorsett (1991) indicated, there are several other structural problems that exist in some companies. For example, organizations may not provide equal opportunities or more important, equal reward structures for their older workers. Worker perceptions strongly influence whether training opportunities will be seized (Noe & Wilk, 1993). Finally, the equipment and training techniques may not be "older user friendly." We focus on the latter situation here because it provides a salient example of the potential for environmental support.

Command Entry for Computers

The current programming emphasis is on the development of user interfaces that make interaction easier and less error-prone. Rather than have the user memorize hundreds of arcane commands through hours of rote learning, programmers spend much effort and ingenuity in building "direct-manipulation" interfaces. Such interfaces minimize typing and command memorization by having the user select an action/command via menus or icons. For instance, rather than have someone type (for a DOS machine) "copy c:\winword\manuscri\compensn.doc a:\winword", the user might instead use a pointing device such as a mouse, a touchscreen stylus, or a lightpen to drag and drop an icon of the file onto another icon representing the diskette drive.

The main advantage to this type of interface is that the environment (menus, icons) provides cues to the user about actions that can be performed, rather than forcing the user to rely on recalling the command from memory. Because older adults are known to learn more slowly and to experience more retrieval failures when learning new material, such as word lists or paired associates (e.g., Craik, 1977; Hultsch & Dixon, 1990; Poon, 1985), having such environmental support (Craik, 1986) should be especially helpful to older trainees.

There have been few empirical tests of alternate interfaces, particularly using older adult samples. We have some preliminary data from an ongoing word processing training study with computer novices (Bosman & Charness, 1992; Kelley, 1993) using Microsoft Word for Windows 1.1™. In it we administered self-paced tutorials with variants of the word processor that permitted three types of command interface: menus, menus plus icons, and keystrokes. Our expectation was that age and condition would interact, such that keystroke commands would be particularly difficult for older adults due to their difficult memorization requirement. Instead, we found that young, middle-aged, and older adults all performed significantly better with either menus or menus plus icons than with keystrokes commands, with the former two conditions being equivalent. There were also main effects of age, with young adults performing better than middle-aged ones, who in turn performed better than older adults. No interaction was evident. Dependent variables included tests of declarative knowledge (a multiple-choice test) and a performance rating based on coding videotapes of trainees performing word processing operations. We are continuing to evaluate these interfaces with experienced users of word processing software who vary in age. What these early results suggest is that modifications to the computer command environment that minimize recall of commands benefit young and old equally. Further, experience compensates for age on final performance measures, except for those involving speed.

REDESIGNING THE WORK ENVIRONMENT

In difficult economic times, the simplest solution to the "older worker problem" is to drop older workers from the company payroll. However, more forward-looking approaches are to prepare job redesign. A good example of such redesign in a production environment is given in Nagamachi (1990). One example involved redesigning to compensate for expected losses in visual acuity and dexterity through the use of a drill jig with a better guide system. Another involved providing transfer equipment to augment the lifting capability of middle-aged female workers. A third innovation involved using automated sensors to detect wrong-way loading by older workers.

Another suggested intervention (e.g., Vassilieff & Dain, 1986) was the prescription of trifocals to accommodate work with computer screens. As people age, they often suffer from loss of accommodation (inability to focus clearly on near objects). Because many people are already nearsighted and require corrective lenses to focus on distant objects, they must now adopt bifocal lens systems. The problem with such systems, which usually have distance vision in the upper part of the lens and near vision in the lower portion, is that intermediate points (around 50–60 cm in distance) are not in focus. As Vassilieff and Dain pointed out, theoretically, working with computer screens should not necessarily be a problem until about 55 years of age. At that point, a trifocal lens system might be needed to enable viewers to maintain a good posture while working with a computer screen. (Without such lenses, operators might have to crane their necks up to view the screen through the lower lens to achieve a clear image.)

All of these suggested interventions are aimed to help older workers with declining perceptual, motoric, and cognitive capabilities. Our hypothesis is that such redesign might also prove helpful to younger workers. We are still lacking in field studies to see how such modifications affect different age groups in the labor force.

CONCLUSIONS

Losses in capabilities are a predictable consequence of aging. Whether these losses translate into disabilities is, in part, determined by the demands made by the environments in which people seek to attain their goals. We have argued that environmental modifications can help prevent impairments from becoming disabilities. We have given examples of how such modifications can potentially compensate for impaired agility, mobility, vision, hearing, memory, and attention. We also pointed out that behavioral modification—training—is a worthy approach to consider. Nonetheless, there are too few formal evaluations of whether the proposed modifications actually work. We need new field studies. It also seems prudent to conduct a cost–benefit analysis before implementing environmental modifications.

Disabilities increase exponentially in old age, and multiple impairments are likely to co-occur. It seems unlikely that society can afford to modify the tools and environments that exist in such a way that the most disabled person can participate fully in the culture. When it comes to mental impairments, such as dementia, no modification of the environment will render the victim unimpaired. The challenge is to balance the costs of environmental modifications with the benefits of having an increasing proportion of the very old participate fully in society. The golden rule may be to provide for better means to goals, rather than force those with impairments to modify their goals. Intelligent compensation should minimize goal modification.

ACKNOWLEDGMENTS

Funding for this research has been provided by the Canadian Aging Research Network, 1 of 15 Networks of Centres of Excellence supported by the government of Canada. We thank Roger Dixon and Lars Bäckman for helpful comments on an earlier draft of this chapter.

REFERENCES

Andre, A. D., Hancock, P. A., & Smith, H. (1993, April). Getting there from here with TravTek. *Ergonomics in Design*, pp. 16–17.

Aubrey, J. B., Li, K. Z. H., & Dobbs, A. R. (1994). Age differences in the interpretation of misaligned "You-Are-Here" maps. *Journal of Gerontology: Psychological Sciences, 49*, P29–P31.

Bäckman, L., & Dixon, R. A. (1992). Psychological compensation: A theoretical framework. *Psychological Bulletin, 112*, 259–283.

Bäckman, L., Mäntylä, T., & Herlitz, A. (1990). The optimization of episodic remembering in old age. In P. B. Baltes & M. M. Baltes (Eds.), *Successful aging: Perspectives from the behavioral sciences* (pp. 118–163). New York: Cambridge University Press.

Baltes, P. B. (1993). The aging mind: Potential and limits. *The Gerontologist, 33*, 580–594.

Belbin, E., & Belbin, R. M. (1972). *Problems in adult retraining*. London: Heineman.

Bosman, E. A. (1993). Age-related differences in motoric aspects of transcription typing skill. *Psychology and Aging, 8*, 87–102.

Bosman, E. A., & Charness, N. (1992, October). *Training older adults in word processing skills.* Paper presented at the Symposium on Promoting Competence in Work and Retirement, Canadian Association on Gerontology Meetings, Edmonton, Canada.

Carstens, D. Y. (1985). *Site planning and design for the elderly: Issues, guidelines, and alternatives*. New York: Van Nostrand Reinhold.

Cerrelli, E. C. (1989). *Older drivers: The age factor in traffic safety*. Washington, DC: National Highway Traffic Safety Administration.

Charness, N., & Bosman, E. A. (1990). Human factors and design for older adults. In J. E. Birren & K. W. Schaie (Eds.), *Handbook of the psychology of aging* (3rd ed., pp. 446–463). San Diego: Academic Press.

Charness, N., & Bosman, E. A. (1992). Age and human factors. In F. I. M. Craik & T. A. Salthouse (Eds.), *The handbook of aging and cognition* (pp. 495–551). Hillsdale, NJ: Lawrence Erlbaum Associates.

Charness, N., & Bosman, E. A. (1994). Age-related changes in perceptual and psychomotor performance: Implications for engineering design. *Experimental Aging Research, 20*, 45–59.

Clark, M. C., Czaja, S. J., & Weber, R. A. (1990). Older adults and daily living task profiles. *Human Factors, 32*, 537–549.

Costa, F. J., & Sweet, M. (1976). Barrier-free environments for older Americans. *The Gerontologist, 16,* 404–409.

Craik, F. I. M. (1977). Age differences in human memory. In J. E. Birren & K. W. Schaie (Eds.), *Handbook of the psychology of aging* (pp. 384–420). New York: Van Nostrand Reinhold.

Craik, F. I. M. (1986). A functional account of age differences in memory. In F. Klix & H. Hagendorf (Eds.), *Human memory and cognitive capabilities: Mechanisms and performances* (pp. 409–422). Amsterdam: North-Holland.

Craik, F. I. M., & Jennings, J. M. (1992). Human memory. In F. I. M. Craik & T. A. Salthouse (Eds.), *The handbook of aging and cognition* (pp. 51–110). Hillsdale, NJ: Lawrence Erlbaum Associates.

Czaja, S. J., Weber, R. A., & Nair, S. N. (1993). A human factors analysis of ADL activities: A capability-demand approach. *Journal of Gerontology, 48,* 44–48.

Davidson, H., Schonfield, D., & Winkelaar, R. (1982). Age differences in the effects of reverberation and pause on sentence intelligibility. *Canadian Journal on Aging, 1,* 29–37.

Dixon, R. A. (1992). Contextual approaches to adult intellectual development. In R. J. Sternberg & C. A. Berg (Eds.), *Intellectual development* (pp. 350–380). New York: Cambridge University Press.

Dixon, R. A., & Bäckman, L. (1992–93). The concept of compensation in cognitive aging: The case of prose processing in adulthood. *International Journal of Aging and Human Development, 36,* 199–217.

Ericsson, K. A., & Simon, H. A. (1993). *Protocol analysis: Verbal reports as data* (rev. ed.). Cambridge, MA: MIT Press.

Evans, L. (1991). *Traffic safety and the driver.* New York: Van Nostrand Reinhold.

Faletti, M. V. (1984). Human factors research and functional environments for the aged. In I. Altman, M. P. Lawton, & J. F. Wohlwill (Eds.), *Human behavior and environment: Advances in theory and research: Vol. 7. Elderly people and the environment* (pp. 191–237). New York: Plenum.

Forbes, W. F., Hayward, L. M., & Agwani, N. (1993). Factors associated with self-reported use, and non-use of assistive devices among impaired elderly residing in the community. *Canadian Journal of Public Health, 84,* 53–57.

Fozard, J. L. (1990). Vision and hearing in aging. In J. E. Birren & K. W. Schaie (Eds.), *Handbook of the psychology of aging* (3rd ed., pp. 150–170). San Diego: Academic Press.

Freedman, M., Zador, P., & Staplin, L. (1993). Effects of reduced transmittance film on automobile rear window visibility. *Human Factors, 35,* 535–550.

Glendenning, F. J., Slavniek, E., & Forbes, W. F. (1992a, August). An evaluation of devices to aid movement: Part 1 Canes. *Rehabilitation Digest,* pp. 15–16.

Glendenning, F. J., Slavniek, E., & Forbes, W. F. (1992b, December). An evaluation of devices to aid movement: Part 2 Walkers. *Rehabilitation Digest,* pp. 21–23.

Government of Canada. (1987). *Housing an aging population: Guidelines for development and design.* National Advisory Council on Aging. Ministry of Supply and Services Canada. Available from National Advisory Council on Aging, Brooke Claxton Building, Ottawa, Ontario, Canada K1A 0K9.

Hultsch, D. F., & Dixon, R. A. (1990). Memory and learning and aging. In J. E. Birren and K. W. Schaie (Eds.), *Handbook of the psychology of aging* (3rd ed., pp. 258–274). San Diego: Academic Press.

Hultsch, D. F., Hertzog, C., & Dixon, R. A. (1987). Age differences in metamemory: Resolving inconsistencies. *Canadian Journal of Psychology, 41,* 193–208.

Kelley, C. L. (1993). Training older and younger adults to use word processors. Unpublished Masters Thesis, University of Waterloo, Waterloo, Ontario, Canada.

Kelley, C. L., & Charness, N. (in press). Issues in training older adults to use computers. *Behaviour and Information Technology.*

Kelly, P. L., & Kroemer, K. H. E. (1990). Anthropometry of the elderly: Status and recommendations. *Human Factors, 32,* 571–595.

Khalil, T. M., Abdel-Moty, E., Diaz, E., Steele-Rosomoff, R., & Rosomoff, H. (1994). Efficacy of physical restoration in the elderly. *Experimental Aging Research, 20,* 189–199.

Kliegl, R., Smith, J., & Baltes, P. B. (1989). Testing-the-limits and the study of adult age differences in cognitive plasticity of a mnemonic skill. *Developmental Psychology, 25,* 247–256.

Kline, D. W., & Fuchs, P. (1993). The visibility of symbolic highway signs can be increased among drivers of all ages. *Human Factors, 35,* 25–34.

Koncelik, J. A. (1976). *Designing the open nursing home.* Stroudsburg, PA: Dowden, Hutchinson & Ross.

Koncelik, J. A. (1982). *Aging and the product environment.* New York: Van Nostrand Reinhold.

Koppa, R. J., Jurmain, M. M., & Congleton, J. J. (1989). An ergonomics approach to refrigerator design for the elderly person. *Applied Ergonomics, 20,* 123–130.

Lawton, M. P. (1977). The impact of the environment on aging and behavior. In J. E. Birren & K. W. Schaie (Eds.), *Handbook of the psychology of aging* (pp. 276–301). New York: Van Nostrand Reinhold.

Lerner, N. (1994). Giving the older driver enough perception-reaction time. *Experimental Aging Research, 20,* 25–33.

Moos, R. H., & Lemke, S. (1984). Supportive residential settings for older people. In I. Altman, M. P. Lawton, & J. F. Wohlwill (Eds.), *Human behavior and environment: Advances in theory and research: Vol. 7. Elderly people and the environment* (pp. 159–190). New York: Plenum.

Morrison, R. E., & Rayner, K. (1985). Legibility of telephone directories: Reduction due to compressed print and disproportionate effects for the aged. In *Proceedings of the Human Factors Society 29th annual meeting* (pp. 231–234). Santa Monica, CA: Human Factors Society.

Moss, M., & Lawton, M. P. (1982). The time budgets of older people: A window on four lifestyles. *Journal of Gerontology, 37,* 115–123.

Nagamachi, M. (1990). Job redesign for senior people. In K. Noro & O. Brown Jr. (Eds.), *Human factors in organizational design and management—III* (pp. 493–496). Amsterdam: Elsevier.

Neisser, U., & Becklen, R. (1975). Selective looking: Attending to visually significant events. *Cognitive Psychology, 7,* 480–494.

Newell, A., & Simon, H. A. (1972). *Human problem solving.* Englewood Cliffs, NJ: Prentice-Hall.

Newman, S. J., Zais, J., & Struyk, R. (1984). Housing older America. In I. Altman, M. P. Lawton, & J. F. Wohlwill (Eds.), *Human behavior and environment: Advances in theory and research: Vol. 7. Elderly people and the environment* (pp. 17–55). New York: Plenum.

Noe, R. A., & Wilk, S. L. (1993). Investigation of the factors that influence employees' participation in developmental activities. *Journal of Applied Psychology, 78,* 291–302.

Plude, D. J., & Doussard-Roosevelt, J. A. (1989). Aging, selective attention, and feature integration. *Psychology and Aging, 4,* 98–105.

Plude, D. J., & Hoyer, W. J. (1985). Attention and performance: Identifying and localizing age deficits. In N. Charness (Ed.) *Aging and human performance* (pp. 47–99). Chichester, England: Wiley.

Poon, L. W. (1985). Differences in human memory with aging: Nature, causes, and clinical implications. In J. E. Birren & K. W. Schaie (Eds.), *Handbook of the psychology of aging* (2nd ed., pp. 427–462). New York: Van Nostrand Reinhold.

Regnier, V., & Pynoos, J. (1987). *Housing the aged.* New York: Elsevier Science.

Roscoe, S. N. (1993). Letters. *Human Factors and Ergonomics Society Bulletin, 39,* 4.

Rothe, J. P. (1990). *The safety of elderly drivers: Yesterday's young in today's traffic.* New Brunswick, NJ: Transaction Publishers.

Salthouse, T. A. (1984). Effects of age and skill in typing. *Journal of Experimental Psychology: General, 13,* 345–371.

Salthouse, T. A. (1990). Cognitive competence and expertise in aging. In J. E. Birren & K. W. Schaie (Eds.). *Handbook of the psychology of aging* (3rd ed., pp. 310–319). San Diego: Academic Press.

Salthouse, T. A. (1992). Reasoning and spatial abilities. In F. I. M. Craik & T. A. Salthouse (Eds.), *The handbook of aging and cognition* (pp. 167–211). Hillsdale, NJ: Lawrence Erlbaum Associates.

Salvendy, G. (Ed.). (1987). *Handbook of human factors.* New York: Wiley.

Sterns, H. L., & Dorsett, J. G. (1991, October). *Career development: A life-span issue.* Presented at Drexel University Conference, Engineering Design for an Aging Society: Current Issues and Future Prospects. Philadelphia, PA.

Stine, E. L., Wingfield, A., & Poon, L.·W. (1986). How much and how fast: Rapid processing of spoken language in later adulthood. *Psychology and Aging, 1,* 303–311.

Stoudt, H. W., Damon, A., McFarland, R. A., & Roberts, J. (1965). *Weight, height, and selected body dimensions of adults. Vital and health statistics, Series 11, Number 8.* Rockville, MD: Public Health Service.

Stoudt, H. W., Damon, A., McFarland, R. A., & Roberts, J. (1973). *Skinfolds, body girths, biacromial diameter and selected anthropometric indices of adults. Vital and health statistics, Series 11, Number 35.* Rockville, MD: Public Health Service.

Transportation. Speed limit reduced in Austria. (1993). *Ageing International, 20*(4), 31.

Vassilieff, A., & Dain, S. (1986). Bifocal wearing and VDU operation: A review and graphical analysis. *Applied Ergonomics, 17,* 82–86.

Verbrugge, L. M., Lepkowski, J. M., & Konkol, L. L. (1991). Levels of disability among U.S. adults with arthritis. *Journal of Gerontology, 46,* S71–S83.

Verrillo, R. T., & Verrillo, V. (1985). Sensory and perceptual performance. In N. Charness (Ed.) *Aging and human performance* (pp. 1–46). Chichester, England: Wiley.

West, R. L. (1988). Prospective memory and aging. In M. M. Gruneberg, P. E. Morris, & R. N. Sykes (Eds.), *Practical aspects of memory: Current research and issues* (Vol. 2, pp. 119–125). Chichester, England: Wiley.

World Health Organization. (1980). *International classification of impairments, disabilities and handicaps: A manual of classification relating to the consequences of disease.* Geneva: World Health Organization.

Yanik, A. J. (1990). New Technology considerations for mature drivers. (SAE Technical Paper Series 900192). Warrandale, PA: SAE International.

Yesavage, J. A., Sheikh, J. I., Friedman, L., & Tanke, E. (1990). Learning mnemonics: Roles of aging and subtle cognitive impairment. *Psychology and Aging, 5,* 133–137.

Zelinski, E. M., Gilewski, M. J., & Thompson, L. W. (1980). Do laboratory tests relate to self-assessment of memory ability in the young and old? In L. W. Poon, J. L. Fozard, L. S. Cermak, D. Arenberg, & L. W. Thompson (Eds.), *New directions in memory and aging* (pp. 519–544). Hillsdale, NJ: Lawrence Erlbaum Associates.

PART THREE

COMPENSATION FOR
NEUROLOGICAL IMPAIRMENTS

CHAPTER EIGHT

Memory Rehabilitation: Compensating for Memory Problems

Barbara A. Wilson

MRC Applied Psychology Unit, England

Memory problems are common after cerebral pathology (Kapur, 1988) and may range from mild forgetfulness to severe amnesia (see Scoville & Milner, 1957; Wilson & Wearing, in press). Whatever the diagnosis, certain common characteristics tend to be seen after brain injury. This remains true when there is a pure amnesic syndrome (i.e., only memory is affected), or when there are more general and widespread cognitive problems. First, there is difficulty in learning and remembering new information. Second, immediate memory is usually normal or almost normal. Third, problems arise after a delay or distraction. Fourth, there is frequently a retrograde amnesia (i.e., loss of memory for events prior to the cerebral insult).

In a long-term follow-up study of 54 people referred for memory rehabilitation some 5–10 years earlier (Wilson, 1991), it was found that most people had learned coping methods that involved the increased use of memory aids and strategies to bypass or compensate for their memory problems. Among this group, there was a significant increase in the mean number of aids used by each individual in comparison with (a) the time before the accident or illness, and (b) the end of rehabilitation. This increase in the use of such aids, in comparison with the numbers used at the end of the formal rehabilitation period, occurred even though much of the emphasis during rehabilitation had been on teaching or encouraging the use of compensatory strategies.

The comparative reluctance or inability of this group to use compensatory strategies during or immediately after rehabilitation might be explained by

171

the lack of relevance of the latter to the daily needs of patients at that time. The fact that ex-patients began using compensatory strategies some time after discharge from rehabilitation could be due to a growing awareness of the mismatch between their impoverished memory skills and the real demands experienced in daily living. This point was made by Bäckman and Dixon (1992) when they wrote: "the first step is typically awareness, without which compensation is unlikely. Awareness of a mismatch may lead to a decision to compensate" (p. 275).

The importance of compensation for people with severe organic memory problems has been stressed by several authors who clearly recognize that restoration of memory functioning after brain injury is almost certainly impossible once the acute stage has passed (Berg, Koning-Haanstra & Deelman, 1991; Glisky, in press; Sohlberg & Mateer, 1989; Wilson, 1991). Berg et al. (1991) made the importance of compensation quite explicit to their head-injured, memory-impaired patients by providing each of them with a book containing a set of rules, one of which states: "Try to accept that a deficient memory cannot be cured; make a more efficient use of your remaining capacities; use external aids when possible" (p. 101).

Despite general agreement that a compensatory approach is probably the most useful one to adopt for people with organic memory problems, there is little general agreement or clarity concerning the nature of those compensations for memory problems experienced in daily life by these people.

The *Concise Oxford English Dictionary* (1990) offers a number of definitions for the verb *compensate* of which the closest in meaning to our present debate would seem to be to: "offset a disability or frustration by development in another direction" (p. 232). However, this begs whether mechanisms should be employed for this development or change to take place. In a recent thoughtful and detailed article, Bäckman and Dixon (1992) provided a theoretical framework for psychological compensation. They distinguished the following four basic steps in the progression of compensatory behavior: (a) origins, (b) mechanisms, (c) forms, and (d) consequences. Each of these stages is worth considering in some detail in light of their application to organic memory impairment.

ORIGINS

According to Bäckman and Dixon, compensatory behavior arises when there is either (a) a decrease in a given skill without an accompanying decrease in the environmental demands placed on a person, or (b) an increase in environmental demands without an increase in the skills required for successful performance. The former is typically seen following organic memory impairment. Any kind of brain injury or disease is likely to cause a decrease in cognitive functioning. Memory impairments are not only common, but deeply handicapping because they are likely to prevent return to work and independent living (British Psychological Society Working Party Report, 1989). Consequently, if a memory-impaired person tries to return to a former lifestyle, there will certainly be a mismatch between the present impoverished level of memory functioning and the demands of everyday life.

Even when environmental demands are reduced in such circumstances, the mismatch may still be there if compensatory mechanisms are not employed. A reduction in environmental demands without accompanying employment of compensatory strategies will be insufficient to overcome difficulties experienced by severely memory-impaired people, who may be quite unable to remember where they are, where they are going, what they have just done or said, or what they are about to do. Even those with milder problems may miss appointments, get lost on journeys, forget people's names, lose their belongings, and so forth.

According to Bäckman and Dixon (1992), compensatory behavior does not always follow when a mismatch occurs. For example, if there is a high degree of contextual support, self-initiated compensation may not be necessary. It is believed that compensatory behavior decreases as a function of increasing contextual support. The latter is similar to environmental adaptations recommended for people with severe intellectual impairment (Wilson, 1989a; 1989b; in press). One of the simplest ways to help such people is to structure the environment so they rely less on memory. Examples include labeling doors, closets, and drawers, or using other people as substitutes for memory. One patient (known to the author) with dense amnesia and Korsakoff's syndrome uses no compensatory strategies, but lives quite comfortably and happily in a hostel for psychiatric patients where the staff members tell him when to get up, when and where to go to breakfast, when and where to go to the sheltered workshop, and so forth.

One could argue that such *contextual support* is a type of compensation because other people are implementing approaches to enable the memory-impaired person to survive better in the environment. In terms of the definition referred to earlier, the contextual support would count as compensation as it is employed to "offset a disability or function" (*Concise Oxford English Dictionary*, 1990, p. 232). Bäckman and Dixon might argue, however, as their framework seems to imply, that compensation has to emanate from the disabled individual.

Another dimension considered important by Bäckman and Dixon, in relation to the origins of compensation, is the severity of any given deficit. Severity is believed to affect the extent to which compensation occurs. They suggest that the likelihood of using compensatory behavior follows a U-shaped curve, with moderately impaired people being more likely to compensate, mildly impaired people unaware of the need to compensate, and those with severe deficits lacking the skills required to implement compensatory behavior. One of the examples given in their 1992 article is that the use of memory aids is more likely to be seen in normal elderly adults who are aware of their memory failures than among younger adults or among people with Alzheimer's disease.

The most severely amnesic patient known to the author is CW (Wilson & Wearing, in press), a musician who developed herpes simplex virus encephalitis in 1985. Although he regularly and frequently makes use of his diary (see Fig. 8.1), his entries are almost entirely devoted to recording his impression that he has just woken up this moment. Thus, the entries cannot be regarded as compensatory measures for his everyday memory failures.

CW is preoccupied with this state of just awakening, and has been like this for over 9 years at the time of writing in April 1994. The only strategies that appear to offer help to this man are the environmental adaptations or contextual support described previously. Wilson (in press) described these in greater detail. Wilson (1991) also reported on six patients in the long-term follow-up study who were using no aids or strategies at all. All six people were in long-term, institutional care, thus possibly providing further support for Bäckman and Dixon's claim that those with severe impairments are less likely to engage in compensatory behavior. It is harder to find evidence for the claim that those with milder impairments are reluctant to use such aids. All those in Wilson's follow-up study had moderate or severe deficits when seen initially, with none having mild deficits.

FIG. 8.1. Part of one page of CW's diaries.

However, one patient who had relatively mild memory problems, and who proved difficult to help, was seen recently by the writer and a colleague, Jonathan Evans. The subject is a 32-year-old man who has a history of epilepsy following a head injury that occurred when he was at school. Nevertheless, he managed to obtain a PhD in mathematics despite certain memory difficulties. He is an intellectually able person, although he is somewhat eccentric and disorganized. We thought we knew how to help him compensate for his memory problems, but we failed in this pursuit. Among the possible reasons for our failure were the following (a): He had sufficient memory for certain everyday activities to be resolved satisfactorily, and therefore he felt he did not need compensatory aids. His reluctance to use efficient compensations may be explained by a partial reinforcement effect (Rimm & Masters, 1979). In other words, he was receiving sufficient reinforcement from certain partial successes in daily life for him to get by. (b) We were unable to identify specific problems faced by this man because he kept shifting the goal posts. On one occasion, his most pressing need was for help in organizing a paper he was writing; on another occasion, he wanted help in remembering people he met at a bridge club. In general, he was vague and nonspecific about his problems. (c) Because we only saw the subject once every 2 weeks, it was impossible to provide the regular prompting and encouragement needed to ensure a more systematic and efficient use of any program we wished him to follow. (d) The man's lifestyle was restricted because he lived at home with his parents and was unemployed, therefore he did not need to change his behavior much to function adequately in those circumstances.

Such an example could be used in support of Bäckman and Dixon's U-shaped model. In general, it is not easy to persuade brain-injured people with memory problems to use compensatory strategies. Many of them think it is cheating in some way or, at least, will prevent natural recovery from occurring, and most will, of course, forget to employ aids without considerable persuasion and teaching.

MECHANISMS

The second step in Bäckman and Dixon's temporal progression is the mechanism by which a match is achieved between the skill deficit and everyday demands. They suggest that most matches are achieved in one of two ways: Either the deficit is counterbalanced by an increase in time and effort, or a substitute skill is employed. A third, less often used, mechanism is adjustment or adaptation to the new situation by changing expectations, selecting new tasks, or relaxing criteria of success. Examples can be found for each of these mechanisms being employed by brain-injured patients.

One head-injured patient of mine returned to work at a demanding post in the civil service after several months at a rehabilitation center. He experienced difficulties coping with the demands of work. He spent long hours at his workplace and brought assignments home so that his wife could help him. He believed he was achieving as much as he had prior to his accident, and at first his employers were sympathetic toward this previously excellent employee. Eventually, however, he was made redundant by his employers who were disatisfied with his work, and thus his efforts to compensate failed to match the demands placed on him.

The second mechanism is to employ a substitutable or different skill to meet environmental demands. This approach is similar to the functional adaptation approach proposed by Luria (1963), or the method Wilson (1989a) described as using an alternative means to achieve a final goal. Such an approach is frequently used by occupational therapists working with people with motor difficulties. For example, if a patient with rheumatoid arthritis is unable to button up clothes, or a hemiplegic patient is unable to peel potatoes, they can achieve these tasks by using alternatives to the usual manner. The clothes of the rheumatoid arthritic patient might be fitted with Velcro, and the hemiplegic patient might be given a spiked potato holder to help keep the potato steady while being peeled with the nonhemiplegic hand.

Similarly, people with memory problems can be given one of a large range of external aids to help them remember in a different way. Thus, they are encouraged to use a substitutable skill. However, there are problems in persuading people to use such aids, or to use them effectively. Sohlberg and Mateer (1989); Zencius, Wesolowski, Krankowski, and Berke (1991); Wilson (1992); Glisky (in press); and Kapur (in press), all provided descriptions of teaching the use of external aids.

An example of the successful use of external memory aids by a memory-impaired person is provided later in this chapter. Suffice it to say here that external aids are probably the most helpful compensations for the greatest number of people, and are most likely to be used in the long term. In the long-term follow-up study referred to earlier (Wilson, 1991), 22 different kinds of compensatory strategies were reported by 38 patients. Of the 22, 14 were external aids (Wilson, in press).

The third mechanism in the compensatory framework of Bäckman and Dixon—whereby people adjust to the mismatch between skill and environmental demand—is to change goals, expectations, or criteria of success. Such adaptation is almost certainly employed by the majority of memory-impaired people who live outside hospital care, in addition to the use of external (or internal) aids and strategies. A young law student, JC, became severely amnesic following a cerebral hemorrhage at the age of 20. After a period of rehabilitation, he was able to live alone and obtain employment. He survives by making efficient use of a number of external memory aids.

However, he needed to adjust to his changed cognitive circumstances; instead of expecting to become a lawyer with a good income, he is now employed making cane chairs. Although he realizes how much his life has changed, he gains self-esteem from the fact that he is independent despite his severe handicap. He is often asked to appear on television or radio as an example of how it is possible to compensate (or partly compensate) for severe memory difficulties, and he is now one of the most active members of a local group composed of memory-impaired people and their families who meet monthly for mutual support, information, and advice.

A different, but equally effective, form of adjustment for some people is to put their changed circumstances down to another cause. For example, one man was a successful television journalist prior to a severe head injury that left him with quite marked memory difficulties. Eventually he returned to his former job, although he was no longer actually seen on television. His memory remained poor, but his explanation for his changed circumstances was that he had suffered a loss of confidence. He believed this was brought on by psychologists, therapists, and other health-service professionals who kept telling him he had a poor memory. The man was coping reasonably well, was in paid employment, had recently married, and was living in a decent house, but his previously good journalistic skills were no longer in evidence.

FORMS OF COMPENSATORY BEHAVIOR

According to Bäckman and Dixon's (1992) theoretical framework, compensatory behavior may be classified in a manner dependent on the extent to which it differs from the behavior of a normal person in a given situation. The difference may be quantifiable, in that the person needing to compensate uses the same skills as those used by the normal population, but more time and effort are needed to achieve results. Alternatively, the difference may be qualitative, in which case substitutable skills are used. These substitutable skills may be ones that normal people possess but typically do not use, or they may be completely new.

We saw earlier how some memory-impaired people exert considerable effort in their attempts to perform as well as they did prior to neurological insult. Indeed, one of the most common findings among patients referred for memory therapy is their reluctance to use any form of compensation because they believe that memory will recover if normal methods are employed. To the question, Do you use anything to help your memory such as a notebook, tape recorder, or personal organizer?, a likely answer is, No, I don't want to rely on things like that; I want my memory to improve on its own.

One may also observe patients making heroic efforts to remember by focusing on the material to be remembered or giving self-instructions. Such attempts may be effective if memory problems are secondary to attentional deficits, but not if there is genuine amnesia. Repetition is another method used by normal people and patients to remember something new. Although it is a widely used method for acquiring skills, repetition on its own is likely to be an inefficient or ineffective method when used by people with significant memory deficits. There are ways in which repetition or repetitive practice can be made more efficient, and this applies to both normal and memory-impaired subjects. One of these is distributed practice, rather than massed practice (Harris, 1992). In the former, practice is distributed over time; this encourages more effective learning than when the same amount of practice is fitted into a short space of time.

Resistance to other forms of compensation, such as external memory aids, should be discouraged because there is no evidence to suggest that using them prevents or slows down recovery of memory, and it is quite normal for people with good memories to use external memory aids and other methods of compensation. For example, Harris (1980) described how common such aids are for students and housewives. By persuading memory-impaired people to use compensatory techniques as a substitutable skill, we encourage them to engage in normal behavior. The difference is that compensations can be the lifeline to independent life for people with amnesia, such as JC mentioned earlier, whereas for most of us they simply make life more convenient.

JC, who is remarkably adept at compensating for his difficulties, claims he could not survive without his compensations. He says that he tries to make the system foolproof and weblike so that it is impossible for anything to slip through. If he misses something with one of his aids, he picks it up with another. His three main aids are a small recorder (dictaphone), a filofax (organizer), and a watch with an alarm. Appointments are recorded on the dictaphone. entered into the filofax, and programmed in the watch alarm. Ongoing information is also recorded on the dictaphone. Each evening he transcribes important information from the dictaphone into a journal. He also uses a series of sticky back ("post it") notes and a menu chart to ensure he does not eat the same food several days in a row.

Unfortunately, most people have far greater difficulty than JC in using compensatory aids so competently. Employing the aids is a memory task, so it is not surprising that problems arise for many people. With sufficient ingenuity, patience, and teaching, however, it is possible to ensure efficient and practical use of external aids.

Internal strategies such as mnemonics are also examples of compensations that are used at one time or another by the majority of the population. For example, in Britain and the United States, we remember how many days are in each month by repeating the rhyme that begins, "Thirty days has September." People in other countries use the knuckles of the hand to remind themselves of the longer months of the year and the dips between the knuckles to remember the shorter months. Such verbal and visual aids enable us to remember material in a particular order. Once again, if we persuade memory-impaired people to use mnemonics as aids to learning, we are encouraging normal behavior. In practice, however, memory-impaired people rarely use mnemonics spontaneously because they cannot remember to put them into practice. Nevertheless, as I have argued elsewhere (e.g., Wilson, 1992), mnemonics can enable memory-impaired to learn some particularly useful information, such as the names of their neighbors. Learning via a mnemonic strategy is almost always quicker than learning through repetition (Wilson, 1987). Moffat (1992) described some of the most commonly used mnemonics in rehabilitation.

In addition to artificial mnemonic systems, Harris (1992) described another category of internal mnemonics—those that are learned naturally, such as the tendency for adults to recall the last few items first when asked for free recall of a word list, and concentrating on items not previously recalled when attempting to learn a list of words. This may seem an obvious thing to do because people would not want to waste time and effort remembering things they had already learned. However, although children show a recency effect, they do not adopt the strategy of spending more time on previously failed items until they are between the ages of 7 and 9 years (Masur, McIntyre, & Flavell, 1973). Harris (1992) suggested that we all use a multitude of natural strategies that are not normally thought of as compensations because they are so much a part of our normal memory skills. This is presumably what Bäckman and Dixon (1992) would call *automatic*, rather than *deliberate*, compensations. Most amnesic subjects with an impaired primacy effect and intact recency effect, when asked for free recall of a list of words, will naturally say the last few first. Some, however, adopt a strategy of rehearsing the first few items because they know they will forget these. Hence, they succeed in reproducing the first one or more items at the expense of forgetting the last two or three.

So far we have discussed compensatory strategies that are used both by those with and without memory deficits. Are there any skills developed by memory-impaired people that are not normally used by people without memory problems? The examples given by Bäckman and Dixon include the Braille system used by people with visual impairments, or the implementation of higher order cognitive systems used by older typists (Salthouse, 1984). In the latter case, however, it is hard to see how these are genuinely new skills, rather than latent skills that are brought into play more and more as the component skills (such as tapping rate or reaction time) deteriorate.

Similarly, various compensatory strategies used by brain-injured people are typically the same as those used by people without brain injury. It is true that some brain-injured people will use certain cognitive strategies to compensate. For example, one of my patients with a short-term memory difficulty will say, "Please can you repeat that," or "please go slower," or "let me make sure I have understood that correctly." The frequency with which he does this may be unusual, but the actual behavior is seen in normal populations. Likewise, JC, the young man with a pure amnesic syndrome described earlier, interrupts regularly to say that he needs to record part of the conversation. Whether we can describe this as a genuinely new skill learned to compensate for amnesia is open to debate.

There are a few compensatory aids or strategies specifically designed for memory-impaired people, and these perhaps come closest to new techniques not normally used by the general population, However, even here we could argue that the component skills are no different from those normal people would use. I am referring to some of the new electronic computer systems that are beginning to be employed as prosthetic memories.

The first of these is the NeuroPage (Hersh & Treadgold, 1992)—a simple and portable paging system that can be attached to a belt. Larry Treadgold, the engineer father of a head-injured son, and Neil Hersh, a neuropsychologist, combined their skills to produce a programmable messaging system utilizing an arrangement of microcomputers linked to a conventional computer memory and, by telephone, to a paging company (see Fig. 8.2).

The scheduling of reminders or cues for each individual is entered into the computer, and from then on no further human interfacing is necessary. At the appropriate time on the appropriate date, the individual user's files

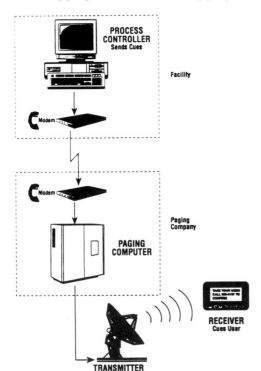

FIG. 8.2. The NeuroPage System (with permission from Hersh and Treadgold).

are accessed to determine which reminder is to be delivered. This is then transmitted by modem to the terminal, where the reminder is converted and transmitted as a wireless radio signal that can only be received by the pager of the particular user. A flashing light and audible chirp alert the user to the incoming message, which is then graphically displayed on the screen of the NeuroPage receiver. Once the message appears, the user is requested to telephone a person or an answer service to confirm the message has been received. Without this confirmation, the message is repeated.

NeuroPage users can control everything with one large button that is easy to control—even for those with motor difficulties. It avoids most existing aids' problems, and it is highly portable—even more so than the Power Book or similar portable computers. NeuroPage has an audible alarm that can be adapted to vibrate if required, together with an accompanying explanatory message, unlike many watch alarms. It is not embarrassing for the majority of users and may even convey prestige. Perhaps the biggest advantage of NeuroPage is that once it is programmed it is easy to use, whereas many other systems require considerable time for memory-impaired people to learn how to handle them—with most being abandoned before this learning is achieved.

The use of computers as prosthetic memories is still in its infancy, but it has significant potential. As Glisky (in press) pointed out, computers have great power for storing and producing on demand all kinds of information relevant to an individual's functioning in everyday life. Some have used computers as aids for activities of daily living. For example, Kirsch, Levine, Fallon-Krueger, and Jaros (1987), and Kirsch, Levine, Lajiness-O'Neill, and Schnyder (1992) used computers as "interactive task guidance systems." These systems provided a series of cues to guide patients through a series of steps needed to perform practical tasks, such as baking and janitorial activities. The computer acts as a compensatory device by providing step-by-step instructions to complete a task. The user needs little knowledge of computer operation and, like NeuroPage, responds by pressing a single key to indicate the instruction has been followed.

Cole and Dehdashti (1990) and Bergman and Kemmerer (1991) also designed individual computer interventions for brain-damaged patients with a variety of cognitive impairments. Each intervention enables the patient to perform an activity of daily living, such as keeping a record of previous telephone conversations and writing a personal check. Glisky (in press) discussed the role of computers in rehabilitation in further detail.

CONSEQUENCES OF COMPENSATORY BEHAVIOR

Basically, the consequences of compensatory behavior can be classified as *successful* or *unsuccessful,* with the former being those that are functional or adaptive. However, as Bäckman and Dixon (1992) pointed out, we do not know whether successful or unsuccessful consequences are more frequent. In the case of memory-impaired, brain-injured people, this probably depends on a number of factors, including: (a) the age of the person, (b) the degree of severity of the memory impairment, (c) the presence or absence of other cognitive impairments, (d) the person's lifestyle (both pre- and post-morbid), (e) individual personality, (f) type of rehabilitation offered, and (g) the amount of time passed since the onset of the problem. We know from the long-term, follow-up study (Wilson, 1991) that those with widespread cognitive deficits are less likely to compensate, and that the use of compensations is likely to increase once the early stages of rehabilitation have passed.

Baltes (1987) discussed the negative trade-off of compensation, whereby compensatory efforts in one domain of functioning may be carried out at the expense of functioning in other areas. An example might be infants who are given a left cerebral hemispherectomy at an early age. Most go on to develop reasonable language functioning in the right cerebral hemsiphere, but the cost is a reduction in the visuospatial skills in which the right hemi-sphere would normally specialize (Dennis & Kohn, 1975). In a language-dominated society, the gains probably outweigh the losses, although in some societies visuospatial skills could be equally or even more important.

In addition to the concept of negative trade-off, Bäckman and Dixon pointed out three other examples in which compensatory behaviors may have maladaptive consequences. First, compensatory behavior hinders, rather than optimizes, efficient utilization of available resources. Eaves and Klonoff (1970) provided the example of people with visual handicaps who concentrate all efforts on using their residual visual capacities, thus hindering the utilization of substitutable skills. A similar example would be the physically handicapped person who puts so much effort into learning to walk that he or she misses out on the opportunities for life satisfaction offered if he or she were to become wheelchair independent. CW, the densely amnesic patient described pre-viously, provides another example. He is constantly trying to capture the moment of just awakening by writing in his diary, but this leads nowhere and he refuses to accept previous entries as evidence that he must have been awake to record.

LeVere and LeVere (1982) suggested that, following brain injury, a patient's compensatory behavior may interfere with the residual capacities of the injured system. Patterson and Wilson (1990) reported on a patient who lost the ability to read initial letters of words through the visual route. However, he was able to read these if he traced the letters with his fingers (i.e., used a tactile route). He would only do this if prompted by the psychologists. When left alone, he tried to read in the way he had always read and believed his problem could be solved by the prescription of new reading glasses. Thus, he was compensating by putting all his efforts into the normal procedure and inhibiting development of a more skilled tactile reading system.

Second, compensatory behaviors intended to have positive consequences may instead have negative repercussions for the producer as well as other people. The illustration offered in support of this involves the parent of a physically handicapped child. The former compensates for the child in social-cognitive situations by initiating and prompting, rather than by helping to develop the child's social and verbal development. An example from memory therapy would be the relative who acts as the main memory compensation rather than allowing the memory-impaired person to develop strategies that would lead to independence.

Third, and perhaps most relevant as far as memory rehabilitation is concerned, compensatory behavior may be primarily positive for the individual concerned, but may have negative consequences for that individual's environment. The amnesic patient who is constantly interrupting to record something on a tape recorder or in a diary is acting sensibly on the one hand, but disruptively on the other hand. Such behavior can be infuriating, and might lead to loss of friends or avoidance of social interaction from members of the community.

Despite the problems outlined herein, and notwithstanding that any particular piece of compensatory behavior is less than optimal, "it may still reduce the mismatch between accessible skills and environmental demands" (Bäckman & Dixon, 1992, p. 277). Partial success or satisfaction is consistent with the concept of *compensation*. This would certainly seem true for memory-impaired people. Although the compensatory behavior might be less than perfect and less efficient than the behavior of people with normal memory functioning, it would seem to enable memory-impaired people to lead a life of reasonable quality and independence. Wilson (1991) demonstrated that memory-impaired people who were independent (i.e., in paid employment, living alone, or in full-time education) were likely to be using more than five memory aids, techniques, or strategies. Employing the chi-square test and categorizing the 43 subjects into those using more than five aids and those using five or fewer, there was a significant difference between those who were and were not independent ($\chi^2 = 10.87$, d.f. = 1, $p < .001$).

MAJOR TYPES OF COMPENSATORY AIDS
FOR MEMORY-IMPAIRED PEOPLE

Kapur (in press) classified external memory aids into two major types: those that are part of a person's environment, and those that are portable and external. Kapur subdivided the former into: (a) personal environmental cues, (b) proximal environmental cues, and (c) distal environmental cues. Examples of personal environmental cues include putting a ring or a watch on the wrong hand, or writing a message on the back of the hand. Such tactics are of limited value, especially for people with organic memory problems who may not remember the purpose of the cue, and for whom sensory habituation may set in.

Proximal environmental cues refer to features in the design of a machine or in the layout of a room or vehicle that could aid memory. For example, storage units could be clearly labeled, be of distinct shape and size, and be in a special position. Machines such as cars, ovens, photocopiers, or computers can have built-in alarms to remind users to do something they need to do at an appropriate time. The consequences of poor ergonomic design can be frustrating for all of us, as Norman (1988) pointed out so succinctly. These consequences are even more extreme for people with severe memory problems.

Distal environmental cues refer to those inherent in the design of homes, other buildings, streets, towns, or transportation networks. The likelihood of memory lapses can be increased or reduced by environmental design. Norman's example of the lack of a distal environmental cue is a door that does not indicate whether it is to be pushed, pulled, or slid open. Colored lines in hospitals, airports, or factories that lead a person from one area or department to another are examples of distal environmental cues. Such cues can remind a person where to go and what to do.

Under the category of *portable external memory aids*, Kapur (in press) discussed a range of stationery aids such as "post it" notes, telephone message pads, and "things to do" lists. He also considered mechanical aids such as alarm clocks and timers. In a further section, Kapur dealt with electronic memory aids, and considered features such as size, power supply, transfer of data to personal computers and printers, price, manufacturer, screen, keyboard, memory capacity, ease of learning, text-storage features, and the nature of alarm systems.

Kapur considered in some detail the application of memory aids in rehabilitation settings. Although few systematic studies have been carried out (Fowler, Hart, & Sheehan, 1982; Naugle, Naugle, Prevey, & Delaney, 1988), certain factors are likely to be important in determining the success or otherwise of these aids as applied to real-life settings. Some of these were discussed earlier. Age, educational level, and premorbid knowledge and skills will probably play a role in whether such aids are used effectively. I found that only 2 of the 44 people in my long-term follow-up study were using a personal organizer (a filofax), and none was using an electronic organizer. Both of the subjects using a filofax were well educated and young. However, during the time of neurological insult of the 44 subjects (between 1978 and 1985), neither filofax nor electronic organizers were in common usage. Because they are used much more widely now, I would expect a similar follow-up study—held in 10 years, of people who sustained brain injury in the years 1985–1990—to indicate much more usage of both nonelectronic and electronic organizers. A young head-injured man who was seen by the author recently was in fact using a filofax efficiently. His mother pointed out that because he had used one before his accident, it was natural that he should continue to use it in changed circumstances.

Employing this same argument, if we can identify the aids or compensatory strategies used in the immediate past by brain-injured patients, we may be more successful in encouraging their use to alleviate some of the problems encountered after brain injury.

At present, we have some information on the particular strategies and aids favored by a group of memory-impaired people several years after cerebral insult (Wilson, 1991). In a group of 44 subjects, the most widely used aids were notebooks and written notes, with 29 subjects claiming to use this method, 28 claiming to use mental retracing of events, 25 using a wall calendar or chart, 25 writing lists of things to do or buy, 23 using an alarm clock, 22 asking other people to remind them to do something, 21 using a watch with the date, and 19 using an appointments diary.

The stategies used the least were first-letter mnemonics (3 people), personal organizers (2), leaving notes in special places so as not to miss them (2), using rhymes (1), using a daily timetable (1), making a rating about pleasantness (1), chunking (1), and tying a knot in a handkerchief (1). In the United States, tying string round a finger is analagous to the British knot in the handkerchief.

The increased use of memory aids and strategies since discharge from rehabilitation suggests that many memory-impaired people are able to learn to compensate for their memory difficulties. However, specialist help may be needed to increase the effectiveness or efficiency of compensatory techniques.

TEACHING THE USE OF COMPENSATIONS

The reason memory-impaired people have difficulty using external memory aids is because *remembering* to use them is a memory task. If relatives or therapists simply provide an aid and expect the patient to do all the rest, failure is highly likely. As Intons-Peterson and Newsome (1992) pointed out, a number of different cognitive processes are involved in using even a simple external memory aid. Users need to be able to identify situations in which a memory aid will be particularly useful, they need to be motivated to use the aid, and they require an aid that is appropriate to the task in hand. They must also remember how to use the particular aid to operate it effectively.

Sohlberg and Mateer (1989) described a method for teaching the use of memory notebooks. They employed a purpose-built notebook with five different sections, each one of which was distinguished by its own specific color. Contents included orientation, memory log, calendar, things to do, and transportation. Training was divided into the three areas: acquisition, application, and adaptation. Kapur (in press) argued that the latter can be combined into two stages: (a) learning about the aid and its features, and (b) using the aid in everyday situations.

Teaching memory-impaired people to use electronic organizers requires a specific training program according to Kapur (in press). He recommends: (a) the use of backward chaining (breaking a task down into small steps) for teaching a particular procedure such as how to enter a telephone number into the machine, (b) the incorporation of certain principles such as the method of vanishing cues (Glisky & Schacter, 1987) and errorless learning (Wilson, Baddeley, Evans, & Shiel, 1994) to enhance learning, (c) feedback and encouragement, and (d) the use of helpcards that summarize the steps involved in a particular operation and can form a backup if problems arise outside the therapy session. Kapur also recommended that training in the clinic should resemble real-life situations as much as possible by referring to concrete examples from each patient's daily routine.

Kapur's approach does not differ greatly from the recommendations of Wilson (1989b, 1992), which follow principles from behavior modification combined with findings from cognitive psychology. For example, in planning a treatment program for memory-impaired people, the following steps are helpful: (a) define the problem, (b) identify the goals or aims of treatment, (c) measure the deficit to obtain a baseline, (d) decide on the most suitable treatment strategy, (e) plan the treatment, (f) begin the treatment, (g) monitor and evaluate progress, (h) change the procedure if necessary, and (i) plan for generalization. Examples are provided in which these steps teach new information, but they could just as easily teach the use of an external memory aid.

The use of errorless learning for teaching new skills and information to people with severe memory impairment has been investigated in recent years by Baddeley and Wilson (Baddeley, 1992; Baddeley & Wilson, 1994; Wilson et al., 1994). We set out to answer the question, Do amnesic subjects learn better when prevented from making mistakes during the learning process? In an experimental study with 16 densely amnesic subjects and 16 young control subjects, we attempted to teach two lists of words using a stem-completion procedure. With one list we encouraged guessing, and in the other list we prevented guessing from occurring as far as this was possible. For example, in the guessing or errorful list, the tester said, "I am thinking of a five-letter word beginning with *TH*. Can you guess what it is?" Following several guesses, the correct answer was provided and the subject wrote it down. We ensured that at least one error was made for each word. In the second condition, we prevented errors from occurring by providing the correct answer immediately.

For example, the tester would say, "I am thinking of a five-letter word beginning with *TH* and the word is *thumb*. Please write that down." Words and conditions were counterbalanced across subjects.

The main difference was this: In one condition, errors were present during initial learning, in the other condition, errors were prevented during that time. Nine test trials followed the original learning trials. Test trials were spread over a 30-minute period. On each test trial, subjects were asked, "One of the words you wrote down just now began with *TH*. Can you remember what it was?" Feedback was provided for each word. All 16 amnesic subjects recalled more words correctly under the errorless learning condition (Baddeley & Wilson, 1994).

Our explanation for this robust phenomenon was that explicit memory is required to eliminate errors. Amnesic subjects have to rely on implicit memory, which is poor at error elimination. Once errors are made, amnesic subjects have little ability to eliminate them, and the errors may become strengthened or reinforced. Therefore, it would seem better to prevent errors from occurring in the first place.

The next step was to see if the principle of errorless learning could be applied to real-life problems faced by memory-impaired people. We carried out several single-case experiments with a number of neurologically impaired people with different diagnoses, differing degrees of severity of brain injury, and at different times postinsult. We also employed a variety of tasks from learning people's names, to learning items of general knowledge, to learning to program an electronic organizer. In each case, errorless learning proved superior to errorful or trial-and-error learning (Wilson et al., 1994).

The electronic aid experiment was conducted with a 35-year-old man diagnosed as having Korsakoff's syndrome. His general level of ability was in the low-average range, and he had some executive or frontal lobe difficulties in addition to his amnesia. Two tasks were selected, both of which involved programming an electronic memory aid. Each task was composed of six steps. One task was to enter a telephone number into the machine, and the other task was to enter a memo. The two tasks were randomly allocated to an errorful (write a memo) or errorless (enter a telephone number) learning condition. In the errorful condition the six steps were demonstrated to the subject, who was then asked to enter the new memo number himself. He was given feedback after each of the six steps, and was corrected when necessary. Thirteen trials were given. Following the first nine trials, there was a 5-minute break before the last four trials were given. The subject did not learn the task.

In the errorless condition, the subject was prevented from making mistakes during the first nine trials by following a list of written instructions. A 5-minute break followed, and then the subject was asked to complete the last four trials alone. He needed minimal help with the first of these, but the final three trials were completed independently. Thus, the subject failed to learn the task under the errorful condition, but succeeded under the errorless condition.

While we are waiting for the results from a larger study investigating errorless learning with memory-impaired people in 13 different centers, it would seem fair to suggest that the principle of enhancing learning in people with severe memory problems by preventing errors during the learning process seems promising.

CONCLUSIONS AND FUTURE DIRECTIONS

This chapter has described the nature of memory problems following brain injury. Bäckman and Dixon's (1992) theoretical framework of psychological compensation was used to illustrate the origins, mechanisms, forms, and consequences of compensatory behavior seen in people with severe memory problems. The major kinds of compensatory aids for this population were described, and consideration was given to the best ways to teach or encourage compensatory behavior.

Although memory-impaired people and their families should not be led to believe that restoration of memory functioning can occur once the period of natural recovery is over, they can nevertheless be taught how to compensate for some of the problems arising from their impairment.

Advances are being made in the design and implementation of external aids and on better structuring of the environment, hence reducing the load on memory. It is hoped that these advances will continue with evermore sophistication. Additionally, further development of the errorless learning technique described earlier, as well as other methods of improving learning, can be developed and implemented to teach people to compensate more efficiently.

REFERENCES

Bäckman, L., & Dixon, R. A. (1992). Psychological compensation: A theoretical framework. *Psychological Bulletin, 112,* 259–283.

Baddeley, A. D. (1992). Implicit memory and errorless learning: A link between cognitive theory and neuropsychological rehabilitation? In L. Squire & N. Butters (Eds.), *Neuropsychology of memory* (2nd ed., pp. 309–314). New York: Guilford Press.

Baddeley, A. D., & Wilson, B. A. (1994). When implicit learning fails: Amnesia and the problem of error elimination. *Neuropsychologia, 32,* 53–68.

Baltes, P. B. (1987). Theoretical propositions of life-span development psychology: On the dynamics between growth and decline. *Developmental Psychology, 23,* 611–626.

Berg, I. J., Koning-Haanstra, M., & Deelman, B. (1991). Long term effects of memory rehabilitation: A controlled study. *Neuropsychological Rehabilitation, 1,* 97–111.

Bergman, M. M., & Kemmerer, A. G. (1991). Computer enhanced self sufficiency: Part 2. Uses and subjective benefits of a text writer for an individual with traumatic brain injury. *Neuropsychology, 5*, 25–28.

British Psychological Society Working Party Report (1989). *Services for young adult patients with acquired brain damage.* Leicester: Author.

Cole, E., & Dehdashti, P. (1990). Interface design as a prosthesis for an individual with a brain injury. *SIGCHI Bulletin, 22*, 28–32.

Concise Oxford English Dictionary (1990). New York: Oxford University Press.

Dennis, M., & Kohn, B. (1975). Comprehension of syntax in infantile hemiplegics after cerebral hemidecortication; left hemisphere superiority. *Brain and Language, 2*, 472–482.

Eaves, L., & Klonoff, H. A. (1970). A comparison of blind and sighted children on a tactual and performance test. *Exceptional Children, 37*, 269–273.

Fowler, R. S., Hart, J., & Sheehan, M. (1982). A prosthetic memory: An application of the prosthetic environment concept. *Rehabilitation Counselling Bulletin, 16*, 80–85.

Glisky, E. L. (in press). Computers in memory rehabilitation. In A. D. Baddeley, B. A. Wilson, & F. N. Watts (Eds.), *Handbook of memory disorders.* Chichester: Wiley.

Glisky, E. L., & Schacter, D. L. (1987). Acquisition of domain specific knowledge in organic amnesia: Training for computer related work. *Neuropsychologia, 25*, 893–906.

Harris, J. E. (1980). Memory aids people use: Two interview studies. *Memory and Cognition, 8*, 31–38.

Harris, J. E. (1992). Ways to help memory. In B. A. Wilson & N. Moffat (Eds.), *Clinical management of memory problems* (2nd ed., pp. 59–85). London: Chapman & Hall.

Hersh, N. A., & Treadgold, L. G. (1992). *Prosthetic memory and cueing for survivors of traumatic brain injury.* Unpublished manuscript.

Intons-Peterson, M. J., & Newsome, G. I. (1992). External memory aids: effects and effectiveness. In D. J. Herrman, H. Weingartner, A. Searleman., & C. McEvoy (Eds.), *Memory improvement: Implications for memory theory* (pp. 101–121). New York: Springer-Verlag.

Kapur, N. (1988). *Memory disorders in clinical practice.* London: Butterworths.

Kapur, N. (in press). Memory aids in the rehabilitation of memory disordered patients. In A. D. Baddeley, B. A. Wilson, & F. N. Watts (Eds.), *Handbook of memory disorders.* Chichester: Wiley.

Kirsch, N. L., Levine, S. P., Fallon-Krueger, M., & Jaros, L. A. (1987). The microcomputer as an "orthotic" device for patients with cognitive deficits. *Journal of Head Trauma Rehabilitation, 2*, 77–86.

Kirsch, N. L., Levine, S. P., Lajiness-O'Neill, L., & Schnyder, M. (1992). Computer assisted interactive task guidance: Facilitating the performance of a simulated vocational task. *Journal of Head Trauma Rehabilitation, 7*, 13–25.

LeVere, N. D., & LeVere, T. E. (1982). Recovery of function after brain damage: Support for the compensation theory of the behavioral deficit. *Physiological Psychology, 10*, 165–174.

Luria, A. R. (1963). *Restoration of function after brain injury.* New York: Macmillan.

Masur, E. F., McIntyre, C. W., & Flavell, J. H. (1973). Developmental changes in appointment of study time in a multi trial free recall task. *Journal of Experimental Child Psychology, 15*, 237–246.

Miller, E. (1984). *Recovery and management of neuropsychological impairments.* Chichester: Wiley.

Moffat, N. (1992). Strategies of memory therapy. In B. A. Wilson & N. Moffat (Eds.), *Clinical management of memory problems* (2nd ed., pp. 86–119). London: Chapman and Hall.

Naugle, R., Naugle, C., Prevey, M., & Delaney, R. (1988). New digital watch as a compensatory device for memory dysfunction. *Cognitive Rehabilitation, 6*, 22–23.

Norman, D. A. (1988). *The psychology of everyday things.* New York: Basic Books.

Patterson, K. E., & Wilson, B. A. (1990). A rose is a rose or a nose: A deficit in initial letter identification. *Cognitive Neuropsychology, 7*, 447–477.

Rimm, D. C., & Masters, J. C. (1979). *Behaviour therapy: Techniques and empirical findings* (2nd ed.). New York: Academic Press.

Salthouse, T. A. (1984). Effects of age and skill in typing. *Journal of Experimental Psychology: General, 113*, 345–371.

Scoville, W. B., & Milner, B. (1957). Loss of recent memory after bilateral hippo-campal lesions. *Journal Neurology, Neurosurgery and Psychiatry, 20*, 11–21.

Sohlberg, M., & Mateer, C. (1989). Training use of compensatory memory books: A three stage behavioral approach. *Journal of Clinical and Experimental Neuropsychology, 11*, 871–891.

Wilson, B. A. (1987). *Rehabilitation of memory.* New York: Guilford Press.

Wilson, B. A. (1989a). Models of cognitive rehabilitation. In R. L. Wood & P. Eames (Eds.), *Models of brain injury rehabilitation* (pp. 117–141). London: Chapman and Hall.

Wilson, B. A. (1989b). Designing memory therapy programmes. In L. W. Poon, D. C. Rubin, & B. A. Wilson (Eds.), *Everyday cognition in adulthood and late life* (pp 615–638). Cambridge, England: Cambridge University Press.

Wilson, B. A. (1991). Long term prognosis of patients with severe memory disorders. *Neuropsychological Rehabilitation, 1*, 117–134.

Wilson, B. A. (1992). Memory therapy in practice. In B. A. Wilson & N. Moffat (Eds.), *Clinical management of memory problems* (2nd ed., pp. 120–153). London: Chapman Hall.

Wilson, B. A. (in press). Management and remediation of memory problems in brain injured adults. In A. D. Baddeley, B. A. Wilson, & F. N. Watts (Eds.), *Handbook of memory disorders.* Chichester: Wiley.

Wilson, B. A., Baddeley, A. D., Evans, J. J., & Shiel, A. (1994). Errorless learning in the rehabilitation of memory impaired people. *Neuropsychological Rehabilitation, 4*, 307–326.

Wilson, B. A., & Wearing, D. (in press). Prisoner of consciousness: A state of just awakening following encephalitis. In R. Campbell & M. Conway (Eds.), *Broken memories.* Oxford: Blackwell.

Zencius, A., Wesolowski, M. D., Krankowski, T., & Berke, W. H. (1991). Memory notebook training with traumatically brain injured clients. *Brain Injury, 5*, 321–325.

CHAPTER NINE

Plasticity and Compensation in Brain Memory Systems in Aging

Diana S. Woodruff-Pak
Temple University and Philadelphia Geriatric Center

Catherine Hanson
Temple University

Just as Nobel laureate, Rita Levi-Montalcini found it challenging to change perspectives in the field of developmental neurobiology to accept the phenomenon of cell death, researchers in the field of aging and neurobiology have experienced resistance in promoting the occurrence of brain plasticity in older organisms. Until the late 20th century, investigators did not include adult or older animals in their brain plasticity studies because they thought it was useless to even test plasticity in older organisms. This reluctance to investigate the effect of aging in studies of brain plasticity attests to the degree to which scientists form premature conclusions about adaptation in the older nervous system.

Behavioral, electrophysiological, and morphological evidence documents the continued expression of plasticity in the brains of adult mammals, including humans (Singer, 1992). The term *plasticity* is used in this chapter to represent adaptive capacity to change, including to learn and remember. At the neurobiological level, plasticity can be supported by numerous mechanisms. For example, profound modifications in the responses of individual neurons recorded electrophysiologically are observed when pharmacological agents are applied to them. In this circumstance, plasticity might be changes in neuronal firing rates resulting from the increased availability of specific neurotransmitters. Morphological substrates of brain plasticity have been observed as increased density of dendritic spines in the cortex of animals exposed to an enriched environment (e.g., Turner & Greenough, 1985). Another physical form of brain plasticity occurs as functional reorganization after brain lesions. Cortical tissue adjacent to the zone of destruction can recover functions in a use-dependent manner (Singer, 1992). Discussion of plasticity includes the capacity for behavioral change as represented in new learning and memory, along with the underlying chemical-structural-organizational changes that support learning and memory.

Compensation is a term that denotes a response to loss or deficiency. In the field of neuroscience, at present, it is challenging to find means to compensate once neurons are lost. Neurons are born with the individual and age with him or throughout the life span. A great difficulty in Alzheimer's disease (AD) is the tremendous loss of neurons—especially neurons in the medial-temporal lobes where memory systems reside. When we compensate, we must compensate using the neurons that remain. In the case of AD, compensation may be augmenting the neurohumoral factors in the brain to support the remaining neurons. In normal aging, there is a much greater brain substrate with which to work.

As measured on a behavioral level, processes of aging differentially affect aspects of learning and memory. Some components of encoding and retrieval appear relatively spared, whereas other components are impaired in every individual who survives to the age of 60 or older. Identification of the components of learning and memory, and their underlying brain memory systems that are relatively spared, may provide insights about interventions for compensation in learning and memory in old age. The possibility exists that preserved components of learning and memory, and preserved structures of brain memory systems, might be used to compensate for the components particularly impaired by aging processes.

Human long-term memory systems have been classified into two major forms: declarative (or explicit) and nondeclarative (or implicit; Cohen & Squire, 1980; Graf & Schacter, 1985; Squire, 1992). *Declarative memory* can be conceptualized as learning with awareness. It refers to the acquisition and retention of information about events and facts, and it is assessed by accuracy on recall and recognition tests (e.g., word-list learning). Four decades of research support the conclusion that medial-temporal/diencephalic memory circuits are critical for establishing long-term memory for events and facts (Squire, 1992). In contrast, there is considerable evidence that medial-temporal/diencephalic memory circuits are not critical for nondeclarative memory (Schacter, 1987; Shimamura, 1986; Solomon, Solomon, Vander Schaaf, & Perry, 1983). *Nondeclarative memory* may be conceptualized as learning without awareness that is measured by changes in performance. It consists of multiple, dissociable processes, including: (a) repetition priming effects; (b) acquisition and retention of motor, perceptual, or problem-solving skills; (c) simple classical conditioning; and (d) non-associative learning. Several independent brain memory systems have been identified that underlie these different forms of nondeclarative memory. Whereas declarative memory is significantly impaired by aging processes, some forms of non-declarative memory are relatively spared.

The first aim of this chapter is to establish that plasticity exists in cognition and its neural substrates in the aging brain. A second aim is to describe the effect of aging on various brain memory systems in an attempt to identify learning and memory components that are relatively spared by aging. A third aim is to consider the potential for compensation using the components that are spared to compensate for the components impaired by aging processes.

FACILITATORS OF BRAIN PLASTICITY

A most important point to be made in this chapter is that adaptability in the form of brain plasticity is present throughout adulthood and old age. Intervention strategies, such as enriching the environment, can reverse some of the deleterious performance observed in older organisms. Placing animals in enriched environments causes changes in behavior and physical changes in the brain including increased brain weight and dendritic branching. Previous behavioral experience is another prophylactic that appears to maintain performance in older organisms at the level of young organisms. Exposing an organism to a cognitive task at one point in the life span appears to preserve performance in later life. The mechanisms by which previous behavioral experiences protect later performance have yet to be discovered. A third means to achieve behavioral and brain plasticity is the use of cognition-enhancing compounds. These substances ameliorate cognitive function with a variety of mechanisms, such as affecting ion channels, neurotransmitter release, brain receptors, and second messengers.

Enriched Environments

There is a wealth of evidence that rearing mammals in an enriched environment results in a persisting increase in the structural complexity of neuronal elements in certain brain regions, and in improved performance in a variety of learning and memory tasks (Thompson, Donegan, & Lavond, 1985). Specifically, increased dendritic branching, spine densities, and spines (by implication, increased numbers of synapses) have been seen in cerebral cortex and cerebellar cortex in animals (usually rats, but also monkeys) raised in enriched versus individual-cage environments (e.g., Diamond, Linder, Johnson, Bennett, & Rosenzweig, 1975; Floeter & Greenough, 1979; Turner & Greenough, 1985). Such changes have been reported even when environmental enrichment is not initiated until middle age (Green, Greenough, & Schlumpf, 1983) or old age (Diamond, Johnson, Protti, Ott, & Kajisa, 1985).

Summary

The important contribution that these enrichment studies have made is that structural changes occur in the brain resulting from manipulations of the environment, and these structural changes have the potential to occur at any point in the life span. The brain retains its potential for plasticity from conception to death. Environmental and social enrichment are potentially effective compensations for isolation throughout life.

Previous Behavioral Experience

Cross-sectional studies of spatial abilities, such as maze learning in rodents and visual-spatial tasks in humans, have demonstrated large age differences in performance. In rats, these age-related impairments have been associated with deterioration of critical neural systems, typically involving hippocampal circuits (Barnes, 1979, 1988; de Toledo-Morrell, Morrell, & Fleming, 1984). Spatial impairment in humans with AD has often been interpreted to result as a consequence of hippocampal cholinergic dysfunction.

Beatty (1988) called explanations proposing neurobiological causes for age-related memory deficits hypotheses about the neural *hardware*. He also pointed out that studies of age differences in human memory implicate changes in strategies the subjects use. Cognitive strategies are identified as *software* in this scheme. Data from Beatty's laboratory suggest that old rats, like old humans, may modulate performance on spatial tasks by strategies or software.

Beatty, Bierley, and Boyd (1985) demonstrated that deficits in spatial working memory are not inevitable concomitants of aging in rats. Whereas 22-month-old rats first introduced to the eight-arm radial maze in old age typically show severe decrements in performance when compared with 3-month-old rats, deficits that are readily apparent in naive older rats can be prevented by training early in life. Rats first trained on an eight-arm radial maze at 3 months of age performed just as accurately at the age of 22 months.

From the perspective of Beatty and his associates, older rats perform well because they have learned to identify and process the salient extra-maze cues. They have acquired efficient software to perform this task. Another way to interpret these data is to suggest that the rats performing well on the task make use of external contextual cues.

An alternative or additional mechanism for the maintenance of optimal performance is that prior experience might retard processes of aging in the brain directly in a structural manner. Experience may protect the hardware as well as facilitating the development of efficient software. Port, Murphy, and Magee (1994) used the term, *use-induced plasticity* to suggest a neurobiological mechanism underlying retained ability in animals trained in early life. They pointed out that spatial learning in rats is highly correlated with general excitability of the hippocampal formation, and that experimental induction of hippocampal excitability with long-term potentiation (LTP) or kindling facilitates simple learning. Use-induced plasticity likely changes the brain itself, thus maintaining performance levels at the level of the younger organism.

In another study, aged rats exposed to long-term instrumental conditioning performed remarkably well in subsequent maze training (Port, Murphy, Magee, & Burns, 1993). Analysis of second-order facilitation at the perforant path-dentate synapse in the hippocampus of these young and older rats revealed no significant differences. Studies comparing untrained young and older rats showed significant differences in hippocampal responses (de Toledo-Morrell et al., 1984), although the capacity for structural plasticity in the hippocampus was demonstrated to remain in older rats (Geinisman, de Toledo-Morrell, Morrell, Persina, & Rossi, 1992). As a consequence of observing facilitated maze performance in instrumentally conditioned aged rats and hippocampal responses in these older rats that were comparable to the hippocampal responses of young rats, Port et al. (1993) concluded that use-induced plasticity may have a general positive effect on neurobiological function and learning performance. With use, the hardware (in this case, measured as hippocampal electrophysiological responses) was maintained so that it was not different in young and old rats.

Behavioral experience early in life facilitated performance in later life in rhesus monkeys. Novak, Suomi, Bowman, and Mohr (1991) tested four monkeys ranging in age from 23 to 27 years. These old animals had prior experience with the Wisconsin General Test Apparatus when they were adolescent or young adult monkeys (8–12 years previously). The performance of these monkeys was compared with naive old monkeys over 20 years of age, and with 15- and 2-year-old monkeys. Among the naive monkeys, the 15-year-olds performed best. However, the test-sophisticated monkeys over 23 years of age performed as well or better than their naive younger counterparts on every test except the visual acuity and delayed object recognition tasks. Limited experience with similar tests many years earlier apparently protected elderly monkeys from demonstrating typical age-related deficits. Mechanisms that account for the preservation of performance remain to be discovered.

In older rabbits, Coffin and Woodruff-Pak (1993) demonstrated that training on eyeblink classical conditioning (EBCC) at the age of 36 months resulted in excellent retention. Performance in the older rabbits 13 months after initial testing was not different from retention in rabbits aged 7 months at the time of the initial acquisition and 20 months in the first retention period. Although there were significant differences in acquisition between the 36- and 7-month-old rabbits, there were no significant differences in retention. Port et al. (1994) pointed out that enhancement or potentiation of hippocampal synaptic transmission has been observed during EBCC, as well as during instrumental conditioning. Training rabbits at the age of 36 months on the EBCC task may have resulted in use-induced plasticity similar to that observed in the Port et al. (1993) and Beatty et al. (1985) studies in rats, and even in the Novak et al. (1991) study in monkeys. Similarly, Port et al. (1994) observed age-related impairment in instrumental conditioning in 18-month-old rats as compared with 3-month-old rats, but there were no age differences in retention.

Summary

Learning and practicing a mental skill relatively early in life apparently protects the skill from impairment in later life. To compensate for documented age-related decline in some cognitive abilities, individuals might "exercise" these abilities in young adulthood and middle age. Just as physical skills benefit from exercise, the behavioral neuroscience data now indicate that mental skills are preserved with practice. Muscles atrophy from disuse, and neural circuits may also deteriorate when they are not activated. Training and testing of learning and memory tasks at one point in the life span preserve the ability when it is tested later in the life span.

Cognition-Enhancing Compounds

Compounds are being identified that enhance the plasticity for learning in the older mammalian brain. In the first author's rabbit laboratory, several compounds have been tested as potential cognition-enhancing drugs in older (and, in some cases, young) animals. Although these compounds are biochemically diverse, at least one dose level in all but one of the compounds significantly facilitated learning of EBCC in older rabbits. The compound with which we did not have success is a hormone. Of the compounds that facilitated acquisition, two are nootropic agents, one is a nicotinic cholinergic agonist, and one is a calcium channel blocker. Here we briefly present results with the hormone, one of the nootropic agents, and a nicotinic cholinergic agonist.

Hormones

Dehydroepiandrosterone sulfate (DHEAS) is a major secretory product of the adrenal cortex with no major biological action. In peripheral tissues, DHEAS is hydrolyzed to dehydroepiandrosterone (DHEA), a known precursor for the androgens and estrogens. Although DHEA has no apparent hormonal effects, the blood level of DHEAS is one of the highest of any steroid found in humans. This is the case until the second decade of life, when the level of DHEAS begins to fall: the level eventually falls to 10%–20% of its maximum values by the seventh grade.

DHEA has been shown to exhibit a number of beneficial effects in laboratory animals. For example, DHEA's regenerative ability was demonstrated when it reversed cell damage resulting from artificially induced lung tumors and breast cancer (Schwartz, Lawbart, & Pashko, 1988). In addition, DHEA and DHEAS have been shown to lessen the effect of diabetes and obesity (Roberts, Bologa, Flood, & Smith, 1987). In tissue culture, DHEA promotes the sprouting of neurites of newborn mouse hypothalamic/preoptic neurons. Roberts et al. viewed this finding as indicative of DHEA's possible role in regenerative processes.

Scopolamine is a compound used in earlier studies in animals and humans to model the anticholinergic effects of AD. Scopolamine creates a memory impairment in humans paralleling that seen in AD patients (Sunderland et al., 1986). DHEA and DHEAS improve the memory of young laboratory mice treated with scopolamine, suggesting that this steroid operates on the cholinergic neurotransmitter system (Flood, Smith, & Roberts, 1988). DHEAS improved retention in middle-aged and older mice to levels obtained in young mice (Flood & Roberts, 1988). As mentioned previously, DHEA levels decline dramatically in normal aging, and recently Sunderland et al. (1989) demonstrated that DHEAS levels are, on the average, 48% lower in AD patients than in age-matched controls.

We tested the cognition-enhancing effects of DHEA on EBCC in older rabbits (Flannery, Williams, & Woodruff-Pak, 1991) and found that, at a dose of 1.58 mg/kg, it had no effect on acquisition (see Fig. 9.1). Rabbits between the age of two and three years treated with vehicle (15% polyethylene glycol in sterile water) conditioned at the same rate as rabbits treated with DHEA. It is possible that other dose levels of DHEA would facilitate acquisition in older rabbits—but at a dose level effective in reversing scopolamine in mice, DHEA did not facilitate acquisition in older rabbits.

Nootropic Agent

The compound, DM-9384 recently named Nefiracetam (Anonymous, 1990), is a nootropic compound developed to improve impaired cognitive functioning in old age. This compound has demonstrated efficacy in facilitating learning

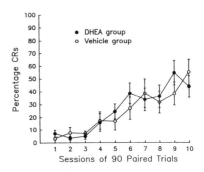

FIG. 9.1. Acquisition over 10 training days (90 paired tone and corneal airpuff trials per day) in the delay classical conditioning paradigm with a 750-msec interval between the tone-conditioned stimulus and corneal airpuff unconditioned stimulus. Subjects include 12 female retired breeder rabbits injected daily with 1.58 mg/kg DHEA, and 14 age and gender matched rabbits treated with polyethylene glycol vehicle (Woodruff-Pak, unpublished data).

and memory in laboratory animals (see review in Sarter, Hagen, & Dudchenko, 1992). Nefiracetam stimulates release of acetylcholine via the GABAergic system, at least in rat cortex (Watabe, Yamaguchi, & Ashida, 1990). Following oxygen and glucose deprivation, Nefiracetam protected membrane dysfunction in hippocampal CA1 neurons (Nakamura, Higashi, Nishi, & Nakazawa, 1991). Pyramidal cells in CA1 layer of hippocampus fire in a pattern contiguous with the conditioned and unconditioned NM response (Berger, Alger, & Thompson, 1976; Berger & Thompson, 1978a, 1978b). Disruption of the septo-hippocampal cholinergic system impairs acquisition of the conditioned nictitating membrane (NM) response (Harvey, Gormezano, & Cool-Hauser, 1983; Solomon et al., 1983; Woodruff-Pak, Li, Kazmi, & Kem, 1994) and eliminates pyramidal cell activity in conjunction with the NM response (Salvatierra & Berry, 1989). Because older rabbits show impaired acquisition in EBCC and delayed hippocampal responding in the conditioned response period (Woodruff-Pak et al., 1987), and because facilitation in hippocampus can expedite acquisition (Berger, 1984), it was anticipated that Nefiracetam would enhance acquisition of EBCC in older rabbits.

In two experiments using retired breeder rabbits, Nefiracetam at some doses had a facilitatory effect on acquisition in EBCC (Woodruff-Pak & Li, 1994; see Fig. 9.2). All dependent measures indicated significantly better conditioning in rabbits treated with 10 mg/kg Nefiracetam, but this dose did not elevate motor responding. Nefiracetam facilitated acquisition of EBCC in older rabbits. EBCC is performed poorly by older humans and is seriously impaired in AD. These preclinical data—in an animal model with clear parallels in humans—suggest that Nefiracetam may prove effective as a cognition enhancer in clinical trials.

Nicotinic Cholinergic Agonists and Antagonists

Nicotinic receptors are significantly reduced in cerebral cortex and hippocampal regions of the brain in AD (Araujo, Lapchak, Robitaille, Ganthier, & Quirion, 1988; Kellar & Wonnacott, 1990; London, Ball, & Waller, 1989; Schroder, Giacobini, Struble, Zilles, & Maelicke, 1991; Sugaya, Giacobini, & Chiappinelli, 1990; Whitehouse et al., 1986). Preliminary investigations using acute administration of nicotine suggests that stimulation of remaining nicotinic receptors alleviates some cognitive deficits in AD (Jones, Sahakian, Levy, Warburton, & Gray, 1992; Newhouse, Potter, & Lenox, 1993; Sahakian, Jones, Levy, Gray, & Warburton, 1989). Chronic nicotine administration may be more effective as a cognition-enhancing agent for age-related impairment in attention and memory and for attention and memory disorders associated with AD. We wanted to determine if nicotinic as well as muscarinic cholinergic receptors were involved in EBCC in rabbits. Our results would determine whether the rabbit EBCC model could be used for preclinical tests of nicotinic agonists to treat memory dysfunction in AD.

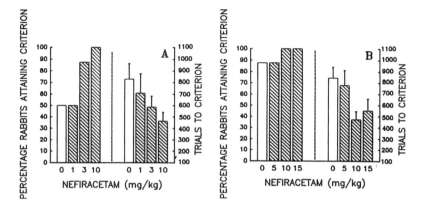

FIG. 9.2. Experiment 1. A (Left panel). Percentage of older rabbits attaining a criterion of eight conditioned responses (CRs) in nine consecutive trials in four conditions of paired tone and airpuff EBCC: (a) sterile saline vehicle (0 mg/kg Nefiracetam); (b) 1 mg/kg Nefiracetam; (c) 3 mg/kg Nefiracetam; and (d) 10 mg/kg Nefiracetam. A (Right panel). Mean number of trials to learning criterion (eight CRs in nine consecutive trials) in the four conditions described previously. Error bars are standard deviation. Experiment 2. B (Left panel). Percentage of older rabbits attaining a criterion of eight conditioned responses (CRs) in nine consecutive trials in four conditions of paired tone and airpuff EBCC: (a) sterile saline vehicle (0 mg/kg Nefiracetam); (b) 5 mg/kg Nefiracetam; (c) 10 mg/kg Nefiracetam; (d) 15 mg/kg Nefiracetam. B (Right panel). Mean number of trials to learning criterion (eight CRs in nine consecutive trials) in the four conditions described earlier. Error bars are standard deviation (Woodruff-Pak & Li, 1994).

First, Woodruff-Pak, Li, Kazmi, and Kem (1994) tested the effect of the nicotinic receptor antagonist, mecamylamine, on EBCC in young rabbits. A dose of 0.5 mg/kg of mecamylamine was injected subcutaneously daily 15 minutes before EBCC. Rabbits receiving mecamylamine were slow to acquire conditioned responses (CRs), and they had a learning profile strikingly similar to the learning profile of older rabbits (see Fig. 9.3). They took an average of 780 trials to reach learning criterion. Saline-treated rabbits learned almost twice as rapidly and to a higher level of conditioned responding than did mecamylamine-treated rabbits. Control animals given mecamylamine and presented with tones and airpuffs unpaired did not show nonspecific effects of the drug. Motor responses of all animals as measured by the NM response to the airpuff (the unconditioned response, UR) were comparable, indicating that mecamylamine affected associative learning, rather than nonassociative aspects of performance.

Administration of nicotine or compounds that activate nicotinic cholinergic receptors facilitates acquisition of CRs in older rabbits. We tested the nicotinic agonist GTS-21 using EBCC (Woodruff-Pak, Li, & Kem, 1994). Older rabbits were administered three different doses of GTS-21, and then they

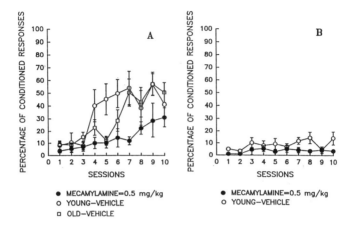

- ● MECAMYLAMINE=0.5 mg/kg
- ○ YOUNG—VEHICLE
- □ OLD—VEHICLE

- ● MECAMYLAMINE=0.5 mg/kg
- ○ YOUNG—VEHICLE

FIG. 9.3. A. Acquisition measured by percentage of conditioned responses (CRs) in 10 daily sessions of 90 paired tone and corneal airpuff presentations in the 750-msec delay EBCC paradigm. Each group has eight rabbits. The filled circles represent young rabbits treated with 0.5 mg/kg of the nicotinic cholinergic antagonist, mecamylamine. Open circles represent young rabbits ($N = 8$) treated with sterile saline vehicle. Open squares represent older rabbits ($M = 30$ months of age) treated with sterile saline vehicle. Error bars are standard error of the mean. B. Acquisition measured by percentage of CRs in 10 daily sessions of 180 explicitly unpaired tone and corneal airpuff presentations. Filled circles represent young rabbits ($N = 4$) treated with 0.5 mg/kg of mecamylamine. Open circles represent young rabbits ($N = 8$) treated with sterile saline vehicle. Error bars are standard error of the mean (Woodruff-Pak, Li, Kazmi, & Kern, 1994).

were compared with vehicle-treated rabbits. At two of the three dose levels, GTS-21 ameliorated learning deficits in older rabbits (see Fig. 9.4). We concluded that the nicotinic agonist, GTS-21, served as a cognition-enhancing agent in older rabbits on EBCC—a task that is seriously impaired in AD. Given that nicotinic cholinergic receptors are significantly reduced in AD brains, and that acute nicotine administration facilitates cognition in AD, we suspect that chronic administration of nicotinic agonists will significantly improve several dimensions of cognition in AD, including EBCC. We also suspect that nondemented elderly adults aged matched to patients diagnosed with probable AD will show cognition-enhancing effects from chronic administration of nicotinic agonists; this assumption is based on our observations of older rabbits.

Summary

With aging, there is a decline in some aspects of neuronal metabolism and information transfer that, among other things, affects learning and memory. To compensate for these losses, cognition-enhancing compounds are

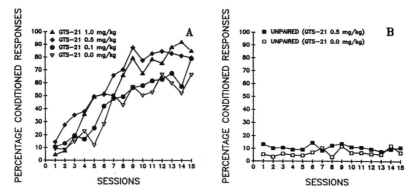

FIG. 9.4. A. Percentage of conditioned responses (CRs) in four treatment groups of older rabbits: Paired presentations of tone and airpuff and dosages of 0.0 (vehicle), 0.1, 0.5, and 1.0 mg/kg GTS-21. Each of the 15 EBCC training sessions was composed of 90 trials of paired tone and airpuff presentations. B. Percentage of CRs in two treatment groups of older rabbits: unpaired presentations of 90 tones or airpuffs, and dosages of 0.0 and 0.5 mg/kg GTS-21 (Woodruff-Pak, Li, & Kem, 1994).

under development to facilitate learning and memory. Many of these compounds are of demonstrated utility in animal models, and they have the potential to ameliorate dysfunction in brain memory systems.

UNDERSTANDING AGING IN BRAIN MEMORY SYSTEMS TO IDENTIFY SITES FOR COMPENSATION

There is no universal effect of aging on all aspects of learning and memory. Rather, processes of aging affect components of learning and memory differentially. Some components of encoding and retrieval are relatively spared, whereas other components are impaired consistently in most older adults. Indeed, cognitive theorists have incorporated the empirical observation that some aspects of memory are relatively spared by aging, in contrast to other aspects that are severely impacted by aging as one rationale in the identification of major memory systems.

Memory has at least two major forms or aspects, although we recognize that dichotomizing memory in this fashion has serious limitations. From the perspective of the dichotomy, one type of memory (declarative, or explicit) requires conscious recollection of specific learning episodes. This type of memory is impaired in old age. The other type of memory (nondeclarative, or implicit) involves the expression of learning that is automatic, without conscious or deliberate recollection. Age differences on some components of this type of memory are small or nonexistent.

Clearly, of the two types of memory, declarative memory is seriously impaired in amnesics, but a number of forms of nondeclarative memory remain intact. In normal aging, the empirical results are less consistently dichotomized. Older adults show large deficits on declarative memory, and some forms of nondeclarative memory are relatively well preserved in aging (e.g., priming, motor skills, nonassociative learning). However, other forms of nondeclarative memory are impaired in normal aging earlier in the adult life span than are declarative memory abilities (EBCC). For example, Woodruff-Pak and Thompson (1988) demonstrated large age differences in EBCC that are first apparent in the decade of the 40s; in the adult sample of Solomon, Pomerleau, Bennett, James, and Morse (1989), the significant effect of age appeared in the decade of the 50s.

In his review of research on nondeclarative memory, Schacter (1987) classified modern studies of nondeclarative memory in amnesia into two broad categories: skill learning and repetition priming. He pointed out that research on skill learning in amnesia was initiated by Milner and Corkin and their colleagues in the 1960s (Corkin, 1965, 1968; Milner, 1965; Milner, Corkin, & Teuber, 1968). For example, Corkin trained HM—the most thoroughly studied neuropsychological patient with bilateral, medial-temporal lobe resection—on a variety of manual-tracking and coordination tasks. Although he had no memory of performing the task before, HM showed normal improvement from session to session. He had no explicit memory of the learning, but his performance improved in a fashion similar to that of individuals with intact medial-temporal regions. Amnesic patients have been able to show robust learning on a number of motor skills (e.g., Starr & Phillips, 1970) as well as perceptual and cognitive skills (e.g., Cohen & Squire, 1980). On repetition priming, Warrington and Weiskrantz (1974, 1978) demonstrated that amnesic patients could show normal retention of a list of familiar words when tested with word-stem or fragment cues, whereas these same patients were profoundly impaired on free recall and recognition tests. Warrington and Weiskrantz commented that the patients frequently did not remember that the words had been presented to them as a study list, and thus treated the subsequent fragment test as a kind of guessing game.

In addition to dissociations between nondeclarative and declarative memory in amnesics in skill learning and repetition priming, these subjects show dissociations between implicit and explicit memory in various other situations including EBCC. EBCC is nondeclarative because it can occur even when the subject is not aware that learning is occurring. Since the 1940s, investigators have documented that there is little relationship between a subject's reported awareness and conditioning performance (Grant, 1973; Kimble, 1962; Norris & Grant, 1948; Spence, 1966). Thompson (1989) elaborated on the aspects of EBCC that qualify it as a nondeclarative or explicit task. Along with any discrete behavioral response learned by mammals to deal with an aversive event, EBCC is a category of associative learning that appears to use the cerebellum for acquisition and storage.

Studies in humans have examined EBCC in subjects with global amnesia, which results from bilateral lesions of the medial-temporal lobe/diencephalic system, and in subjects (presumably without global amnesia) who had unilateral lesions of the temporal-lobe. In a study of two amnesic subjects, Weiskrantz and Warrington (1979) reported evidence of EBCC in the delay paradigm, with retention at 10 minutes and 24 hours. However, the subjects' performance was not compared to that of normal control subjects. The measures of conditioning consisted of subjective judgments about the occurrence of CRs and URs made from a videotape. Daum, Channon, and Canavan (1989) tested three amnesic subjects on EBCC using a delay paradigm with a 720 msec interval between the conditioned stimulus (CS) and unconditioned stimulus (US). Responses were recorded and analyzed by computer and indicated that acquisition in the delay paradigm was intact. Unfortunately, data on control subjects were not provided in this study. In a subsequent study, Daum, Channon, Polkey, and Gray (1991) investigated electrodermal and discrimination conditioning in 17 normal control subjects and 17 subjects who had undergone unilateral en bloc resection of the right or left temporal lobe for the relief of intractable epilepsy. Daum et al. found that the acquisition of CRs was comparable in these unilateral hippocampectomized subjects to the normal control group.

HM (with bilateral removal of medial-temporal lobe structures and profound amnesia) performed EBCC for 21 ninety-trial sessions in the 400-msec delay and 900-msec trace paradigms (Woodruff-Pak, 1993). At the time of the initial testing, HM was 62 years old. A second amnesic subject, 57 years of age, with temporal lobe lesions and age-matched normal control subjects were also conditioned. Acquisition occurred in both paradigms for all subjects. Acquisition in the delay paradigm was prolonged in HM (perhaps due to his cerebellar degeneration in vermis and hemispheres) but not in the second amnesic subject. Amnesic subjects and normal controls showed more rapid acquisition in the trace than in the delay paradigm. Two years after initial EBCC, HM attained learning criterion in the trace paradigm in one tenth as many trials. No recollection of the experimenters, apparatus, instructions, or procedure was manifested by HM. Results suggest that humans can perform EBCC with the hippocampus radically excised.

Amnesics have difficulty with declarative memory, and typically they have experienced hippocampal damage. The hippocampus is a brain structure impaired by normal aging processes. The neural system subserving declarative memory encompasses the relevant sensory-association cortex, medial-temporal and diencephalic structures, and is connected to prefrontal cortex. In particular, the hippocampus and temporal lobe structures are involved as indicated by Milner and Corkin's dramatic studies of HM (Corkin, 1984; Milner, 1966), Mishkin's work on the monkey (Mishkin, 1978; Mishkin & Appenzeller, 1987), and Squire's work on humans and primates (Zola-Morgan & Squire,

1990). The prefrontal cortex in conjunction with the hippocampus subserves working memory, which involves the temporary use of knowledge to guide behavior. A major deficit in patients with prefrontal cortex lesions is reduced performance in problem-solving tasks, which require flexibility in response strategies and are assumed to tax working memory (Milner & Petrides, 1984). Parallel deficits have been observed in normal aging, along with selective neural degeneration in frontal cortex (Albert & Kaplan, 1980).

Nondeclarative memory includes a number of different types of learning and memory tasks. The proposed common denominator of these learning tasks is a certain acquired "automaticity" in response (Dudai, 1989). Different types of nondeclarative memory are likely subserved by different brain systems: (a) EBCC involves cerebellar circuitry; (b) motor skill learning engages the basal ganglia, motor, and premotor cortex; and (c) repetition priming appears to involve occipital cortex and parietal-temporal cortex in the case of conceptual priming.

Summary

Essential sites for declarative memory are medial-temporal lobe structures—in particular, the hippocampus. Plasticity is clearly present in these structures throughout the life span, but they appear less efficient in later life. At present, cognition-enhancing compounds are a means to facilitate these structures and achieve compensation. However, much remains to be discovered about mechanisms of plasticity and compensation in the hippocampus. Nondeclarative memory systems do not have a common brain substrate. It may be that repetition priming is relatively preserved because its brain substrates (occipital cortex and partietal-temporal cortex) are well preserved. Motor skill learning is maintained quite well in aging, as are the basal ganglia. However, in elderly adults with Parkinson's disease, basal ganglia function is extremely impaired, as is motor skill learning. EBCC shows age-related impairment as early as the decade of the 40s. In rabbits, impairment of this form of learning is highly correlated with cerebellar Purkinje cell loss (Woodruff-Pak, Cronholm, & Sheffield, 1990), which also occurs in normal human aging. At present, there is no documented technique for preserving Purkinje cells in cerebellar cortex. Compensation on a neurobiological level for this cerebellar loss may be through compounds that enhance activity of remaining cerebellar circuitry.

COMPENSATION IN BRAIN MEMORY SYSTEMS: FUNCTIONS THAT ARE RELATIVELY SPARED

Age-related impairment in cognitive performance appears to be less evident when tasks do not require explicit retrieval or processing of information. That is, although older adults may not be able to consciously recall having seen material previously, they can demonstrate memory for that material when probed indirectly. Much of the evidence for relatively preserved memory performance stems from work examining the priming effect, that is, the facilitation of performance in a given task as a function of prior exposure to material without deliberate retrieval of that material. For example, priming has occurred when the ability to complete word stems is greater for those words previously seen than for those not seen previously in the experimental context.

Priming effects appear to be intact for older adults across a wide range of tasks, including word completion (Howard, 1988; Light & Singh, 1987; Light, Singh, & Capps, 1986), perceptual identification of words (Light & Singh, 1987), picture naming (Mitchell, 1989), reading degraded or transformed text (Moscovitch, Winocur, & McLachlan, 1986), lexical decision (Moscovitch, 1982), spelling of homophones (Howard, 1988), and generation of category exemplars (Light & Albertson, 1989). Although there are studies that have shown a significant deleterious effect of age on priming (Chiarello & Hoyer, 1988; Hulsch, Masson, & Small, 1991), age differences on this nondeclarative memory task are much smaller than when the subjects are required to recall or recognize the stimuli using their declarative memory system.

A cognitive interpretation of the priming effect attributes it to activation of memory representations and their associates. Activation of a given concept occurs during initial encoding and subsequent retrieval. If a concept is sufficiently activated during retrieval, it will be recognized. Whether a concept is sufficiently activated may depend on the extent to which the concept was initially activated and the duration of the activation. Assuming a decay function for any activation, if a concept is weakly activated initially, its strength at retrieval may be insufficient for retrieval. Even if the initial activation was fairly strong, if the delay between initial activation and subsequent retrieval is too long, retrieval will also be impaired. In addition to the activation of the target concept, activation is also assumed to spread to other associated concepts. Evidence for spreading activation is seen in the response times produced to targets primed with related or unrelated concepts. Related primes produce faster response times than do unrelated primes (Fischler, 1977; Meyer & Schvaneveldt, 1971; Neely, 1976). Thus, the priming effect may also reflect the strength and/or speed of activation among related concepts in semantic memory.

These various components of the priming effect appear to be intact in older adults. For example, the magnitude and duration of the priming effect in older adults were comparable to those for younger adults in a picture naming task, even after 21 days (Mitchell, Brown, & Murphy, 1990). Similar priming effects for older and younger adults have also been demonstrated with lexical decision tasks (Moscovitch, 1982), category judgments and letter detection (Rabbitt, 1982), partial word identification (Light & Singh, 1987), homophone spelling (Howard, 1988), and category generation (Light & Albertson, 1989).

Semantic priming paradigms have also been used to examine age-related effects on the rate of activation buildup and the strength of activation between concepts. In this paradigm, the prime is not the same stimulus as the target; rather, it is related to the target semantically. Concepts that are highly related semantically should produce stronger activation (i.e., faster response times) than those that are less closely related. Varying the presentation time (called *stimulus onset asynchrony*—SOA) between primes and targets provides some measure of the time taken to build up activation. This paradigm indicates that both the strength and the buildup of activation are similar for older and younger adults (Balota & Duchek, 1988, 1989; Hasher & Zacks, 1988).

The activation of newly associated prime-target pairs has been examined with an episodic priming paradigm. This paradigm compares response times to targets primed with items that were or were not presented in close temporal proximity to the targets. By manipulating the association between prime and target within the experimental setting, activation strength can be examined independently of preexisting semantic associations. Work in this area supports the conclusion that activation strength is similar for younger and older adults (Howard, Heisey, & Shaw, 1986; Rabinowitz, 1986). Moreover, Balota and Duchek (1989) demonstrated that younger and older adults do not differ in activation buildup or the strength of prime-target association based on temporal contiguity.

The relatively intact memory performance demonstrated by the priming studies contrasts sharply with the impairments in declarative memory that are generally observed in older adults. One difference between priming tasks and more traditional declarative tasks, such as recall, is that context is provided in the priming task. The priming stimulus provides a context. Admittedly, the term *context* is somewhat amorphous. We will the term to refer to information that is associated with episodic memory such as temporal and spatial information, and, in more general terms, to any information that can be used to differentiate one event from others similar in kind. Context, in the form of the prime, initiates memory activation, and thereby greatly constrains the search of memory. Thus, the presence of an externally provided context eliminates the need for deliberate, internally driven, selective activation by the rememberer.

Performance on memory tasks reflects the ability to retrieve a record or representation of to-be-remembered information. A failure to remember reflects an inability to retrieve a targeted memory record. Whether a failure to retrieve a targeted memory record reflects impairment of the initial encoding processes (formation of the record) or the retrieval processes is difficult to determine. However, evidence of remembering—when memory is tested with indirect or nondeclarative tasks—indicates that some record of the to-be-remembered event was formed. In other words, some aspect of the encoding process—some degree of consolidation—remains unimpaired by factors (e.g., aging) that apparently disrupt performance as measured by more direct or declarative memory tasks. Memory failure in these cases may appear to be localized to retrieval processes. However, although retrieval failure may reflect an isolated breakdown in retrieval processes, it is also quite possible that a disruption of encoding processes could lead to a retrieval failure.

Retrieval-deficit models of amnesia, in which the memory dysfunction is isolated to retrieval processes, cannot account for unimpaired retrieval (both declarative and nondeclarative) of prelesion information (see Hirst, 1982). It is also apparent that a general failure of encoding processes cannot adequately account for preserved retention of information such as that observed when memory is tested indirectly. How then does one account for failures in the selective retrieval of a targeted memory record?

Consider that the memory record includes the to-be-remembered fact or event (i.e., the core information), as well as the context in which that fact or event occurred. Context provides the basis for distinguishing Event A from similar Event A^0. To-be-remembered events that are not associated with a unique context in the memory record are events that are difficult to selectively retrieve. Failure to integrate core and context of to-be-remembered events during encoding will clearly affect the success of subsequent retrieval.

Converging evidence from research with humans and animals implicates the hippocampus as playing a primary role in the integration of co-occurring information associated with any given event. Hippocampal damage in humans leads to the dissociations in memory performance demonstrated by comparisons of declarative and nondeclarative memory tasks (e.g., Squire, 1987). Moreover, humans with hippocampal damage generally fail to transfer or generalize to new contexts. In animal studies, lesioning of the hippocampus leads to inappropriate conditioning to background context in a Pavlovian conditioning paradigm (Winocur, Rawlins, & Gray, 1987), overreliance on context during conditioning (Winocur & Olds, 1978), and impaired performance in spatial tasks (Gallagher & Holland, 1992). Regardless of whether the role of the hippocampus is to identify co-occurring elements in a stimulus event (Wickelgren, 1979), to provide the basis for acquisition and storage of configural cues (Sutherland & Rudy, 1989), to represent relational stimulus components in novel situations (Eichenbaum & Buckingham, 1991), or to provide a "contextual tag" for events (Penick & Solomon, 1991; Winocur et al., 1987), it is clear that compensatory mechanisms will be necessary if this structure is damaged.

MARSHALING SPARED FUNCTIONS TO SUPPORT AGE-IMPAIRED FUNCTIONS

Skill acquisition is often found to be unimpaired for individuals who demonstrate impaired declarative task performance. This is one reason that preserved skill acquisition has been categorized as nondeclarative memory performance by many researchers (e.g., Light & Burke, 1988; Schacter, 1987; Squire, 1986). However, there is considerable diversity in the results obtained from studies examining skill acquisition in older adults. Some research indicates comparable effects of practice for older and younger adults (e.g., Charness & Campbell, 1988; Howard & Howard, 1989; Leonard & Newman, 1965; Madden & Nebes, 1980), whereas other studies suggest that older adults benefit more from practice than do younger adults (e.g., Jordan & Rabbitt, 1977; Murrell, 1970; Salthouse & Somberg, 1982), or that older adults show less improvement with practice (e.g., Elias, Elias, Robbins, & Gage, 1987; Moscovitch et al., 1986; Wright & Payne, 1985).

Hashtroudi, Chrosniak, and Schwartz (1991) recently examined repetition priming and skill learning in younger and older adults. They found no difference between the two age groups in repetition priming in either an inverted word reading task (Experiment 1) or a partial word identification task (Experiment 2). However, when skill learning in these tasks were examined, older subjects did not improve across trials, whereas younger subjects did. Older adults showed improvement across trials in the two tasks only when additional perceptual information was provided—that is, by increasing exposure duration (Experiments 1a) or by decreasing stimulus degradation (Experiment 2a). These results suggest that even nondeclarative memory performance (skill acquisition) can be improved in older adults when additional information is made available.

Context is widely known to have considerable influence on cognitive performance, ranging from perception to problem solving. In some cases, context acts in a bottom-up fashion. For example, a selective attention task is performed more easily when targets and foils are perceptually dissimilar than when they share a number of physical features. In other cases, context appears to have a more top-down effect. For example, perception of ambiguous figures (such as the man-rat figure) is readily biased toward one possible view or another as a function of the setting (faces or animals) in which the ambiguous figure is presented. Regardless of whether context acts in a bottom-up or a top-down fashion, its primary effect seems to be to constrain potential associations or, in other words, to focus selective retrieval.

On the one hand, older adults encode context poorly (e.g., Schacter, Kaszniak, Kihlstrom, & Valdiserri, 1991). On the other hand, it is possible that older adults benefit from additional information or context when tasks require access to memory. They may benefit from context because, during retrieval, they process context to a greater extent than do younger adults.

Evidence for more extensive processing of context by older adults is found in lexical decision studies, which have shown that older subjects gain more from less predictive primes than do younger subjects (Bowles & Poon, 1988; Cohen & Faulkner, 1983). There is also some evidence that older adults benefit as much or more than do younger adults from context in speech recognition and recall (Cohen & Faulkner, 1983; Hutchinson, 1989; Wingfield, Poon, Lombardi, & Lowe, 1985), in speech repetition (Borod, Goodglass, & Kaplan, 1980), and in both spoken (Wingfield, Aberdeen, & Stine, 1991) and visual word recognition (Madden, 1988). For example, Hutchinson (1989) compared older and younger subjects' speech perception in background noise. Targeted words completed sentences with either high or low predictability. Hutchinson found older and younger subjects benefitted from contexts of high predictability.

Another possible explanation for the apparent usefulness of context to older adults is that semantic associations are stronger and more extensive for these individuals than for younger adults. Older adults may be expected to have richer conceptual networks than younger adults, given that they have had more exposure to both repeated and diverse experiences. Moreover, if use strengthens connections among conceptual nodes, as MacKay and Burke (1990) argued, then older adults (who have had more opportunity to access their conceptual network than younger adults) may also have stronger semantic associations. A stronger and more extensive conceptual network could compensate for failures in tasks requiring selective retrieval.

Assuming that the conceptual network in older adults is intact, or even superior to that of younger adults, the failure to selectively retrieve information—as is required in explicit memory tasks—demonstrates some dissociation between memory for core information (the fundamental event or fact that is to be remembered) and contextual information (the information that co-exists with the to-be-remembered event and that distinguishes it from others of the same class). The fact that older adults often demonstrate poor memory for context (Bartlett, Strater, & Fulton, 1991; Cohen & Faulkner, 1989; Dywan & Jacoby, 1990; Hastroudi, Johnson, & Chrosniak, 1989; McIntyre & Craik, 1987; Schacter et al., 1991; however, see Hastroudi et al., 1989; Schacter et al., 1991, for exceptions), although core information is retrievable (via nondeclarative tasks), further indicates that core and context information is dissociated. This dissociation may exist because context is not recorded during encoding, or because the context record is inadequately linked to the core record. Further research is needed to determine which possibility best accounts for the observed dissociation between memory for core and memory for context.

Summary

Bäckman and Dixon (1992) suggested a number of ways in which an individual may compensate for what they called a *skill-demand mismatch*. An individual may invest more time and effort in the same skill, may substitute a latent skill, or may develop a new skill to meet task demands when existing skills or strategies are perceived to be inadequate. A decline in declarative memory performance appears to be an inevitable consequence of aging, and older adults may rely more heavily on intact skills and cognitive processes than do younger adults. Preserved processes underlying semantic association and conceptual activation may provide one means of compensating for the loss of other, less primitive processes associated with declarative memory performance.

When explicit access to memory is disrupted (as evidenced by poor declarative memory performance), impaired individuals may capitalize on intact conceptual activation processes by relying on externally provided cues to trigger that activation. The disrupted encoding of context associated with hippocampal damage (resulting in inadequate representation of core-context associations) could lead to increased processing of available context during retrieval. In this way, external context may be used to constrain conceptual activation during retrieval, thereby providing a compensatory mechanism when internal representation of context is inadequate.

CONCLUSIONS

Impaired memory performance may occur through natural aging processes, as well as through more traumatic means (e.g., accident or disease). Compensation for lost abilities can be accomplished at the neurobiological and behavioral levels. A major point of emphasis has been that the capacity for structural and chemical change in the form of neural plasticity exists in the brain throughout the life span. At the neurobiological level, brain plasticity provides a mechanism for new learning, as well as a means to compensate for loss.

Enriching the environment of an organism has direct consequences for brain function and behavior. Placing an animal—including a very old animal—in an enriched social or physical environment will increase synapses, dendritic branching, and brain weight. Structural changes have been measured in the brain resulting from manipulations of the environment, and the brain plasticity for development of these structural changes is retained throughout the life span.

The brain responds to behavioral experience. Mental skills are preserved with practice, but neural circuits may deteriorate when they are not activated. Learning and practicing a mental skill relatively early in life apparently protects the skill from impairment in later life. The mechanisms by which previous behavioral experience protect later performance have yet to be discovered. Nevertheless, to compensate for documented age-related decline in some cognitive abilities, individuals might "exercise" these abilities in young adulthood and middle age.

Behavioral and brain plasticity can be changed dramatically through the use of cognition-enhancing compounds. With aging, there is a decline in some aspects of neuronal metabolism and information transfer that, among other things, affect learning and memory. To compensate for these losses, cognition-enhancing compounds are under development to facilitate learning and memory. These substances ameliorate cognitive function with a variety of mechanisms. For example, the compounds affect ion channels, neurotransmitter release or reuptake, brain receptors, and second messengers.

To identify learning and memory components that are relatively spared by processes of aging, the effects of aging on various brain memory systems were examined. Declarative memory involves medial-temporal lobe structures, including the hippocampus. Whereas plasticity is present in declarative memory structures throughout the life span, in later life declarative memory is somewhat impaired. At present, cognition-enhancing compounds are a means to facilitate these structures and achieve compensation. However, most of these compounds are not yet available for humans, and much remains to be discovered about mechanisms of plasticity and compensation in the hippocampus.

Nondeclarative memory systems do not have a common brain substrate. Repetition priming is a nondeclarative task that is relatively preserved. Its brain substrates (occipital cortex and partietal-temporal cortex) are well preserved in normal aging. Motor skill learning is maintained quite well in aging, as are the basal ganglia, which are structures thought to be the substrate of this nondeclarative task. Human performance on EBCC shows age-related impairment in middle age. In middle-aged and older rabbits, impairment of this form of learning is highly correlated with cerebellar Purkinje cell loss (Woodruff-Pak et al., 1990), which also occurs in normal human aging. Neuronal cell loss is not a phenomenon for which direct neurobiological compensatory strategies exist. At present, the strategy might be to use drugs to facilitate activity of the remaining neural circuitry.

From a cognitive neuroscience perspective, compensation may be achieved in both a bottom-up and a top-down fashion. The plasticity of the brain provides a structural means through which intact neural substrates can be strengthened or extended. Practice and use of cognitive facilities in adulthood and old age may preserve the neural memory systems. It may be that intact brain memory systems, such as those associated with nondeclarative memory performance, may be able to be used for cognitive compensation. Top-down compensatory mechanisms include strategies that can be used with or without conscious awareness. One such strategy apparently used by older adults is the allocation of more processing effort to contextual support during retrieval. At the behavioral level, reliance on external contextual support may compensate for lost internal representations.

ACKNOWLEDGMENTS

Portions of the research described in this chapter were supported by grants from the National Institute on Aging (1 RO1 AG09752), the Alzheimer's Disease and Related Disorders Association (IIRG-91-059), Daiichi Pharmaceutical Co., Ltd., and Taiho Pharmaceutical Co., Ltd.

REFERENCES

Albert, M. S., & Kaplan, E. F. (1980). Organic implications of neuropsychological deficits in the elderly. In L. W. Poon, J. Fozard, L. Cermak, D. Arenberg, & L. W. Thompson (Eds.), *New directions in memory and aging: Proceedings of the George A. Tall and memorial conference* (pp. 403–422). Hillsdale, NJ: Lawrence Erlbaum & Associates.

Anonymous. (1990). Proposed international nonproprietary names (Prop. INN): List 64. *World Health Organization Drug Information, 4*, 203.

Araujo, D. M., Lapchak, P. A., Robitaille, Y., Ganthier, S., & Quirion, R. (1988). Differential alteration of various cholinergic markers in cortical and subcortical regions of human brain in Alzheimer's disease. *Journal of Neurochemistry, 50*, 1914–1923.

Bäckman, L., & Dixon, R. A. (1992). Psychological compensation: A theoretical framework. *Psychological Bulletin, 112*, 259–283.

Balota, D. A., & Duchek, J. M. (1988). Age-related differences in lexical access, spreading activation, and simple pronunciation. *Psychology and Aging, 3*, 84–93.

Balota, D. A., & Duchek, J. M. (1989). Spreading activation in episodic memory: Further evidence for age independence. *Quarterly Journal of Experimental Psychology, 41A*, 849–876.

Barnes, C. A. (1979). Memory deficits associated with senescence: A behavioral and physiological study in the rat. *Journal of Comparative and Physiological Psychology, 93*, 74–104.

Barnes, C. A. (1988). Aging and the physiology of spatial memory. *Neurobiology of Aging, 9*, 563–568.

Bartlett, J. C., Strater, L., & Fulton, A. (1991). False recency and false fame of faces in young adulthood and old age. *Memory & Cognition, 19*, 177–188.

Beatty, W. W. (1988). Preservation and loss of spatial memory in aged rats and humans: Implications for the analysis of memory dysfunction in dementia. *Neurobiology of Aging, 9*, 557–561.

Beatty, W. W., Bierley, R. A., & Boyd, J. G. (1985). Preservation of accurate spatial memory in aged rats. *Neurobiology of Aging, 6*, 219–225.

Berger, T. W., Alger, B. E., & Thompson, R. F. (1976). Neuronal substrates of classical conditioning in the hippocampus. *Science, 192*, 483–485.

Berger, T. W., & Thompson, R. F. (1978a). Identification of pyramidal cells as the critical elements in hippocampal neuronal plasticity during learning. *Proceedings of the National Academy of Sciences, 75*, 1572–1576.

Berger, T. W., & Thompson, R. F. (1978b). Neuronal plasticity in the limbic system during classical conditioning of the rabbit nictitating membrane response. I. The hippocampus. *Brain Research, 145*, 323–346.

Borod, J. C., Goodglass, H., & Kaplan, E. (1980). Normative data on the Boston Diagnostic Aphasia Examination, Parietal Lobe Battery, and the Boston Naming Test. *Journal of Clinical Neuropsychology, 2*, 209–215.

Bowles, N. L., & Poon, L. W. (1988). Age and context effects in lexical decision. An age by context interaction. *Experimental Aging Research, 14*, 201–205.

Charness, N., & Campbell, J. I. D. (1988). Acquiring skill at mental calculation in adulthood: A task decomposition. *Journal of Experimental Psychology: General, 117,* 115–129.

Coffin, J. M., & Woodruff-Pak, D. S. (1993). Delay classical conditioning in young and older rabbits: Acquisition and retention at 12 and 18 months. *Behavioral Neuroscience, 107,* 63–71.

Cohen, G., & Faulkner, D. (1983). Word recognition: Age differences in contextual facilitation effects. *British Journal of Psychology, 74,* 239–251.

Cohen, G., & Faulkner, D. (1989). Age differences in source forgetting: Effects on reality monitoring and on eyewitness testimony. *Psychology and Aging, 4,* 10–17.

Cohen, N. J., & Squire, L. R. (1980). Preserved learning and retention of pattern-analyzing skill in amnesia: Dissociation of "knowing how" and "knowing that." *Science, 210,* 207–209.

Corkin, S. (1965). Tactually-guided maze-learning in man: Effects on unilateral cortical excisions and bilateral hippocampal lesions. *Neuropsychologia, 3,* 339–351.

Corkin, S. (1968). Acquisition of motor skill after bilateral medial temporal-lobe excision. *Neuropsychologia, 6,* 255–265.

Daum, I., Channon, S., & Canavan, A. G. M. (1989). Classical conditioning in patients with severe memory problems. *Journal of Neurology, Neurosurgery, and Psychiatry, 52,* 47–51.

Daum, I., Channon, S., Polkey, C. E., & Gray, J. A. (1991). Classical conditioning after temporal lobe lesions in man: Impairment in conditional discrimination. *Behavioral Neuroscience, 105,* 396–408.

de Toledo-Morrell, L., Morrell, F., & Fleming, S. (1984). Age-dependent deficits in spatial memory are related to impaired hippocampal kindling. *Behavioral Neuroscience, 98,* 902–907.

Diamond, M. C., Johnson, R. E., Protti, A. M., Ott, C., & Kajisa, L. (1985). Plasticity in 904-day-old male rat cerebral cortex. *Experimental Neurology, 87,* 309–317.

Diamond, M. C., Linder, B., Johnson, R., Bennett, E. L., & Rosenzweig, M. R. (1975). Differences in occipital cortical synapses from environmentally enriched, impoverished, and standard colony rats. *Journal of Neuroscience Research, 1,* 109–119.

Dudai, Y. (1989). *The neurobiology of memory.* New York: Oxford University Press.

Dywan, J., & Jacoby, L. L. (1990). Effects of aging and source monitoring: Differences in susceptibility to false fame. *Psychology and Aging, 3,* 379–387.

Eichenbaum, H., & Buckingham, J. (1991). Studies on hippocampal processing: Experiment, theory, and model. In M. Gabriel & J. Moore (Eds.), *Neurocomputation and learning: Foundations of adaptive networks* (pp. 21–48). Cambridge, MA: MIT Press.

Elias, P. K., Elias, M. F., Robbins, M. A., & Gage, P. (1987). Acquisition of word-processing skills by younger, middle-age, and older adults. *Psychology and Aging, 2,* 340–348.

Fischler, I. (1977). Semantic facilitation without association in a lexical decision task. *Memory & Cognition, 5,* 335–339.

Flannery, B., Williams, J. R., & Woodruff-Pak, D. S. (1991). The effect of DHEA on acquisition of the nictitating membrane response in older rabbits. *Third IBRO World Congress of Neuroscience Abstracts, 3,* 424.

Floeter, M. K., & Greenough, W. T. (1979). Cerebellar plasticity: Modification of Purkinje cell structure by differential rearing in monkeys. *Science, 206,* 227–229.

Flood, J. F., & Roberts, E. (1988). Dehydroepiandrosterone sulfate improves memory in aging mice. *Brain Research, 462,* 178–181.

Flood, J. F., Smith, G. E., & Roberts, E. (1988). Dehydroepiandrosterone and its sulfate enhance memory retention in mice. *Brain Research, 477,* 269–278.

Gallagher, M., & Holland, P. (1992). Preserved configural learning and spatial learning impairment in rats with hippocampal lesions. *Hippocampus, 2,* 1–6.

Geinisman, Y., de Toledo-Morrell, L., Morrell, F., Persina, I. S., & Rossi, M. (1992). Structural synaptic plasticity associated with the induction of long-term potentiation is preserved in the dentate gyrus of aged rats. *Hippocampus, 2,* 445–456.

Graf, P., & Schacter, D. L. (1985). Implicit and explicit memory for new associations in normal and amnesic subjects. *Journal of Experimental Psychology: Learning, Memory, and Cognition, 11*, 45–53.

Green, E. J., Greenough, W. T., & Schlumpf, B. E. (1983). Effects of complex or isolated environments on cortical dendrites of middle-aged rats. *Brain Research, 264*, 233–240.

Grant, D. A. (1973). Cognitive factors in eyelid conditioning. *Psychophysiology, 10*, 75–81.

Harvey, J. A., Gormezano, I., & Cool-Hauser, V. A. (1983). Effects of scopolamine and methyl-scopolamine on classical conditioning of the rabbit nictitating membrane response. *Journal of Pharmacology and Experimental Therapeutics, 225*, 42–49.

Hasher, L., & Zacks, R. T. (1988). Working memory, comprehension, and aging: A review and a new view. In G. Bower (Ed.), *The psychology of learning and motivation* (Vol. 22, pp. 193–225). New York: Academic Press.

Hashtroudi, S., Chrosniak, L. D., & Schwartz, B. L. (1991). Effects of aging on priming and skill learning. *Psychology and Aging, 6*, 605–615.

Hashtroudi, S., Johnson, M. K., & Chrosniak, L. D. (1989). Aging and source monitoring. *Psychology and Aging, 4*, 106–112.

Hirst, W. (1982). The amnesic syndrome: Descriptions and explanations. *Psychological Bulletin, 91*, 435–460.

Howard, D. V. (1988). Aging and memory activation: The priming of semantic and episodic memories. In L. L. Light & D. M. Burke (Eds.), *Language, memory, and aging* (pp. 77–99). New York: Cambridge University Press.

Howard, D. V., & Howard, J. H., Jr. (1989). Age differences in learning serial patterns: Direct versus indirect measures. *Psychology and Aging, 4*, 357–364.

Howard, D. V., Heisey, J. G., & Shaw, R. J. (1986). Aging and the priming of newly learned associations. *Developmental Psychology, 22*, 78–85.

Hutchinson, K. M. (1989). Influence of sentence context on speech perception in young and older adults. *Journal of Gerontology, 44*, 36–44.

Jones, G. M. M., Sahakian, B. J., Levy, R., Warburton, D. M., & Gray, J. A. (1992). Effects of acute subcutaneous nicotine on attention, information processing and short-term memory in Alzheimer's disease. *Psychopharmacology, 108*, 485–494.

Jordan, T. C., & Rabbitt, P. M. A. (1977). Response times to stimuli of increasing complexity as a function of ageing. *British Journal of Psychology, 68*, 189–201.

Kimble, G. A. (1962). Classical conditioning and the problem of awareness. *Journal of Personality, 30*, 27–45.

Leonard, J. A., & Newman, R. C. (1965). On the acquisition and maintenance of high speed and high accuracy in a keyboard task. *Ergonomics, 8*, 281–304.

Light, L. L., & Albertson, S. A. (1989). Direct and indirect tests of memory for category exemplars in young and older adults. *Psychology and Aging, 4*, 487–492.

Light, L. L., & Burke, D. M. (1988). Patterns of language and memory in old age. In L. L. Light & D. M. Burke (Eds.), *Language, memory, and aging* (pp. 244–271). New York: Cambridge University Press.

Light, L. L., & Singh, A. (1987). Implicit and explicit memory in young and older adults. *Journal of Experimental Psychology: Learning, Memory, and Cognition, 13*, 531–541.

Light, L. L., Singh, A., & Capps, J. L. (1986). Dissociation of memory and awareness in young and older adults. *Journal of Clinical Experimental Neuropsychology, 8*, 62–74.

MacKay, D. G., & Burke, D. M. (1990). Cognition and aging: A theory of new learning and the use of old connections. In T. M. Hess (Ed.), *Aging and cognition: Knowledge organization and utilization* (pp. 213–264). Amsterdam: North Holland.

Madden, D. J. (1988). Adult age differences in the effects of sentence context and stimulus degradation during visual word recognition. *Psychology and Aging, 3*, 167–172.

Madden, D. J., & Nebes, R. D. (1980). Aging and the development of automaticity in visual search. *Developmental Psychology, 16*, 377–384.

McIntyre, J. S., & Craik, F. I. M. (1987). Age differences for item and source information. *Canadian Journal of Psychology, 41,* 175–192.

Meyer, D., & Schvaneveldt, R. (1971). Facilitation in recognizing pairs of words: Evidence of a dependence between retrieval operations. *Journal of Experimental Psychology, 90,* 227–234.

Milner, B. (1965). Visually-guided maze learning in man: Effects of bilateral hippocampal, bilateral frontal, and unilateral cerebral lesions. *Neuropsychologia, 3,* 317–338.

Milner, B., Corkin, S., & Teuber, H.-L. (1968). Further analysis of the hippocampal amnesic syndrome: 14-year follow up study of H. M. *Neuropsychologia, 6,* 215–234.

Milner, B., & Petrides, M. (1984). Behavioral effects of frontal-lobe lesions in man. *Trends in Neuroscience, 7,* 403–407.

Mishkin, M. (1978). Memory in monkeys severely impaired by combined but not by separate removal of amygdala and hippocampus. *Nature, 273,* 297–298.

Mishkin, M., & Appenzeller, T. (1987). The anatomy of memory. *Scientific American, 256,* 62–71.

Mitchell, D. B. (1989). How many memory systems? Evidence from aging. *Journal of Experimental Psychology: Learning, Memory, and Cognition, 15,* 31–49.

Mitchell, D. B., Brown, A. S., & Murphy, D. R. (1990). Dissociations between procedural and episodic memory: Effects of time and aging. *Psychology and Aging, 5,* 264–276.

Moscovitch, M. (1982). Multiple dissociation of function in amnesia. In L. Cermak (Ed.), *Human memory and amnesia* (pp. 337–370). Hillsdale, NJ: Lawrence Erlbaum Associates.

Moscovitch, M., Winocur, G., & McLachlan, D. (1986). Memory as assessed by recognition and reading time in normal and memory impaired people with Alzheimer's disease and other neurological disorders. *Journal of Experimental Psychology: General, 115,* 331–346.

Murrell, F. H. (1970). The effect of extensive practice on age differences in reaction time. *Journal of Gerontology, 25,* 268–274.

Nakamura, J., Higashi, H., Nishi, S., & Nakazawa, Y. (1991). DM-9384, a pyrrolidone derivative, protects the membrane dysfunction induced by deprivation of oxygen and glucose in guinea-pig hippocampal neurons in vitro. *Biological Psychiatry, 29,* 29–36.

Neely, J. (1976). Semantic priming and retrieval from lexical memory. Evidence for facilitatory and inhibitory processes. *Memory & Cognition, 4,* 648–654.

Newhouse, P. A., Potter, A., & Lenox, R. (1993). The effects of nicotinic agents on human cognition: Possible therapeutic applications in Alzheimer's and Parkinson's diseases. *Medical and Chemical Research, 2,* 628–642.

Norris, E. B., & Grant, D. A. (1948). Eyelid conditioning as affected by verbally induced inhibitory set and counter-reinforcement. *American Journal of Psychology, 61,* 37–49.

Novak, M. A., Suomi, S. J., Bowman, R. E., & Mohr, D. (1991). Problem solving in elderly sophisticated and naive monkeys. *Journal of Gerontology: Psychological Sciences, 46,* 102–108.

Penick, S., & Solomon, R. (1991). Hippocampus, context, and conditioning. *Behavioral Neuroscience, 105,* 611–617.

Port, R. L., Murphy, H. A., & Magee, R. A. (1994). *Age-related impairment in instrumental conditioning is restricted to initial acquisition.* Manuscript submitted for publication.

Port, R. L., Murphy, H. A., Magee, R. A., & Burns, L. (1993). Long-term instrumental training greatly facilitates spatial cognition in young and aged rats. *Society for Neuroscience Abstracts, 19,* 602.

Rabbitt, P. M. A. (1982). How do old people know what to do next? In F. I. M. Craik & S. Trehub (Eds.), *Aging and cognitive processes* (pp. 79–98). New York: Plenum Press.

Rabinowitz, J. C. (1986). Priming in episodic memory. *Journal of Gerontology, 41,* 204–213.

Roberts, E., Bologa, L., Flood, J. F., & Smith, G. E. (1987). Effects of dehydroepiandrosterone and its sulfate on brain tissue in culture and on memory in mice. *Brain Research, 406,* 357–362.

216

WOODRUFF-PAK AND HANSON

Sahakian, B., Jones, G., Levy, R., Gray, J., & Warburton, D. (1989). The effects of nicotine on attention, information processing, and short-term memory in patients with dementia of the Alzheimer's type. *British Journal of Psychiatry, 154*, 797–800.

Salthouse, T. A., & Somberg, B. L. (1982). Skilled performance: Effects of adult age and experience on elementary processes. *Journal of Experimental Psychology: General, 11*, 176–207.

Salvatierra, A. T., & Berry, S. D. (1989). Scopolamine disruption of septo-hippocampal activity and classical conditioning. *Behavioral Neuroscience, 103*, 715–721.

Sarter, M., Hagen, J., & Dudchenko, P. (1992). Behavioral screening for cognition enhancers: From indiscriminate to valid tasting: Part I. *Psychopharmacology, 107*, 144–159.

Schacter, D. L. (1987). Implicit memory: History and current status. *Journal of Experimental Psychology: Learning, Memory, and Cognition, 13*, 501–518.

Schacter, D. L., Kaszniak, A. W., Kihlstrom, J. F., & Valdiserri, M. (1991). On the relation between source memory and aging. *Psychology and Aging, 6*, 559–568.

Schwartz, R. D., Lawbart, M. L., & Pashko, L. L. (1988). Novel dehydroepiandrosterone analogues with enhanced biological activity and reduced side effects in mice and rats. *Cancer Research, 48*, 4817–4822.

Shimamura, A. P. (1986). Priming effects in amnesia: Evidence for a dissociable memory function. *Quarterly Journal of Experimental Psychology, 38A*, 619–644.

Singer, W. (1992). Adult visual cortex—Adaptation and reorganization. In L. R. Squire (Ed.), *Encyclopedia of learning and memory* (pp. 453–454). New York: Macmillan.

Solomon, P. R., Pomerleau, D., Bennett, L., James, J., & Morse, D. L. (1989). Acquisition of the classically conditioned eyeblink response in humans over the life span. *Psychology and Aging, 4*, 34–41.

Solomon, P. R., Solomon, S. D., Vander Schaaf, E., & Perry, H. E. (1983). Altered activity in the hippocampus is more detrimental to classical conditioning than removing the structure. *Science, 220*, 329–331.

Spence, K. W. (1966). Cognitive and drive factors in the extinction of the conditioned eyeblink in human subjects. *Psychological Review, 73*, 445–458.

Squire, L. R. (1986). Mechanisms of memory. *Science, 232*, 1612–1619.

Squire, L. R. (1987). *Memory and brain*. New York: Oxford University Press.

Squire, L. R. (1992). Memory and the hippocampus: A synthesis from findings with rats, monkeys, and humans. *Psychological Review, 99*, 195–231.

Starr, A., & Phillips, L. (1970). Verbal and motor memory in the amnesic syndrome. *Neuropsychologia, 16*, 339–348.

Sunderland, T., Merril, C. R., Harrington, M. G., Lawlon, B. A., Molchan, S. E., Martinez, H., & Murphy, D. L. (1989, September). Reduced plasma dehydroepiandrosterone concentrations in Alzheimer's disease. *Lancet*, p. 2, 570.

Sunderland, T., Tariot, P. N., Weingartner, H., Murphy, D. L., Newhouse, P. A., Mueller, E. A., & Cohen, R. M. (1986). Pharmacologic modelling of Alzheimer's disease. *Progress in Neuro-Psychopharmacological and Biological Psychiatry, 10*, 599–610.

Sutherland, R. J., & Rudy, J. W. (1989). Configural association theory: The role of the hippocampal formation in learning, memory, and amnesia. *Psychobiology, 17*, 129–144.

Thompson, R. F. (1989). A model system approach to memory. In P. R. Solomon, J. B. Goethals, C. M. Kelly, & B. R. Stephens (Eds.), *Memory: Interdisciplinary approaches* (pp. 17–32). New York: Springer-Verlag.

Thompson, R. F., Donegan, N., & Lavond, D. G. (1985). The psychobiology of learning and memory. In R. C. Atkinson, R. J. Herrinstein, G. Lindzey, & R. D. Luce (Eds.), *Stevens' handbook of experimental psychology* (2nd ed., pp. 245–351). New York: Wiley.

Turner, A. M., & Greenough, W. T. (1985). Differential rearing effects on rat visual cortex synapses: I. Synaptic and neuronal density and synapses per neuron. *Brain Research, 329*, 195–203.

Warrington, E. K., & Weiskrantz, L. (1974). The effect of prior learning on subsequent retention in amnesic patients. *Neuropsychologia, 12,* 419–428.

Warrington, E. K., & Weiskrantz, L. (1978). Further analysis of the prior learning effect in amnesic patients. *Neuropsychologia, 16,* 169–176.

Watabe, S., Yamaguchi, H., & Ashida, S. (1990). Effects of DM-9384, a new cognition-enhancing agent, on cholinergic system in rat cortex. *Society for Neuroscience Abstracts, 16,* 137.

Weiskrantz, L., & Warrington, E. K. (1979). Conditioning in amnesic patients. *Neuropsychologia, 17,* 187–194.

Whitehouse, P. J., Martino, A. M., Antuono, P. G., Lowenstein, P. R., Coyle, J. T., Price, D. L., & Kellar, K. J. (1986). Nicotinic acetylcholine binding sites in Alzheimer's disease. *Brain Research, 371,* 146–151.

Wickelgren, W. A. (1979). Chunking and consolidation: A theoretical synthesis of semantic networks, configuring in conditioning, S-R versus cognitive learning, normal forgetting, the amnesic syndrome and the hippocampal arousal system. *Psychological Review, 86,* 44–60.

Wingfield, A., Aberdeen, J. S., & Stine, E. A. L. (1991). Word-onset gating and linguistic context in spoken word recognition by young and elderly adults. *Journal of Gerontology: Psychological Sciences, 46,* 127–129.

Wingfield, A., Poon, L. W., Lombardi, L., & Lowe, D. (1985). Speed of processing in normal aging: Effects of speech rate, linguistic structure, and processing time. *Journal of Gerontology, 40,* 579–585.

Winocur, G., Rawlins, J., & Gray, J. R. (1987). The hippocampus and conditioning to contextual cues. *Behavioral Neuroscience, 101,* 617–625.

Winocur, G., & Olds, J. (1978). Effects of context manipulation on memory and reversal learning in rats with hippocampal lesions. *Journal of Comparative and Physiological Psychology, 92,* 312–321.

Woodruff-Pak, D. S. (1993). Eyeblink classical conditioning in H. M.: Delay and trace paradigms. *Behavioral Neuroscience, 107,* 911–923.

Woodruff-Pak, D. S., Cronholm, J. F., & Sheffield, J. B. (1990). Purkinje cell number related to rate of classical conditioning. *NeuroReport, 1,* 165–168.

Woodruff-Pak, D. S., & Li, Y.-T. (1994). Nefiracetam (DM-9384): Effect on eyeblink classical conditioning in older rabbits. *Psychopharmacology, 114,* 200–208.

Woodruff-Pak, D. S., Li, Y.-T., Kazmi, A., & Kem, W. R. (1994). Nicotinic cholinergic system involvement in eyeblink classical conditioning in rabbits. *Behavioral Neuroscience, 108,* 486–493.

Woodruff-Pak, D. S., Li, Y.-T., & Kem, W. R. (1994). A nicotinic agonist (GTS-21), eyeblink classical conditioning, and nicotinic receptor binding in rabbit brain. *Brain Research, 645,* 309–317.

Woodruff-Pak, D. S., & Thompson, R. F. (1988). Classical conditioning of the eyeblink response in the delay paradigm in adults aged 18–83. *Psychology and Aging, 3,* 219–229.

Wright, B. M., & Payne, R. B. (1985). Effects of aging on sex differences in psychomotor reminiscence and tracking proficiency. *Journal of Gerontology, 40,* 179–184.

Zola-Morgan, S., & Squire, L. R. (1990). Neuropsychological investigations of memory and amnesia: Findings from humans and nonhuman primates. In A. Diamond (Ed.), *The development and neural bases of higher cognitive functions* (pp. 434–456). New York: New York Academy of Sciences.

CHAPTER TEN

Behavioral Compensation in the Case of Treatment of Acquired Language Disorders Resulting From Brain Damage

Leslie J. Gonzalez Rothi
Gainesville Veterans Affairs Medical Center
University of Florida College of Medicine

Compensation can be inferred when an objective or perceived mismatch between accessible skills and environmental demands is counterbalanced (either automatically or deliberately) . . . so that a change in the behavioral profile occurs, either in the direction of adaptive attainment, maintenance, or surpassing of normal levels of proficiency or of maladaptive outcome behaviors or consequences.
—Bäckman & Dixon, 1992, p. 272

For anyone who has worked with patients with cognitive deficits resulting from acquired brain damage, it is clear that, in the majority of cases, some measure of compensation occurs over time—with or without intervention. That is, a patient seen immediately after the onset of brain damage is most often behaviorally different than the same patient 6 weeks postonset, who is different than the same patient 6 months postonset, 6 years postonset, and so forth. As stated in the opening quote, although many deficiencies noted at onset may improve, some maladaptive behaviors may emerge with time. In addition, gains that occur in the early stages of recovery may diminish subsequently as well (Geschwind, 1974; Hamlin, 1970). This chapter's premise is that the role of the cognitive rehabilitation clinician (e.g., speech/language pathologist, clinical neuropsychologist) working with brain-damaged patients is to maximize adaptive compensations and to minimize the emergence of (or to extinguish existing) maladaptive compensations for deficits in higher cortical function. Although I address treatment of some

219

acquired language disorders specifically, the principles used in this approach are the same as those used in the rehabilitation of other neuropsychological syndromes, such as neglect, amnesia, apraxia, and so forth.

References to treatment of deficits of higher cortical functions (most predominately spoken language) can be found in the literature as far back as biblical times. Although these early efforts focused on such things as herbal potions or the placing of stones in the mouth, it was not until World War II that we began to look to behavioral manipulations for the management of these various neuropsychological deficits. Then between 1965 and 1985 the major research attention in disordered language treatment targeted studies of "treatment efficacy" in which the intention was to answer the question best stated by Darley (1972): "Does language rehabilitation accomplish measurable gains in language function beyond what can be expected to occur as a result of spontaneous recovery?" (p. 4). However, researchers such as Siegel (1987) suggested that these early behavioral treatment efficacy studies were pursued "not to learn about therapy, but rather to satisfy the skeptics . . ." (p. 310). Although speech/language pathologists have continuously studied "treatment efficacy," a recent increase in interest in language therapy is notable in the search for particular "efficacious treatments" (as opposed to "treatment efficacy"). One such effort is the study of cognitive-neuropsychological models in treatment planning. Most significantly, this treatment research focus spans professions (speech/language pathologists, linguistics, psychologists, neurologists) representing a marriage between cognitive theoreticians and clinicians alike.

Some research teams say that treatment studies using cognitive-neuropsychological models can inform us about the adequacy of these models, as well as the efficacy of particular model-driven treatments (for example, see Berndt, 1992). The use of information-processing models has recently been advocated by researchers who strongly feel that the specificity of "deficit definition" provided by these models allows better specificity of treatment task selection (Byng & Coltheart, 1986). This is especially true of treatment of acquired reading and/or writing disorders because cognitive-psychological models developed to explain normal processing were first applied, tested, confirmed, and modified in a population of acquired alexic patients (J. C. Marshall & Newcombe, 1973). Unfortunately, more controversies have been raised than answered with some questioning the role of cognitive models in treatment planning (Caramazza, 1989). That is, models have been proposed that specify the processes needed to read a word aloud; when used as an infrastructure to guide assessment, clinicians can arrive at conclusions regarding which specific components of the reading system are deficient in a particular patient. The implication is that treatment would then be tailored to address the identified deficiency. For example, if an acquired alexic patient had particular difficulty with a "grapheme/phoneme conversion module," identification of that deficiency would lead the clinician to choose a particular treatment "suited for" remediating that deficiency. But Hillis (1993) has shown that two patients with qualitatively different problems (as determined by assessments based on cognitive-neuropsychological models) can respond to the same treatment designed to address a single level of processing dysfunction. In turn, Hillis has shown that a single patient can respond to two treatments, each of which is designed to address a putatively different level of processing dysfunction. If treatments should be directly linked to information-processing models, such as those of cognitive neuropsychology, why would there not be a more invariant link between model-defined deficits and treatment result? Maybe it is that our perspective is limited in scope to those principles emanating exclusively from behavioral science, all but ignoring the principles emanating from any other relevant perspective such as a physical science perspective of the human nervous system and its dysfunction and recovery (Fazzini, Bachman, & Albert, 1986). In fact, Finger and Stein (1982) cited this as one of the major frustrations that led them to write their book entitled *Brain Damage and Recovery: Research and Clinical Perspectives:*

> Almost everyone is aware of the tragedy that can occur when someone is afflicted with a brain injury or a disease of the central nervous system. In many cases, all that seems to be available are words of comfort for the family and hospitalization or pity for the victim. Why should the outcome of . . . injury to the central nervous system be seen in such a pessimistic light? . . . As we continued our exploration of the literature we realized that part of the problem was communicative. That is, the individuals who were studying recovery of function were not effectively conveying their findings to those who could make the most use of the new observations and information. There was no professional society devoted to the study of recovery from brain damage, no journal, and not even a monograph dealing with recovery from integrated anatomical, physiological, and behavioral perspectives. (p. ix)

It is my primary assumption that behavior is supported by the action and/or the interaction of neurons. Damage to the nervous system (more specifically, the neurons) disrupts the normal functioning of neural systems or networks, the balance of these systems one to another (LeVere, 1988), and, in turn, the behaviors these neural systems subserve. Accepting the intimacy of neurons and neural systems, and accepting the intimacy of neural systems and behavior, it seems logical that principles emanating from a neuronal perspective of recovery, from a systemic perspective of recovery, and from a behavioral perspective of recovery would need to be compatible. Therefore, to speak of recovery from or treatment of behavioral deficits resulting from brain damage, we should begin by understanding the putative, physiological mechanisms of neuronal recovery, and by striving to achieve a measure of the integration referred to earlier by Finger and Stein (1982).

PHYSIOLOGICAL EXPLANATIONS OF RECOVERY

The natural history of recovery from lesions in the nervous system can be organized into those physiological mechanisms that can be considered "restitutive" and those that can be considered "substitutive" (Finger, 1978). Each is discussed separately herein.

Physiological Restitution

Restitution assumes that functional recovery results from recovery of the health of damaged neurons and neural systems. As such, there is a quality and a chronology to the changes resulting from restitution that are dependent on the physiology of an individual's neural system. To briefly review (see Finger & Stein, 1982, for a thorough review), it is important to know that not all cells associated with a particular lesion necessarily die. In fact, there may be a clear differential between the integrity of cells within the lesion "core"—those within the lesion "penumbra"—and those of distant locations that collectively and collaboratively support functions (and cells) related to the affected lesion site (Zivin & Choi, 1991). That is, cell loss is more complete in the lesion core, less so but still significant in the penumbra, and, less so but potentially significant in the distant but functionally associated sites (Siesjo, 1992). In addition to cell death, some cells in the lesion portions may not be dead, but alive and rendered dysfunctional. To appreciate the potential of restitution, it is helpful to understand physiological changes occurring in those cells local to a lesion site that are left living but not functioning, the physiological capabilities of cells local to the lesion site left living and functioning, and finally the physiological capabilities of those cells distant to a lesion site. For example, neurons distant to the lesion site might degenerate when they are deprived of their normal afferent input; this process is called *transneuronal* or *transsynaptic degeneration* (Geschwind, 1974). As such, the function supported by particular neurons undergoing this process (and, in turn, possibly the behavior supported by the affected neural system) would potentially be disrupted even further and later than that disturbance directly produced by the lesion. But this speaks to loss of function. What of recovery?

One mechanism of restitution distinguishes between damage to the cell body (which usually results in cell death) and damage to the axon. If the cell body is spared and the axon is severed, it is possible that the axon will regenerate and connect with postsynaptic membranes of communicating neurons, a process called *axonal regeneration* (Aguayo, 1985; Bjorklund & Stenevi, 1971; 1972; Katzman, Bjorklund, Owman, Stenevi, & West, 1971). A derivative of this is called *collateral sprouting* where a new axon is generated from a previously uninvolved cell and synapses with the membrane of a cell deprived of input from an injured cell (Goodman & Horel, 1966; Raisman, 1969). These processes, collectively called *synaptogenesis*, are thought to represent a physiological process that normally occurs throughout the life span in the central nervous system (CNS) of mammals, and that is possibly related to ". . . whatever dormant structural and chemical substrates are left over from developmental days" (Ebbesson, 1988, p. 197), but is a process that is "accelerated" in the pathological state (Matthews, Cotman, & Lynch, 1976). Relevant to the situation of recovery from brain damage, it should be noted that the process of axonal remodeling, such as axonal or collateral sprouting, has a time course. The Matthews et al. work with adult rats shows that these processes occur quickly initially, but drop in rate dramatically. This suggests that a window of opportunity may be available for this type of physiological process.

Another restitutive process that should be included is *denervation supersensitivity.* It has been noted that remaining neurons local to the lesion site or those distant but linked (within 24 hours of lesion onset) can become up to 20 times more sensitive to their respective neurotransmitters than normal (J. F. Marshall, 1984; Ungerstedt, 1971).

But do the physiological changes associated with restitution, such as denervation supersensitivity or the alternate forms of reactive synaptogenesis, conceivably facilitate at least some level of recovery of function? Because neurotransmitters are the vehicle by which neurons communicate with one another, a hypersensitive cell or portion of a neural system might conceivably be able to carry a larger functional burden than normal. Finger and Stein (1982) stated:

> The concept of supersensitivity can make a certain amount of sense if one thinks in terms of design principles. Neural structures can be thought of as "modules" that have a greater capacity than would ordinarily be needed. When normally innervated, this excess capacity will go unnoticed. Following the loss of innervation, whether due to a lesion or to the normal loss of cells over a lifetime, this excess capacity may be called upon to maintain a relatively normal level of functioning of the modules. (p. 273)

Consistent with this notion, studies of supersensitivity in both animals (Glick & Greenstein, 1972; Glick, Greenstein, & Zimmerberg, 1972) and humans (Stavraky, 1961), and studies of reactive synaptogenesis in animals (Goldberger & Murray, 1978; Loesche & Steward, 1977), have suggested that these mechanisms do support some behavioral improvement or sparing in the damaged CNS (although this conclusion remains controversial; see Freed, de Medinaceli, & Wyatt, 1985). However, it is clear that each of these processes also has the potential for aberrant functional consequences. For example, it has been suggested that anomalous reactive synaptogenesis contributes to the development of spasticity (muscular hypertonia; Liu & Chambers, 1958), and that supersensitivity contributes to the development of tardive dyskinesia (a movement disorder; Tarsy & Baldessarini, 1974), sensory ataxia (a condition of incoordination), and paraesthesia and hyperaesthesia (disorders of sensation; Stavraky, 1961) as the result of brain damage.

Although some portion of the behavioral recovery seen subsequent to brain damage may result from these restitutive processes, all forms of this behavioral recovery cannot be contingent upon restitution (Almli & Finger, 1992). Therefore, I turn to the substitution theory of recovery in the next section.

Physiological Substitution

Two versions of substitution theories of recovery are given. One involves what Finger and Stein (1982) called the *theory of vicariation*, which assumes that recovery results from neural system reorganization. The early proponents of this form of substitution were, of course, Munk (1881), Lashley (1929), and, more recently, Kertesz (1988). Three possible explanations of this kind of recovery are: (a) that the function of a deficient neural system is taken up by homologous regions of the opposite hemisphere, (b) that function is taken up by previously "uncommitted" areas of the same hemisphere, or (c) that function is taken up by a different level of neuroanatomic organization (i.e., higher or lower order structures; Finger & Stein, 1982). In other words, vicariative recovery involves parts of the brain not incorporated in the lesion and not previously involved in the "lost" function assuming responsibility for the "lost" function. It would seem that the time course and limits in degree of this form of recovery would be susceptible to the normal variations in brain morphology (or structure and organization) noted across individuals. Would this form of physiological recovery result in functional changes over the recovery interval? As with restitution theories, the notion that vicariation explains behavioral recovery from brain damage is controversial; it has been so for many years with those who have supported this notion (classically described by Kennard, 1936, 1938) and with those who have not (Carville & Duret, 1875).

The second form of substitutive recovery is behavioral compensation (a notion discussed extensively by Luria, 1963, 1966), which obviously has no time course or degree limitations, and instead can continue as long as learning potential is present. Behavioral compensation involves altering the task strategy such that spared brain regions, previously uninvolved functionally, now support the behavior (see Almli & Finger, 1988). This is not accomplished by altering their function to assume the lost function. Instead, previously uninvolved brain regions maintain their function, and the task demands are altered such that the maintained (but previously uninvolved) function is used in a new way to support the accomplishment of the task.

For example, memory failure may be behaviorally compensated for by giving the amnesic person a visual cue (i.e, a calendar) or an auditory cue (i.e., a watch with an alarm set to go off at a particular time to remind the patient of an event). Another example would be the use of pantomime or gesture in place of word production in a case of anomia. In each of these examples, the compensating behavior was not previously typically used to accomplish the task, but becomes useful in a compensatory way. Behavioral compensation can occur either as a self-initiated process or one managed and encouraged by therapeutic intervention. Again, although there are those who strongly support this notion—that behavioral recovery can be explained by a behavioral compensation theory of recovery (Gazzaniga, 1978)—it has its critics as well (Finger & Stein, 1982).

In summary, although we have a number of alternative theories about the physiological basis of recovery, no one theory seems to hold the exclusive answer to how recovery from brain damage occurs. However, none of the theories reviewed has been completely discounted, and it is most likely that a combination of all three is nearer to the truth.

Further research on these forms of recovery and their behavioral implications is clearly needed. The important notion to carry into the clinic is this: Each recovery theory has its limits as to what can be hoped to be accomplished behaviorally, each has distinctive implications for how treatment should be approached strategically, and each has a time course as to when it would potentially be relevant. For example, it would seem (although it is not proved) that restitution would occur relatively early in recovery, whereas substitution would be available continuously after brain damage. In addition, within substitutive theories, vicariation has been related, to some extent, to the processes of reactive synaptogenesis as well, and one might hypothesize that these changes would be time and extent limited in comparison with behavioral compensation. Therefore, it appears important to relate these assumptions (time-course limitation, recovery extent limits) to our selection of behavioral treatments.

BEHAVIORAL TREATMENT APPROACHES

It seems important to differentiate among the terms *treatment task, treatment goal*, and *treatment strategy*. To begin, let us define a *treatment goal* as the behavior we wish to achieve (i.e., the target behavior). The *treatment task* is simply the context in which we place the patient, such that the occurrence of the target behavior is warranted. This leads to the important notion that the treatment task is *not* the therapy. In contrast, a *treatment strategy* is what clinicians do so that, on the next occasion in which the target behavior would be appropriate, the patient is more likely to achieve the treatment goal.

Therefore, the treatment strategy (restitution, vicariation, compensation) is really the therapy. Although admittedly controversial, it is my contention (Rothi, 1992; Rothi & Horner, 1983) that the design of behavioral treatments, and thus the choice of treatment strategies, must consider principles emanating from the proposed mechanisms of recovery as conceptualized by Finger (Finger, 1978; Finger & Stein, 1982). The two most obvious of these principles is that: (a) restitutive physiological recovery may be constrained in the time course and in the maximal degree of recovery that can be accomplished with our current state of knowledge, and (b) substitutive strategies may not be thus constrained. With this in mind, I contend (Rothi, 1992; Rothi & Horner, 1983) that behavioral treatment strategies might be better selected if done so in a manner compatible with the suspected state of the physiological recovery of each individual. That is, if the majority of restitutive recovery we can expect is concentrated in the early stages of recovery, it would seem prudent to emphasize these treatment strategies during the early postonset period. In anticipation that this type of recovery may be limited in degree, it would also seem important to anticipate that the patient may be left with some deficits, and to simultaneously encourage strategies to circumvent potential residual problems. Therefore, in the early stages of recovery, both restitutive and substitutive treatment strategies should be used. In contrast, in the chronic case, when resources are likely to be limited, it would seem prudent to focus treatment efforts on those strategies that may have the most potential for yielding a positive result (i.e., the successful attainment of a behavioral goal). Therefore, in cases in the later stages of their recovery, restitutive strategies might be emphasized less and less, whereas, all forms of substitutive strategies might be increasingly emphasized.

Does this approach lead to the pessimism that Finger and Stein spoke of? For example, does this mean that in the chronic aphasic case, potential for verbal recovery as the result of treatment would likely be minimal? A common recommendation for a patient who has had aphasia for years is that therapy is not warranted—as if the length of time with a deficit implies whether treatment is warranted. However, I believe that the physiological mechanisms of recovery suggest that the length of time one has a deficit of higher cortical function implies *which strategy* needs to be emphasized, *not whether* treatment is indicated. In fact, if treatments emphasizing return of verbal communication to the aphasic patient are indeed warranted in a chronic aphasic, the amount of time postonset dictates that emphasis might be better placed exclusively on substitutive strategies (vicariative or compensatory) for supporting a deficient verbal system.

With this in mind, what might be restitutive, vicariative, or compensatory treatments for behavioral deficits resulting from brain damage such as aphasia? Restitutive treatment would be "deficit-directed" therapy that attempts to encourage the patient to approximate a premorbid manner of performance. For example, the "stimulation" treatments—commonly referred to in the literature on aphasia treatment during the 1950s and 1960s—are typical of restitutive treatments. Philosophically, their goal is to place the aphasic patient in a linguistically enriched environment controlled by the clinician. In contrast, substitutive treatments may be deficit oriented or may be oriented toward maximizing the use of spared functions. The hallmark of a substitutive treatment is that it assumes that the patient will perform the behavioral goal in a new way—that he or she will not arrive at this goal in a manner that precisely reconstructs normal performance. Instead, the patient will either mimic normal performance by having a previously uninvolved system (vicariation) take up the "lost function," or by reformatting the behavior using new functions to accomplish the behavioral goal (compensation).

When selecting treatments for patients, it quickly becomes obvious that there are multiple ways to solve a single problem. For each treatment goal, restitutive, vicariative, and compensatory strategies should all be possible. For example, if a patient cannot retrieve a word during conversation, we may choose treatment tasks that focuses on word retrieval—where the treatment strategy is to encourage the patient to internalize a cuing hierarchy that approximates the way we normally retrieve words (restitutive treatment strategy). First, we might tell the patient to think of the physical attributes of a target object, what it is used for, who might use it, or where it may be found. Then we might ask the patient to think of the first sound of the target, how many syllables it may contain, a rhyming word, and so on. These steps roughly approximate the stage progression of normal object recognition and naming, including identification of: (a) structural descriptions, (b) semantic attributes, and finally, (c) phonological representation. Alternatively, we may choose to teach this patient a strategy that does not reconstruct the way we normally retrieve words. One such treatment might be Melodic Intonation Therapy (a vicariative treatment initially described by Sparks, Helm, & Albert, 1974), where the normal melodic line of an utterance is embellished such that putative right-hemisphere, intonational mechanisms can be recruited to support (at least in theory) more accurate verbal productions. With time, the exaggerated intonational patterns are faded, and the hope is that the more accurate verbal productions will continue, assuming that the right hemisphere may then be sponsoring verbal production (a new, not previously supported function of that region). A third alternative is teaching patients a compensatory strategy, where they self-cue by writing the word first (assuming that written spelling is spared) and then reading it aloud. No attempt is made to structure this process as it would be found in the normal system. That is, in the normal state, people do not write words down to say them aloud. The difference between this compensatory strategy and one that is vicariative is that, at some point in the vicariative approach, the cue is ultimately removed, whereas in the compensatory approach the cue always remains. We always intend to provide that bridge, thus it is compensatory in nature. In each of the approaches described, the treatment goal is the same: that the aphasic is able to communicate a word to the person who needs to receive the information. What differs is the treatment strategy by which the treatment goal of successful lexical retrieval is accomplished.

What determines which of these behavioral strategies (restitution, vicariation, compensation) should be used in any particular case at any particular point in time? At this time, we have no hard and fast evidence upon which to base the strategy selection. But if we look to the physiological mechanisms reviewed earlier, the hints of time course and extent that might be extrapolated could be used, as suggested previously. Admittedly, the extrapolation and application of these principles might be imprecise at this stage in our understanding of these physiological processes. However, despite these potential flaws, this information provides at least a theoretical framework upon which to base our rehabilitation attempts.

CONCLUSIONS

In summary, although it is clearly controversial and premature to say that the physiologic mechanisms of recovery described in this chapter support the behavioral change we see in the days, weeks, and months after acquired brain damage in human adults, it is possible and logical that these physiologic processes may support some of the behavioral change noted herein. Because each physiologic process has particular attributes that can be applied to the choice of behavioral treatment strategies, it seems appropriate that the clinician be aware of these attributes (such as time course, etc.) and try to develop compatible behavioral treatment strategies. Unfortunately, because the study of these physiologic mechanisms is in its infancy, the empirical study of strategically comparable behavioral treatments is nonexistent. That is, although there are many studies looking at aphasia treatment efficacy, none exists that matches the treatment strategy to the putative physiologic mechanisms of recovery. This remains a frontier of future treatment research.

REFERENCES

Aguayo, A. J. (1985). Axonal regeneration from injured neurons in the adult mammalian central nervous system. In C. W. Cotman (Ed.), *Synaptic plasticity* (pp. 457–484). New York: Guilford.

Almli, C. R., & Finger, S. (1988). Toward a definition of recovery of function. In S. Finger, T. E. LeVere, R. Almli, & D. G. Stein (Eds.), *Brain injury and recovery* (pp. 1–14). New York: Plenum.

Almli, C. R., & Finger, S. (1992). Brain injury and recovery of function: Theories and mechanisms of functional reorganization. *Journal of Head Trauma Rehabilitation, 7*, 70–77.

Bäckman, L., & Dixon, R. A. (1992). Psychological compensation: A theoretical framework. *Psychological Bulletin, 112*, 259–283.

Berndt, R. S. (1992). Using data from treatment studies to elaborate cognitive models: Non-lexical reading, an example. In J. Cooper (Ed.), *Aphasia therapy: Current trends and research opportunities* (pp. 47–64). Bethesda, MD: NIH Monographs.

Bjorklund, A., & Stenevi, U. (1971). Growth of central catecholamine neurons into mesencephalon. *Brain Research, 31*, 1–20.

Bjorklund, A., & Stenevi, U. (1972). Nerve growth factor: Stimulation of regenerative growth in central noradrenergic neurons. *Science, 125*, 1251–1253.

Byng, S., & Coltheart, M. (1986). Aphasia therapy research: Methodological requirements and illustrative results. In E. Hjelmquist & L.-G. Nilsson (Eds.), *Communication handicap: Aspects of psychological compensation and technical aids* (pp. 191–213). New York: North-Holland.

Caramazza, A. (1989). Cognitive neuropsychology and rehabilitation: An unfulfilled promise? In X. Seron & G. Deloche (Eds.), *Cognitive approaches in neuropsychological rehabilitation* (pp. 383–398). Hillsdale, NJ: Lawrence Erlbaum Associates.

Carville, C., & Duret, H. (1875). Sur le fonction des hemispheres cerebraux. *Archiv der Physiologie, 7*, 352–490.

Darley, F. L. (1972). The efficacy of language rehabilitation in aphasia. *Journal of Speech and Hearing Disorders, 37*, 3–21.

Ebbesson, S. O. (1988). The parcellation theory and alterations in brain circuitry after injury. In S. Finger, T. E. LeVere, R. Almli, & D. G. Stein (Eds.), *Brain injury and recovery* (pp. 191–199). New York: Plenum.

Fazzini, E., Bachman, D., & Albert, M. L. (1986). Recovery of function in aphasia. *Journal of Neurolinguistics, 2*, 15–46.

Finger, S. (Ed.). (1978). *Recovery from brain damage: Research and theory*. New York: Plenum.

Finger, S., & Stein, D. G. (1982). *Brain damage and recovery: Research and clinical perspectives*. New York: Academic Press.

Freed, W. J., de Medinaceli, L., & Wyatt, R. J. (1985). Promoting functional plasticity in the damaged nervous system. *Science, 227*, 1544–1552.

Gazzaniga, M. S. (1978). Is seeing believing? Notes on clinical recovery. In S. Finger (Ed.), *Recovery from brain damage: Research and theory* (pp. 409–414). New York: Plenum.

Geschwind, N. (1974). Late changes in the nervous system: An overview. In D. G. Stein, J. J. Rosen, & N. Butters (Eds.), *Plasticity and recovery of function in the central nervous system* (pp. 203–215). New York: Academic Press.

Glick, S. D., & Greenstein, S. (1972). Facilitation of recovery after lateral hypothalamic damage by prior ablation of frontal cortex. *Nature New Biology, 239*, 187–188.

Glick, S. D., Greenstein, S., & Zimmerberg, B. (1972). Facilitation of recovery by alpha-methyl-p-tyrosine after lateral hypothalamic damage. *Science, 177*, 534–535.

Goldberger, M. E., & Murray, M. (1978). Recovery of movement and axonal sprouting may obey some of the same laws. In C. W. Cotman (Ed.), *Neuronal plasticity* (pp. 73–96). New York: Raven.

Goodman, D. C., & Horel, J. (1966). Sprouting of optic tract projections in the brain stem of the rat. *Journal of Comparative Neurology, 127*, 71–88.

Hamlin, R. M. (1970). Intellectual functions 14 years after frontal lobe surgery. *Cortex, 6*, 299–307.

Hillis, A. E. (1993). The role of models of language processing in rehabilitation of language impairments. *Aphasiology, 7*, 5–27.

Katzman, R., Bjorklund, A., Owman, C., Stenevi, U., & West, K. A. (1971). Evidence for regenerative axon sprouting of central catecholamine neurons in the rat mesencephalon following electrolytic lesions. *Brain Research, 25*, 579–596.

Kennard, M. A. (1936). Age and other factors in motor recovery from precentral lesions in monkeys. *American Journal of Physiology, 115,* 138–146.

Kennard, M. A. (1938). Reorganization of motor function in the cerebral cortex of monkeys deprived of motor and premotor areas in infancy. *Journal of Neurophysiology, 1,* 477–497.

Kertesz, A. (1988). What do we learn from recovery from aphasia? In S. G. Waxman (Ed.), *Advances in neurology: Vol 47. Functional recovery in neurological disease* (pp. 277–292). New York: Raven.

Lashley, K. S. (1929). *Brain mechanisms and intelligence.* Chicago: University of Chicago Press.

LeVere, T. E. (1988). Neural system imbalances and the consequence of large brain injuries. In S. Finger, T. E. LeVere, R. Almli, & D. G. Stein (Eds.), *Brain injury and recovery* (pp. 15–28). New York: Plenum.

Liu, C.-N., & Chambers, W. W. (1958). Intraspinal sprouting of dorsal root axons. *Archives of Neurology and Psychiatry, 79,* 46–61.

Loesche, J., & Steward, O. (1977). Behavioral correlates of denervation and reinnervation of the hippocampal formation of the rat: Recovery of alternation performance following unilateral entorhinal cortex lesions. *Brain Research Bulletin, 2,* 31–39.

Luria, A. R. (1963). *Restoration of function after brain injury.* New York: Macmillan.

Luria, A. R. (1966). *Higher cortical functions in man.* New York: Basic Books.

Marshall, J. C., & Newcombe, F. (1973). Patterns of paralexia: A psycholinguistic approach. *Journal of Psycholinguistic Research, 2,* 175–199.

Marshall, J. F. (1984). Brain function: Neural adaptation and recovery from injury. *Annual Review of Psychology, 35,* 277–308.

Matthews, D. A., Cotman, C., & Lynch, G. (1976). An electron microscopic study of lesion-induced synaptogenesis in the dentate gyrus of the adult rat: II. Reappearance of morphologically normal synaptic contacts. *Brain Research, 115,* 23–41.

Munk, H. M. (1881). *Ueber die Funktion der Grosshirnrinde. Gesammelte Mittheilungen aud den Jahren 1877–80.* Berlin: Hirschwald.

Raisman, G. (1969). Neuronal plasticity in the septal nuclei of the adult brain. *Brain Research, 14,* 25–48.

Rothi, L. J. G. (1992). Theory and clinical intervention: One clinicians view. In J. Cooper (Ed.), *Aphasia treatment: Current approaches and research opportunities* (pp. 91–98). U.S. Department of Health and Human Services, Public Health Service, National Institutes of Health, NIH Publication No. 93-3424.

Rothi, L. J., & Horner, J. (1983). Restitution and substitution: Two theories of recovery with application to neurobehavioral treatment. *Journal of Clinical Neuropsychology, 5,* 73–81.

Siegel, G. M. (1987). The limits of science in communication disorders. *Journal of Speech and Hearing Disorders, 52,* 306–312.

Siesjo, B. K. (1992). Pathophysiology and treatment of focal cerebral ischemia: Part 1. Pathophysiology. *Journal of Neurosurgery, 77,* 169–184.

Sparks, R., Helm, N., & Albert, M. (1974). Aphasia rehabilitation resulting from melodic intonation therapy. *Cortex, 10,* 303–316.

Stavraky, G. W. (1961). *Supersensitivity following lesions of the nervous system.* Toronto, Canada: University of Toronto Press.

Tarsey, D., & Baldessarini, R. J. (1974). Behavioural supersensitivity to apomorphine following chronic treatment with drugs which interfere with the synaptic functions by catecholamines. *Neuropharmacology, 13,* 927–940.

Ungerstedt, U. (1971). Postsynaptic supersensitivity after 6-Hydroxydopamine induced degeneration of the nigro-striatel dopamine system. *Acta Physiologica Scandinavica Suppl, 367,* 69–93.

Zivin, J. A., & Choi, D. W. (1991). Stroke therapy. *Scientific American, 265,* 56–63.

CHAPTER ELEVEN

Functional Compensation in Alzheimer's Disease

Cheryl L. Grady
Laboratory of Neuroscience, NIA

Raja Parasuraman
The Catholic University of America

Alzheimer's disease (AD) is the most common cause of dementia in the elderly, accounting for 50%–80% of patients with dementia (Chui, 1989; Evans et al., 1989). As recently as the 1970's, AD was considered to be a widespread degenerative disease affecting all cognitive functions in a global manner. However, more recent neuropathological (Kemper, 1984; Morrison et al., 1990; Van Hoesen & Damasio, 1987) and neuroimaging studies (Grady et al., 1988; Grady et al., 1990; Haxby et al., 1990; Haxby et al., 1988; Kumar et al., 1991; McGeer et al., 1990) have shown that AD does not affect all parts of the brain equally. Moreover, a more accurate view of the cognitive functioning of patients with AD is that this disease, particularly in its early stages, leads to a selective breakdown of particular cognitive functions rather than to a global loss (Schwartz, 1990). In addition, some cognitive functions may be spared until relatively late in the course of the disease.

These findings provide growing evidence for the relative sparing or preservation of both structure and function in the AD brain. To account for these findings, suggestions have been put forward that the brain possesses a reserve capacity or is able to compensate for damage and maintain function for some period of time despite disease progression. In this chapter we review the patterns of deficit and sparing in cognitive functioning seen in AD patients, and how these patterns are related to neuroimaging measures of brain metabolism and neuropathological features of the disease. We discuss how preservation of function, in which the neural elements responsible for a particular function are spared, and functional compensation, in which the

231

brain adapts to loss of neural elements by various types of plasticity, may both lead to preserved cognitive function in early AD. Finally, we discuss the possible mechanisms by which preservation and compensation occur.

EVIDENCE OF FUNCTIONAL COMPENSATION IN AD: COGNITIVE MEASURES

Although severe dementia is characterized by impairments of all or almost all types of cognitive processing, early in the course of AD some cognitive operations are spared, suggesting that some brain areas or networks are more resistant or less vulnerable to the effects of the disease. Parasuraman and Nestor (1993) recently reviewed evidence for preserved cognitive operations underlying memory, attention, language, and motor processes in patients with AD. In their analysis *preservation* was used to refer to elementary operations (e.g., response selection, or disengagement of attention from a spatial location) underlying a particular cognitive function, rather than to sparing of cognitive task performance as a whole. Whereas whole task performance may not be preserved in even mildly demented patients, performance of some of the underlying information-processing operations may be preserved. Such a proposal is consistent with a distributed, neural-systems view of cognitive functioning (e.g., Mesulam, 1990; Posner, Petersen, Fox, & Raichle, 1988). In this section we briefly review the evidence for sparing of cognitive operations in AD. Additional details can be found in the review by Parasuraman and Nestor (1993).

Memory

Impaired memory is one of the hallmarks of AD, and reductions in episodic, semantic, and working memory are early symptoms of the disease (Martin & Fedio, 1983; Morris & Baddeley, 1988; Nebes, 1989). Nevertheless, there are some types of memory that are relatively unaffected in mildly demented patients. Implicit memory, which can be demonstrated using priming paradigms, can be preserved in AD (Nebes, Boller, & Holland, 1986). For example, priming for lexical decisions (Chertkow, Bub, & Seidenberg, 1989) and implicit learning of repeating sequences of lights that cue a positional response (Knopman & Nissen, 1987) are reportedly unaffected early in AD. However, priming during word stem tasks or other tasks that require the retrieval of a given word is impaired in early AD (Salmon, Shimamura, Butters, & Smith, 1988). Procedural memory, such as motor skill learning, also is preserved in AD patients (Biondi & Kaszniak, 1991), and may account for the findings of preserved priming; that is, the preserved priming reflects the learning of a behavioral connection between stimulus and response and does not depend on a semantic or symbolic ability (Nebes, 1989). Nebes et al. (1984) also argued that semantic knowledge was preserved in AD and that difficulties in retrieval (which is attentionally demanding) accounted for the object-naming and word-finding deficits shown by AD patients (see also Nebes, 1989). However, there is a growing body of evidence indicating that semantic knowledge is degraded in AD (see Martin, 1992) and that the semantic memory deficit in AD cannot be attributed solely to retrieval or attentional problems (Parasuraman & Martin, 1994).

Another aspect of memory, working memory, also appears to be affected unevenly in mildly impaired AD patients. The articulatory loop, which is responsible for rehearsing the recently presented material, is only slightly affected in early AD (Morris, 1984), whereas the central executive, a module hypothesized to organize the processing and storage components of working memory, is markedly affected, resulting in impairments in remembering material under distracting conditions (Morris et al., 1988). These findings suggest that different components of memory or perhaps different memory systems have differential vulnerability to the effects of AD, which may reflect differential regional damage or more effective compensation of brain areas subserving these spared memory components.

Language

Language abilities also are unevenly affected by AD. The semantic aspects of language are prominently affected in AD patients, as are fluency, comprehension, and naming (Appel, Kertesz, & Fisman, 1982; Huff, 1989), but other aspects, such as phonological processing and word reading are spared until late in the course of the disease (Bayles, 1982; Cummings, Houlihan, & Hill, 1986). The semantic deficits do not appear to be related to perceptual difficulties, but rather reflect a breakdown of the symbolic structure of language. However, not even all aspects of semantic structure are affected, as AD patients have a loss of specific knowledge and an abnormal organization of associations within semantic categories, but show preservation of superordinate categories (Chan et al., 1993; Martin et al., 1983). Thus, the sphere of language also reflects loss of some components, with sparing of others, again suggesting differential vulnerability or compensation ability within the various brain networks responsible for these components.

Attention

Although attention in AD patients has been a focus for direct research only recently, several aspects of attentional functioning in AD have been described (for a review see Parasuraman, & Haxby, 1993). Mildly demented AD patients have pronounced difficulties under conditions requiring divided attention

(Grady et al., 1989; Morris et al., 1988; Nestor, Parasuraman, Haxby, & Grady, 1991). These are not modality specific, being present in auditory, visual, and motor tasks. These results are consistent with the notion of a generalized attentional capacity deficit in AD, or, alternatively, what Baddeley and Wilson (1988) have termed the *dysexecutive syndrome*. However, not all cognitive operations may be uniformly affected by a capacity deficit or loss of executive control in AD, and a basis for determining which operations are consistently affected and which are not has not been identified. As a result, the usefulness of these approaches to understanding attentional functioning in AD patients has been questioned (Parasuraman & Haxby, 1993). The related view espoused by Jorm (1986)—that cognitive processes that are automatic in normal adults may be less vulnerable to AD than are controlled or effortful processes—is also not fully supported by the evidence (Parasuraman & Haxby, 1993).

More clear-cut, though still incomplete evidence for preservation and impairment of attentional functions has emerged from studies that have examined more specific attentional mechanisms involved in visual detection and search tasks (Parasuraman & Haxby, 1993). For example, the focusing of attention on the basis of either stimulus location (Parasuraman, Greenwood, Haxby, & Grady, 1992) or color (Nebes, & Brady, 1989) is relatively well preserved in the mild stages of AD. However, selection on the basis of more complex features or conjunctions of features is impaired in AD (Panicker, Greenwood, Parasuraman, & Haxby, 1993). Attentional switching between spatial locations (Parasuraman et al., 1992), sensory modalities (Berardi, 1994), and between different stimulus-response "sets" (Grady et al., 1988) is also affected early in the disease. Finally, whereas the development of phasic alertness following a warning stimulus (Nebes & Brady, 1993) and sustained attention to simple targets are normal in mild AD, sustained attention is impaired under conditions requiring effortful processing of visual stimuli (Berardi, 1994).

The brain systems involved in the control of these attentional functions in normal subjects are currently the focus of intense research (Posner & Dehaene, 1994). In the review of this literature, Parasuraman and Haxby (1993) suggested that some attentional functions may operate normally in the AD brain because they are mediated by relatively local networks that are not markedly affected by pathological processes affecting communication between networks, which disrupt other attentional operations. For example, AD may not impair focusing of attention to single visual features because this function is mediated by local interactions in extrastriate perceptual processing areas (e.g., Corbetta, Miezin, Dobmeyer, Shulman, & Petersen, 1990). In contrast, attentional switching between locations, modalities, or response sets may involve interaction and coordination of more distant cortical and subcortical areas, for example, between the superior parietal cortex, prefrontal cortex, and the pulvinar for switching between locations (Corbetta, Miezin, Shulman, & Petersen, 1993; Desimone, Wessinger, Thomas, & Schneider, 1990; LaBerge, & Buchsbaum, 1990). There is neuropathological evidence for disconnection between these areas in the AD brain (Morrison et al., 1990).

Perception

Patients with AD show impairments of visual perception such as contrast sensitivity, particularly at low spatial frequencies (Cronin-Golomb et al., 1991; Mendez, Turner, Gilmore, Remler, & Tomsak, 1990; Nissen et al., 1985), visual tracking (Hutton, Nagel, & Loewenson, 1984), stereopsis (Cronin-Golomb et al., 1991), visually-guided reaching, (Hof, Bouras, Constantinidis, & Morrison, 1989; Hof, Bouras, Constantinidis, & Morrison, 1990; Mendez et al., 1990), the visual perception of objects, distinct from naming deficits (Hof & Bouras, 1991; Mendez, Mendez, Martin, Smyth, & Whitehouse, 1990), and visuoconstructive abilities, such as drawing or block design (Haxby et al., 1986). However, color and face perception are much less affected than are other visual abilities (Haxby et al., 1990; Mendez et al., 1990), suggesting sparing of ventral occipital and occipitotemporal areas known to mediate color and face perception (Haxby et al., 1991; Sergent, Ohta, & MacDonald, 1992; Zeki et al., 1991).

Auditory perception has not been examined widely in patients with AD, although one study found that some types of auditory processing were spared, such as phoneme discrimination and tone memory, whereas other types of auditory perception were impaired, such as sound localization and timbre discrimination (Kurylo, Corkin, Allard, Zatorre, & Growden, 1993). Thus, as with other cognitive processes, sensory perceptual abilities reflect a pattern of sparing and loss of components that await explanation in terms of functional sparing or compensation.

EVIDENCE OF FUNCTIONAL COMPENSATION IN AD: METABOLIC MEASURES

In addition to the perceptual and cognitive changes discussed above, patterns of sparing and loss also have been reported in neuroimaging studies of baseline or resting cerebral metabolism in AD patients. The consensus in the literature is that the parietal and temporal association cortex usually show the most diminution of glucose or oxygen utilization (Duara et al., 1986; Foster et al., 1984; Frackowiak et al., 1981; Friedland et al., 1983; Grady et al., 1990; Haxby, Duara, Grady, Rapoport, & Cutler, 1985; Kumar et al., 1991; McGeer et al., 1986), although reductions in frontal association cortex are also seen, particularly later in the course of the disease (Chase, 1987; Grady et al., 1990; Haxby et al., 1988). Primary cortical and subcortical regions are relatively spared (Benson et al., 1983; Haxby et al., 1988; Metter, Riege, Kameyama, Kuhl, & Phelps, 1984). This pattern of damage in association cortex and relative sparing of primary sensorimotor areas also is seen in the neuropathological lesions that form the basis of the diagnosis of AD (Brun & Gustafson, 1976; Kemper, 1984). Within the association neocortical areas that are primarily affected,' there is a considerable amount of heterogeneity in the areas that show the greatest reductions in metabolism. For example, right/left asymmetries of metabolism are found in association cortex in AD patients (Friedland, Budinger, Koss, & Ober, 1985; Haxby et al., 1985; Kumar et al., 1991), such that some patients show disproportionately greater left hemisphere reductions, and others have greater reductions in the right hemisphere. Intrahemispheric (anterior/posterior) heterogeneity also is found in AD patients (Chase, 1987; Grady et al., 1990; Haxby et al., 1988), such that although 50% or more of patients show greater reductions in parietal cortex with relative sparing of frontal cortex, a large fraction of patients shows the opposite pattern (Grady et al., 1990).

Correlations between metabolic rates measured at rest in various regions of cortex also have been examined in patients with AD. Mildly to moderately demented patients show fewer significant correlations between frontal and parietal metabolic rates than do healthy older controls (Horwitz, Grady, Schlageter, Duara, & Rapoport, 1987). In addition, the number of significant correlations between glucose metabolism in right/left homologous regions is significantly reduced in AD, which is of interest since these homologous correlations were among the largest correlations found in both old and young healthy subjects (Horwitz, Duara, & Rapoport, 1986). Other inter-regional correlations of resting metabolism are spared, such as those between temporal and occipital regions. Thus, early in the course of AD, there appears to be an alteration in the functional coupling of brain regions that reflects impaired communication between areas known to be part of an attentional network, namely, frontal and parietal cortex (Bushnell, Goldberg, & Robinson, 1981; Goldberg & Bruce, 1985; Goldberg & Bushnell, 1981; Mesulam, 1985; Morecraft, Geula, & Mesulam, 1993; Pardo, Fox, & Raichle, 1991), but other networks remain unaffected.

The cognitive functions that are spared in AD may be explained at least in part by their dependence on brain regions that are relatively unaffected. This can be seen in correlations among the patterns of sparing and loss in both resting metabolism and neuropsychological impairments that are seen in AD patients. For example, metabolic right/left asymmetry measures in frontal and parietal cortices are significantly correlated with measures of right/left neuropsychological discrepancy, such that those patients with disproportionate left hemisphere hypometabolism have greater language impairment compared to visuospatial function, and those with disproportionate right hemisphere hypometabolism have more impairment of visuoconstructive abilities (Foster et al., 1983; Friedland et al., 1985; Haxby et al., 1985). Parietal/frontal metabolic measures and discrepancies between performance on neuropsychological tests mediated by parietal or frontal cortex also are significantly correlated (Haxby et al., 1988). In addition, attentional measures are related to metabolic measures in AD patients: for example, divided attention to speech stimuli is correlated with left temporal lobe metabolism (Grady et al., 1989), and measures of divided or shifting attention in dual task paradigms are correlated with metabolism in right parietal and frontal cortex (Nestor et al., 1991; Parasuraman et al., 1992).

Evidence for functional compensation can be found in the relation between the behavioral deficits and metabolic abnormalities. Mildly affected patients have abnormal memory performance, but often score in the normal range on neocortically-mediated cognitive tests of attention, executive function, language and visuospatial function (Grady et al., 1988; Haxby et al., 1986), whereas moderately demented patients are significantly impaired on all of these tests. Nevertheless, both mildly and moderately demented patients show reductions in baseline measures of parietal glucose metabolism, and have significantly increased metabolic asymmetry in frontal, parietal and temporal association cortex. In a group of mildly demented AD patients followed longitudinally (Grady et al., 1988), neocortical metabolic abnormalities preceded, by as few as 8 or as many as 36 months, the appearance of impairments on the neuropsychological tests that are most sensitive to changes early in AD. These results show that in mildly affected AD patients, metabolic changes in neocortex are seen prior to changes in neocortically mediated neuropsychological performance, and suggest that the brain is able to compensate for the metabolic dysfunction and maintain performance for sometimes considerable lengths of time.

MECHANISMS OF PRESERVED FUNCTION

Spared Areas of the Brain: Local Versus Distributed Networks

One explanation for preserved cognitive functioning in AD patients could be that the preserved functions rely on localized cortical circuits or networks that remain undamaged early in the disease, whereas affected functions rely on communication between these circuits, which is altered by the neuropathological changes in the brain. Support for this explanation can be found in the study of Grady et al. (1988), in which attention switching between response sets was affected before language or visuoconstructive abilities. Attention is thought to depend not only on the integrity of frontal and parietal cortex, but also on the interactions between anterior and pos-

terior cortex (Mesulam, 1981). As discussed previously, Parasuraman and
Haxby (1993) offered a similar explanation for preservation of single-feature
focused attention and impairment of attentional switching in AD patients.
Language and visuospatial function may be more localized to perisylvian
and parietal cortex, respectively, and thus affected later in the disease when
the local circuits are damaged. Changes in the functional connections between anterior and posterior brain regions early in the course of AD, as
indicated by the reductions in significant frontal-parietal correlations and
the increased heterogeneity of parietal/frontal metabolic ratios, may impair
the ability to attend to abstract and complex aspects of the environment. In
addition, there is evidence from neuropathological studies that the cortical
layers and cells most affected by AD are the pyramidal cells in layers III
and V, those which have the greatest number of long intracortical connections (Lewis, Campbell, Terry, & Morrison, 1987; Morrison et al., 1990; Pearson, Esiri, Hiorns, Wilcock, & Powell, 1985; Rogers & Morrison, 1985). Thus,
those functions most sensitive to a disconnection between regions would show
impairment before functions more dependent on local or regional circuits.

Reorganization of Cortical Networks

Recent evidence from experiments involving measurement of regional cerebral blood flow (rCBF) during cognitive activation using positron emission
tomography (PET) has suggested a possible mechanism for functional compensation—that of reorganization of the cortical networks that are utilized
during task performance. The evidence suggests that reorganization may
occur in both normal older adults and in patients with AD. In a series of studies
designed to examine the effects of age and dementia on the areas of the brain
activated in object and spatial vision (Grady et al., 1993; Grady et al., 1992;
Grady et al., 1994; Haxby et al., 1991), it was demonstrated that using PET one
could identify two functionally distinct pathways in extrastriate visual cortex—
namely, ventral occipitotemporal activation during the perception of objects
and dorsal occipitoparietal activation during the perception of spatial relations
among objects, similar to the pathways identified in non-human primates
(Desimone & Ungerleider, 1989; Mishkin, Ungerleider, & Macko, 1983;
Ungerleider & Mishkin, 1982; Van Essen, 1985). In the studies in question, a
face matching task was used as the object vision task and a location matching
task as the spatial vision task. The dissociations in rCBF activation were found
in both young and old subjects; however, there were some interesting age
differences between the groups. Young subjects showed more activation of
prestriate cortex in the lingual gyrus in both the face and location matching
tasks. These prestriate regions are early in the visual pathway, possibly before
the ventral/dorsal dissociation. Old subjects, on the other hand, had more
activation in occipitotemporal cortex during both face and location matching,

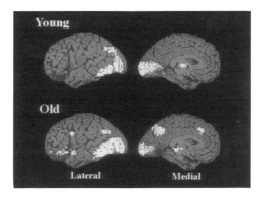

FIG. 11.1.   Cortical areas of significantly ($p < .001$) increased blood flow during
a face matching task compared to a control task in old and young subjects,
shown on medial and lateral schematics of the left hemisphere. Young subjects
had significantly greater activation in prestriate occipital cortex (seen in the
medial projections) and old subjects had greater activation in lateral
occipitotemporal and prefrontal cortex. Reaction time was significantly slower
in the old subjects (3422 ± 940 v. 2196 ± 669 msec, $p < .001$), but accuracy
was equivalent in the two groups ($76 \pm 7\%$ v. $81 \pm 9\%$ correct). (Adapted
from Grady et al., 1994.)

and there also were age-related changes in middle prefrontal cortex of the left
hemisphere during both tasks (see Fig. 11.1). During location matching there
were additional areas of prefrontal cortex, as well as in inferior and medial
parietal cortex, that showed more activation in the old subjects. These results
suggest that the neurobiological changes which underlie the performance
decrements of old subjects on these visual tasks are a reduction in the
processing efficiency of prestriate occipital cortex, leading to increased
utilization of one or more cortical networks to compensate for this inefficiency.
This functional reorganization may also indicate a difference in strategy used
by the two groups. For example, given the role of prefrontal cortex in working
memory (particularly Brodmann's area 46), activation of this region in the old
subjects suggests that these visual tasks place a greater demand on working
memory in old subjects than in young subjects—possibly on the organizational
function of the central executive.

Using a face matching task similar to the one mentioned above that was
used to study normal aging, Grady et al. (1993) examined rCBF activation
in mildly demented AD patients and healthy age-matched controls. Both
patients and controls showed bilateral rCBF increases in occipitotemporal
extrastriate cortex during face matching, compared to a control task, replicating the occipitotemporal activation seen in young and old healthy subjects
(see Fig. 11.2). In addition, the patients showed greater rCBF activation in
dorsal prefrontal cortex just anterior to the precentral sulcus. Greater activation of dorsal prefrontal cortex in the patients may reflect an increased

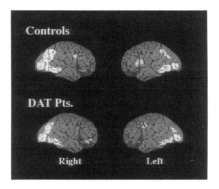

FIG. 11.2. Cortical areas of significantly ($p < .01$) increased blood flow during a face matching task compared to a control task in patients with dementia of the Alzheimer type and controls, shown on lateral schematics of the right and left hemispheres. Patients had greater activation in dorsal prefrontal cortex in the left hemisphere, and slower reaction times compared to the control subjects (3393 ± 1284 v. 2040 ± 560 msec, $p < .005$). Accuracy was equivalent in the two groups ($88 \pm 4\%$ v. $92 \pm 4\%$ correct). (Adapted from Grady et al., 1993.)

attentional load during face matching due to their reduced cognitive capacity, and may indicate greater use of the frontal segment of the attentional network, referred to above, in their performance of this task. In a test of this hypothesis, correlations between rCBF in anterior and posterior regions were examined in this group of AD patients (Horwitz et al., 1994). Whereas the control subjects showed strong correlations between rCBF in occipital and occipitotemporal areas and frontal cortex, the AD patients had signficant correlations only among frontal regions. This finding supports the idea of alterations in functional networks in AD brains during visual processing and is evidence for a compensatory mechanism that enables the patients to perform the task.

These studies taken together suggest that both aging and dementia are characterized by some degree of reorganization of functional networks during visual perceptual tasks, and perhaps during other types of cognitive processing. The degree to which this reorganization helps maintain cognitive performance remains to be determined. Prefrontal cortex seems to play a special role in this reorganization, and may hold the key for understanding how a wide range of cognitive abilities are spared in both aging and AD.

Plasticity of Neural Elements

Plasticity of neural elements such as dendrites and synapses is another factor that could play a role in functional sparing or compensation in AD. Plasticity of synapses has been found in AD brains (DeKosky & Scheff, 1990), such that the numbers of synapses is decreased, but the remaining synapses are increased in size, presumably in an attempt to maintain synaptic efficacy. How well this works is unknown, but this is an indication that the synapses may be able to function more or less normally under some conditions, despite the beginnings of neuropathological changes. Some behavioral evidence consistent with this notion can be found in the neuroimaging study of face perception in mildly demented AD patients referred to in the previous section (Grady et al., 1993). All of the patients had increased rCBF in occipitotemporal cortex during the face matching task, as did a group of controls—even those patients with significant baseline flow reductions in this area. For example, in patients with decreased occipitotemporal flow during the control task, the rCBF activation in occipitotemporal cortex was 12% in one patient and 10% in another—increases that were well within the normal range of increases seen in the control subjects for this region of cortex (8%–25%). Duara and colleagues have reported a similar result in AD patients performing various memory tasks during measurement of cerebral glucose utilization (Duara et al., 1992), that is, activation in those areas with reduced baseline metabolism. These findings, that early in the course of AD, regions of cortex with low flow or metabolism—presumably due to damage from the disease process—can show appropriate activation during cognitive tasks, suggest that the functional failure is at least partially reversible and may be related to changes in synaptic efficacy or other forms of synaptic plasticity.

Neural plasticity may also be related to age. Patients with early onset of AD have been reported to show significantly greater metabolic reductions in parietal regions, but these were not associated with greater impairments in performance on neuropsychological tests of parietal lobe function until some time later (Grady, Haxby, Horwitz, Berg, & Rapoport, 1987; Small et al., 1989). These data suggest that younger AD patients (i.e. in their 60's) are better able to compensate cognitively for metabolic dysfunction than are older patients, perhaps because of greater plasticity of neural elements (Horwitz, 1988). In the parahippocampal and dentate gyri, plasticity—in the form of increased dendrites—was found to increase with age (Buell & Coleman, 1981; Flood, Buell, DeFiore, Horwitz, & Coleman, 1985), but only up to a certain age (around 80 years), after which it declined (Flood et al., 1985). Similarly, in the monkey, dendrites in prefrontal cortex were found to be increased in older monkeys and to be decreased in very old animals (Cupp & Uemura, 1980). Dendritic changes in the human association cortex have not been examined in many areas, although there is a report of decreasing, rather than increasing, dendritic length with age in Wernicke's area in the superior temporal gyrus up to age 80 (Jacobs, & Scheibel, 1993). The future exploration of this relation between neural plasticity and age in human association cortex could be critical for our understanding of functional compensation in both healthy aging and dementia.

Threshold Effects and Redundancy

The concept of thresholds of neuronal damage in degenerative diseases has been invoked primarily in the case of Parkinson's disease. It has often been suggested that the symptoms of Parkinson's disease only become manifest when the number of dopaminergic neurons in the substantia nigra falls below 20% of pre-morbid levels (Bernheimer, Birkmayer, Hornykiewicz, Jellinger, & Seitelberger, 1973). It has been suggested that the known ability of dopaminergic neurons to increase the synthesis and release of neurotransmitter in response to a loss of cells (Snyder, Keller, & Zigmond, 1990) may be a compensatory mechanism responsible for this threshold effect (Calne & Zigmond, 1991). Similar mechanisms might be at work in AD in areas of the brain that supply vital neurotransmitters, for example, the nucleus basalis of Meynert, explaining at least in part the observed patterns of sparing and loss.

One factor that may be related to degree of neuropathological damage and thresholds for symptom appearance in AD is that of educational level of the patient. It has been suggested that more education may raise the threshold for behavioral impairment in AD by increasing the reserve capacity of the brain (perhaps through increased redundancy or increased propensity for functional reorganization), thus prolonging the time between the onset of neuropathological changes and the onset of symptoms (Satz, 1993). There is some evidence in support of this notion—more years of education are associated with more severe reductions of glucose metabolism in the parietal lobes (Stern, Alexander, Prohovnik, & Mayeux, 1992) but not more severe dementia. Education may therefore provide some protection early in the course of AD against the damage occurring in the brain and may delay the onset of symptoms, accounting in part for the patterns of spared functions that are observed. However, the relation between education and the specific components of the various cognitive processes that are spared is not known.

CONCLUSIONS

The behavioral evidence in patients with AD clearly shows that early in the course of the disease, numerous components of different cognitive processes are either completely or relatively unaffected, despite marked impairments in other components of the same processes. With this review we have attempted to present a convincing argument that, although some of these sparings are probably the result of sparing of the critical brain circuits, other spared functions are due to the efforts of the brain to compensate for loss of circuits or of critical components of circuits. It is unclear at the present time which of the various compensatory mechanisms is responsible for which particular spared function, although it is likely that more than one mechanism, for example synaptic plasticity and reorganization of networks, may be occuring simultaneously. Future research should focus on more fully defining the specific components of cognition that are spared, which brain circuits are responsible for these components, and finally how the operation of these circuits is spared, reorganized, or otherwise modified in response to the effects of AD.

REFERENCES

Appel, J., Kertesz, A., & Fisman, M. (1982). A study of language function in Alzheimer patients. *Brain and Language, 17*, 73–91.

Baddeley, A. D., & Wilson, B. (1988). Frontal amnesia and the dysexecutive syndrome. *Brain and Cognition, 7*, 212–230.

Bayles, K. A. (1982). Language function in senile dementia. *Brain and Language, 16*, 265–280.

Benson, D. F., Kuhl, D. E., Hawkins, R. A., Phelps, M. E., Cummings, J. L., & Tsai, S. Y. (1983). The fluorodeoxyglucose 18F scan in Alzheimer's disease and multi-infarct dementia. *Archives of Neurology, 40*, 711–714.

Berardi, A. (1994). *Varieties of attention in mild dementia of the Alzheimer type and in healthy aging: Behavioral and positron emission tomography studies.* University of Lausanne, Switzerland: Unpublished PhD dissertation.

Bernheimer, H., Birkmayer, W., Hornykiewicz, O., Jellinger, K., & Seitelberger, F. (1973). Brain dopamine and the syndromes of Parkinson and Huntington: Clinical, morphological and neurochemical correlations. *Journal of the Neurological Sciences, 20*, 415–455.

Biondi, M. S., & Kaszniak, A. (1991). Implicit and explicit memory in Alzheimer's disease and Parkinson's disease. *Journal of Clinical and Experimental Neuropsychology, 13*, 339–358.

Brun, A., & Gustafson, L. (1976). Distribution of cerebral degeneration in Alzheimer's disease. *Archiv fuer Psychiatrie und Nervenkrankheiten, 223*, 15–33.

Buell, S. J., & Coleman, P. D. (1981). Quantitative evidence for selective dendritic growth in normal human aging but not in senile dementia. *Brain Research, 214*, 23–41.

Bushnell, M. C., Goldberg, M. E., & Robinson, D. L. (1981). Behavioral enhancement of visual responses in monkey cerebral cortex: I. Modulation in posterior parietal cortex related to selective visual attention. *Journal of Neurophysiology, 46*, 755–772.

Calne, D. B., & Zigmond, M. J. (1991). Compensatory mechanisms in degenerative neurologic diseases. *Archives of Neurology, 48*, 361–363.

Chan, A. S., Butters, N., Paulsen, J. S., Salmon, D. P., Swenson, M. R., & Maloney, L. T. (1993). An assessment of the semantic network in patients with Alzheimer's disease. *Journal of Cognitive Neuroscience, 5*, 254–261.

Chase, T. N. (1987). Cortical glucose utilization patterns in primary degenerative dementia of the anterior and posterior types. *Archives of Gerontology and Geriatrics, 6*, 289–297.

Chertkow, H., Bub, D., & Seidenberg, M. (1989). Priming and semantic memory in Alzheimer's disease. *Brain and Language, 36*, 420–446.

Chui, H. C. (1989). Dementia. A review emphasizing clinicopathologic correlation and brain-behavior relationships. *Archives of Neurology, 46*, 806–814.

Corbetta, M., Miezin, F. M., Dobmeyer, S., Shulman, G. L., & Petersen, S. E. (1990). Attentional modulation of neural processing of shape, color, and velocity in humans. *Science, 248*, 1556–1559.

Corbetta, M., Miezin, F. M., Shulman, G. L., & Petersen, S. E. (1993). A PET study of visuospatial attention. *Journal of Neuroscience, 13*, 1202–1226.

Cronin-Golomb, A., Corkin, S., Rizzo, J. F., Cohen, J., Growdon, J. H., & Banks, K. S. (1991). Visual dysfunction in Alzheimer's disease: Relation to normal aging. *Annals of Neurology, 29*, 41–52.

Cummings, J. L., Houlihan, J. P., & Hill, M. A. (1986). The pattern of reading deterioration in dementia of the Alzheimer type: Observations and implications. *Brain and Language, 29*, 315–322.

Cupp, C. J., & Uemura, E. (1980). Age-related changes in prefrontal cortex of macaca mulatta: Quantitative analysis of dendritic branching patterns. *Experimental Neurology, 69*, 143–163.

DeKosky, S. T., & Scheff, S. W. (1990). Synapse loss in frontal cortex biopsies in Alzheimer's disease: Correlation with cognitive severity. *Annals of Neurology, 27*, 457–464.

Desimone, R., & Ungerleider, L. G. (1989). Neural mechanisms of visual processing in monkeys. In H. Goodglass, & A. R. Damasio (Ed.), *Handbook of neuropsychology* (pp. 267–300). Amsterdam: Elsevier.

Desimone, R., Wessinger, M., Thomas, L., & Schneider, W. (1990). Attentional control of visual perception: Cortical and subcortical mechanisms. *Cold Spring Harbor Symposia on Quantitative Biology, 55*, 963–971.

Duara, R., Barker, W. W., Chang, J., Yoshii, F., Loewenstein, D. A., & Pascal, S. (1992). Viability of neocortical function shown in behavioral activation state PET studies in Alzheimer Disease. *Journal of Cerebral Blood Flow and Metabolism, 12*, 927–934.

Duara, R., Grady, C. L., Haxby, J. V., Sundaram, M., Cutler, N. R., Heston, L., Moore, A. M., Schlageter, N. L., Larson, S., & Rapoport, S. I. (1986). Positron emission tomography in Alzheimer's disease. *Neurology, 36*, 879–887.

Evans, D. A., Funkenstein, H., Albert, M. S., Scher, P. A., Cook, N. R., Chown, M. J., Hebert, L. E., Hennekens, C. H., & Taylor, J. O. (1989). Prevalence of Alzheimer's disease in a community population of older persons. Higher than previously reported. *Journal of the American Medical Association, 262*, 2551–2556.

Flood, D. G., Buell, S. J., DeFiore, C. H., Horwitz, G. J., & Coleman, P. D. (1985). Age-related dendritic growth in dentate gyrus of human brain is followed by regression in the 'oldest old'. *Brain Research, 345*, 366–368.

Foster, N. L., Chase, T. N., Fedio, P., Patronas, N. J., Brooks, R. A., & DiChiro, G. (1983). Alzheimer's disease: Focal cortical changes shown by positron emission tomography. *Neurology, 33*, 961–965.

Foster, N. L., Chase, T. N., Mansi, L., Brooks, R., Fedio, P., Patronas, N. J., & DiChiro, G. (1984). Cortical abnormalities in Alzheimer's disease. *Annals of Neurology, 16*, 649–654.

Frackowiak, R. S. J., Pozzilli, C., Legg, N. J., Du Boulay, G. H., Marshall, J., Lenzi, G. L., & Jones, T. (1981). Regional cerebral oxygen supply and utilization in dementia. A clinical and physiological study with oxygen-15 and positron tomography. *Brain, 104*, 753–778.

Friedland, R. P., Budinger, T. F., Ganz, E., Yano, Y., Mathis, C. A., Koss, E., Ober, A. B., Heusman, R. H., & Derenzo, S. E. (1983). Regional cerebral metabolic alterations in dementia of the Alzheimer type: Positron emission tomography with (18F)fluoro-deoxyglucose. *Journal of Computer Assisted Tomography, 7*, 590–598.

Friedland, R. P., Budinger, T. F., Koss, E., & Ober, B. A. (1985). Alzheimer's disease: Anterior-posterior and lateral hemispheric alterations in cortical glucose utilization. *Neuroscience Letters, 53*, 235–240.

Goldberg, M. E., & Bruce, C. J. (1985). Cerebral cortical activity associated with the orientation of visual attention in the monkey. *Vision Research, 25*, 471–481.

Goldberg, M. E., & Bushnell, M. C. (1981). Behavioral enhancement of visual responses in monkey cerebral cortex. II. Modulation in frontal eye fields specifically related to saccades. *Journal of Neurophysiology, 46*, 773–787.

Grady, C. L., Grimes, A. M., Patronas, N., Sunderland, T., Foster, N. L., & Rapoport, S. I. (1989). Divided attention, as measured by dichotic speech performance, in dementia of the Alzheimer type. *Archives of Neurology, 46*, 317–320.

Grady, C. L., Haxby, J. V., Horwitz, B., Berg, G. W., & Rapoport, S. I. (1987). Neuropsychological and cerebral metabolic function in early vs late onset dementia of the Alzheimer type. *Neuropsychologia, 25*, 807–816.

Grady, C. L., Haxby, J. V., Horwitz, B., Gillette, J., Salerno, J. A., Gonzalez-Aviles, A., Carson, R. E., Herscovitch, P., Schapiro, M. B., & Rapoport, S. I. (1993). Activation of cerebral blood flow during a face perception task in patients with dementia of the Alzheimer type. *Neurobiology of Aging, 14*, 35–44.

Grady, C. L., Haxby, J. V., Horwitz, B., Sundaram, M., Berg, G., Schapiro, M. B., Friedland, R. P., & Rapoport, S. I. (1988). Longitudinal study of the early neuropsychological and cerebral metabolic changes in dementia of the Alzheimer type. *Journal of Clinical and Experimental Neuropsychology, 10*, 576–596.

Grady, C. L., Haxby, J. V., Horwitz, B., Ungerleider, L. G., Schapiro, M. B., Carson, R. E., Herscovitch, P., Mishkin, M., & Rapoport, S. I. (1992). Dissociation of object and spatial vision in human extrastriate cortex: age-related changes in activation of regional cerebral blood flow measured with [^{15}O]water and positron emission tomography. *Journal of Cognitive Neuroscience, 4*, 23–34.

Grady, C. L., Haxby, J. V., Schapiro, M. B., Gonzalez-Aviles, A., Kumar, A., Ball, M. J., Heston, L., & Rapoport, S. I. (1990). Subgroups in dementia of the Alzheimer type identified using positron emission tomography. *Journal of Neuropsychiatry and Clinical Neurosciences, 2*, 373–384.

Grady, C. L., Maisog, J. M., Horwitz, B., Ungerleider, L. G., Mentis, M. J., Salerno, J. A., Pietrini, P., Wagner, E., & Haxby, J. V. (1994). Age-related changes in cortical blood flow activation during visual processing of faces and location. *Journal of Neuroscience, 14*, 1450–1462.

Haxby, J. V., Duara, R., Grady, C. L., Rapoport, S. I., & Cutler, N. R. (1985). Relations between neuropsychological and cerebral metabolic asymmetries in early Alzheimer's disease. *Journal of Cerebral Blood Flow and Metabolism, 5*, 193–200.

Haxby, J. V., Grady, C. L., Duara, R., Schlageter, N. L., Berg, G., & Rapoport, S. I. (1986). Neocortical metabolic abnormalities precede non-memory cognitive deficits in early Alzheimer-type dementia. *Archives of Neurology, 43*, 882–885.

Haxby, J. V., Grady, C. L., Horwitz, B., Ungerleider, L. G., Mishkin, M., Carson, R. E., Herscovitch, P., Schapiro, M. B., & Rapoport, S. I. (1991). Dissociation of object and spatial visual processing pathways in human extrastriate cortex. *Proceedings of the National Academy of Science (USA), 88*, 1621–1625.

Haxby, J. V., Grady, C. L., Koss, E., Horwitz, B., Heston, L. L., Schapiro, M. B., Friedland, R. P., & Rapoport, S. I. (1990). Longitudinal study of cerebral metabolic asymmetries and associated neuropsychological patterns in early dementia of the Alzheimer type. *Archives of Neurology, 47*, 753–760.

Haxby, J. V., Grady, C. L., Koss, E., Horwitz, B., Schapiro, M. B., Friedland, R. P., & Rapoport, S. I. (1988). Heterogeneous anterior-posterior metabolic patterns in Alzheimer's type dementia. *Neurology, 38*, 1853–1863.

Hof, P. R., & Bouras, C. (1991). Object recognition deficit in Alzheimer's disease: Possible disconnection of the occipito-temporal component of the visual system. *Neuroscience Letters, 122*, 53–56.

Hof, P. R., Bouras, C., Constantinidis, J., & Morrison, J. H. (1989). Balint's syndrome in Alzheimer's disease: Specific disruption of the occipito-parietal visual pathway. *Brain Research, 493*, 368–375.

Hof, P. R., Bouras, C., Constantinidis, J., & Morrison, J. H. (1990). Selective disconnection of specific visual association pathways in cases of Alzheimer's disease presenting with Balint's syndrome. *Journal of Neuropathology and Experimental Neurology, 49*, 168–184.

Horwitz, B. (1988). Neuroplasticity and the progression of Alzheimer's disease. *International Journal of Neuroscience, 41*, 1–14.

Horwitz, B., Duara, R., & Rapoport, S. I. (1986). Age differences in intercorrelations between regional cerebral metabolic rates for glucose. *Annals of Neurology, 19*, 60–67.

Horwitz, B., Grady, C. L., Schlageter, N. L., Duara, R., & Rapoport, S. I. (1987). Intercorrelations of regional cerebral glucose metabolic rates in Alzheimer's disease. *Brain Research, 407*, 294–306.

Horwitz, B., McIntosh, A. R., Haxby, J. V., Kurkjian, M., Salerno, J. A., Schapiro, M. B., Rapoport, S. I., & Grady, C. L. (1994). Altered brain functional interactions during visual processing in Alzheimer-type dementia. *submitted.*

Huff, F. J. (1989). Language in normal aging and age-related neurological diseases. In R. D. Nebes, & S. Corkin (Ed.), *Handbook of neuropsychology* (pp. 251–264). Amsterdam: Elsevier.

Hutton, J. T., Nagel, J. A., & Loewenson, R. B. (1984). Eye tracking dysfunction in Alzheimer-type dementia. *Neurology, 34*, 99–102.

Jacobs, B., & Scheibel, A. B. (1993). A quantitative dendritic analysis of Wernicke's area in humans. I. Lifespan changes. *Journal of Comparative Neurology, 327*, 83–96.

Jorm, A. F. (1986). Automatic and controlled information processing in senile dementia. *Psychological Medicine, 16*, 77–88.

Kemper, T. (1984). Neuroanatomical and neuropathological changes in normal aging and in dementia. In M. Albert (Ed.), *Clinical neurology of aging* (pp. 9–52). New York: Oxford Univ. Press.

Knopman, D. S., & Nissen, M. J. (1987). Implicit learning in patients with probable Alzheimer's disease. *Neurology, 37*, 784–788.

Kumar, A., Schapiro, M. B., Grady, C., Haxby, J. V., Wagner, E., Salerno, J. A., Friedland, R. P., & Rapoport, S. I. (1991). High-resolution PET studies in Alzheimer's disease. *Neuropsychopharmocology, 4*, 35–46.

Kurylo, D. D., Corkin, S., Allard, T., Zatorre, R. J., & Growden, J. H. (1993). Auditory function in Alzheimer's disease. *Neurology, 43*, 1893–1899.

LaBerge, D., & Buchsbaum, M. S. (1990). Positron emission tomographic measurements of pulvinar activity during an attention task. *Journal of Neuroscience, 10*, 613–619.

Lewis, D. A., Campbell, M. J., Terry, R. D., & Morrison, J. H. (1987). Laminar and regional distributions of neurofibrillary tangles and neuritic plaques in Alzheimer's disease: A quantitative study of visual and auditory cortices. *Journal of Neuroscience, 7*, 1799–1808.

Martin, A. (1992). Degraded knowledge representations in patients with Alzheimer's disease: Implications for models of semantic and repetition priming. In L. R. Squire, & N. Butters (Ed.), *Neuropsychology of memory* (2nd ed.) (pp. 220–232.). New York: The Guilford Press.

Martin, A., & Fedio, P. (1983). Word production and comprehension in Alzheimer's disease: The breakdown of semantic knowledge. *Brain and Language, 26*, 181–185.

McGeer, E. G., Peppard, R. P., McGeer, P. L., Tuokko, H., Crockett, D., Parks, R., Akiyama, H., Calne, D. B., Beattie, B. L., & Harrop, R. (1990). 18-Fluorodeoxyglucose positron emission tomography studies in presumed Alzheimer cases, including 13 serial scans. *Canadian Journal of the Neurological Sciences, 17*, 1–11.

McGeer, P. L., Kamo, H., Harrop, R., Li, D. K. B., Tuokko, H., McGeer, E. G., Adam, M. J., Ammann, W., Beattie, B. L., Calne, D. B., Martin, W. R. W., Pate, B. D., Rogers, J. G., Ruth, T. J., Sayre, C. I., & Stoessl, A. J. (1986). Positron emission tomography in patients with clinically diagnosed Alzheimer's disease. *Canadian Medical Association Journal, 134*, 597–607.

Mendez, M. F., Mendez, M. A., Martin, R., Smyth, K. A., & Whitehouse, P. J. (1990). Complex visual disturbances in Alzheimer's disease. *Neurology, 40*, 439–443.

Mendez, M. F., Turner, J., Gilmore, G. C., Remler, B., & Tomsak, R. L. (1990). Balint's syndrome in Alzheimer's disease: visuospatial functions. *International Journal of Neuroscience, 54*, 339–346.

Mesulam, M. M. (1981). A cortical network for directed attention and unilateral neglect. *Annals of Neurology, 10*, 309–325.

Mesulam, M.-M. (1985). Attention, confusional states, and neglect. In M.-M. Mesulam (Ed.), *Principles of behavioral neurology* (pp. 125–168). Philadelphia: F. A. Davis.

Mesulam, M.-M. (1990). Large-scale neurocognitive networks and distributed processing for attention, language, and memory. *Annals of Neurology, 28,* 597–613.

Metter, E. J., Riege, W. H., Kameyama, M., Kuhl, D. E., & Phelps, M. E. (1984). Cerebral metabolic relationships for selected brain regions in Alzheimer's, Huntington's and Parkinson's diseases. *Journal of Cerebral Blood Flow and Metabolism, 4,* 500–506.

Mishkin, M., Ungerleider, L. G., & Macko, K. A. (1983). Object vision and spatial vision: Two cortical pathways. *Trends in Neuroscience, 6,* 414–417.

Morecraft, R. J., Geula, C., & Mesulam, M. M. (1993). Architecture of connectivity within a cingulo-fronto-parietal neurocognitive network for directed attention. *Archives of Neurology, 50,* 279–284.

Morris, R. G. (1984). Dementia and the functioning of the articulatory loop. *Cognitive Neuropsychology, 1,* 143–157.

Morris, R. G., & Baddeley, A. D. (1988). Primary and working memory in Alzheimer-type dementia. *Journal of Clinical and Experimental Neuropsychology, 10,* 279–296.

Morrison, J. H., Hof, P. R., Campbell, M. J., DeLima, A. D., Voigt, T., Bouras, C., Cox, K., & Young, W. G. (1990). Cellular pathology in Alzheimer's disease: Implications for cortico-cortical disconnection and differential vulnerability. In S. I. Rapoport, H. Petit, D. Leys, & Y. Christen (Ed.), *Imaging, cerebral topography, and Alzheimer's disease* (pp. 19–40). Berlin: Springer Verlag.

Nebes, R. D. (1989). Semantic memory in Alzheimer's disease. *Psychological Bulletin, 106,* 377–394.

Nebes, R. D., Boller, F., & Holland, A. (1986). Use of semantic context by patients with Alzheimer's disease. *Psychology and Aging, 1,* 261–269.

Nebes, R. D., & Brady, C. B. (1989). Focused and divided attention in Alzheimer's disease. *Cortex, 25,* 305–315.

Nebes, R. D., & Brady, C. B. (1993). Phasic and tonic alertness in Alzheimer's disease. *Cortex, 29,* 77–90. Nebes, R. D., Martin, D. C., & Horn, L. C. (1984). Sparing of semantic memory in Alzheimer's disease. *Journal of Abnormal Psychology, 93,* 321–330.

Nestor, P. G., Parasuraman, R., Haxby, J. V., & Grady, C. L. (1991). Divided attention and metabolic brain dysfunction in mild dementia of the Alzheimer's type. *Neuropsychologia, 29,* 379–387.

Nissen, M. J., Corkin, S., Buonanno, F. S., Growdon, J. H., Wray, S. H., & Bauer, J. (1985). Spatial vision in Alzheimer's disease: general findings and a case report. *Archives of Neurology, 42,* 667–671.

Panicker, S., Greenwood, P. M., Parasuraman, R., & Haxby, J. V. (1993). Cued visual search in Alzheimer's disease. *Society for Neuroscience Abstracts, 19,* 564.

Parasuraman, R., Greenwood, P. M., Haxby, J. V., & Grady, C. L. (1992). Visuospatial attention in dementia of the Alzheimer type. *Brain, 115,* 711–733.

Parasuraman, R., & Haxby, J. V. (1993). Attention and brain function in Alzheimer's disease: A review. *Neuropsychology, 7,* 242–272.

Parasuraman, R., & Martin, A. (1994). Cognition in Alzheimer's disease: Disorders of attention and semantic knowledge. *Current Opinion in Neurobiology, 4,* 237–244.

Parasuraman, R., & Nestor, P. G. (1993). Preserved cognitive operations in early Alzheimer's disease. In J. Cerella, J. Rybash, W. Hoyer, & M. L. Commons (Ed.), *Adult information processing: Limits on loss* (pp. 77–111). San Diego, CA: Academic Press.

Pardo, J. V., Fox, P. T., & Raichle, M. E. (1991). Localization of a human system for sustained attention by positron emission tomography. *Nature, 349,* 61–64.

Pearson, R. C. A., Esiri, M. M., Hiorns, R. W., Wilcock, G. K., & Powell, T. P. S. (1985). Anatomical correlates of the distribution of the pathological changes in the neocortex in Alzheimer disease. *Proceedings of the National Academy of Sciences, USA, 82,* 4531–4534.

Posner, M., & Dehaene, S. (1994). Attentional networks. *Trends in Neuroscience, 17,* 75–79.

Posner, M. I., Petersen, S. E., Fox, P. T., & Raichle, M. E. (1988). Localization of cognitive operations in the human brain. *Science, 240*, 1627–1631.

Rogers, J., & Morrison, J. H. (1985). Quantitative morphology and regional and laminar distributions of senile plaques in Alzheimer's disease. *Journal of Neuroscience, 5*, 2801–2808.

Salmon, D. P., Shimamura, A. P., Butters, N., & Smith, S. (1988). Lexical and semantic priming deficits in patients with Alzheimer's disease. *Journal of Clinical and Experimental Neuropsychology, 10*, 477–494.

Satz, P. (1993). Brain reserve capacity on symptom onset after brain injury: A formulation and review of evidence for threshold theory. *Neuropsychology, 7*, 273–295.

Schwartz, M. F. (1990). *Modular deficits in Alzheimer-type dementia*. Cambridge, MA: Bradford Press.

Sergent, J., Ohta, S., & MacDonald, B. (1992). Functional neuroanatomy of face and object processing. A positron emission tomography study. *Brain, 115*, 15–36.

Small, G. W., Kuhl, D. E., Riege, W. H., Fujikawa, D. G., Ashford, J. W., Metter, E. J., & Mazziotta, J. C. (1989). Cerebral glucose metabolic patterns in Alzheimer's disease. Effect of gender and age at dementia onset. *Archives of General Psychiatry, 46*, 527–532.

Snyder, G. L., Keller, R. W., & Zigmond, M. J. (1990). Dopamine efflux from striatal slices after intracerebral 6-hydroxydopamine: Evidence for compensatory hyperactivity of residual terminals. *Journal of Pharmacology and Experimental Therapeutics, 253*, 867–876.

Stern, Y., Alexander, G. E., Prohovnik, I., & Mayeux, R. (1992). Inverse relationship between education and parietotemporal perfusion deficit in Alzheimer's disease. *Annals of Neurology, 32*, 371–375.

Ungerleider, L. G., & Mishkin, M. (1982). Two cortical visual systems. In D. J. Ingle, M. A. Goodale, & R. J. W. Mansfield (Ed.), *Analysis of visual behavior* (pp. 549–586). Cambridge: MIT Press.

Van Essen, D. C. (1985). Functional organization of primate visual cortex. In A. Peters, & E. G. Jones (Ed.), *Cerebral Cortex* (pp. 259–328). New York: Plenum Press.

Van Hoesen, G. W., & Damasio, A. R. (1987). Neural correlates of cognitive impairment in Alzheimer's disease. In F. Plum, & V. Mountcastle (Ed.), *Handbook of physiology. The nervous system* (pp. 871–898). Washington D.C.: American Physiological Society.

Zeki, S., Watson, J. D. G., Lueck, C. J., Friston, K. J., Kennard, C., & Frackowiak, R. S. J. (1991). A direct demonstration of functional specialization in human visual cortex. *Journal of Neuroscience, 11*, 641–649.

PART FOUR

COMPENSATION IN SENSORY
AND SKILL DOMAINS

CHAPTER TWELVE

Perceptual Compensation in the Deaf and Blind: Myth or Reality?

Jerker Rönnberg
Linköping University, Sweden

This chapter is about perceptual compensation in the blind and deaf. Perceptual compensation draws on the development of sensory as well as cognitive compensatory abilities. To this end, the chapter consists of three conceptually distinct parts. The first deals with the sensory aspects of the input to the perceptual process. The second focuses on the perceptual processing of tasks that are ecologically meaningful to the blind and deaf. The third addresses the conceptually and cognitively driven aspects of perceptual compensation. Obviously, a sensory impairment delimits the possible input to the perceptual process. In some conditions, such perceptual processing is supported by the architecture of the cognitive system that is involved in extracting meaning from perceptually degraded and distorted signals. The overall emphasis of the chapter is on psychological compensation, rather than technical compensation, although some attention is devoted to successful cases of technical compensation when they illustrate general perceptual or cognitive principles.

Perceptual compensation is dependent on that/those psychological or neurological process(es) or mechanism(s) that, due to partial or complete loss of sensory input in one modality, stimulate(s) development or improvement of a perceptual function in another modality (qualitatively or quantitatively). To qualify as a compensatory process, it is also necessary that perceptual performance is either quantitatively superior to, or qualitatively different from, that of a matched control group. The reason for this conservative compensatory criterion is threefold.

First, when normal levels of performance are surpassed, the compensatory pressure toward change can be assumed to have been high, resulting not only in a supernormal quantitative change, but sometimes in a qualitatively new perceptual skill as well. The conditions that cause and maintain such compensatory change are important to chart and analyze.

Second, such a substantial change in perceptual function may also give an indication of the malleability of the function in question; extreme cases of compensation can tell us interesting stories of how far the limits of human potential can be stretched. Thus, a dynamic perceptual change of such magnitude and quality hints at important perceptual possibilities toward which educational and interventional practices may formulate goals.

Third, in keeping with the previous definition, a more general point is that the concept of *compensation* should be dissociated from the concept of *normality*. Underlying the concept of compensation is that normality is not necessarily the goal toward which to strive. Normality is a useful reference point, but does not represent any obvious perceptual or communicative end state. A case in point is sign language use. For cultural, social, and perceptual reasons, congenitally deaf individuals do not view the acquisition of sign language as compensation—sign language is part and parcel of their linguistic community. From a hearing perspective, sign language use presents one means to compensate for deafness. Still, its assessment does not require quantitative measurement sticks—it represents a qualitatively new skill. This reasoning is applicable to alternative communicative skills that are not based primarily on speech (e.g., communication by means of pictograms). However, once the hearing-impaired or profoundly deaf individual attempts to restore speech perception (e.g., by means of a hearing aid, a cochlear implant, or a speech-based tactile aid), normality is the prime goal. In this case, research focuses on how far perceptual improvement can reach toward normality. The mechanisms of such perceptual substitution are also relevant to sensory-compensation research, but do not, according to the present argument and definition, equate with a compensatory change.

From the perspective of research on sensory impairments, compensatory processes that are initiated by the lack of input in one sensory modality forms one important basis for the study of psychological compensation. The need and opportunity for perceptual compensation is definitely present. The putative cause for compensatory behavior to occur is present in the sense that the mismatch between perceptual skill level and environmental demands can be objectively assessed and subjectively reported (Bäckman & Dixon, 1992). Given such a mismatch, and given ecologically meaningful criterial tasks, the study of intrinsic, spontaneous developments of compensatory perceptual mechanisms must be considered fundamental to compensation research. The reason is that the degree of spontaneous improvement in a nonimpaired perceptual modality informs us about its malleability and potential. This constitutes important information with regard to the necessity of structured training of that function, or to the possibility of acquiring new, alternative skills. Thus, variability in quantitative and qualitative compensatory, spontaneous improvements should be scrutinized and evaluated with regard to the relative success of additional educational, communicative, and technical means.

The forms and consequences of compensation can vary depending on the impairment discussed. Again, the analysis focuses on those spontaneous compensatory processes emanating from the impaired individual's long-term everyday interaction with the environment, not on systematic training programs. In this context, it is also necessary to distinguish between impairment-related and individually related compensation. *Impairment-related compensation* means that improvement in other perceptual functions is related to the degree and type of impairment, as well as to the duration of impairment. For example, a recent study on speech-reading skill showed that partialing out for decibel loss and duration of hearing impairment did not change the correlation between chronological age and speech-reading performance (Rönnberg, 1990). However, if it can be shown that improvement in perceptual function can be attributed to individual abilities, independent of the degree and type of impairment, individual compensation is present.

The conditions for spontaneous compensation that are examined in this chapter are the following: the extent to which compensation can be accomplished when stimuli are poor and relatively meaningless (i.e., *sensory compensation*), relative to (a) when stimuli are meaningful and interwoven with the communicative process (i.e., *perceptual compensation*), and (b) when cognitive skills are accounted for as contributors and/or extractors of meaning (i.e., *cognitive compensation*).

THE SENSORY-COMPENSATION HYPOTHESIS

The evidence pertinent to sensory compensation deals with performance in relatively simple sensory tasks, where extraction of meaning from stimuli typically is not the defining characteristic. Early auditory deprivation in animals suggests that neither simple black-white discrimination tasks nor more complex pattern-discrimination tasks reveal any evidence of sensory compensation (MacDoughall & Rabinovitch, 1971). Human data on visuosensory compensation falsify the sensory-compensation hypothesis: In an early survey of the sensory-compensation hypothesis, Hayes (1934) concluded that absolute auditory thresholds are either higher (i.e., less sensitive) or equal when the blind are compared with the sighted, suggesting no sensory compensation. Sakurabayashi, Sato, and Uehara (1956) did not find any differences between blind and sighted subjects on several parameters of the

Seashore Measure of Musical Talent Test, including discriminations of loudness, pitch, rhythm, timbre, and tonal memory. More recent research reaffirms this position: Bross (1979a, 1979b) has shown that visual sensitivity in brightness discrimination may even be inferior in the deaf. Bross and Sauerwein (1980) also demonstrated that the lack of sensory compensation was generalizable to perception of visual flicker (i.e., a measure to assess the temporal resolution of the visual system) for congenitally deaf: The flicker-fusion values for the deaf and hearing groups were almost identical. Bross and Borenstein (1982) also presented results suggesting that blind subjects' auditory flutter fusion do not exhibit any significant compensatory trends, nor does loudness perception of the blind differ from that of the sighted (Yates, Johnson, & Starz, 1972). Thus, from a group perspective and based on the relatively limited number of variables scrutinized, both blind and deaf people show no compelling evidence for sensory compensation.

Neurophysiological Aspects
of Sensory Compensation

Using electroencephalographic indices, Wolff and Thatcher (1990) collected data that suggest that cortical reorganization can be observed in prelingually deaf children. More precisely, there is the distinct possibility that early childhood deafness decreases cerebral differentiation in the left hemisphere, whereas right-hemisphere functions are enhanced due to increased interneuronal differentiation in the right hemisphere. These data are also in general agreement with various kinds of evidence that suggest that lateralization of function may differ due to deafness, and also due to communication mode (see Wolf & Thatcher, 1990, for review of the evidence).

Neville (1990) suggested a mechanism whereby compensation may be achieved by changing attentional foci of modality-specific stimuli as a consequence of early sensory deprivation in one modality to the other, rather than intramodal enhancement of sensory thresholds or acuity measures (cf. the lack of evidence for sensory compensation). This mechanism of the major cortical changes should occur in the nonprimary, amodal, "association" regions of the brain. Likely candidates are the parietal and superior temporal cortices (Neville, 1990). Testing this hypothesis, Neville, Smith and Kutas (1983) showed that flashing a white square (while the subjects were watching a black video) resulted in attentional changes over temporal cortex, primarily as a result of congenital deafness and not as a result of mastery of American sign language per se. Also, the effects were only present for peripherally, as opposed to centrally, presented stimuli (i.e., when the stimulus was presented 8 degrees to the right or left of the visual field). Neville's data on detection of motion in the peripheral visual field (also see Neville & Lawson, 1987a, 1987b, 1987c, for details) suggest that deaf subjects respond more quickly than hearing subjects, thus replicating that the attentional changes are found chiefly in the peripheral visual field, and that sensory deprivation from birth is the key factor involved. Concomitant event-related potentials support the link between neurophysiology and behavior.

As one explanation of the results, Neville (1990) hypothesized that the periphery effect may occur within the superior temporal sulcus, where so-matosensory, auditory, and visual· inputs converge. If one sensory system does not function properly, the others compete for computational brain capacity, thus compensating for this lack of information by changing attentional foci. In relative terms, peripheral space receives greater representation in the superior temporal sulcus, which constitutes one explanation for the attentional shift.

To reiterate, compensation can be observed in the peripheral attentional field as a result of intermodal cortical reorganization, but not as a consequence of more sensitive intramodal sensory thresholds per se (Neville, 1990). One additional explanation for the general lack of intramodal sensory compensation comes from a study by Benedetti and Loeb (1972), in which sensory compensation in terms of auditory thresholds between blind and sighted subjects was not observed, but compensation in a vigilance task involving detection of auditory pulses was found. As suggested by the authors, the factor most likely to be responsible for blind subjects' superior auditory vigilance is necessary reliance and practice on discrimination of critical aspects of auditory stimulation. The authors suggest that the term *sensory compensation* should be replaced by the term *perceptual compensation*.

PERCEPTUAL COMPENSATION

One further reason that sensory compensation has not been considered a viable hypothesis in the blind and deaf is that the criterial tasks usually have been devoid of communicative meaning. Once meaningfulness is introduced in the task, even with simple stimuli, some form of compensation may occur (Benedetti & Loeb, 1972). Following this notion, the strategy of simplifying the stimuli and the task—to the extent that they become stripped of meaning—may undermine the possibility of detecting perceptual compensation. If spontaneous compensation exists in the blind and deaf, it seems likely that only rich, meaningful contexts have the potential to activate schemata relevant to the perceptual task (Samuelsson, 1993; Samuelsson & Rönnberg, 1991, 1993). Only in such situations may the individual have a realistic chance to discover, explore, and learn about the perceptual possibilities that exist. Thus, when addressing perceptual compensation, the perceptual meaning and communicative setting must be considered.

Two fundamental perceptual domains for blind and deaf individuals that can allow for spontaneous compensatory processes are perception of, and orientation in, space for the blind and perception of speech for the deaf. The perceptual task for the blind is to use nonvisual information to apprehend the spatial layout of rooms and objects and to be able to move about in that space. The perceptual task for the deaf is to use nonauditory information to extract meaning from the speech signal. The extent to which these two tasks can be solved must depend on the substitutability of one type (or types) of sensory information for another, and the degree to which the individual has come to master processing of that particular type of information in relation to other sources of information.

As we focus on speech perception for the deaf, it should be noted that we are not primarily focusing on compensatory processes in the congenitally deaf individual. In Sweden, the pendulum between the oral and manual approaches to teaching the deaf is in relative balance; sign language is perceived as a rather self-evident compensatory means for the congenitally deaf child, whereas a speech-based type of rehabilitation is preferred for the older, adventitiously deaf individual (Öhngren, 1992). Thus, compensation for the congenitally deaf is an integral part of the process of sign language acquisition and socialization into deaf culture. Given that the congenitally deaf also lack the necessary verbal skills, the need to develop speech-reading proficiency should not be as pronounced for this group as for the adventitiously or postlingually deaf individuals. For the blind, this distinction may be less important because perception of space is ubiquitous for all blind individuals and, irrespective of etiology, the blind individual is left with the same basic compensatory means: tactually and haptically mediated perception (Kennedy, Gabias, & Heller, 1992), as well as echolocation and vibratory exploration/guidance by means of the long cane (Jansson, 1991). Nevertheless, the degree of compensation may become more fully developed when blindness occurs early in life (Veraart & Wanet-DeFalque, 1987).

Speech Perception

Adventitiously deaf lipreaders (or speech-readers) rely primarily on visual information from speech gestures and body language, as well as complementary information inherent in the communicative setting (i.e., context, conversational postulates; Rommetveit, 1974). The simple and straightforward hypothesis is that speech-readers who have been hearing impaired or deaf for a large part of their adult lives should spontaneously compensate by becoming more skilled than matched controls. However, in a series of experimental studies by Rönnberg and colleagues (Lyxell & Rönnberg, 1989; Rönnberg, 1990; Rönnberg, Öhngren, & Nilsson, 1982, 1983), this hypothesis did not receive any support. In other words, daily dependence on lipreading in a variety of social situations does not seem to suffice as a trigger for the development of speech-reading skill. This lack of compensation is generalizable across test materials (digits, words, or sentences), test form (live vs. recorded materials), average hearing loss, and duration of handicap (see also Cowie & Douglas-Cowie, 1992; Mogford, 1987). Compensation is also absent when more complex test situations are employed, such as following a conversation in noise. The benefit of speech-reading support in such a task, measured in gains in signal-to-noise ratio, is constant across normal hearing and hearing-impaired subjects (Hygge, Rönnberg, Larsby, & Arlinger, 1992). Thus, the hearing-impaired subjects do not compensate in the sense that they accept a relatively greater decrement in signal strength relative to the noise background, when visual information is added to the auditory signal.

To examine the generality of this negative outcome further, we conducted a set of studies that investigate the role of emotional expression in the talker's face, his or her body language, as well as emotional content. The hypothesis was that the deaf speech-reader has formed perceptual habits that utilize facial and body-language cues. The results do not suggest any systematic effects of facial expression (Johansson & Rönnberg, in press) or body language (Johansson & Rönnberg, 1993) on speech readability, independent of the emotional content of the message. There is also no difference in data pattern when deafened adults are compared to normal hearing individuals (Johansson & Rönnberg, in press). Rather, what accounts for the data is the way in which a certain message content is related to the scenario or script in which it is embedded. Emotionally neutral messages that are typical of a particular script, as well as being at a level of abstraction compatible with the contextual constraints, are the most powerful (Johansson & Rönnberg, in press; Samuelsson & Rönnberg, 1991, 1993). Thus, the results indicate that the role played by facial expression and body language is not as informative to the speech-reader as first suspected. Thus, content and script are superordinate to facial expression and body language. Generally speaking, then, speech-readers who have become adventitiously hearing impaired or deaf do not compensate for their hearing loss by developing a speech-reading skill that is superior to normal, matched controls.

The previous results may suggest that the information conveyed by lip movements is relatively poor and not sufficiently specific. Therefore, there is not much more to be extracted from the speech signal by the deaf that cannot be picked up by normal hearing people as well. The effects of speech-reading training are also limited and speaker dependent (see Lyxell, 1989, for a review). However, from a Gibsonian point of view, which views perception as the active exploration of meaningful patterns of information in the environment (i.e., affordances, J. Gibson, 1979) that are specified without reference to cognitive mediation, visual speech (natural and dynamic as it is) should, at least in principle, suffice for direct information pickup (see Runeson, 1990, for an explanation in terms of informational constraints). Unfortunately, this principle has not gained any empirical support for speech-reading. Even the very skilled lipreader seldom attains perfect performance. Discrimination accuracy of phonemes varies between 10% and 25% (Lyxell, 1989). Without contextual support, speech-reading performance for unrelated sentences is usually below 10% (Risberg, 1979; Samuelsson & Rönnberg, 1991). Hence, the question is this: Why is the perceptual system not fine tuned enough to pick up the dynamics of facial speech gestures?

One suggestion is provided by Summerfields (1987) analysis of audiovisual speech perception. On the one hand, there is a complementarity between visual and auditory confusability of phonemes, such that those phonemes that are easy to speech-read (i.e., where place of articulation varies) are hard to discriminate in noise. On the other hand, those phonemes that stress manner of articulation are easier to discriminate in noise, but speech-reading of such phonemes is much harder. The task seems to be to arrange speech perception conditions for the deaf that can optimize this complementarity in such a way that a deeper perception of articulatory dynamics, not kinematics, is accomplished (Studdert-Kennedy, 1983).

Tactually supported speech-reading can be very effective, presumably because it optimizes this complementarity. In a recent case study on the adventitiously deaf adult GS (a 55-year-old male), it was found that almost perfect speech-reading can be attained with the tactiling method. Tactiling involves placing the hand on the talker's shoulder and the thumb on the neck/collarbone (Rönnberg, 1993). By this method, GS is able to pick up the prosodic elements of speech through laryngeal vibrations, which are simultaneously combined with speech-reading of visual information. With tactiling, GS performs at ceiling in the Lyxell and Rönnberg (1989) sentence-based speech-reading test, and he performs at a level that is functionally similar to that of the normally hearing in a speech-tracking task (Öhngren, 1992). He has also learned to speak English fluently and intelligibly without ever having heard a spoken English word. By means of tactiling his own laryngeal vibrations, while watching what his mouth produces in the mirror, this could be accomplished. GS is atypical. However, as discussed later, his skill is also partially explained by the characteristics of his higher order cognitive skills.

To assess whether tactiling is a method worth pursuing, a generalization experiment was carried out with an updated version of the Lyxell and Rönnberg test (Öhngren, Rönnberg, & Lyxell, 1992). It was found that all subjects benefited on average 25% (without practice) by means of tactiling compared, with visual speech-reading conditions. In addition, the effect was independent of the speaker. In a further case study on GS (Öhngren, Kassling, & Risberg, in press), consonant perception was evaluated by means of speech-reading, tactiling, and by the tactilator. The tactilator is a technical tactile aid that is constructed and based on the same principle as tactiling. Vibrations are transmitted wirelessly to a vibrator element from a larynxmicrophone held against the throat. The tactilator, as well as tactiling, seems to effectively create a perceptual complementarity of the kind Summerfield (1987) reported: Voicing, stops, nasals, and fricatives were all perceived with almost 100% accuracy. Notably, voicing and nasality are hard to perceive without tactile information.

In a final generalization study, with speech tracking as the main dependent variable, it was shown that for all 16 deaf subjects the tactilator gave a significant additional benefit over tracking from speech-reading only (Öhngren, 1992). Interestingly enough, a rhyme test constituted the best predictor of tracking with the tactilator, suggesting an interesting confluence between tactually supported speech-reading and some type of internal speech representation (Conrad, 1979; Lyxell, Rönnberg, & Samuelsson, 1994). The phonological aspects of internal speech can mediate perception of articulatory dynamics. Perceiving articulatory dynamics is a question of perceiving articulatory gestures—the movements of the articulators, which to some extent can be picked up from the larynx by means of tactiling (cf. Studdert-Kennedy, 1983). Thus, internal speech plays the same role as tactile information—they both, albeit in different ways, utilize information associated with the articulators.

The tactilator and tactiling represent one-channel methods of conveying tactile information, mainly in the form of a tactile, fundamental frequency contour. Other studies of tactually supported speech-reading do not necessarily indicate that there is a superiority due to an increased number of channels for information coding (e.g., Plant, 1989), but there are examples of efficient multichannel, laboratory models (e.g., Brooks, Frost, Mason, & Gibson, 1986a, 1986b). There are several possible reasons for this state of affairs. First, the complementarity is not necessarily as efficient when the signal is preprocessed and coded into different channels. The multichannel information must then be decoded, hence the involvement of combining learning of place of stimulation with, for example, frequency of information. This may be an example of a cognitive-perceptual conflict. This way, attention will not solely be devoted to speech comprehension as such. Second, the signal-to-noise ratio is solved with our one-channel methods. Third, the data are compatible with the results, which suggest that auditory fundamental frequency supplements the visual speech signal effectively (Breeuwer & Plomp, 1986; Grant, Ardell, Kuhl, & Sparks, 1986; Risberg, 1974; Risberg & Lubker, 1978).

Thus, substituting auditory information with tactile information is successful when speech perception in adventitiously deaf or hearing-impaired adults is concerned. This represents improvement via principles of visuo-tactile integration, which presumably are generalizable to the normal hearing, as is the case for visuo-auditory integration (Massaro, 1987). Utilizing the properties of such integrations leaves us with perceptual mechanisms that facili-tate perceptual improvement. However, the mechanisms seem to be general and not specific to the degree of hearing impairment, or, for that matter, characteristic of a certain compensatory process. Such normal, although sometimes undiscovered, perceptual mechanisms are important to utilize in handicap research, as well as in an individual's everyday activities, but they do not represent the result of compensatory mechanisms or processes that go beyond these normal levels of functioning.

Space Perception

Research on the perception of space has focused on the relation between haptics (i.e., the sense of touch in relation to body position and action) and spatial awareness in the blind. Kennedy, Gabias, and Heller (1992) argued that extensions of J. Gibson's (1966, 1979) principles of communalities in process-ing of sensory patterns, and thus substitutability of one type of information for another, are applicable to haptic perception of space in the blind. For example, in a version of Piaget's classic three-mountain task, in which the observer has to identify different arrays of three objects produced by different vantage points, the problem is solved equally (by means of line drawings for the blind and pictures for the sighted) by congenitally blind, adventitiously blind, and blindfolded sighted subjects (Heller & Kennedy, 1990). This result suggests that geometry of space is relatively normal in the blind. Klatsky, Loomis, Golledge, Fujita, and Pellegrino (1990) found that navigation in the absence of landmarks was equally efficient in the blind as in the blindfolded, as well as in the face of a change of scale. In this vein, picture identification by outline drawings is slower in the congenitally blind, but is as accurate (Heller & Kennedy, 1990). Spatial imagery is present when familiar objects are recalled (Hollins, 1989), and verbal description of routes are equally interfered with by spatial distractors in blind as in sighted subjects. Thus, the spatial layout of surfaces is apprehended with relative accuracy in the blind, and blind individuals can substitute visually for tactually mediated information, at least to some extent. However, in the same way as for speech perception in the deaf, there are no signs of spontaneous compensation.

Previous non-Gibsonian research has been relatively consistent in sug-gesting that the role of visual experience is important in the spatial repre-sentation of the blind. As discussed and reviewed by Veraart and Wanet-DeFalque (1987), the spatial abilities of early-blind subjects have been found to be inferior to those of late-blind and sighted subjects in many studies. This is clearly expressed in locomotor and spatial-localization tasks. One principal difference between the Gibsonian and non-Gibsonian approaches is that, in the former case, the emphasis is on demonstrating the existence of skilled individuals who can solve certain tasks where spatial representation is less dependent on visual experience (e.g., Landau, Gleitman, & Spelke, 1981); and in the latter case, more universal hypotheses have been falsified. From a compensatory perspective, both are equivalent: No compensation can be detected such that blind subjects improve their spatial concepts relative to sighted controls.

Although compensation is lacking, there are still interesting avenues for research that pertain to, for example, blind children's spontaneous locomotor activity. It is well known that blind children are delayed in their locomotor activity (Warren, 1984). This may also prove to have deleterious effects on the children's cognitive development (E. Gibson, 1988; Hatwell, 1985). However, blind children's exploratory activities can be improved by means of auditory stimulation (Aitken & Bower, 1982). Nielsen (1988) found that when the environment was arranged so that the children's movements easily produced sounds, the development of spatial concepts was promoted. Thus, interesting possibilities lay ahead in research on the development of children's concep-tions of space by means of auditory information (G. Jansson, 1988a).

A special perceptual problem related to the perception of space is the perception of tactile pictures. Presumably, these pictures work as long as they are simple and stereotypical. But when complexity increases, several problems arise (G. Jansson, 1988b; G. Jansson & Hämäläinen, 1991). It is hard for the haptic observer to: (a) get a fast overview of the tactile picture, (b) extract details, and (c) pick up three-dimensional aspects of the tactile picture. The technical problems associated with solutions to these problems are discussed by G. Jansson and Hämäläinen (1991) and by G. Jansson (1992). For example, soft-copy displays—where points within a matrix are vibrating, or where electrical current is applied—have problems because of low spatial resolution and because too little of the display is represented on the skin. These factors greatly reduce possibilities for three-dimensional perception because of inaccurate representations of texture and luminance gradients. This is compensated for by hard-copy alternatives to some extent (G. Jansson & Hämäläinen, 1991).

The principle of substituting visual information with tactile information for the blind, displayed on a matrix on vibrotactile vibrators, was addressed explicitly by Bach-y-Rita (1972, 1982). These systems appear to have met with some success, even though the information provided is relatively crude. Some of the low-pass filter characteristics of the tactile system can be com-pensated for by allowing the subject to manipulate the camera by scanning and zooming the display; the subject also must be able to distinguish virtual camera movement from real object movement. Then subjects are usually trained with image-processing tasks of various complexities (e.g., recognition of line orientation, discrimination of straight vs. curved lines, identification of objects). More complex information, such as perspective and size con-stancy, was also introduced for the blind. Such tactile-vision substitution systems (TVSS) have also been applied to the restoration of sight (after a keratoprosthesis implant) following long-term visual deprivation (Apkarian, 1983). By the 7th postoperative week, case CM (an 11-year-old female) could discriminate between a square and a triangle; by the 10th week, simple objects could be recognized. After 7 months, CM could match one familiar shape with one of three others. CM could neither perceive the Müller-Lyer illusion nor experience the rotating spiral effect. In all, after 11 months of training, CM's visual acuity remained at a low level, whereas her spatial concepts improved dramatically, as illustrated by her drawings. This reminds us again of the possibility of development of space perception by means of taction. Nonetheless, Apkarian (1983) cautioned that it is hard to draw definite conclusions from only one case. Further examples of TVSS experiments were reviewed by G. Jansson (1983). The tasks used so far are relatively simple and the more ecological possibilities of active touch remain to be explored before more definite conclusions can be made with such substitution systems.

One further area of research that is tangential to perception of space—by means of taction and haptics—is the area of echolocation (cf. Cotzin & Dallenbach, 1950; Supa, Cotzin, & Dallenbach, 1944). In a discussion of the area, G. Jansson (1986) concluded that the special ability of echolocation is used by the adventitiously blind rather spontaneously. But the ability is restricted to "moving along" an edge rather than "moving toward" an object. It is also hard to locate objects in space more than a few meters away (Arias, 1989; G. Jansson, 1991; Schenkman, 1985). However, with travel aids such as the long cane, location of objects and edges can be achieved by means of parameters not inherently spatial: angle of rod to surface, its length, and the moment of inertia (Barac-Cikoja & Turvey, 1991; Chan & Turvey, 1991). It is as if we could speak of "echovibration" in parallel with echolocation. Thus, spatial distance can be perceived by nonspatial parameters that are physically related to space, although it may put great demands on the perceiver (Schenkman & Jansson, 1986).

Curtis and Winer (1969) demonstrated that expert blind travelers, compared with homebound travelers and sighted subjects, make finer intensity discrimination of auditory stimuli. Intensity is informative with respect to relative distance to objects, texture, and size. Using ultrasonic echolocating devices, it has been shown that early- and late-blind subjects improve their performance, primarily in distance assessments (Veraart & Wanet-DeFalque, 1987). However, the lack of visual experience in the early blind is still less substituted for by the prosthesis than for the late blind. Thus, substitution is quite possible with auditory stimulation, but not to the degree of compensation. With respect to the criterial tasks of space perception, it is questionable whether improvements in some simple auditory abilities actually predict enhanced spatial performance.

INTERIM SUMMARY

The evidence presented so far does not paint an optimistic picture with respect to spontaneous compensatory processes in the blind and deaf. We have adopted a rather stringent criterion for compensation: Individuals must spontaneously develop sensory or perceptual skills related to speech and space that are superior to comparative controls. This does not exclude the possibility that systematic training can fulfill compensatory purposes. However, potential effects of systematic training programs is not the topic of the present chapter.

One exception was found for attention and vigilance data on simple sensory stimulation, with some support from neurophysiological indices. But once the stimulation is made more meaningful and ecologically relevant, typically perceptual compensation is lacking. Nevertheless, the data suggest that perceptual improvement can occur by substituting one type of information for another—i.e., by utilizing the human propensity to process information amodally, near normal performance can be attained. In addition, the principles and mechanisms of substitutability can obviously be modeled technically with some success.

COMPENSATION BY COGNITIVE SKILLS VS. SENSORY SUBSTITUTION

As we have seen so far, compensation is not generally the case in the domains of speech and space perception. Such compensation is lacking, although the tasks are ecologically meaningful. The rule seems to be perceptual learning up to the level of normal functioning, or improvement by means of sensory-substitution principles. Once sensory substitution is achieved, and thus an approximation of what is considered normal for that particular perceptual function is attained, there may be no need for further compensation. One reason for this is the rather direct effects (i.e., without training) that can be discovered when perceptual complementarity between two nondamaged senses is optimized (cf. Summerfield's, 1987, principle). Direct effects may have a negative effect reducing the individual's motivation for further skill improvement beyond the level of normality (i.e., compensatory developments). Nevertheless, other ways to discover "smart" perceptual mechanisms seem to represent important domains for substitution research (cf. Runeson, 1977).

Compensatory, amodal cortical changes may also indirectly serve as a stimulus for development of higher order cognitive functions. The taking over of brain capacity in amodal cortical areas may have something to do with, for example, working memory functions (e.g., Engle, Cantor, & Carullo,

1992; Schneider & Detweiler, 1988)—compensatory developments that, at this stage, have only a speculative status. However, it is still likely that central-capacity functions are individually based capacity predictors of certain criterial tasks in the deaf and blind, and not necessarily as operationalizations of general cortical compensatory reorganizations. At present, these possibilities have not been empirically tested.

Despite the conclusion from cortical reorganization and development of higher order cognitive functions, the problem can be viewed from another perspective: individual ways of dealing with information processing in highly complex and demanding situations. Recent research on speech-reading suggests that decoding skills and information-processing speed (Lyxell, 1989; Rönnberg, 1990) represent low-level bottlenecks of perceptual information processing that are general for all kinds of speech-reading tasks, whereas higher order cognitive functions (i.e., guesssing and working memory) only come into play in certain tasks (e.g., when contextual support is low). Given this argument, higher order cognitive skills represent strategic resources that an individual can deploy in certain tasks. The conditions that can be particularly conducive to compensatory behavior via individually based higher order cognitive skills are proposed to be present when: (a) stimuli are relatively poorly specified, or contextual support is low for a certain communicative situation and form; and (b) the task draws heavily on preexperimental knowledge and expertise. Both conditions demand a continuous updating of knowledge in a working memory system, which can utilize various kinds of redundancy (e.g., in language) and open up the possibilities for meaningful inferences. Condition *a* is illustrated by means of data on speech-reading in the adventitiously deaf, and condition *b* is illustrated by chess skill in the blind.

Compensation by Individual Cognitive Skill

Cognitive compensation occurs when the general perceptual possibilities of substitution are exhausted or not available for the individual. The argument is that cognitive compensation is task specific, strategy dependent, and consequently related to variations in individual cognitive skills and task experience. Consequently, compensation is more selective, task dependent, and independent of impairment-related factors (Rönnberg, 1990; Rönnberg & Lyxell, 1986) than is improvement by substitution.

The Deaf. As was discussed already, visual speech-reading skill is not critically related to auditory impairment per se. In other laboratories as well as our own, it has been shown that the cognitive architecture underlying skilled visual speech-reading is multifactorial (cf. DeFilippo, 1982; Gailey, 1987; Lyxell, 1989) and mainly based on three cognitive predictors. Decoding ability (i.e., when naming of a spoken word is required) and information-processing speed (i.e., especially when lexical access is required) are most important for the population as a whole (Lyxell, 1989; Lyxell & Rönnberg, 1991a, 1991b; Lyxell, Johansson, Lidestam, & Rönnberg, 1993; Lyxell, Rönnberg, Andersson, & Linderoth, 1993; Rönnberg, 1987, 1990, 1993, in press), and are generalizable to different communicative settings. Verbal inference-making (guessing) ability (i.e., when sentence completion is required under heavy time pressure) is important in specific situations, such as when contextual support is relatively low for the speech-reading task (Lyxell & Rönnberg, 1987a, 1987b, 1989; Rönnberg, Arlinger, Lyxell, & Kinnefors, 1989).

Although only an indirectly important predictor for the population as a whole, a capacious working memory (i.e., measured by the working memory-span task; Baddeley, Logie, Nimmo-Smith, & Brereton, 1985) constitutes an important measure of storage and processing capacity necessary for inference making (guessing; Lyxell & Rönnberg, 1989). The same holds true for vocabulary size (Lyxell & Rönnberg, 1992).

To attain extreme speech-reading skill (cf. Lyxell, 1994; Rönnberg, 1993; Rönnberg, Andersson, Samuelsson, Söderfeldt, & Risberg, 1994), it seems important that a low-level cognitive-processing threshold (i.e., decoding and speed) be surpassed and complemented by high-level processing in working memory (Lyxell & Rönnberg, 1993). Thus, from an individual compensatory perspective, decoding skill and high speed of lexical access are necessary cognitive prerequisites, but presumably not sufficient to communicate at a high level of efficiency (Rönnberg & Archer, 1992). A capacious working memory is necessary for spare capacity for prospective guesswork, as are reserves for updating and disambiguation of previously decoded fragments of information (for a detailed theoretical discussion of the roles of decoding, phonology, and working memory capacity, see Rönnberg, in press). Based on these cognitive resources, the individual may develop qualitatively different speech-reading strategies that further serve compensatory purposes (Lyxell, 1994; Rönnberg, 1993). Thus, the intimate interplay between capacity and strategy can help the individual to previously unforeseen levels of skill.

The Blind. Ohlsson (1986) found that blind subjects did not outperform blindfolded, sighted subjects when the task was to map an initial chess configuration (that they had tactilely explored for some time) onto a matching board. This task entails the subject to keep a memory record of the pieces explored, hold the pieces placed on the matching board active in memory, compare what pieces have been placed with those remembered to be remaining from the configuration, and so on. Task-specific cognitive representations of chess-specific configurations come into play in such a task. The data show that there is no compensation for unskilled chess players, especially not for adventitiously blind individuals. In fact, for unskilled subjects, the blindfolded performed better than the blind. Independent evidence also suggests that blindfolded subjects are better than blind subjects in complex spatial tasks (Millar, 1975; OConnor & Hermelin, 1978). However, blind subjects can become experts of the game. Chess skill develops through extensive practice and knowledge of the game, independent of sensory impairment. We know from the previous discussion that it is possible for the blind to develop spatial concepts, thus laying the groundwork for chess skill. Although not discussed in the Ohlsson study, the task employed obviously draws on deployment of complex working memory resources.

The situation for blind individuals' chess playing is similar to that of deaf individuals' visual speech-reading. Cognitive compensation is achieved by means of individual resources, sometimes complemented with preexperimental, task-relevant strategies and knowledge, and not primarily by some spontaneous compensation for the impairment as such. In addition, the independent evidence on auditory short-term/working memory is inconsistent. For tonal memory (Pitman, 1965) as well as melody memory (Drake, 1954), data suggest compensation for the blind, whereas more recent data (Rönnberg & Nilsson, 1987; Stankow & Spilsbury, 1978) suggest a lack of compensation. Thus, impairment-related compensation cannot be unequivocally claimed for the blind, neither in a criterial task demanding working memory resources nor in separate tests assessing short-term/working memory. What are left are task-relevant, individual resources. The same pattern of data holds true for deaf individuals' speech-reading skills.

But there is also one important difference between research on the blind and the deaf. Tests of a particular sensory or cognitive function in the blind have not been regularly used to predict skill in the main criterion variable under scrutiny. Thus, the perspective of predicting skill in a criterion variable on the basis of individual differences in theoretically important perceptual and cognitive abilities has not been systematically advocated for the blind. Orientation by means of echolocation has usually been examined separately from abilities related to hearing, but there are exceptions (Riley, Luterman, & Cohen, 1964).

NONADAPTIVE COMPENSATIONS

In those cases where compensation has been found for cognitive testing in deafened adults—in visual short-term memory (Rönnberg & Nilsson, 1982, 1987; Rönnberg et al., 1982; Sharp, 1972) and linguistic abstraction (Rönnberg, Öhngren, & Lyxell, 1987)—this compensation has not proved to serve adaptive functions for speech-reading skill (i.e., we cannot rule out that these compensations can be adaptive and serve functional aspects for other criteria). There is one deviation from this pattern. It seems that deafened adults' internal speech functions (cf. Conrad, 1979) deteriorate with time compared with a control group, which is associated with sentence-based speech-reading performance (Lyxell et al., 1994). But the general conclusion still holds true: Neither speech-reading skills nor cognitive compensations potentially relevant to improve the skill seem to develop with long periods of hearing loss in adults. It is only for those cognitive abilities that are impairment unrelated that we have shown that individual variations have predictive value for speech perception.

It also remains to be proven whether variations in low-level auditory abilities in the blind (e.g., Benedetti & Loeb, 1972; Curtis & Winer, 1969) accurately predict orientation in space by means of sound, or whether these abilities can be classified as *nonadaptive compensations*. However, if we change the criterion variable from space perception to listening comprehension, it may be that some auditory abilities predict comprehension. Niemeyer and Starlinger (1981) showed that congenitally blind subjects were better than controls in identifying meaningful words and sounds in noise. As a follow-up to that study, Sahlman and Koper (1992) demonstrated that perception of devious intent in spoken messages is better in the blind than for matched normal hearing individuals. However, this relatively global and subtle listening-comprehension ability was not accurately predicted by a concomitant increase in rated awareness of specific auditory cues assumed to carry the relevant information. Therefore, the potential individual-difference perspective, whether it be cognitive or perceptual abilities, is not shown empirically for the blind. Nevertheless, there are other signs that suggest that such an analysis may also be profitable for the blind: Blindfolded subjects' ability to orient in culverts has been hypothesized to depend on updating in working memory (Böök, 1982). Notably, braille reading comprehension is dependent on a capacious working memory, and is also correlated with listening-comprehension scores (Daneman, 1988).

Finally, nonadaptive behavior in the blind was observed by U. Jansson and Merényi (1992). They investigated how blind and sighted children in integrated preschools interact with adults and each other. The blind children characteristically rely much more than the sighted children on the adult for help and information seeking. The blind children also seem to be more unspecific in their contact behaviors with their playmates. They spontaneously talk "right out in the air" without having a sense of to whom the talk is directed. These compensations are not adaptive for the development of play among children. However, viewed from the children's perspective, the key thing may be to get the sufficient amount of adult attention and guidance. This may be true even though intellectual, emotional, and social development are enhanced by play activities in children.

GENERAL CONCLUSIONS

The line of argument can be concluded as follows: First, compensation—in the sense of sensory processing superiority in intact modalities—cannot be shown unequivocally for the deaf or the blind. However, attentional and vigilance, as opposed to threshold and sensitivity, indices seem to support the notion of *compensation*; at least for the congenitally deaf, there is a plausible electrophysiological base for the observed intermodal, attentional enhancements. Second, substituting one kind of information for another seems to be a viable and fairly general perceptual principle for improvement that is applicable to space perception in the blind and speech perception in the deaf. These improvements utilize general, "smart" perceptual mechanisms that may (due to the directness of their effects) leave the individual with less motivation for further compensatory improvements. Third, compensation can be achieved by means of individual, strategic cognitive functions, which supposedly are not as general in nature as those mechanisms pertinent to substitution. Among those higher order cognitive functions was postulated a complex working memory system, related to which conditions for individual compensation can be outlined, as exemplified by visual speech-reading in the deaf and chess playing in the blind. Fourth, cognitive abilities related to a working memory system have been thoroughly investigated and found important with respect to speech-reading skill, whereas the picture is less systematic with respect to orientation in space. Fifth, and finally, it is important to be critical with respect to all compensatory signs that are reported in the literature, primarily because all compensations do not serve adaptive or relevant supportive functions with respect to the main criterion variables discussed. It may be that they serve compensatory functions hitherto not conceived of and empirically tested with alternative criterion variables.

Overall, sensory impairment and concomitant perceptual compensation in intact modalities is a cherished myth, rather than a real, robust finding, both for the blind and the deaf. But improvement—in terms of sensory substitution or compensation via impairment-unrelated cognitive functions—represents definite realities for the communicative criteria discussed.

ACKNOWLEDGMENTS

Writing of the chapter was supported by a grant from the Swedish Council for Research in the Humanities and Social Sciences (F 615/93), and from the Swedish Council for Social Research (91-0077). Constructive comments on earlier versions of the chapter by Drs. G. Jansson, B. Lyxell, and the editors are gratefully acknowledged.

REFERENCES

Aitken, S., & Bower, T. G. R. (1982). The use of sonicguide in infancy. *Journal of Visual Impairment and Blindness, 76*, 91–100.

Apkarian, P. A. (1983). Visual training after long-term deprivation: A case report. *International Journal of Neuroscience, 19*, 65–84.

Arias, C. (1989). Human echolocation: Studies of the obstacle perception process in visually-impaired people. *Journal of Visual Impairment and Blindness, 83*, 479–482.

Bach-y-Rita, P. (1972). *Brain mechanisms in sensory substitution.* New York: Academic Press.

Bach-y-Rita, P. (1982). Sensory substitution in rehabilitation. In L. Illis & M. Sedgwick (Eds.), *Rehabilitation of the neurological patient* (pp. 361–383). Oxford: Blackwell Scientific Publications.

Bäckman, L., & Dixon, R. A. (1992). Psychological compensation: A theoretical framework. *Psychological Bulletin, 112*, 259–283.

Baddeley, A., Logie, R., Nimmo-Smith, I., & Brereton, N. (1985). Components of fluent reading. *Journal of Memory and Language, 24*, 119–131.

Barac-Cikoja, D., & Turvey, M. T. (1991). Perceptual aperture size by striking. *Journal of Experimental Psychology: Human Perception and Performance, 17*, 330–340.

Benedetti, J. B., & Loeb, M. (1972). A comparison of auditory monitoring performances in blind subjects with that of sighted subjects in light and dark. *Perception and Psychophysics, 11*, 10–16.

Böök, A. (1982). *Maintenance of environmental orientation during locomotion.* Unpublished doctoral dissertation, Department of Psychology, University of Umeå, Sweden.

Breeuwer, M., & Plomp, R. (1986). Speechreading supplemented with auditorily presented speech parameters. *Journal of Acoustical Society of America, 79*, 481–499.

Brooks, P. L., Frost, B. J., Mason, J. L., & Gibson, D. M. (1986a). Continuing evaluation of the Queens University tactile vocoder: I: Identification of open-set words. *Journal of Rehabilitation Research and Development, 23*, 119–128.

Brooks, P. L., Frost, B. J., Mason, J. L., & Gibson, D. M. (1986b). Continuing evaluation of the Queens University tactile vocoder: II: Identification of open-set sentences and tracking narrative. *Journal of Rehabilitation Research and Development, 23*, 129–138.

Bross, M. (1979a). Response bias in deaf and hearing subjects as a function of motivational factors. *Perceptual and Motor Skills, 49*, 779–782.

Bross, M. (1979b). Sensory compensation in the deaf: A signal detection analysis. *Perceptual and Motor Skills, 48*, 187–194.

Bross, M., & Borenstein, M. (1982). Temporal auditory acuity in blind and sighted subjects: A signal detection analysis. *Perceptual and Motor Skills, 55*, 963–966.

Bross, M., & Sauerwein, H. (1980). Signal detection analysis of visual flicker in deaf and hearing individuals. *Perceptual and Motor Skills, 51*, 839–843.

Chan, T. C., & Turvey, M. J. (1991). Perceiving the vertical distances of surfaces by means of hand-held probe. *Journal of Experimental Psychology: Human Perception and Performance, 17*, 347–358.

Conrad, R. (1979). *The deaf schoolchild.* London: Harper & Row.

Cotzin, M., & Dallenbach, K. M. (1950). "Facial vision": The role of pitch and loudness in the perception of obstacles by the blind. *American Journal of Psychology, 63*, 485–483.

Cowie, R., & Douglas-Cowie, E. (1992). *Postlingually acquired deafness: Speech deterioration and the wider consequences.* New York: Mouton.

Curtis, J. F., & Winer, D. M. (1969). The auditory abilities of the blind as compared with the sighted. *Journal of Auditory Research, 9*, 57–59.

Daneman, M. (1988). How reading braille is both like and unlike reading of print. *Memory & Cognition, 16*, 497–504.

DeFilippo, C. L. (1982). Memory for articulated sequences and lipreading performance of hearing-impaired observers. *Volta Review, 31,* 134–146.

Drake, R. M. (1954). *Manual for Drake Musical Aptitude Test.* Chicago: University of Chicago Press.

Engle, R. W., Cantor, J., & Carullo, J. (1992). Individual differences in working memory and comprehension: A test of four hypotheses. *Journal of Experimental Psychology: Learning, Memory and Cognition, 18,* 972–992.

Gailey, L. (1987). Psychological parameters of lipreading skill. In B. Dodd & R. Campbell (Eds.), *Hearing by eye: The psychology of lipreading* (pp. 115–141). Hove, England: Lawrence Erlbaum Associates.

Gibson, E. J. (1988). Exploratory behavior in the development of perceiving, acting, and the aquiring of knowledge. *Annual Review of Psychology, 39,* 1–41.

Gibson, J. J. (1966). *The senses considered as perceptual systems.* Boston, MA: Houghton Mifflin.

Gibson, J. J. (1979). *The ecological approach to visual perception.* Boston, MA: Houghton Mifflin.

Grant, K. W., Ardell, L. H., Kuhl. P. K., & Sparks, D. W. (1986). The transmission of prosodic information via an electrotactile speechreading aid. *Ear and Hearing, 7,* 328–335.

Hatwell, Y. (1985). *Piagetian reasoning and the blind.* New York: American Foundation for the Blind.

Hayes, S. P. (1934). New experimental data on the old problem of sensory compensation. *Teachers' Forum (Blind), 6,* 22–26.

Heller, M. A., & Kennedy, J. M. (1990). Perspective-taking, pictures and the blind. *Perception & Psychophysics, 48,* 459–466.

Hollins, M. (1989). *Understanding blindness.* Hillsdale, NJ: Lawrence Erlbaum Associates.

Hygge, S., Rönnberg, J., Larsby, B., & Arlinger, S. (1992). Normal and hearing-impaired subjects' ability to just follow conversation in competing speech, reversed speech, and noise backgrounds. *Journal of Speech and Hearing Research, 35,* 208–215.

Jansson, G. (1983). Tactile guidance of movement. *International Journal of Neuroscience, 19,* 37–46.

Jansson, G. (1986). Travelling without vision: On the possibilities of cognitive and perceptual compensation. In E. Hjelmquist & L.-G. Nilsson (Eds.), *Communication and handicap: Aspects of psychological compensation and technical aids* (pp. 103–114). Amsterdam: Elsevier Science.

Jansson, G. (1988a, August). *The start of spontaneous locomotor activity of children born blind.* Paper presented at Realities and Opportunities, international symposium on visually handicapped infants and young children, Edinburgh, Scotland.

Jansson, G. (1988b). What are the problems with tactile pictures, and what can we do to solve them? In C. W. M. Magneé, F. J. M. Vlaskamp, M. Soede, & G. Butcher (Eds.), *Man-machine interfaces, graphics and practical applications* (pp. 18–24). London: Royal National Institute for the Blind.

Jansson, G. (1991). The control of locomotion when vision is reduced or missing. In A. E. Patla (Ed.), *Adaptability of human gait* (pp. 333–357). Amsterdam: Elsevier.

Jansson, G. (1992). 3-D perception from tactile computer displays. In W. Zagler (Ed.), *Computers for handicapped persons* (pp. 233–237). Wien: R. Oldenbourg.

Jansson, G., & Hämäläinen, H. (1991). *Perceptual aspects of displays for pictures and graphics for the blind.* Manuscript.

Jansson, U., & Merényi, A.-C. (1992, August). *Social play between blind and sighted preschool children.* Paper presented at ICEVH Early Childhood Conference, Bangkok, Thailand.

Johansson, K., & Rönnberg, J. (1993). *The effects of facial expression and body language on speechreadability.* Unpublished manuscript, Department of Education and Psychology, Linköping University, Sweden.

Johansson, K., & Rönnberg, J. (in press). The role of emotionality and typicality in speechreading. *Scandinavian Journal of Psychology.*

Kennedy, J. M., Gabias, P., & Heller, M. A. (1992). Space, haptics and the blind. *Geoforum, 23,* 175–189.

Klatsky, R. L., Loomis, J. M., Golledge, R. G., Fujita, N., & Pellegrino, J. W. (1990, November). *Navigation without vision by blind and sighted.* Paper presented at meeting of the Psychonomics Society, New Orleans, LA.

Landau, B., Gleitman, H., & Spelke, E. (1981). Spatial knowledge and geometric representation in a child blind from birth. *Science, 213,* 1275–1278.

Lyxell, B. (1989). *Beyond lips: Components of speechreading skill.* Unpublished doctoral dissertation, Department of Psychology, University of Umeå, Sweden.

Lyxell, B. (1994). Skilled speechreading: A single case study. *Scandinavian Journal of Psychology, 35,* 212–219.

Lyxell, B., Johansson, K., Lidestam, B., & Rönnberg, J. (1993). *Facial expression and speechreading.* Unpublished manuscript. Department of Education and Psychology, Linköping University, Sweden.

Lyxell, B., & Rönnberg, J. (1987a). Guessing and speechreading. *British Journal of Audiology, 21,* 13–20.

Lyxell, B., & Rönnberg, J. (1987b). Necessary cognitive determinants for speechreading skills. In J. G. Kyle (Ed.), *Adjustment to acquired hearing loss: Analysis, change, and learning* (pp. 48–54). Chippenham, Wiltshire: Antony Row.

Lyxell, B., & Rönnberg, J. (1989). Information processing skills and speechreading. *British Journal of Audiology, 23,* 339–347.

Lyxell, B., & Rönnberg, J. (1991a). Visual speech processing: Word decoding and word discrimination related to sentence-based speechreading and hearing-impairment. *Scandinavian Journal of Psychology, 32,* 9–17.

Lyxell, B., & Rönnberg, J. (1991b). Word-discrimination and chronological age related to sentence-based speechreading skill. *British Journal of Audiology, 25,* 3–10.

Lyxell, B., & Rönnberg, J. (1992). Verbal ability and speechreading. *Scandinavian Audiology, 21,* 67–72.

Lyxell, B., & Rönnberg, J. (1993). Background noise, working memory capacity, and speechreading performance. *Scandinavian Audiology, 22,* 67–70.

Lyxell, B., Rönnberg, J., Andersson, J., & Linderoth, E. (1993). Vibrotactile support: Initial effects on visual speech perception. *Scandinavian Audiology, 22,* 179–183.

Lyxell, B., Rönnberg, J., & Samuelsson, S. (1994). Internal speech functioning and speechreading in deafened and normal hearing adults. *Scandinavian Audiology, 23,* 179–185.

MacDoughall, J. C., & Rabinovitch, M. S. (1971). Early auditory deprivation and sensory compensation. *Developmental Psychology, 5,* 368.

Massaro, D. W. (1987). *Speech perception by ear and eye: A paradigm for psychological inquiry.* Hillsdale: NJ: Lawrence Erlbaum Associates.

Millar, S. (1975). Spatial memory by blind and sighted children. *British Journal of Psychology, 66,* 449–459.

Mogford, K. (1987). Lipreading in the prelingually deaf. In B. Dodd & R. Campbell (Eds.), *Hearing by eye: The psychology of lipreading* (pp. 191–211). Hillsdale, NJ: Lawrence Erlbaum Associates.

Neville, H. J. (1990). Intermodal competition and compensation in development: Evidence from studies of the visual system in congenitally deaf adults. In A. Diamond (Ed.), *The development and neural bases of higher cognitive functions* (pp. 71–91). New York: The New York Academy of Sciences.

Neville, H. J., & Lawson, D. (1987a). Attention to central and peripheral visual space in a movement detection task: I. Normal hearing adults. *Brain Research, 405,* 253–267.

Neville, H. J., & Lawson, D. (1987b). Attention to central and peripheral visual space in a movement detection task: II. Congenitally deaf subjects. *Brain Research, 405,* 268–283.

Neville, H. J., & Lawson, D. (1987c). Attention to central and peripheral visual space in a movement detection task: III. Separate effects of auditory deprivation and acquisition of a visual language. *Brain Research, 405*, 284–294.

Neville, H. J., Smith, A., & Kutas, M. (1983). Altered visual evoked potentials in congenitally deaf adults. *Brain Research, 266*, 127–132.

Nielsen, L. (1988). *Spatial relations in congenitally blind infants.* Unpublished masters thesis, University of Aarhus, Denmark.

Niemeyer, W., & Starlinger, I. (1981). Do the blind hear better? Investigations on auditory processing in congenital or early acquired blindness. *Audiology, 20*, 510–515.

O'Connor, N., & Hermelin, B. (1978). *Seeing and hearing and space and time.* London: Academic Press.

Ohlsson, K. (1986). Compensation as skill. In E. Hjelmquist & L.-G. Nilsson (Eds.), *Communication and handicap: Aspects of psychological compensation and technical aids* (pp. 85–101). Amsterdam: Elsevier Science.

Öhngren, G. (1992). *Touching voices: Components of direct tactually supported speechreading.* Unpublished doctoral dissertation, Department of Psychology, Uppsala University, Sweden.

Öhngren, G., Kassling, B., & Risberg, A. (in press). The hand and the tactilator: A comparison between two tactile aids to visual speech perception. *Scandinavian Journal of Psychology.*

Öhngren, G., Rönnberg, J., & Lyxell, B. (1992). Tactiling: A usable support system for speechreading? *British Journal of Audiology, 26*, 167–173.

Pitman, D. J. (1965). The musical ability of blind children. *American Foundation for the Blind Research Bulletin, 11*, 63–79.

Plant, G. (1989). A comparison of five commercially available tactile aids. *Australian Journal of Audiology, 11*, 11–19.

Riley, L. H., Luterman, D. M., & Cohen, M. F. (1964). Relationship between hearing ability and mobility in a blinded adult population. *New Outlook for the Blind, 58*, 139–141.

Risberg, A. (1974). The importance of prosodic speech elements for the lipreader. *Scandinavian Audiology, Suppl. 4*, 153–164.

Risberg, A. (1979). *Assessment of hearing capacity and speech perception ability in the profoundly hearing-impaired.* Unpublished doctoral dissertation. Department of Speech Transmission and Music Acoustics, Royal Institute of Technology, University of Stockholm, Sweden.

Risberg, A., & Lubker, J. (1978). *Prosody and speechreading* (*Tech. Rep. STL-QPSR 4/1978*). Stockholm, Sweden: University of Stockholm Press.

Rommetveit, R. (1974). *On message structure.* London: Wiley.

Rönnberg, J. (1987, September). *The role of lexical speed and working memory capacity in speechreading.* Paper presented at the second conference of the European Society for Cognitive Psychology, Madrid, Spain.

Rönnberg, J. (1990). Cognitive and communicative function: The effects of chronological age and "handicap age." *European Journal of Cognitive Psychology, 2*, 253–273.

Rönnberg, J. (1993). Cognitive characteristics of skilled tactiling: The case of GS. *European Journal of Cognitive Psychology, 5*, 19–33.

Rönnberg, J. (in press). What makes a good speechreader? In G. Plant & K. Spens (Eds.), *Profound deafness and speech communication.* London: Whurr.

Rönnberg, J., & Archer, T. (1992). Purposive behavior in cognition and perception: Considerations of awareness in memory. *Scandinavian Journal of Psychology, 33*, 86–91.

Rönnberg, J., & Lyxell, B. (1986). Compensatory strategies in speechreading. In E. Hjelmquist & L.-G. Nilsson (Eds.), *Communication and handicap: Aspects of psychological compensation and technical aids* (pp. 19–38). Amsterdam: North-Holland.

Rönnberg, J., & Nilsson, L.-G. (1982). Representation of auditory information based on a functionalistic perspective. In R. Carlsson & B. Granström (Eds.), *The representation of speech in the peripheral auditory system* (pp. 73–79). Amsterdam: Elsevier.

Rönnberg, J., & Nilsson, L.-G. (1987). The modality effect, sensory handicap, and compensatory functions. *Acta Psychologica, 65,* 263–283.

Rönnberg, J., Andersson, J., Samuelsson, S., Söderfeldt, B., & Risberg, J. (1994). *The "bilingual" enrichment hypothesis: The case of MJ.* Unpublished manuscript, Department of Education and Psychology, Linköping University, Sweden.

Rönnberg, J., Arlinger, S., Lyxell, B., & Kinnęfors, C. (1989). Visual evoked potentials: Relation to adult speechreading and cognitive function. *Journal of Speech and Hearing Research, 32,* 725–735.

Rönnberg, J., Öhngren, G., & Lyxell, B. (1987). Linguistic abstraction and hearing handicap. *Scandinavian Audiology, 16,* 95–99.

Rönnberg, J., Öhngren, G., & Nilsson, L.-G. (1982). Hearing deficiency, speechreading and memory functions. *Scandinavian Audiology, 11,* 261–268.

Rönnberg, J., Öhngren, G., & Nilsson, L.-G. (1983). Speechreading performance evaluated by means of TV and real-life presentation: A comparison between a normally hearing, moderately impaired and profoundly hearing-impaired group. *Scandinavian Audiology, 12,* 71–77.

Runeson, S. (1977). On the possibility of smart perceptual mechanisms. *Scandinavian Journal of Psychology, 18,* 172–179.

Runeson, S. (1990). Mode distinctions in knowing: The view from perception. Comments on Rönnberg (1990). *Scandinavian Journal of Psychology, 31,* 223–227.

Sahlman, J. M., & Koper, R. J. (1992, May). *Do you hear what I hear?: Deception detection by the blind.* Paper presented to the Interpersonal Interest Group of the International Communication Association, Miami, FL.

Sakurabayshi, H., Sato, Y., & Uehara, E. (1956). Auditory discrimination of the blind. *Journal of Psychology of the Blind, 1,* 3–10.

Samuelsson, S. (1993). *Scripted knowledge packages: Implicit and explicit constraints on comprehension and memory.* Unpublished doctoral dissertation, Department of Education and Psychology, Linköping University, Sweden.

Samuelsson, S., & Rönnberg, J. (1991). Script activation in lipreading. *Scandinavian Journal of Psychology, 32,* 124–143.

Samuelsson, S., & Rönnberg, J. (1993). Implicit and explicit use of scripted constraints in lipreading. *European Journal of Cognitive Psychology, 5,* 201–233.

Schenkman, B. (1985). *Human echolocation: The detection of objects by the blind.* Unpublished doctoral dissertation, Department of Psychology, Uppsala University, Sweden.

Schenkman, B., & Jansson, G. (1986). The detection and localization of objects by the blind with the aid of long cane tapping sounds. *Human Factors, 28,* 607–618.

Schneider, W., & Detweiler, M. (1988). The role of practice in dual-task performance: Toward workload in a connectionist/control architecture. *Human Factors, 30,* 539–566.

Sharp, E. Y. (1972). The relationship of visual closure to speechreading. *Exceptional Children, 38,* 729–734.

Stankow, L., & Spilsbury, G. (1978). The measurement of auditory abilities of blind, partially sighted, and sighted children. *Applied Psychological Measurement, 2,* 491–503.

Studdert-Kennedy, M. (1983). On learning to speak. *Human Neurobiology, 2,* 191–195.

Summerfield, Q. (1987). Some preliminaries to a comprehensive account of audiovisual speech perception. In B. Dodd & R. Campbell (Eds.), *Hearing by eye: The psychology of lipreading* (pp. 3–51). Hillsdale, NJ: Lawrence Erlbaum Associates.

Supa, M., Cotzin, M., & Dallenbach, K. M. (1944). "Facial vision": The perception of obstacles by the blind. *American Journal of Psychology, 57,* 133–183.

Veraart, C., & Wanet-DeFalque, M. C. (1987). Representation of locomotor space by the blind. *Perception and Psychophysics, 42,* 132–139.

Warren, D. H. (1984). *Blindhood and early childhood development* (2nd ed.). New York: American Foundation for the Blind.

Wolff, A. B., & Thatcher, R. W. (1990). Cortical reorganization in deaf children. *Journal of Clinical and Experimental Psychology, 12*, 209–221.

Yates, J. T., Johnson, R. M., & Starz, W. J. (1972). Loudness perception of the blind. *Audiology, 11*, 368–376.

CHAPTER THIRTEEN

Compensatory Processes in Reading

Richard F. West
James Madison University

Keith E. Stanovich
Ontario Institute for Studies in Education

Anne E. Cunningham
University of Washington

In the reading literature, the concept of *compensation* is usually discussed in two different contexts. The first is the process of compensation that occurs during online reading—compensations that occur when, during the act of reading, the processing system compensates for inefficient cognitive operations by drawing on other knowledge sources and/or processing operations. There is a considerable literature in the reading field on this type of compensation, which we term *online compensation*.

A second type of compensation—one much less studied—refers to situations where reading itself is the compensatory mechanism. That is, attention has recently focused on the importance of reading experience as a mechanism of cognitive growth and as a means of building knowledge structures. Recent research has addressed the question of whether exposure to print could—through building knowledge bases and exercising malleable cognitive components—compensate for deficiencies in relatively nonmalleable cognitive capacities, at least in certain domains. There is less evidence on this type of compensation, which we term *experiential compensation*, but our research group has collected some intriguing correlational data on this issue, which we discuss later. For example, vocabulary growth depends on certain basic abilities to elucidate relations, compare semantic features (Sternberg, 1985; Sternberg & Powell, 1983), and maintain codes in working memory (Gathercole & Baddeley, 1989; Gathercole, Willis, Emslie, & Baddeley, 1992). Deficiencies in these basic processes will impair vocabulary growth (see Gathercole et al., 1992). Individuals with deficiencies in these basic processes will require more exposure to a given word before forming an integrated representation of it in semantic memory. However, greater exposure to print provides more opportunities for inducing the meaning of unknown words from context, and this is true of all readers regardless of their level of basic abilities (Anderson, Wilson, & Fielding, 1988; Nagy, Herman, & Anderson, 1985; Stanovich, 1986, 1993). Thus, the concept of *experiential compensation* raises the issue of whether greater exposure might compensate for deficiencies in the basic abilities relevant to vocabulary induction. We present some preliminary evidence that suggests the possibility that some experiential compensations might be mediated by exposure to print.

ONLINE COMPENSATION

Contextual Facilitation Processes in Reading

One of the clearest cases of online compensation—and the one on which there exists the most empirical evidence—concerns the compensatory relation between word-recognition efficiency and processes of contextual facilitation that operate during reading. It is now well established that as a reader's word-recognition processes decrease in efficiency, there is a tendency for the reader to rely more on prior textual and sentential context to aid in lexical access. In short, the poorer the word-recognition process, the greater the reliance on contextual information.

The discovery of this online compensation was an experimental surprise— a finding that confounded many reading theorists and was predicted by few investigators when it first appeared in the literature in the late 1970s. In fact, the finding falsified the strong predictions of the major models of reading development that were influential at that time. During the mid-1970s, models of reading acquisition and individual differences in reading ability were dominated by top-down conceptualizations (e.g., F. Smith, 1971) that borrowed heavily from the New Look movement in perceptual research (Henderson, 1987). These models strongly emphasized the contribution of expectancies and contextual information. According to such models, the word-recognition process was heavily penetrated by background knowledge and higher-level cognitive expectancies. Reading theorists were considerably influenced by analysis-by-synthesis models of speech perception and interactive models of recognition that derived from artificial intelligence work in speech perception (Rumelhart, 1977).

With hindsight, the problem here is apparent. The analogy from speech to written language is simply not apt. The ambiguity in decontextualized speech is well known. For example, excised words from normal conversation are often not recognized out of context. This does not hold for written language, obviously. A fluent reader can identify written words with near perfect accuracy out of context. In short, the physical stimulus alone completely specifies the lexical representation in writing, whereas this is not always true in speech. The greater diagnosticity of the external stimulus in reading, as opposed to listening, puts a greater premium on an input system that can deliver a complete representation of the stimulus to higher-level cognitive systems.

One particular prediction derived from the top-down reading models, which turned out to be of considerable importance, concerned individual differences. Theorists who developed top-down models of reading consistently predicted that skilled readers would rely less on graphic cues and more on contextual information than less skilled readers (F. Smith, 1971, 1973, 1975). Smith's well-known hypothesis was that good readers were especially sensitive to the redundancy afforded by sentences, were particularly good at developing hypotheses about upcoming words, and were thus able to confirm the identity of a word by sampling only a few features in the visual array. According to this hypothesis, good readers processed words faster, not because their processes of lexical access were more efficient, but because their use of redundancy lightened the load on their stimulus-analysis mechanisms. In short, the skilled reader was less reliant on graphic cues and more reliant on contextual information than the less skilled reader:

> As the child develops reading skill and speed, he uses increasingly fewer graphic cues. (Goodman, 1976, p. 504)

> The more difficulty a reader has with reading, the more he relies on visual information; this statement applies to both the fluent reader and the beginner. (F. Smith, 1971, p. 221)

> One difference between the good beginning reader and the one heading for trouble lies in the overreliance on visual information that inefficient— or improperly taught—beginning readers tend to show, at the expense of sense. (F. Smith, 1973, p. 190)

> It is clear that the better reader barely looks at the individual words on the page. (F. Smith, 1973, p. 190)

The last conjecture has been uniformly contradicted by eye-movement research in the last two decades. Research consistently indicates that the vast majority of content words in text receive a direct visual fixation (Balota, Pollatsek, & Rayner, 1985; Just & Carpenter, 1987; Perfetti, 1985; Rayner & Pollatsek, 1989). Short function words and highly predictable words are more likely to be skipped, but even the majority of these are fixated. In short, the sampling of visual information in reading, as indicated by fixation points, is relatively dense. Likewise, the study of the processing of visual information within a fixation has indicated that the visual array is rather completely processed during each fixation. It appears that visual features are not minimally sampled, but are exhaustively processed even when the word is highly predictable (Balota et al., 1985; Rayner & Bertera, 1979; Zola, 1984).

More important, however, is that the theoretical prediction embodied in the first three quotes—that word recognition in the skilled reader will display more contextual dependency—has been decisively falsified by much empirical data. The falsifying data revealed instead a pattern of compensatory processing: It is less skilled readers who appear to be more reliant on contextual information, presumably to speed a process of lexical access that is proceeding slowly on the basis of the stimulus information alone.

Many discrete-trial reaction-time (RT) studies have been conducted to investigate the effect of context on word recognition. Most of these studies have used priming paradigms, where a context (sometimes an associated word, sometimes a sentence, and sometimes several sentences or paragraphs) precedes a target word to which the subject must make a naming or lexical-decision response. Although this paradigm does not completely isolate the word-recognition level of processing (see Balota & Chumbley, 1984; Seidenberg, Waters, Sanders, & Langer, 1984; West & Stanovich, 1982, 1986), it does so more than other methodologies that have been used. The finding has consistently been that poorer readers show somewhat larger contextual effects than do the better readers (Becker, 1985; Ben-Dror, Pollatsek, & Scarpati, 1991; Briggs, Austin, & Underwood, 1984; Bruck, 1988, 1990; Perfetti, 1985; Pring & Snowling, 1986; Schvaneveldt, Ackerman, & Semlear, 1977; Schwantes, 1985, 1991; Simpson & Foster, 1986; Simpson, Lorsbach, & Whitehouse, 1983; Stanovich, 1980, 1986; Stanovich, Nathan, West, & Vala-Rossi, 1985; Stanovich, Nathan, & Zolman, 1988; Stanovich, West, & Feeman, 1981; West & Stanovich, 1978; West, Stanovich, Feeman, & Cunningham, 1983).

Some investigators have employed oral-reading error analyses to examine individual differences in the use of context to facilitate word recognition. However, the use of the technique for this purpose is problematic because oral-reading errors often implicate levels of processing beyond word recognition (Bowey, 1985; Kibby, 1979; Leu, 1982; Wixson, 1979). For example, self-corrections, in part, reflect comprehension monitoring. Nevertheless, analyses of initial substitution errors have been used to throw light on the facilitation of word recognition by context, and it is likely that these errors partially implicate processes operating at the word-recognition level. Fortunately, the results of oral-reading error studies largely converge with those of RT studies. When skilled and less skilled readers are reading materials of comparable difficulty (an important control; see Stanovich, 1986), the reliance on contextual information relative to graphic information is often greater for the less skilled readers (Allington & Fleming, 1978; Biemiller, 1970, 1979; Harding, 1984; Juel, 1980; Lesgold, Resnick, & Hammond, 1985;

Leu, DeGroff, & Simons, 1986; Nicholson & Hill, 1985; Nicholson, Lillas, & Rzoska, 1988; Perfetti & Roth, 1981; Richardson, DiBenedetto, & Adler, 1982; Simons & Leu, 1987; Whaley & Kibby, 1981).

The results from studies of text-disruption effects, timed text reading, and a variety of other paradigms also display a similar pattern (Allington & Strange, 1977; Biemiller, 1977–1978; Ehrlich, 1981; Lovett, 1986; Nicholson, 1991, 1993; Schwartz & Stanovich, 1981; Stanovich, Cunningham, & Feeman, 1984; Strange, 1979). Thus, the results from a variety of different paradigms indicate that the effects of background knowledge and contextual information attenuate as the efficiency of word-recognition processes increases.

The consistent trend indicating that contextual effects on word recognition decrease as reading skill increases has led several theorists to conceptualize the logic of contextual facilitation on word recognition as compensatory in nature (Perfetti, 1985; Perfetti & Roth, 1981; Stanovich, 1980, 1984, 1986). It is hypothesized that the information processing system is arranged so that when the bottom-up stimulus-analysis processes that result in word recognition are deficient, the system compensates by relying more heavily on other knowledge sources (e.g., contextual information). Thus, "the compensatory assumption states that a deficit in any knowledge source results in a heavier reliance on other knowledge sources regardless of their level in the processing hierarchy" (Stanovich, 1980, p. 63).

Although the compensatory data pattern in studies of context effects is well established empirically, theoretical explanations of the pattern are less well developed. Nevertheless, some progress has been made in elucidating what Bäckman and Dixon (1992) termed the *three dimensions of compensatory behavior*: (a) whether the compensation is automatic or deliberate; (b) whether the compensating behavior is functional or maladaptive; and (c) whether the compensation is qualitatively, or merely quantitatively, different from the performance of the same task by a noncompensating individual. On the third question, there is a reasonable amount of empirical data, and the results are reasonably consistent. When the word-recognition processes of fluent readers are disrupted—either by using various forms of stimulus degradation or by using more difficult words—the magnitude and pattern of their contextual effects largely mirror those of less skilled readers (Durgunoglu, 1988; Perfetti, Goldman, & Hogaboam, 1979; Perfetti & Roth, 1981; Stanovich & West, 1983; Stanovich et al., 1981), although in some studies there has been a slight tendency for the contextual effects of less skilled readers to be larger even when equated on word recognition efficiency (Stanovich et al., 1984; Stanovich et al., 1988). Thus, contextual compensation appears to be a case of "normal" quantitative adjustment, rather than a qualitative reorganization of subskills. The compensation in contextual facilitation of word recognition does not involve the use of substitutable subskills, but instead "the use of the same skills as the normal population to solve the task at hand" (Bäckman & Dixon, 1992, p. 275).

The issue of whether online contextual compensation of word recognition in reading is automatic has also been addressed in some research. Many priming studies in the late 1970s and early 1980s were interpreted within the context of Posner and Snyder's (1975) two-process model of expectancy (e.g., Briggs et al., 1984; Neely, 1977; Stanovich & West, 1983; Stanovich et al., 1981; Stanovich et al., 1985; Vitek & Schwantes, 1989). For example, subjects in Stanovich and West's study named target words that had been preceded by incomplete sentences. The incomplete sentences provided either a congruous context (e.g., "the skier was buried in the"), neutral context ("they said it was the"), or incongruous context ("the bodyguard drove the") for the subsequent target words (e.g., snow). The contextual effects in these sentence-context experiments were partitioned into a facilitation component (the difference between performance in the neutral context and the congruous context) and an inhibition component (the difference between performance in the incongruous context and the neutral context). According to the Posner-Snyder two-process view, facilitation can arise from an automatic spreading-activation process or an attentional-prediction mechanism, whereas inhibition arises only from the operation of the conscious-attention mechanism. Results indicating that skilled readers displayed contextual facilitation in the absence of inhibition (Stanovich et al., 1981; Stanovich et al., 1985; West & Stanovich, 1978) led to the conclusion that contextual effects were an automatic facilitative mechanism in relatively fluent readers. That this mechanism was compensatory in nature was supported by the finding that contextual effects were larger for words that were more difficult to recognize in isolation (e.g., Stanovich & West, 1981). Conversely, indications that poorer readers displayed contextual inhibition as well as facilitation (e.g., West & Stanovich, 1978) were taken to indicate that contextual effects in the less-fluent reader reflected conscious compensatory strategies. These conclusions are less secure now because subsequent results have not always been consistent with the two-process theory, and because models of expectancy and priming have evolved since the early studies on context effects (see Durgunoglu, 1988; King & Just, 1991; Morris, 1994; Neely & Keefe, 1989; Smith, Besner, & Miyoshi, 1994; Stanovich & West, 1983; West & Stanovich, 1986, 1988). Nevertheless, a more modest conclusion still seems warranted—that contextual compensation of online word recognition during reading is relatively more automatic in the more skilled reader.

On the third dimension of compensatory behavior—whether the compensating behavior is functional or maladaptive—any conclusion drawn must be even more speculative. There is undoubtly a negative correlation between contextual reliance during word recognition and reading skill. Better readers rely less on context than do less skilled readers. Therefore, signs of contextual dependence are predictive of reading difficulty. But the causal status of this association is less secure. It is well known that poor readers have difficulties with phonological processing (e.g., Rack, Snowling, & Olson, 1992; Siegel & Ryan, 1988; Stanovich, 1988, 1991; Stanovich & Siegel, 1994), and, as a result, are slow to develop decoding skills. Their reliance on context might serve to maintain levels of word-recognition efficiency that are sufficient to sustain comprehension processes. Therefore, the use of context by poor readers might be viewed as an adaptive response. However, a recurring fear often voiced in the reading literature (e.g., Biemiller, 1970; Frith, 1985; Nicolson, 1993; Stanovich, 1980, 1986, 1992) is that such contextual dependence tempts the child to develop a nonanalytic processing style that ultimately interferes with the learning of spelling-sound correspondences.

However, some investigators (e.g., Share, in press; Tunmer & Hoover, 1992) have argued that some level of contextual prediction in early reading acquisition might be efficacious for long-term reading growth because it "facilitates the development of phonological recoding skill by enabling children to use context to identify unfamiliar words, which in turn increases their knowledge of grapheme-phoneme correspondences" (Tunmer & Hoover, 1992, p. 201). However, such a conjecture requires some fine theoretical distinctions—distinctions that probably outrun the empirical evidence. For example, a contextual prediction that maintains the comprehensibility of the passage, but is nevertheless incorrect, will result in a misleading learning trial (see Jorm & Share, 1983; Share, in press; Tunmer & Hoover, 1992) from the standpoint of learning correspondences between orthographic and phonological information. If a contextual prediction aids in decoding the correct orthographic form, only then will it be a mechanism associated with long-term growth in decoding ability, and hence reading skill. Which of these two situations predominates is presently unknown, but most reading researchers probably feel that the greater danger is from too much reliance on context, rather than too little (Adams, 1990; Gough, 1983; McKenna, Robinson, & Miller, 1993; Nicolson, 1993; Stanovich, 1986, 1992). Online contextual compensation—as efficacious as it might be for the current reading act—is, in the long term, more likely to be maladaptive.

Orthographic and Phonological Coding in Word Recognition

The second example of online compensation that has been extensively investigated in the reading literature is the trade-off between phonological coding and orthographic coding in word recognition. A strong caveat is in order before discussing this literature, however. Theoretical conceptualization in this area has recently evolved quite markedly with the advent of several influential connectionist models of word recognition (e.g., Brown, 1987; Brown & Watson, 1991; Hinton & Shallice, 1991; Seidenberg, 1992; Seidenberg & McClelland, 1989a, 1989b; Sejnowski & Rosenberg, 1986, 1988; Van Orden, Pennington, & Stone, 1990). In contrast, most of the literature on the compensatory relationship of phonological and orthographic coding was developed using the classic dual-route model of lexical access (see later discussion) as a theoretical background. We maintain much of the implicit dual-route language in our discussion, although we acknowledge that theoretical developments in this area are in flux. Nevertheless, the issues are far from resolution, and dual-route architectures remain viable theoretical contenders (Besner, Twilley, McCann, & Seergobin, 1990; Castles & Coltheart, 1993; Coltheart, Curtis, Atkins, & Haller, 1993; Paap, Noel, & Johansen, 1992). However, the discussion of the compensatory relationship would not be drastically altered regardless of how this dispute is resolved.

As classically formulated, dual-route models (Coltheart, 1978; Forster & Chambers, 1973; Meyer, Schvaneveldt, & Ruddy, 1974) posit two alternate recognition pathways to the lexicon: a direct visual/orthographic access route that does not involve phonological mediation, and an indirect route through phonology that utilizes stored spelling-sound correspondences. The size of the spelling-sound correspondences that make up the phonological route differ from model to model. Versions of dual-route models also differ in assumptions about the various speeds of the two access mechanisms involved, and how conflicting information is resolved. Excellent discussions of the many variants of this type of model are contained in several review articles (see Carr & Pollatsek, 1985; Coltheart et al., 1993; Humphreys & Evett, 1985; Paap et al., 1992; Patterson & Coltheart, 1987; Rayner & Pollatsek, 1989). In all such models, the phonological route may or may not become implicated in performance, depending on the status of the other route (Patterson, Marshall, & Coltheart, 1985) and the nature of the words being read. Two important factors in the latter class are the frequency and the spelling-sound regularity of the words used as stimuli. Indeed, studies of the spelling-sound regularity effect in word recognition have become a major source of data for addressing questions about the role of phonological coding in word recognition.

Spelling-sound regularity refers to the consistency of the mapping between the letters in the word and the sounds in its pronunciation. Regular words are those whose pronunciations reflect common spelling-sound correspondences (e.g., *made, rope*); irregular words are those with pronunciations that reflect atypical correspondences (e.g., *sword, pint, have, aisle*). Regularity is, of course, a continuous variable, not a discrete category (Barber & Millar, 1982; Patterson & Coltheart, 1987; Rosson, 1985; Venezky & Massaro, 1987), and the issue of how best to define regularity is a complex and contentious issue (Brown, 1987; Henderson, 1982, 1985; Humphreys & Evett, 1985; Kay & Bishop, 1987; Patterson et al., 1985; Rosson, 1985; Venezky & Massaro, 1987). Disagreement about how to classify words in terms of spelling-sound regularity is common because the degree of regularity assigned depends greatly on the size of the coding unit that is assumed for spelling-sound correspondences (Kay & Bishop, 1987). Simply put, many more words are regular when large-unit mappings are employed (Henderson, 1982; Ryder & Pearson, 1980; Treiman, 1992; Venezky, 1970).

Nevertheless, the finding of primary interest to us here is not dependent on any of these disputes, because it holds up despite differing definitions of *regularity*. The finding concerns the so-called spelling-sound regularity effect in word recognition: the tendency for regular words to be read faster and more accurately than exception words. It has been consistently found that highly skilled readers display very small regularity effects, presumably because their fast-acting visual/orthographic access mechanism operates too rapidly for the slower-acting phonological coding process to become implicated in performance (Backman, Bruck, Hebert, & Seidenberg, 1984; Seidenberg, 1985b; Seidenberg, Waters, Barnes, & Tanenhaus, 1984; Waters & Seidenberg, 1985). In contrast, poorer readers display much larger regularity effects, presumably because their slower visual/orthographic access route allows time for the phonological coding process to become implicated in performance. Thus, we have a compensatory processing situation similar to that involving context described previously. There, individuals with slower word-recognition processes displayed larger context effects. Likewise, individuals with slower mechanisms of direct visual access display larger effects of the phonological route on word processing.

Some research has addressed Backman and Dixon's (1992) three dimensions of compensatory behavior in this domain. Most investigators view this particular tradeoff in processing subskills as representing an automatic compensation (e.g., Seidenberg, 1985a), but the use of the phonological route may necessitate expenditure of some processing capacity (Paap et al., 1992). As was the case with context effects, the compensatory use of phonological information appears to represent a case of "normal" quantitative adjustment, rather than a qualitative reorganization of subskills for poor readers. When the visual/orthographic route of fluent readers is slowed by using low-frequency words, the magnitude of their spelling-sound regularity effect largely mirrors that of less skilled readers (Backman et al., 1984; Seidenberg, 1985b; Seidenberg, Waters, Barnes, & Tanenhaus, 1984). Finally, there is little direct evidence indicating whether compensatory use of phonological information is functional or maladaptive. However, given the critical role of phonological processing in several different subprocesses of reading (e.g., Siegel & Ryan, 1988; Stanovich, 1986, 1991; Stanovich & Siegel, 1994; Vellutino & Scanlon, 1987), there is reason to believe that it probably represents a functional and adaptive compensation.

EXPERIENTIAL COMPENSATION

In our research program, we have also investigated whether there was empirical evidence for experiential compensation: situations where reading itself served to compensate for other cognitive deficiencies. With respect to print exposure, there is a curious asymmetry in the research literature. Re-searchers studying the cognitive psychology of reading have attempted to specify individual differences in the cognitive processes that support efficient reading performance (Carr & Levy, 1990; Daneman, 1991; Just & Carpenter, 1987; Perfetti, 1985; Rayner & Pollatsek, 1989). A popular research strategy has been the cognitive-correlates approach (see Pellegrino & Glaser, 1979; Sternberg, 1990), in which investigators attempt to determine whether indi-vidual differences in particular cognitive processes or knowledge bases can serve as predictors of reading ability (e.g., Jackson & McClelland, 1979). The causal model that is implicit in such analyses locates individual differences in the cognitive subprocesses that support the reading act.

In cognitive psychology, little attention has been focused on what might be termed a form of *reciprocal causation*—that is, on the possibility that differences in exposure to print might affect the development of cognitive processes and declarative knowledge bases. In contrast, for decades anthro-pologists, sociologists, and historians have been intensely preoccupied with speculations on how the exercise of literacy affects knowledge acquisition, belief systems, cognitive processes, and reasoning (e.g., Goody, 1977, 1987; Havelock, 1963, 1980; Kaestle, 1991; Olson, 1977, 1986; Ong, 1967, 1982; Stock, 1983). It is not clear why the division of labor between cognitive psychologists and other social scientists in the domain of literacy should have developed in such an extreme fashion. Reading is a special type of interface with the environment, providing the organism with unique oppor-tunities to acquire declarative knowledge. Furthermore, the processing mechanisms exercised during reading receive an unusual amount of practice. Certain microprocesses of reading that are linked to words or groups of words are repeatedly exercised. From at least the fifth grade, an avid reader is seeing literally millions of words a year (Anderson et al., 1988). Thus, whatever cognitive processes are engaged over word or word-group units (phonological coding, semantic activation, parsing, induction of new vo-cabulary items) are being exercised hundreds of times a day. It is possible that this amount of cognitive muscle flexing will have some specific effects. Yet the dominant framework in the cognitive psychology of reading con-tinues to be the cognitive-correlates approach, with its bias toward viewing cognitive processes as causally prior to the reading act, which is almost exclusively perceived as an outcome variable. In our research, we have reversed this pattern by examining the extent to which differences in the exercise of reading skills may be viewed as causally prior to certain cognitive outcomes.

We have spent considerable research effort developing measures of ex-posure to print that are valid and that can be administered efficiently. How-ever, this part of our research program is tangential to the issues of the present chapter, so the reader is referred to a series of articles in which we established the construct validity of the measures of print exposure that we employ (Allen, Cipielewski, & Stanovich, 1992; Stanovich, 1993; Stanovich & Cunningham, 1992; West & Stanovich, 1991; West, Stanovich, & Mitchell, 1993). Here, we present analyses in which we pit—in a correlational sense—general ability measures against print exposure as predictors of cognitive outcomes in the verbal domain. Although never losing sight of the correlational nature of the data, we may ask, for example, whether print exposure can compensate for modest levels of general cognitive abilities, at least in a statistical sense.

The results of some relevant comparisons are presented in Table 13.1 (see also Stanovich, 1993; Stanovich & Cunningham, 1992). Two groups that were mismatched on print exposure and nonverbal cognitive ability were formed in the following manner. A large sample ($N = 300$) of college subjects was classified according to a median split of performance on the Raven Progressive Matrices and a composite print-exposure measure. The resulting 2×2 matrix revealed 118 subjects who were discrepant: 56 subjects who were low in print exposure but high on the Raven (LoPrint/HiAbility), and 62 subjects who were high in print exposure but low on the Raven (HiPrint/LoAbility). These two groups were then compared on seven verbal-outcome measures. As indicated in Table 13.1, the HiPrint/LoAbility group outperformed the LoPrint/HiAbility group on every variable in the study, which included two measures of vocabulary (Nelson-Denny and Peabody Picture Vocabulary Tests), two measures of general knowledge, a verbal-fluency task, a spelling measure, and the Nelson-Denny Reading Comprehension subtest. Four of the seven differences were statistically significant. Thus, as regards performance on these measures of declarative knowledge and verbal skill, print exposure was a more potent predictor than a general ability indicator. It appears that low ability need not necessarily hamper the acquisition of vocabulary and knowledge as long as the individual is an avid reader.

TABLE 13.1
Differences Between Subjects With High Ability but Low Print Exposure
($N = 56$), and Subjects With Low Ability but High Print Exposure ($N = 62$)

Variable	LoPrint/HiAbility	HiPrint/LoAbility	t(116)
Nelson-Denny Vocabulary	14.3	15.5	1.90
Peabody Picture Vocabulary Test	10.1	12.5	4.11**
History and Literature (NAEP)	12.1	13.9	3.24*
Cultural Literacy Recognition	.367	.517	6.57**
Nelson-Denny Comprehension	22.5	23.3	1.34
Spelling Composite	−.16	.27	2.67*
Verbal Fluency	30.6	32.8	1.66

*$p < .05$. **$p < .001$.

TABLE 13.2
Differences Between Subjects High in Comprehension Ability
but Low in Print Exposure ($N = 38$), and Subjects Low
in Comprehension Ability but High in Print Exposure ($N = 44$)

Variable	LoPrint/HiComp	HiPrint/LoComp	t(80)
Nelson-Denny Vocabulary	15.1	14.4	−0.94
Peabody Picture Vocabulary Test	10.6	12.1	2.06*
History and Literature (NAEP)	12.7	13.4	0.99
Cultural Literacy Recognition	.396	.483	3.86**
Spelling Composite	.16	−.05	−1.12
Verbal Fluency	31.6	32.0	0.30

*$p < .05$. **$p < .001$.

Table 13.2 displays an analysis of an even more unusual mismatch: that between print exposure and reading-comprehension ability. This analysis takes advantage of the fact that, although print exposure is positively correlated with Nelson-Denny Reading Comprehension performance, the relationship is far from perfect. There are individuals who, despite having modest comprehension skills, seem to read avidly; and there are other individuals who, despite good comprehension skills, seem not to exercise their abilities.

What are the cognitive correlates of a mismatch between abilities and the exercise of those abilities? To investigate this issue, the sample was classified according to a median split of performance on the Nelson-Denny Reading Comprehension subtest and a composite print-exposure variable. The resulting 2 × 2 matrix revealed 82 subjects who were discrepant: 38 subjects who were low in print exposure but high in comprehension (LoPrint/HiComp), and 44 subjects who were high in print exposure but low in comprehension (HiPrint/LoComp). These two groups were then compared on all the variables in the study (see Table 13.2). Despite comprehension differences favoring the LoPrint/HiComp group, as well as nonverbal cognitive abilities favoring this group (they were also higher on the Raven), LoPrint/HiComp individuals were not superior on any of the other variables. In fact, on one measure of vocabulary (the Peabody Picture Vocabulary Test) and one measure of general knowledge (a cultural literacy test), the HiPrint/LoComp group performed significantly better. Although inferences from these correlational analyses must be tentative, the results do suggest that low ability need not necessarily hamper the development of vocabulary and verbal knowledge as long as the individual is exposed to a lot of print.

In another study (Stanovich & Cunningham, 1993), we found that measures of general knowledge were more strongly associated with print exposure when it was mismatched with reading-comprehension ability. A sample of 268 college subjects was classified according to a median split of performance on the Nelson-Denny Reading Comprehension subtest and on measures of print exposure. The resulting 2 × 2 matrix revealed 77 subjects who were discrepant: 44 subjects who were below the median in print exposure but scored above the median on the Nelson-Denny (LoPrint/Hi-Comp), and 33 subjects who were high in print exposure but were low on the Nelson-Denny (HiPrint/LoComp). These two groups were then compared on five measures of general declarative knowledge. There were differences favoring the HiPrint/LoComp group on all five measures, and three of these differences were statistically significant (see Stanovich & Cunningham, 1993). The results suggest that low comprehension ability does not necessarily lead to low levels of knowledge as long as an individual has considerable print exposure.

In a final study illustrating experiential compensation (Stanovich, West, & Harrison, in press), we compared the performance of 133 college students ($M = 19.1$ years of age) and 49 older individuals ($M = 79.9$ years of age) on two general knowledge tasks, a vocabulary task, a working memory task, a syllogistic reasoning task, and several measures of exposure to print. The older individuals outperformed the college students on the measures of general knowledge and vocabulary, but did significantly less well than the college subjects on the working memory and syllogistic reasoning tasks.

Much attention has focused on the psychometric theory of fluid-crystallized intelligence in the study of intellectual growth and decline (Carroll, 1993; Horn, 1982; Horn & Cattell, 1967; Horn & Hofer, 1992; see also Baltes, 1987; Smith & Baltes, 1990). Fluid abilities are processes such as memory and reasoning, which operate across a range of domains and which are posited to be relatively independent of specific environmental experiences. In contrast, "crystallized abilities are postulated to reflect one's experiential history, and are assessed by tests of vocabulary, general information, and nearly all types of acquired knowledge" (Salthouse, 1988, p. 239). Fluid abilities are known to decline substantially with age, whereas crystallized abilities either decline much less or exhibit continual growth throughout most of the adult years (Baltes, 1987; Horn, 1982; Horn & Donaldson, 1980; Horn & Hofer, 1992). The results from Stanovich et al. (in press) were consistent with this trend in the literature for crystallized abilities, which are presumably reflected in the knowledge and vocabulary measures, to continue to grow with age, and for measures of fluid ability, which are presumably reflected in the working memory and syllogistic reasoning measures, to decline with age. However, a series of hierarchical regression analyses indicated that when measures of exposure to print were used as control variables, the positive relationships between age and vocabulary, and age and declarative knowledge, were eliminated (in contrast, the negative relationships between age and fluid abilities were largely unattenuated). The results suggest that, in the domain of verbal abilities, print exposure helps compensate for the normally deleterious effects of aging.

In terms of characterizing the experiential compensation of reading in terms of Backman and Dixon's (1992) three dimensions of compensatory behavior, the situation is clear with respect to two of the three dimensions. The compensating behavior is clearly functional. It is also somewhat clear that the compensation is quantitative, rather than qualitative, in nature. That is, no one has demonstrated that individuals high in print exposure think in a qualitatively different way than individuals low in print exposure. Although there have been conjectures that the cognitive processes of completely illiterate individuals might be qualitatively different from those of literates (e.g., Olson, 1977, 1986, 1994), these conjectures are still controversial and, in any case, do not represent the comparison that we have examined in our work. On the third dimension—of whether the compensation is automatic or conscious—a few conceptual distinctions are necessary. First, the act of reading is certainly sometimes engaged in as the result of a conscious decision by the subject (i.e., it is not always a mindless act; see Brown & Langer, 1990). So clearly the decision to engage in reading is sometimes conscious. However, the effects of the reading behavior on cognitive processes may, in fact, arise as an automatic side effect of reading. Again, the extent to which knowledge building during reading is a conscious or automatic process (e.g., is the induction of a new vocabulary item from context conscious or automatic?) is a largely uninvestigated issue.

SUMMARY

In the area of reading, two different types of psychological compensation have been investigated: online compensation and experiential compensation. Two examples of online compensation that have been extensively studied were examined in this chapter. The compensatory use of contextual information to supplement inefficient word-recognition processes appears to be a "normal" use of a compensatory mechanism, in the sense that it does not involve the use of substitutable subskills, but instead represents the use of the same skills as the normal population to aid processing. Such a compensation is probably automatic in most cases, but is probably maladaptive at the higher levels of reading skill. The compensatory use of phonological information to aid the visual-orthographic route during word recognition is, in contrast, probably an adaptive compensation. It too, is probably primarily an automatic compensation.

The long-term, experiential, compensatory effects of reading behavior have recently become the subject of empirical investigation. So far, all of the experiential compensations involving print exposure have been adaptive in nature. It appears that, as regards the development of declarative knowledge bases such as vocabulary, a large amount of exposure to print can compensate for modest levels of general comprehension abilities. Likewise, it appears that the absence of normally deleterious effects of aging in the domain of crystallized abilities is due, to some extent, to the compensatory effects of print exposure.

ACKNOWLEDGMENTS

This research was supported by grant #410-92-0397 from the Social Sciences and Humanities Research Council of Canada to Keith E. Stanovich, by a James Madison University Program Faculty Assistance Grant to Richard F. West, and by a James S. McDonnell Foundation Postdoctoral Fellowship to Anne E. Cunningham.

REFERENCES

Adams, M. J. (1990). *Beginning to read: Thinking and learning about print.* Cambridge, MA: MIT Press.

Allen, L., Cipielewski, J., & Stanovich, K. E. (1992). Multiple indicators of children's reading habits and attitudes: Construct validity and cognitive correlates. *Journal of Educational Psychology, 84,* 489–503.

Allington, R. L., & Fleming, J. T. (1978). The misreading of high-frequency words. *Journal of Special Education, 12,* 417–421.

Allington, R. L., & Strange, M. (1977). Effects of grapheme substitutions in connected text upon reading behaviors. *Visible Language, 11,* 285–297.

Anderson, R. C., Wilson, P. T., & Fielding, L. G. (1988). Growth in reading and how children spend their time outside of school. *Reading Research Quarterly, 23,* 285–303.

Backman, J., Bruck, M., Hebert, M., & Seidenberg, M. (1984). Acquisition and use of spelling-sound correspondences in reading. *Journal of Experimental Child Psychology, 38,* 114–133.

Bäckman, L., & Dixon, R. A. (1992). Psychological compensation: A theoretical framework. *Psychological Bulletin, 112,* 259–283.

Balota, D., & Chumbley, J. I. (1984). Are lexical decisions a good measure of lexical access? The role of word frequency in the neglected decision stage. *Journal of Experimental Psychology: Human Perception and Performance, 10,* 340–357.

Balota, D., Pollatsek, A., & Rayner, K. (1985). The interaction of contextual constraints and parafoveal visual information in reading. *Cognitive Psychology, 17,* 364–390.

Baltes, P. B. (1987). Theoretical propositions of life-span developmental psychology: On the dynamics between growth and decline. *Developmental Psychology, 23,* 611–626.

Barber, P. J., & Millar, D. G. (1982). Subjective judgments of spelling-sound correspondences: Effects of word regularity and word frequency. *Memory & Cognition, 10,* 457–464.

Becker, C. A. (1985). What do we really know about semantic context effects during reading? In D. Besner, T. Waller, & G. MacKinnon (Eds.), *Reading research: Advances in theory and practice* (Vol. 5, pp. 125–166). New York: Academic Press.

Ben-Dror, I., Pollatsek, A., & Scarpati, S. (1991). Word identification in isolation and in context by college dyslexic students. *Brain and Language, 40,* 471–490.

Besner, D., Twilley, L., McCann, R., & Seergobin, K. (1990). On the association between connectionism and data: Are a few words necessary? *Psychological Review, 97,* 432–446.

Biemiller, A. (1970). The development of the use of graphic and contextual information as children learn to read. *Reading Research Quarterly, 6,* 75–96.

Biemiller, A. (1977–1978). Relationships between oral reading rates for letters, words and simple text in the development of reading achievement. *Reading Research Quarterly, 13,* 223–253.

Biemiller, A. (1979). Changes in the use of graphic and contextual information as functions of passage difficulty and reading achievement level. *Journal of Reading Behavior, 11,* 307–319.

Bowey, J. A. (1985). Contextual facilitation in children's oral reading in relation to grade and decoding skill. *Journal of Experimental Child Psychology, 40,* 23–48.

Briggs, P., Austin, S., & Underwood, G. (1984). The effects of sentence context in good and poor readers: A test of Stanovich's interactive-compensatory model. *Reading Research Quarterly, 20,* 54–61.

Brown, G. (1987). Resolving inconsistency: A computational model of word naming. *Journal of Memory and Language, 26,* 1–23.

Brown, G. D. A., & Watson, F. L. (1991). Reading development in dyslexia: A connectionist approach. In M. Snowling & M. Thomson (Eds.), *Dyslexia: Integrating theory & practice* (pp. 165–182). London: Whurr.

Brown, J., & Langer, E. (1990). Mindfulness and intelligence: A comparison. *Educational Psychologist, 25,* 305–335.

Bruck, M. (1988). The word recognition and spelling of dyslexic children. *Reading Research Quarterly, 23,* 51–69.

Bruck, M. (1990). Word-recognition skills of adults with childhood diagnoses of dyslexia. *Developmental Psychology, 26,* 439–454.

Carr, T. H., & Levy, B. A. (Eds.). (1990). *Reading and its development: Component skills approaches.* San Diego: Academic Press.

Carr, T. H., & Pollatsek, A. (1985). Recognizing printed words: A look at current models. In D. Besner, T. G. Waller, & G. E. MacKinnon (Eds.), *Reading research: Advances in theory and practice* (Vol. 5, pp. 1–82). Orlando, FL: Academic Press.

Carroll, J. B. (1993). *Human cognitive abilities: A survey of factor-analytic studies.* Cambridge, England: Cambridge University Press.

Castles, A., & Coltheart, M. (1993). Varieties of developmental dyslexia. *Cognition, 47,* 149–180.

Coltheart, M. (1978). Lexical access in simple reading tasks. In G. Underwood (Ed.), *Strategies of information processing* (pp. 151–216). London: Academic Press.

Coltheart, M., Curtis, B., Atkins, P., & Haller, M. (1993). Models of reading aloud: Dual-route and parallel-distributed-processing approaches. *Psychological Review, 100,* 589–608.

Daneman, M. (1991). Individual differences in reading skills. In R. Barr, M. L. Kamil, P. Mosenthal, & P. D. Pearson (Eds.), *Handbook of reading research* (Vol. 2, pp. 512–538). New York: Longman.

Durgunoglu, A. Y. (1988). Repetition, semantic priming, and stimulus quality: Implications for the interactive-compensatory model. *Journal of Experimental Psychology: Learning, Memory, and Cognition, 14,* 590–603.

Ehrlich, S. (1981). Children's word recognition in prose context. *Visible Language, 15,* 219–244.

Forster, K. I., & Chambers, S. (1973). Lexical access and naming time. *Journal of Verbal Learning and Verbal Behavior, 12,* 627–635.

Frith, U. (1985). Beneath the surface of developmental dyslexia. In K. Patterson, J. Marshall, & M. Coltheart (Eds.), *Surface dyslexia* (pp. 301–330). Hove, England: Lawrence Erlbaum Associates.

Gathercole, S. E., & Baddeley, A. D. (1989). Evaluation of the role of phonological STM in the development of vocabulary in children: A longitudinal study. *Journal of Memory and Language, 28,* 200–213.

Gathercole, S. E., Willis, C., Emslie, H., & Baddeley, A. D. (1992). Phonological memory and vocabulary development during the early school years: A longitudinal study. *Developmental Psychology, 28,* 887–898.

Goodman, K. S. (1976). Reading: A psycholinguistic guessing game. In H. Singer & R. B. Ruddell (Eds.), *Theoretical models and processes of reading* (pp. 497–508). Newark, DE: International Reading Association.

Goody, J. (1977). *The domestication of the savage mind.* New York: Cambridge University Press.

Goody, J. (1987). *The interface between the written and the oral.* Cambridge, England: Cambridge University Press.

Gough, P. B. (1983). Context, form, and interaction. In K. Rayner (Ed.), *Eye movements in reading* (pp. 203–211). New York: Academic Press.

Harding, L. M. (1984). Reading errors and style in children with a specific reading disability. *Journal of Research in Reading, 7*, 103–112.

Havelock, E. A. (1963). *Preface to Plato.* Cambridge, MA: Harvard University Press.

Havelock, E. A. (1980). The coming of literate communication to Western culture. *Journal of Communication, 30*, 90–98.

Henderson, L. (1982). *Orthography and word recognition in reading.* London: Academic Press.

Henderson, L. (1985). Issues in the modeling of pronunciation assembly in normal reading. In K. E. Patterson, J. C. Marshall, & M. Coltheart (Eds.), *Surface dyslexia* (pp. 459–508). Hove, England: Lawrence Erlbaum Associates.

Henderson, L. (1987). Word recognition: A tutorial review. In M. Coltheart (Ed.), *Attention and performance* (Vol. 12, pp. 171–200). Hove, England: Lawrence Erlbaum Associates.

Hinton, G., & Shallice, T. (1991). Lesioning an attractor network: Investigations of acquired dyslexia. *Psychological Review, 98*, 74–95.

Horn, J. L. (1982). The theory of fluid and crystallized intelligence in relation to concepts of cognitive psychology and aging in adulthood. In F. I. M. Craik & S. Trehub (Eds.), *Aging and cognitive processes* (pp. 847–870). New York: Plenum.

Horn, J. L., & Cattell, R. B. (1967). Age differences in fluid and crystallized intelligence. *Acta Psychologica, 26*, 1–23.

Horn, J. L., & Donaldson, G. (1980). Cognitive development in adulthood. In O. Brim & J. Kagan (Eds.), *Constancy and change in human development* (pp. 91–123). Cambridge, MA: Harvard University Press.

Horn, J. L., & Hofer, S. (1992). Major abilities and development in the adult period. In R. J. Sternberg & C. A. Berg (Eds.), *Intellectual development* (pp. 44–99). Cambridge, England: Cambridge University Press.

Humphreys, G. W., & Evett, L. J. (1985). Are there independent lexical and nonlexical routes in word processing? An evaluation of the dual-route theory of reading. *Behavioral and Brain Sciences, 8*, 689–740.

Jackson, M., & McClelland, J. (1979). Processing determinants of reading speed. *Journal of Experimental Psychology: General, 108*, 151–181.

Jorm, A., & Share, D. (1983). Phonological recoding and reading acquisition. *Applied Psycholinguistics, 4*, 103–147.

Juel, C. (1980). Comparison of word identification strategies with varying context, word type, and reader skill. *Reading Research Quarterly, 15*, 358–376.

Just, M., & Carpenter, P. A. (1987). *The psychology of reading and language comprehension.* Boston: Allyn & Bacon.

Kaestle, C. F. (1991). *Literacy in the United States.* New Haven, CT: Yale University Press.

Kay, J., & Bishop, D. (1987). Anatomical differences between nose, palm, and foot, or, the body in question: Further dissection of the processes of sub-lexical spelling-sound translation. In M. Coltheart (Ed.), *Attention and performance* (Vol. 12, pp. 449–469). Hove, England: Lawrence Erlbaum Associates.

Kibby, M. W. (1979). Passage readability affects the oral reading strategies of disabled readers. *The Reading Teacher, 32*, 390–396.

King, J., & Just, M. (1991). Individual differences in syntactic processing: The role of working memory. *Journal of Memory and Language, 30,* 580–602.

Lesgold, A., Resnick, L., & Hammond, K. (1985). Learning to read: A longitudinal study of word skill development in two curricula. In G. MacKinnon & T. Waller (Eds.), *Reading research: Advances in theory and practice* (Vol. 4, pp. 107–138). London: Academic Press.

Leu, D. (1982). Oral reading error analysis: A critical review of research and application. *Reading Research Quarterly, 17,* 420–437.

Leu, D. J., DeGroff, L., & Simons, H. D. (1986). Predictable texts and interactive-compensatory hypotheses: Evaluating individual differences in reading ability, context use, and comprehension. *Journal of Educational Psychology, 78,* 347–352.

Lovett, M. W. (1986). Sentential structure and the perceptual spans of two samples of disabled readers. *Journal of Psycholinguistic Research, 15,* 153–175.

McKenna, M., Robinson, R., & Miller, J. (1993). Whole language and research: The case for caution. In D. Leu & C. Kinzer (Eds.), *Examining central issues in literacy research, theory, and practice: 42nd NRC yearbook* (pp. 141–152). Chicago, IL: National Reading Conference.

Meyer, D. E., Schvaneveldt, R. W., & Ruddy, M. G. (1974). Functions of graphemic and phonemic codes in visual word recognition. *Memory & Cognition, 2,* 309–321.

Morris, R. (1994). Lexical and message-level sentence context effects on fixation times in reading. *Journal of Experimental Psychology: Learning, Memory, and Cognition, 20,* 92–103.

Nagy, W. E., Herman, P. A., & Anderson, R. C. (1985). Learning words from context. *Reading Research Quarterly, 20,* 233–253.

Neely, J. H. (1977). Semantic priming and retrieval from lexical memory: Roles of inhibitionless spreading activation and limited-capacity attention. *Journal of Experimental Psychology: General, 106,* 226–254.

Neely, J. H., & Keefe, D. E. (1989). Semantic context effects on visual word processing: A hybrid prospective-retrospective processing theory. In G. H. Bower (Ed.), *The psychology of learning and motivation* (pp. 207–248). San Diego, CA: Academic Press.

Nicholson, T. (1991). Do children read words better in context or in lists? A classic study revisited. *Journal of Educational Psychology, 83,* 444–450.

Nicholson, T. (1993). The case against context. In G. B. Thompson, W. Tunmer, & T. Nicholson (Eds.), *Reading acquisition processes* (pp. 91–104). Philadelphia: Multilingual Matters.

Nicholson, T., & Hill, D. (1985). Good readers don't guess—Taking another look at the issue of whether children read words better in context or in isolation. *Reading Psychology, 6,* 181–198.

Nicholson, T., Lillas, C., & Rzoska, M. (1988). Have we been misled by miscues? *The Reading Teacher, 42*(1), 6–10.

Olson, D. R. (1977). From utterance to text: The bias of language in speech and writing. *Harvard Educational Review, 47,* 257–281.

Olson, D. R. (1986). The cognitive consequences of literacy. *Canadian Psychology, 27,* 109–121.

Olson, D. R. (1994). *The world on paper.* Cambridge, England: Cambridge University Press.

Ong, W. J. (1967). *The presence of the word.* Minneapolis: University of Minnesota Press.

Ong, W. J. (1982). *Orality and literacy.* London: Methuen.

Paap, K., Noel, R., & Johansen, L. (1992). Dual-route models of print to sound: Red herrings and real horses. In R. Frost & L. Katz (Eds.), *Orthography, phonology, morphology, and meaning* (pp. 293–318). Amsterdam: North-Holland.

Patterson, K., & Coltheart, V. (1987). Phonological processes in reading: A tutorial review. In M. Coltheart (Ed.), *Attention and performance* (Vol. 12, pp. 421–447). Hove, England: Lawrence Erlbaum Associates.

Patterson, K., Marshall, J., & Coltheart, M. (1985). *Surface dyslexia.* Hove, England: Lawrence Erlbaum Associates.

Pellegrino, J. W., & Glaser, R. (1979). Cognitive correlates and components in the analysis of individual differences. In R. J. Sternberg & D. K. Detterman (Eds.), *Human intelligence: Perspectives on its theory and measurement* (pp. 61–88). Norwood, NJ: Ablex.

Perfetti, C. A. (1985). *Reading ability.* New York: Oxford University Press.

Perfetti, C. A., Goldman, S., & Hogaboam, T. (1979). Reading skill and the identification of words in discourse context. *Memory & Cognition, 7,* 273–282.

Perfetti, C. A., & Roth, S. (1981). Some of the interactive processes in reading and their role in reading skill. In A. Lesgold & C. Perfetti (Eds.), *Interactive processes in reading* (pp. 269–297). Hillsdale, NJ: Lawrence Erlbaum Associates.

Posner, M. I., & Snyder, C. R. R. (1975). Facilitation and inhibition in the processing of signals. In P. Rabbitt & S. Dornic (Eds.), *Attention and performance* (Vol. 5, pp. 669–682). London: Academic Press.

Pring, L., & Snowling, M. (1986). Developmental changes in word recognition: An information-processing account. *Quarterly Journal of Experimental Psychology, 38A,* 395–418.

Rack, J. P., Snowling, M. J., & Olson, R. K. (1992). The nonword reading deficit in developmental dyslexia: A review. *Reading Research Quarterly, 27,* 28–53.

Rayner, K., & Bertera, J. H. (1979). Reading without a fovea. *Science, 206,* 468–469.

Rayner, K., & Pollatsek, A. (1989). *The psychology of reading.* Englewood Cliffs, NJ: Prentice-Hall.

Richardson, E., DiBenedetto, B., & Adler, A. (1982). Use of the decoding skills test to study differences between good and poor readers. In K. Gadow & I. Bialer (Eds.), *Advances in learning and behavioral disabilities* (Vol. 1, pp. 25–74). Greenwich, CT: JAI.

Rosson, M. B. (1985). The interaction of pronunciation rules and lexical representations in reading aloud. *Memory & Cognition, 13,* 90–99.

Rumelhart, D. E. (1977). Toward an interactive model of reading. In S. Dornic (Ed.), *Attention and performance* (Vol. 6, pp. 573–603). New York: Academic Press.

Ryder, R., & Pearson, P. D. (1980). Influence of type-token frequencies and final consonants on adults' internalization of vowel digraphs. *Journal of Educational Psychology, 72,* 618–624.

Salthouse, T. A. (1988). Resource-reduction interpretations of cognitive aging. *Developmental Review, 8,* 238–272.

Schvaneveldt, R., Ackerman, B., & Semlear, T. (1977). The effect of semantic context on children's word recognition. *Child Development, 48,* 612–616.

Schwantes, F. M. (1985). Expectancy, integration, and interactional processes: Age differences in the nature of words affected by sentence context. *Journal of Experimental Child Psychology, 39,* 212–229.

Schwantes, F. M. (1991). Children's use of semantic and syntactic information for word recognition and determination of sentence meaningfulness. *Journal of Reading Behavior, 23,* 335–350.

Schwartz, R. M., & Stanovich, K. E. (1981). Flexibility in the use of graphic and contextual information by good and poor readers. *Journal of Reading Behavior, 13,* 263–269.

Seidenberg, M. S. (1985a). The time course of information activation and utilization in visual word recognition. In D. Besner, T. Waller, & G. MacKinnon (Eds.), *Reading research: Advances in theory and practice* (Vol. 5, pp. 199–252). New York: Academic Press.

Seidenberg, M. S. (1985b). The time course of phonological code activation in two writing systems. *Cognition, 19,* 1–30.

Seidenberg, M. S. (1992). Dyslexia in a computational model of word recognition in reading. In P. B. Gough, L. C. Ehri, & R. Treiman (Eds.), *Reading acquisition* (pp. 243–273). Hillsdale, NJ: Lawrence Erlbaum Associates.

Seidenberg, M. S., & McClelland, J. L. (1989a). A distributed, developmental model of word recognition and naming. *Psychological Review, 96,* 523–568.

Seidenberg, M. S., & McClelland, J. L. (1989b). Visual word recognition and pronunciation: A computational model of acquisition, skilled performance, and dyslexia. In A. M. Galaburda (Ed.), *From reading to neurons* (pp. 256–305). Cambridge, MA: MIT Press.

Seidenberg, M. S., Waters, G. S., Barnes, M. A., & Tanenhaus, M. K. (1984). When does irregular spelling or pronunciation influence word recognition? *Journal of Verbal Learning and Verbal Behavior, 23,* 383–404.

Seidenberg, M. S., Waters, G. S., Sanders, M., & Langer, P. (1984). Pre- and post-lexical loci of contextual effects on word recognition. *Memory & Cognition, 12,* 315–328.

Sejnowski, T. J., & Rosenberg, C. R. (1986). *NETtalk: A parallel network that learns to read aloud* (Tech. Rep. No. JHU/EECS-86/01). Baltimore, MD: Department of Electrical Engineering and Computer Science, The Johns Hopkins University.

Sejnowski, T. J., & Rosenberg, C. R. (1988). Learning and representation in connectionist models. In M. S. Gazzaniga (Ed.), *Perspectives in memory research* (pp. 135–178). Cambridge, MA: MIT Press.

Share, D. L. (in press). Phonological recoding and self-teaching: Sine qua non of reading acquisition. *Cognition.*

Siegel, L. S., & Ryan, E. B. (1988). Development of grammatical-sensitivity, phonological, and short-term memory skills in normally achieving and learning disabled children. *Developmental Psychology, 24,* 28–37.

Simons, H. D., & Leu, D. J. (1987). The use of contextual and graphic information in word recognition by second-, fourth-, and sixth-grade readers. *Journal of Reading Behavior, 19,* 33–47.

Simpson, G. B., & Foster, M. R. (1986). Lexical ambiguity and children's word recognition. *Developmental Psychology, 22,* 147–154.

Simpson, G. B., Lorsbach, T., & Whitehouse, D. (1983). Encoding and contextual components of word recognition in good and poor readers. *Journal of Experimental Child Psychology, 35,* 161–171.

Smith, F. (1971). *Understanding reading.* New York: Holt, Rinehart & Winston.

Smith, F. (1973). *Psycholinguistics and reading.* New York: Holt, Rinehart & Winston.

Smith, F. (1975). The role of prediction in reading. *Elementary English, 52,* 305–311.

Smith, J., & Baltes, P. B. (1990). A life-span perspective on thinking and problem-solving. In M. Schwebel, C. Maher, & N. Fagley (Eds.), *Promoting cognitive growth over the life span* (pp. 47–69). Hillsdale, NJ: Lawrence Erlbaum Associates.

Smith, M. C., Besner, D., & Miyoshi, H. (1994). New limits to automaticity: Context modulates semantic priming. *Journal of Experimental Psychology: Learning, Memory, and Cognition, 20,* 104–115.

Stanovich, K. E. (1980). Toward an interactive-compensatory model of individual differences in the development of reading fluency. *Reading Research Quarterly, 16,* 32–71.

Stanovich, K. E. (1984). The interactive-compensatory model of reading: A confluence of developmental, experimental, and educational psychology. *Remedial and Special Education, 5,* 11–19.

Stanovich, K. E. (1986). Matthew effects in reading: Some consequences of individual differences in the acquisition of literacy. *Reading Research Quarterly, 21,* 360–407.

Stanovich, K. E. (1988). Explaining the differences between the dyslexic and the garden-variety poor reader: The phonological-core variable-difference model. *Journal of Learning Disabilities, 21,* 590–612.

Stanovich, K. E. (1991). Discrepancy definitions of reading disability: Has intelligence led us astray? *Reading Research Quarterly, 26,* 7–29.

Stanovich, K. E. (1992). Speculations on the causes and consequences of individual differences in early reading acquisition. In P. Gough, L. Ehri, & R. Treiman (Eds.), *Reading acquisition* (pp. 307–342). Hillsdale, NJ: Lawrence Erlbaum Associates.

Stanovich, K. E. (1993). Does reading make you smarter? Literacy and the development of verbal intelligence. In H. Reese (Ed.), *Advances in child development and behavior* (Vol. 24, pp. 133–180). San Diego, CA: Academic Press.

Stanovich, K. E., & Cunningham, A. E. (1992). Studying the consequences of literacy within a literate society: The cognitive correlates of print exposure. *Memory & Cognition, 20,* 51–68.

Stanovich, K. E., & Cunningham, A. E. (1993). Where does knowledge come from? Specific associations between print exposure and information acquisition. *Journal of Educational Psychology, 85,* 211–229.

Stanovich, K. E., Cunningham, A. E., & Feeman, D. (1984). Relation between early reading acquisition and word decoding with and without context: A longitudinal study of first-grade children. *Journal of Educational Psychology, 76,* 668–677.

Stanovich, K. E., Nathan, R. G., West, R. F., & Vala-Rossi, M. (1985). Children's word recognition in context: Spreading activation, expectancy, and modularity. *Child Development, 56,* 1418–1429.

Stanovich, K. E., Nathan, R. G., & Zolman, J. E. (1988). The developmental lag hypothesis in reading: Longitudinal and matched reading-level comparisons. *Child Development, 59,* 71–86.

Stanovich, K. E., & Siegel, L. S. (1994). The phenotypic performance profile of reading-disabled children: A regression-based test of the phonological-core variable-difference model. *Journal of Educational Psychology, 86,* 24–53.

Stanovich, K. E., & West, R. F. (1983). On priming by a sentence context. *Journal of Experimental Psychology: General, 112,* 1–36.

Stanovich, K. E., West, R. F., & Feeman, D. J. (1981). A longitudinal study of sentence context effects in second-grade children: Tests of an interactive-compensatory model. *Journal of Experimental Child Psychology, 32,* 185–199.

Stanovich, K. E., West, R. F., & Harrison, M. R. (in press). Knowledge growth and maintenance across the life span: The role of print exposure. *Developmental Psychology.*

Sternberg, R. J. (1985). *Beyond IQ: A triarchic theory of human intelligence.* Cambridge, England: Cambridge University Press.

Sternberg, R. J. (1990). *Metaphors of mind: Conceptions of the nature of intelligence.* Cambridge, England: Cambridge University Press.

Sternberg, R. J., & Powell, J. (1983). Comprehending verbal comprehension. *American Psychologist, 38,* 878–893.

Stock, B. (1983). *The implications of literacy.* Princeton, NJ: Princeton University Press.

Strange, M. (1979). The effect of orthographic anomalies upon reading behavior. *Journal of Reading Behavior, 11,* 153–161.

Treiman, R. (1992). The role of intrasyllabic units in learning to read and spell. In P. B. Gough, L. C. Ehri, & R. Treiman (Eds.), *Reading acquisition* (pp. 65–106). Hillsdale, NJ: Lawrence Erlbaum Associates.

Tunmer, W. E., & Hoover, W. (1992). Cognitive and linguistic factors in learning to read. In P. B. Gough, L. C. Ehri, & R. Treiman (Eds.), *Reading acquisition* (pp. 175–214). Hillsdale, NJ: Lawrence Erlbaum Associates.

Van Orden, G. C., Pennington, B. F., & Stone, G. O. (1990). Word identification in reading and the promise of subsymbolic psycholinguistics. *Psychological Review, 97,* 488–522.

Vellutino, F., & Scanlon, D. (1987). Phonological coding, phonological awareness, and reading ability: Evidence from a longitudinal and experimental study. *Merrill-Palmer Quarterly, 33,* 321–363.

Venezky, R. L. (1970). *The structure of English orthography.* The Hague, Netherlands: Mouton.

Venezky, R. L., & Massaro, D. W. (1987). Orthographic structure and spelling-sound regularity in reading English words. In A. Allport, D. MacKay, W. Prinz, & E. Scheerer (Eds.), *Language perception and production* (pp. 159–179). London: Academic Press.

Vitek, D., & Schwantes, F. M. (1989). Automatic spreading activation effects following children's reading of complete sentences. *Journal of Reading Behavior, 21,* 181–194.

Waters, G., & Seidenberg, M. (1985). Spelling-sound effects in reading: Time-course and decision criteria. *Memory & Cognition, 13,* 557–572.

West, R. F., & Stanovich, K. E. (1978). Automatic contextual facilitation in readers of three ages. *Child Development, 49*, 717–727.

West, R. F., & Stanovich, K. E. (1982). Sources of inhibition in experiments on the effect of sentence context on word recognition. *Journal of Experimental Psychology: Learning, Memory, and Cognition, 8*, 385–399.

West, R. F., & Stanovich, K. E. (1986). Robust effects of syntactic structure on visual word processing. *Memory & Cognition, 14*, 104–112.

West, R. F., & Stanovich, K. E. (1988). How much of sentence priming is word priming? *Bulletin of the Psychonomic Society, 26*, 1–4.

West, R. F., & Stanovich, K. E. (1991). The incidental acquisition of information from reading. *Psychological Science, 2*, 325–330.

West, R. F., Stanovich, K. E., Feeman, D., & Cunningham, A. (1983). The effect of sentence context on word recognition in second- and sixth-grade children. *Reading Research Quarterly, 19*, 6–15.

West, R. F., Stanovich, K. E., & Mitchell, H. R. (1993). Reading in the real world and its correlates. *Reading Research Quarterly, 28*, 34–50.

Whaley, J., & Kibby, M. (1981). The relative importance of reliance on intraword characteristics and interword constraints for beginning reading achievement. *Journal of Educational Research, 74*, 315–320.

Wixson, K. L. (1979). Miscue analysis: A critical review. *Journal of Reading Behavior, 11*, 163–175.

Zola, D. (1984). Redundancy and word perception during reading. *Perception & Psychophysics, 36*, 277–284.

CHAPTER FOURTEEN

Compensation in Athletic Sport

M. J. Stones
University of Waterloo

Albert Kozma
Memorial University of Newfoundland

This chapter examines compensation in athletic sport. Bäckman and Dixon (1992) described a general model of compensation that is composed of components of external demand, personal expectation of performance, and accessible skill. They reasoned that compensation begins with a mismatch between demands and skill, with performance expectations initially matched to demand. Faced with an imbalance between demand and skill, three classes of option are available. First, a person can try to compensate by changing skill to match demand. Possible mechanisms include raising the level of effort, using latent aspects of skill, or finding an alternative skill. A second category of option is to compensate by changing expectations to match skill rather than demand. Third, noncompensatory options are not to change behavior at all, but to acquiesce with grace or rancour to the demand–skill discrepancy. Unlike the latter, both the compensatory options involve behavioral change that restores the balance between skill and expectations.

Bäckman and Dixon emphasized three clarifications to the preceding scheme. First, only behaviors arising from a demand–skill mismatch exemplify compensation. Second, such a mismatch does not always result in compensatory behavior. Third, they suggested the behavior to be different between a compensating person and a normal person in a given situation. The latter raises some intriguing issues for research design.

Successful athletes are supranormal in their expertise, being both selected for ability and extensively trained for technique and fitness. Appropriate referents for aging athletes include equally gifted but younger peers, or their

297

own performances at earlier times. However, compensatory behavior mainly occurs at critical stages within an athletic career. The success curve in sport, even among athletes competing in veterans events, is typically not linear but ∩-shaped: ascent followed by a plateau around the age of peak performance, with ultimate decline (Stones & Kozma, 1984). Consequently, a sensitive monitoring of compensation may require a temporal tracking of behavior, particularly around times when the gradients of success curves change. Before and after monitoring is also appropriate if the collective performances by athletes evolve to a new plateau. Such evolution was observed in race walking after the 1968 Mexico City Olympics, when improved technique and more effortful training lopped minutes off the best times of the leading walkers.

This chapter analyzes compensation at the level of the individual athlete, as well as how it concerns communal change. First, we introduce our readers to a range of compensatory behaviors observed among competitors, termed by Bäckman and Dixon (1992) as *mechanisms of compensation*. Second, we examine the evolution of modern sport as a form of social compensation. Beginning about two centuries ago, philosophers began to advocate sport as a means to rectify perceived mismatches between the required and then-existing forms of national character. The present century witnessed a wider professionalization of sport, with compensatory changes required of athletes and administrators to meet the demands for higher performance. Third, we discuss individual differences in motivation among athletes, and associated implications for compensation. Fourth, we examine compensation in relation to the diversity in skill and expertise.

ILLUSTRATIONS OF COMPENSATION

Athletic proficiency owes some debt to natural ability. However, expertise in sport develops with experience *and* the maturation of physical and psychological processes (French & Nevett, 1993). Family members, fellow competitors, and (increasingly in recent eras) coaches contribute to the regulation of demands on young athletes. The relationship with an experienced coach is an undoubted stepping stone toward superior performance (cf. Butt, 1987). However, some sports commentators decry the kind of coaching that emphasizes team tactics at the expense of promoting individual flair (Lewis, 1993). Another source of demand, especially on professional athletes, is the fans. Garry Charles, a promising young soccer defender, repeatedly incurred the displeasure of Nottingham Forest's supporters during the 1992–1993 season, in which the team suffered relegation from England's Premier Division. Because the abuse from the terraces caused him to lose confidence, he compensated by transferring to a neighboring club whose fans were less demanding of his skill.

The demands on established athletes are rarely static, but change frequently within the span of a career. One reason is progress in technique—high jumping changed forever after Dick Fosbury introduced his famous "flop" at the 1968 Olympics. A second reason is superior performance by upcoming athletes. Female race walking provides a recent example of evolving standards. A third reason is changing strategies. Team manager Sir Alf Ramsey replaced traditional wingers by overlapping fullbacks to win the World Cup for England's soccer team in 1966. All these examples suggest success in sport to be reactive to changing demands, with the athlete expected to compensate accordingly.

Bäckman and Dixon (1992) identified four mechanisms of compensation: modifying expectations, working to improve skill, substituting a latent skill, or using a new skill. All four mechanisms are capable of objective measurement. Self-report data can reflect changing aspirations. Data on the intensity, type, and time spent training allow for measurement of the effort expended to improve or maintain skill with age. Designs to study these mechanisms could include a cross-sectional sampling of athletes of different ages, or longitudinal analysis of training diaries. An understanding of the skill components is a prerequisite for evaluating the use of latent or new skills. The former might be indexed quantitatively, for example, by an analysis of the frequency with which power pitchers in baseball change to become finesse pitchers with age. In soccer, an analysis of former goal scorers who take on defensive roles has relevance to the substitution of latent skills.

The following examples illustrate these mechanisms in different sports. However, we offer them with two main qualifications. First, the data are verified anecdotes about individual athletes. Because the data are idiographic rather than nomothetic, we make no pretense about generalization. Second, individual athletes may compensate by using more than one mechanism at the same or different times. We have illustrated only the mechanism that predominated at a specific stage in the athlete's career.

Changes in Aspirations

The first mechanism is to modify expectations to accord with accessible skill. French and Nevett (1993) discussed aspects of skill development in youth sport. Most young athletes not progressing as they had hoped become reconciled to be other than a star. Some find a niche with minor teams, in the middle of the pack, or contribute as a substitute player. Similarly, older athletes in decline may lower their sights. They adjust to not running from the front, to competition against lesser opposition, or to performing with less flair. Even the legendary Muhammad Ali lowered his lofty ambitions when fighting to regain the world heavyweight boxing championship from Leon Spinks in 1978. The young Ali was prideful of his flamboyance, whereas with Spinks (12 years his junior) he simply hit and ran.

Training to Improve Skill

The second form of compensation is to train to improve aspects of skill. Then-upcoming tennis star Steffi Graf suffered humiliation from Martina Navratilova's left-handed sliced serve to her backhand in the 1987 Wimbledon final. "I didn't have to go for big serves," Martina said after. "It seemed that my spin bothered her more than the pace, which enabled me to get most of my first serves. With some second serves she had a harder time timing it than with my first serves" (cited in Frayne, 1990, p. 97). Journalist Trent Frayne (1990) later told of the rumor that Steffi's coach and father, Peter Graf, had found a left-hander with a serve like Navratilova's. This hired hand "lay endless serves against Steffi's backhand until she could whack them back in her sleep (and while wide awake)" (Frayne, 1990, p. 97). It worked for Steffi, who drilled powerful backhands to win Wimbledon from Martina in 1988 and 1989.

Changing Tactics or Strategy

Other athletes substitute latent skills or modify tactics. Nigel Clough, the England soccer striker, compensated for a low scoring rate by setting up goals for others to score, creating openings for them from just behind the main attack. Marcel Jobin, the Canadian race walker, ended a world-class career by competing in longer races that required more endurance but less speed. Prizefighter Sam Longford knew well the sports lore lesson that "the legs go first." In 1929, almost at age 50 and partly blind, he compensated for poor eyes and wobbly legs in the simplest way: "Both my eyes were bad then but I could see a bit. So when I got in there, this fella started swingin' that left hand and I blocked it and he swung again and I blocked it. An' then I knocked him out" (Frayne, 1990, p. 241). In contrast to Ali, who lowered his aspirations when fighting Spinks, Longford compensated for his deficiencies by full-blooded attack.

Doing Something Else

The final form of compensation is to do something else. Commonwealth Games and Pan-Am gold medalist Debbie Brill reacted to Canada's boycott of the 1980 Moscow Olympics in a novel way. She interrupted her career by getting pregnant, later to resume high jumping successfully. However, Brill was unable to overcome the effects of a long-term knee injury with training and therapy. She finally retired from sport just before the 1988 Seoul Olympics.

The "something else" that attracts many older athletes is management or the sports media. Lennie Wilkens was an outstanding basketball player who became an outstanding coach. Franz Beckenbaur was captain of the West

German soccer team when it won the World Cup in 1974; he later managed the national team that won the same trophy in 1990. Baseballer Tony Kebuk, who played shortstop and outfielder for the New York Yankees in six World Series, became a broadcaster with the Toronto Blue Jays until 1990.

SPORT AS SOCIETAL COMPENSATION

Games and sport are pastimes. Veteran sportswriter Trent Frayne (1990) described *sport* as "children's games that seem to enchant millions of grown-ups" (p. 10)). However, sport has broader functions than simply to provide fun. Some philosophers advocated sport to promote positive social change. Others foresaw a potential for anarchy. Irrespective of what these thinkers opined, history records a vigorous evolution in sport's participation, organization, and support over the past two centuries. We apply compensation theory to this evolution at three levels: society as a whole, the athletes, and the fans.

Sport as a Mechanism of Societal Compensation

Philosophers Rousseau and Jahn considered sport a form of training to close the gap between existing and desired traits of national character. Patriotism and militarism were traits that the major nations valued highly around the beginning of the 19th century. Rousseau's (1773) *Considerations on the Government of Poland* reflected on sport as a way to impart patriotic values (cited in McIntosh, 1963, pp. 53–56). He saw a mismatch between the patriotism demanded by society and the product of ongoing education. He thought public sport would promote in children the values of discipline, equality, and fraternity.

Jahn expressed similar views on the social value of sport. He wrote of the German Way of Life in 1810, shortly after Germany's disasters in the Napoleonic Wars (McIntosh, 1963). Jahn advocated sport as an effortful form of training to build military readiness, and hence to restore preeminence to the German people.

Not all philosophers were optimistic that sport could compensate for deficiencies in national character. By the end of the 19th century, the Anglophile Baron de Courbertin, who founded the modern Olympic movement, remained an optimist. Veblen (1899/1953), another writer of that era, was not. More recently, Nobel prize winner Konrad Lorenz (1966) offered an optimistic, but different, philosophy.

Lorenz thought of sport as a means to remedy the mismatch between the demands of the populace for peaceful coexistence and the national (and natural) aggressive traits in humankind. Sport, he wrote, "educates man to a conscious and responsible control of his own fighting behavior" (p. 242). The social demands of Lorenz's era are less to promote militarism than to channel aggression into nondestructive forms, with the alternatives being violence and war. Whereas Rousseau and Jahn considered sport a form of training for war, Lorenz advocated its potential to substitute for war.

Landmarks in the Modern History of Sport

The history of modern sport provides measures of support for all of the preceding philosophers. Although some sport clubs boast of origins in the 18th century (e.g., the Jockey Club—1750, the Royal and Ancient Golf Club—1754, and the Marylebone Cricket Club—1788), participation then was mainly by the aristocracy. Modern sport really began in the early 19th-century public schools of Britain. At first the school authorities tried to suppress sport because of the lawlessness associated with the traditional pastimes of hunting and shooting. The students compensated by more formally organizing the individual and team sports allowed them, consistent with Lorenz's ideas on sport as nondestructive aggression. An evolving educational ethic of that era—self-government by praeposters (i.e., senior pupils, or prefects, to whom authority for aspects of governance was assigned)—became nowhere as well developed as in games. Headmasters at most schools became subsequent converts to the ideals they saw practiced, with the church and business authorities joining them during the latter 19th century. A model of the "muscular Christian" found favor among the clergy, which encouraged sporting pastimes among parishioners. McIntosh (1963) wrote that between 20%–25% of soccer and cricket clubs formed in one city by 1880 had a primary affiliation with a religious body. Alongside the increase in sport participation was an increase in the number of spectators. In 1863, the Football Association (FA) was founded as the governing body for soccer. The first FA Cup Final in 1872 drew 2,000 spectators; in 1901, the attendance was nearly 111,000.

If Rousseau and Jahn anticipated the main reasons for the evolution of sport in the 19th century (i.e., training in patriotism and militarism), Lorenz more accurately described developments in the 20th century: Sport compensates not for too little militarism, but for too much. The late 19th century saw the formation of national sports associations in Europe and North America. Because the Baron de Courbertin upheld the 19th-century ideal that sport breeds character, he wanted to make sport international. However, the International Olympic Committee he founded in 1894 succeeded in making the playing field a substitute battleground for competing nations. Sport became a matter of national prestige, with the aim being to win most medals, rather than just to compete. States and corporations came to invest considerable sums towards such ends, with athleticism becoming more a vocation than a pastime. Lorenz may have been right that sport in this century evolved to compensate for frustrated militarism in an era of disintegrating empires. However, whether this compensation was effective is open to question.

Compensation by Athletes

Athletes in this century came to compensate for the increasing demands placed on their expertise with greater effort and sophistication in training. Bannister's (1955) training schedule in preparation to break the 4-minute mile seems less effortful than that of present-day runners who aspire only to minor competition. It was Bannister's arch rival, Australia's John Landry, who trained with an intensity resembling that of today.

Not all athletes compete fairly. Veblen (1953) foresaw problems arising from cunning and chicanery. He thought that these traits, not the virtues anticipated by Rousseau and de Courbertin, result from competition in sport. Cheating is an unfair way to compensate if the demands on performance exceed accessible skill. In the last century, corruption contributed to the decline of sports such as prize fighting and pedestrianism (i.e., the antecedent to modern race walking). The present century is not immune. A notorious example is the disqualification of Canada's Ben Johnson for steroid use following his first-place finish over 100 meters in the 1988 Seoul Olympics. Another example is the ban subsequently imposed on 1993 European soccer champion Olympic Marseilles following allegations of bribery.

Sports Supporters

Baden-Powell, who founded scouting, anticipated problems among spectators. Early this century, he likened soccer fans to the nation of wasters who hastened the downfall of the Roman Empire. American literary editor Bill Burford joined England's soccer thugs for several seasons during the 1980s. The values he encountered were xenophobic, racist, and militaristic. Burford (1992) recounted befriending a lad from the town of Grimsby (whom he simply calls Grimsby) at an England versus Holland game played at Dusseldorf in 1988. We reproduce what Burford wrote only because it captures so vividly the base values of which Veblen and Baden-Powell forewarned:

> Grimsby believed that he needed to prove his cultural superiority to every foreigner he met; I had forgotten just how violent the violent nationalism of the English football supporter could be, and being in Germany made him vigorously nationalistic. The viciousness of the Germans, the spinelessness of the Dutch, the bulldog bravery of the English: these were the tenets of a fundamental belief, and Grimsby would be an unhappy man if he couldn't go into a battle of some kind to illustrate that they were more—that they were in fact incontestable verities of national character. (Burford, 1992, pp. 230–231)

Grimsby and his ilk are among small minorities of sport fans. Are they, as Goodhart and Chataway (1968) suggested, compensating for a meaningless life by living vicariously through sporting idols? This suggestion seems too simplistic. Their xenophobia portrays a truer interpretation. The group allegiance gives them identity, and their thuggery confers status within the delinquent subculture to which they belong. According to Burford's (1992) book, soccer thuggery is not simply a response to frustration (e.g., the riots by the ice hockey fans of the Montreal Canadians in 1955, and the Vancouver Canucks in 1993), but instead, it exemplifies compensation for low success within the wider culture.

COMPENSATION AND MOTIVATION

Butt (1987) provided a general model of motivation for participation in sport. In this model, the motives derive from two main sources. The first is biological, in which energy finds its outlet in psychological motives of aggression, neurotic conflict, and competence striving. Whichever motive predominates in an athlete is a probable influence on the kinds of compensation made. The second source includes reinforcements contingent on participation. Athletes obtain reinforcement by extrinsic reward (e.g., attention, money, status) and intrinsic reward (e.g., self-esteem). A mismatch between expected and obtained rewards becomes a likely prompt of compensatory behavior.

Aggression as a Motive

Displays of aggression are common in sport. Tennis star John McEnroe's recurrent on-court tantrums are notorious. Swimmer Victor Davis made world headlines at the 1982 Commonwealth Games by angrily kicking away a chair before a primly seated Queen Elizabeth. Indiana University basketball coach Bobby Knight was also captured on video throwing chairs across the court. A British newspaper published a now-famous photo of soccer player Vinnie Jones clasping the genitals of opposing player Paul Gasgoine. Their faces graphically (and not surprisingly) contrast anger with agony. Reigning Olympic and world champion sprinter Linford Christie drew ire from his colleague Derek Redmond: "Linford is the most balanced athlete in Britain: he has a chip on each shoulder" (*Weekly Telegraph*, 1992, p. 52).

Some depictions of professional team sports convey truths with a spice of humor. Rugby may be a game for hooligans played by gentlemen, but soccer is a game for gentlemen played by hooligans. A Melbourne coach described Australian football as a game for men played by beasts. Connie Smythe, who was a dynast of the Toronto Maple Leafs ice hockey organization, uttered a classic line: "If you can't beat 'em outside in the alley, you won't beat 'em inside on the ice" (cited in Frayne, 1990). A comedy troupe, the Royal Canadian Air Farce, cited the main difference between ice hockey and soccer to be whether the fighters are the players or the fans.

Aggression in sport has tactical and strategic aims in the service of winning the game. However, the severe penalties imposed for violence in sports like soccer make it imperative for aggressive players to compensate for their inclinations. Argentinean star Diego Maradona provides a good example. He disgraced himself in the 1982 World Cup by reacting petulantly to fouls. In 1986, he compensated by substituting acting for aggression. Slow-motion video showed him acting out the effects of fouls even when the opposing players were innocent of any misdemeanor. He frequently fooled the match officials, winning for his side many undeserved free kicks, but contributing greatly to their World Cup victory.

Other compensatory styles include inhibiting aggression and expressing it in ways barely, but just, tolerated by the officials. Twice Wimbledon champion Althea Gibson of America described her early career inclination to jump the net and hit an opponent during moments of frustration (Gibson, 1958). Part of her socialization in tennis was to channel her anger into skill. Sweeney Schriner, who played ice hockey with the Toronto franchise, took liberties with rules of fair play: "You had to know how to use your elbows in the corners. But not the sticks. You'd hear the referees say, 'If you use that stick, you're gone.' So ... you'd bring up the elbows" (Frayne, 1990, p. 189).

Aggressive motives may find different levels of expression within an athletic career. As a young player, soccer sweeper Kenny Burns was often in trouble for violence during games. At his peak in the late 1970s, when he helped Nottingham Forest win the European Cup twice, he tackled opposing players fiercely, but without resorting to violence. Long after he retired from professional sport, his violence resurfaced in recreational soccer. In the 1990s, the Nottingham *Football Post* several times mentioned misconduct by Burns, resulting in his dismissal or suspension from games. An athlete who controls aggression at the stage of peak performance may again resort to violence when the performances wane. Other data that we analyzed show this trend within professional ice hockey careers (see Fig. 14.1).

We obtained the data summarized in Fig. 14.1 from the career records of 15 National (Ice) Hockey League (NHL) players. These players are a random selection of registrants with the NHL for 1993–1994 who played continuously with an NHL club from 1980–1981 to 1992–1993 (National Hockey League, 1993). The smoothed curves give the mean trends for: (a) penalties in minutes (PIM) per game, (b) total points (composed of assists and goals) per game, and (c) the number of games played over possible games within a regular season. Figure 14.1 shows the typical ∩-shaped curve for performance, and a late career decline in the number of games played. The curve for penalty minutes per game is sinusoidal, with a decline followed by an increase, followed by subsequent decline.

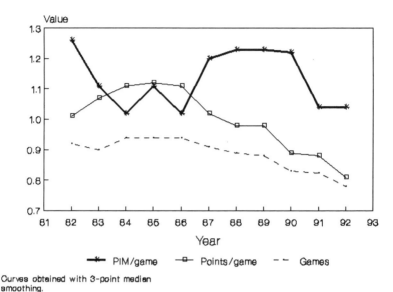

FIG. 14.1. Longitudinal trends for penalties in minutes (PIM) per game, points per game, and games per season (as a proportion of total games) by ice hockey players from 1980–1981 to 1992–1993.

It is instructive to examine the trends for penalties and points from a compensation perspective. An increase in penalty minutes coincides with the beginning of the scoring decline (i.e., both changes occur around 1987). Does the increase in penalties suggest a frustrative reaction to declining performance? Alternatively, are the athletes actively compensating for lower scoring by substituting aggressive play? Evidence supporting the latter includes a significantly positive relationship between penalties and points per game, with age controlled (i.e., accounting for 58% of the variance). Moreover, most correlations between penalty time and points per game were positive when computed with single case data—being statistically significant for 3 of the 15 athletes (i.e., with age controlled). If penalty time mainly indexes aggressive play, these findings suggest overt aggression to accompany higher scoring, with the aggression used to compensate for declines in scoring rates.

Competence Striving

Aggression does not fuel all athletes. Butt (1987) wrote that some strive for competence, but others are merely neurotic. Roger Bannister, the first runner to break the 4-minute mile, was of the former. His autobiography tells of an intrinsic satisfaction in achievement before, during, and after his athletic career. American race walker Ron Laird (1972) illustrated beautifully the theme of competence striving: "For years I had a morbid fear of training. Because of this I could not quit although I promised myself often that I would. I simply could not have gone through life then wondering what I might have accomplished and making up excuses to myself for why I gave it up. Today, many years later, I remain motivated by the same principles" (p. 9).

Butt (1987) predicted that athletes who strongly need to achieve may retain an involvement with sport. This is true of Laird, who won more championships than any other race walker in history (65 U.S. titles from 1958 to 1976, and four Canadian championships). He became an American coach and remains an occasional competitor, recently finishing second in a 15-km event at Grand Island near New York. One of us (MJS) interviewed him at the 1981 World Cup in Valencia, Spain. He said the biggest problem for dedicated amateurs is "what to do when they retire." The hockey star, Gordie Howe, expressed similar sentiments. "I'm going to stick with hockey since I can. It's the only business I know. It's my life. I'd be lost in anything else" (Vipond, 1971, p. 17).

The compensatory mechanisms that allow veteran athletes to remain within sport include a lowering of expectations. Some continue to compete in the minor leagues or in age-class events. American Larry Young, a bronze medalist in the 1968 Mexico City Olympics, provides an example. He began competing in age-class race walking when in his 40s, setting new American records. Other athletes stage comebacks even at advanced ages. Don Thompson, affectionately called the "mighty mouse," won the 50-km walking race in the 1960 Rome Olympics. He gained accolades in 1991 by becoming the oldest full U.K. international, competing over 200 km at Bazencourt, France, at age 58 years.

A few athletes attempt comebacks without lowering their expectations. Skaters Jayne Torville and Christopher Dean set the highest tally of maximum marks to win the World Ice Dance Championships at Ottawa in 1984. They won at the Winter Olympics in Sarajevo the same year. Subsequently, they retired from competition to become entertainers on the professional ice skating circuit. Their comeback began in January 1994. With victories already obtained in the British and European Championships, they hoped to win again at the Winter Olympics 2 months later. However, despite being lauded as best competitors by their fans and media, the judges awarded them the bronze medal, penalizing them over a technical infringement they subsequently disputed. Despite this disappointment, their expectations clearly matched a level of skill they still possessed.

Other retired athletes compensate by using their abilities to benefit others. Many become coaches, managers, or sport administrators. Baseballer Roy Campanella exemplifies this pattern. Following three Most Valuable Player awards in a decade, he suffered paralysis from the chest down after a motor accident in 1958. He was 36 years old at the time. Refusing to relinquish the game he loved, he became a coach and inspiration to subsequent generations of young ball players.

Despite Butt's (1987) predictions, not all competence-driven athletes choose to remain within sport. David Gower made his debut in first-class cricket in 1975, at age 18 years. Upon retiring in 1993, he was ranked sixth in the world for runs ever scored in major international games. His reasons for retiring were as follows: "The key is that I didn't want to carry on playing just for the sake of it. I've enjoyed playing it well and that's the way it had to finish" (*Weekly Telegraph*, 1993, p. 51). Basketball star Michael Jordan, who also retired at the peak of his success, gave similar reasons: "I have nothing more to prove. I have no more challenges that I felt I could get motivated for" (*Life*, 1994, p. 52). Like former England cricket captain Bob Willis, who retired in 1984, competence-driven athletes may choose to try for success in endeavors other than sport.

Neurosis

Neurotic athletes are not hard to find, if *neurosis* is understood by its colloquial use rather than psychiatric nomenclature. Butt (1987) cited many examples of selfish and egocentric behavior styles, with motivations fueled by conflict. Neurosis has relevance to compensation in two respects.

First, such athletes are predicted to compensate by opting out rather than by using mechanisms that allow them to improve or maintain skills. Selye (1981) added that such careers may be foreshortened because of frustrations that physically and mentally wear out the athletes. A prime example is George Best, judged to be the best European soccer player of his era. Best fell prey to fame and predilections for alcohol, partying, and womanizing, and then abruptly and petulantly quit the game when at his peak. It took him years to sort out his life. Commenting on a suggestion that the now portly Best manage his native Northern Ireland squad, former goalkeeper Pat Jennings commented: "George would be a good manager, if only he'd turn up for games" (*Weekly Telegram*, 1993, p. 55).

Second, sports psychology provides examples of how troubled athletes can be helped to compensate in ways other than opting out. Its armory now contains tools to help athletes cope with stress or compensate for excessive demands on ego strength (Meichenbaum, 1977; Nideffer & Sharpe, 1978; Suin, 1980). Had sport psychologists been as readily available three decades earlier, George Best's career might have flourished longer.

COMPENSATION AND EXPERTISE

Different sports require different kinds and combinations of skill. We can distinguish between motor ability and cognitive expertise. The basic motor abilities include speed, endurance, strength, and agility. *Agility* means quickness and deftness in part systems of the body (e.g., the hands or feet), as opposed to *speed*, which means quickness in moving the body as a whole. Games of strategy require the cognitive skills of anticipation and knowledge, both of which develop with experience.

There are differences within and between sports in the demands placed on motor and cognitive skills. Low-strategy sports demanding maximum physical effort include athletics (i.e., track-and-field), swimming, and weight lifting. Other low-strategy sports involve what Poulton (1957) termed *closed motor skills.* In sports like gymnastics, diving, skating, and synchronized swimming, adjudication is of the motor pattern itself, rather than the outcome of the movement sequence (Starkes, 1993). Such sports mainly (although not exclusively) combine agility with speed. High-strategy sports that also require agility and mainly continuous effort include basketball, boxing, football, hockey, judo, racquet sports, rugby, soccer, and wrestling. Other high-strategy sports involve agility and occasional effort. These sports include baseball and cricket. Frayne (1990) wrote of baseball: "Except for the pitcher and catcher, nobody does much of anything for long periods except stand around and wait" (p. 307). Finally, sports like autoracing, billiards, darts, and pool involve high strategy and agility, but require low physical power.

The Ages of Competitors in Different Sports

We anticipate compensatory behavior to vary with the mix of skills required in a sport. Experimental studies show dexterity- and knowledge-based skills to change little with aging per se, but to show retention with continued practice and experience (Leas & Chi, 1993; Spirduso, 1980; Stones & Kozma, 1988). Consequently, careers in sports mainly emphasizing dexterity or strategy, but not excessive physical effort, have the potential to be lengthy. Abernethy, Thomas, and Thomas (1993) proposed similar ideas, in which knowledge and experience both compensate for age changes in motor skill. In contrast, age changes in the underlying physiology cause eventual decline in the effortful skills of speed, strength, and endurance. Stones and Kozma (1986) showed such trends in the performances by older athletes and swimmers. Aging athletes who continue to compete in effortful sports must eventually expect to lower their aspirations.

Figure 14.2 provides illustrative data comparing the ages of the oldest and youngest world-record holders or world champions in selected sports and chess (Matthews, 1993). Chess involves purely cognitive expertise, with the age of the oldest champion (Wilhelm Steinitz) exceeding that in any sport by over 10 years. The sports of boxing, autoracing, and tennis combine strategy and motor expertise. The ages of the oldest champions (i.e., Archie Moore, Juan-Miguel Fangio, and Norman Brookes, respectively) exceed those in the low-strategy, but effortful sports of athletics (Gerhard Weidner) and weight lifting (Norbert Schemansky).

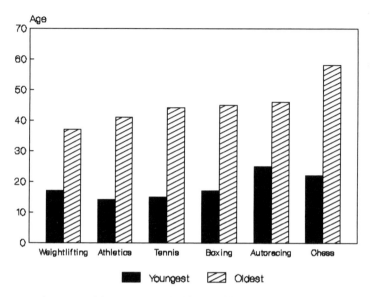

FIG. 14.2. Ages of the youngest and oldest world champions or world-record breakers in selected games and sport (as of 1993).

Figure 14.3 shows how long careers can last in sports that emphasize strategy (Matthews, 1993). For this purpose, the *length of career* was defined from the first to last (or most recent) appearance in international or major domestic competition. Lester Piggott (jockey), Gordie Howe (an ice hockey player), and Wilfred Rhodes and Frank Woolley (cricketers) all had careers exceeding 30 years. Soccer player Peter Shilton's continuing career exceeds 25 years. Kareem Abdul-Jabbar (basketball), Pete Rose (baseball), and Alain Prost (autoracing) all competed at the top level for over 20 years. Other examples include the Hungarian fencer Alardar Gerevich, who won Olympic medals and world championships over a record 28-year span. All these athletes managed to compensate for declining effortful skill through knowledge and experience. We also find evidence within a sport that cognitive skills can compensate for declines in effortful skill. The 10 oldest professional soccer players in the top 6 European nations for 1993 included 6 goalkeepers, 1 defender, and 3 midfielders, but no strikers. Goalkeeping and the midfield positions are those in which anticipation and an ability to "read the game" are more important than speed and strength.

Age and Compensation in Effortful Sport

For sports emphasizing effort rather than strategy, Stones and Kozma's (1986) POrPA model (i.e., Power Output over Power Available) anticipates age trends among veteran athletes. The model posits greater aging effects where

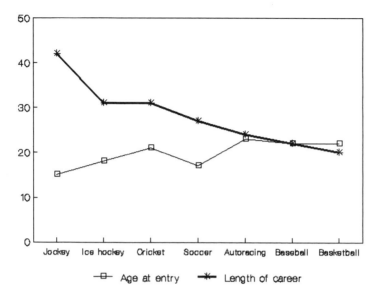

FIG. 14.3. Lengths of career and ages at entry into major competition for selected sports.

the discrete units of movement use more of the available power. Movements that tap more power usually involve larger displacements of the body. Examples include larger displacements in (a) jumping and hurdling than running, (b) running than race walking, and (c) the butterfly than other strokes in swimming. However, the available power is not a constant commodity, but diminishes with the duration of effortful performance. The fuel for brief strenuous effort is not aerobic; however, aerobic sources supply most of the power in prolonged effort. Consequently, the lower displacements per stride or stroke in running or swimming races of beyond sprint distance are more than offset by the reduction in available power. The model finds support from following trends among veteran record holders (see Stones & Kozma, 1986). In swimming, veterans' performance declines most with age in the butterfly events and over the longer distances. In athletics, veteran jumpers, hurdlers, and distance runners have steeper declines than sprinters and race walkers.

We have not previously applied the model to the ages of record holders in open-class competition. What it predicts are younger ages for record holders in events placing higher demands on power (e.g., jumps, throws, and hurdles vs. running events, vs. race walks) and those of longer duration (i.e., events significantly fueled by aerobic metabolism).

Open-class swimmers and track-and-field athletes differ from their veteran counterparts in that the world's best competitors specialize within a narrower spectrum of events and train on a full-time basis. Despite such differences, the ages of the 1993 world-record holders are consistent with the model. Freestyle swimming is the only stroke for which world records are available over distances from 50 to 1,500 m. The ages for each gender decline linearly with event distance (Matthews, 1993). American Tom Jager was 25 years old when he claimed the 50-m record, compared with the 18-year-old Australian John Kieren who holds records at 800 m and beyond. China's Wenyi Yang broke the female 50-m record at age 20 years, compared with America's Janet Evans, who was age 16 or 17 years when she claimed all the records from 400 m upward.

The model also anticipates the records in track-and-field and race walking. As previously stated, the trend among veteran athletes is for lower age differences in the sprints and race walks than for performance in the power events and longer runs. By extrapolation, the ages of the open-class record holders should be older for the sprints and race walks than for the jumps, throws, hurdles, and longer runs, if aging least affects the former categories. Figure 14.4 provides confirmatory evidence. It summarizes the mean ages (when the records were broken) of the 1993 male and female world-record holders for all track-and-field and road-walk events in which both gender compete (Matthews, 1993). Although gender had no significant effect, the ages for the sprints and walks are significantly older than for the other events, with this difference accounting for a quarter of the variance.

Race walking may seem an unlikely complement to sprinting. However, the findings on age trend pair them against other events. The rationale

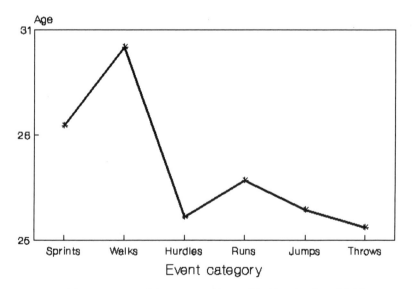

FIG. 14.4. Mean ages of the 1993 world-record holders (track-and-field) or fastest performers (road walks) in five categories of athletic event.

provided by the POrPA model is that, despite the obvious differences in form and function, there are similarities in the underlying energetics. Sprinters use less power than competitors in other short-duration events, but the available power is greater than in the longer runs. Race walkers use short strides to comply with the rules, with lower power expended per stride than by sprinters and runners. We next examine the kinds of compensation used by race walkers.

Race walking is not primarily an endurance activity to its exponents, but rather "a technique event that happens to go on for a long time" (Burrows, 1992, p. 12). The training includes an apprenticeship in technique to ensure legality and promote speed, and endurance workouts to sustain that technique over long periods. There are two main compensatory mechanisms available to a walker whose performance falls below expectations: to work on technique to improve speed, or to work on endurance to sustain a given speed for longer. An analysis of data from the 1993 World Championships, held in Stuttgart, suggest that older walkers may adopt the latter.

The finishers were 46 women in the 10-km event, 33 men in the 20-km race, and 35 men in the 50-km race. Figure 14.5 shows a significant effect of age on

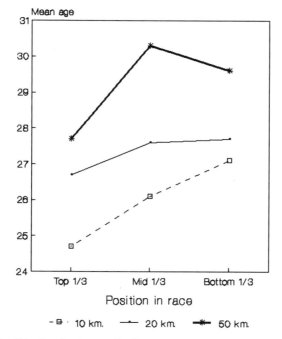

The 10 km. is a female event. The 20 km. and 50 km. are both male events.

FIG. 14.5. Mean ages of competitors finishing in the top, middle, and bottom third positions in the 1993 world race walking championships.

performance in the women's event, with the younger walkers more frequently finishing in the top third and the more older walkers finishing in the bottom third positions. In the men's competition, the ages are significantly older in the longer event (50 km) than the shorter race (20 km), irrespective of where in the pack the walker finished. This finding is consistent with a hypothesis that race walkers compensate for insufficient or declining speed by upping their racing distance, with contingent changes in training to emphasize sustained technique rather than improved technique.

We commented previously on this form of compensation, using as examples Marcel Jobin and Don Thompson, both of whom raised their event distances late in their careers. Another example is the Italian Maurizo Damilano, who won the gold medal over 20 km in the 1980 Moscow Olympics. At age 35 years in 1992, he raised his distance to the less frequently contested 30 km, setting a new world record. The will to win or to set new records is a potent motivator, and athletes compensate by modifying their choice of competition to accord with a higher probability of success.

CONCLUSIONS

To conclude this chapter, we highlight some general issues that emerged. In sequence, these concern: (a) origins of compensation at different levels of analysis, (b) diversity in demands, and (c) designs to study compensation in aging athletes.

We applied the principles of Bäckman and Dixon's (1992) compensation theory at several levels. At an ideational level, philosophers believed sport to provide training (e.g., Rousseau, Jahn) or a compensatory alternative (e.g., Lorenz) for militaristic traits. The origins of such advocations were discrepancies between the existing and demanded attributes of nationalism in the respective eras. Sociohistorically, athleticism was a pastime that became a vocation. The Industrial Revolution of the last century led to a concentration of workers in cities, many of whom came to adopt sports spectatorship as a leisure activity. A result was a demand for greater proficiency in performance among athletes, with the latter emerging as a distinct vocational group. Professionalism allowed athletes to use the compensatory mechanism of greater practice to meet the demand for higher skill, although some also resorted to breaking or bending the rules. Compensation principles also apply to athletes at critical stages in their careers. A critical stage may have origins in advances in technique or tactics within a sport, or in the effects of aging on the capacity to function at the highest level. Age effects tend to be high in sports demanding considerable expenditure of physical power, but with relatively prolonged careers in activities involving higher strategy.

An issue in compensation theory concerns the diversity in demand, and the development of empirical methods to differentiate between demands and expectations. Objective demands coexist on a multiplicity of levels. Sport fans believe they know more than coaches, who believe they know more than the athletes, who also react to demands from their peers. These demands are frequently in conflict. Because Bäckman and Dixon specified that compensation must originate from a demand-skill discrepancy, it becomes critical to identify the relative salience of different demands. This issue became apparent in our discussion of the soccer thugs. Their behavior is more influenced by the demands of a delinquent subculture than by those of lawful society. A form of resolution lies in self-report instrumentation, in which the measures include the range and importance given to nominal demands and the appraisal of personal performance expectations.

Finally, we refer to the material used to study compensation. We used secondary analysis of existing data. We inferred compensation in the ice hockey statistics using longitudinal changes in penalty minutes and points scoring. Data on the ages of world-record holders and the length of athletic careers clarified the compensatory value of cognitive skill. Data on the age differences of race walkers competing in shorter or longer events provided evidence on compensatory goal selection. A subsequent level of research may be experimental. For example, a molar equivalence-molecular decompensation strategy could be applied to runners. The POrPA model suggests that older runners become slower because of declining power, which should result in a shorter stride. Can they compensate by increasing their frequency of strides? An analysis of stride length by frequency in younger and older runners, either matched for speed or with speed used as a covariate, should answer this question.

The preceding illustrate the flexibility of compensation theory to generate inferences with different designs and dependent variables. Applications to expert performance, of which athletic sport is a prime example, should also be mindful of the uses of self-reported and anecdotal evidence. Although nomothetic research provides safeguards against error when testing general laws, evidence from case studies frequently illuminates those laws worth testing.

REFERENCES

Abernethy, B., Thomas, K. T., & Thomas, J. T. (1993). Strategies for improving understanding of motor expertise [or mistakes we have made and things we have learned!!]. In J. L. Starkes & F. Allard (Eds.), *Cognitive issues in motor expertise* (pp. 317–358). Amsterdam: Elsevier Science.

Bäckman, L., & Dixon, R. A. (1992). Psychological compensation: A theoretical framework. *Psychological Bulletin, 112,* 259–283.

Bannister, R. (1955). *First four minutes.* London: Putnam.

Burrows, R. (1992). *Race walking: An overview for athletics coaches.* Ottawa: Athletics Canada.

Butt, D. S. (1987). *Psychology of sport: The behavior, motivation, personality, and performance of athletes.* New York: Van Nostrand Reinhold.

French, K. E., & Nevett, M. E. (1993). The development of expertise in youth sport. In J. L. Starkes & F. Allard (Eds.), *Cognitive issues in motor expertise* (pp. 255–272). Amsterdam: Elsevier Science.

Frayne, T. (1990). *The tales of an athletic supporter.* Toronto: McClelland & Stewart.

Gibson, A. (1958). *I always wanted to be a somebody.* New York: Perennial.

Goodhart, P., & Chataway, C. (1968). *War without weapons.* London: W. H. Allen.

Laird, R. (1972). *Competitive race walking.* Los Altos, CA: Tafnews.

Leas, R. R., & Chi, M. T. H. (1993). Analyzing diagnostic expertise of competitive swimming coaches. In J. L. Starkes & F. Allard (Eds.), *Cognitive issues in motor expertise* (pp. 75–94). Amsterdam: Elsevier Science.

Lewis, T. (1993). Rugby is suffocating in a straightjacket of method. *Weekly Telegraph, 128*, 14.

Life (1994). January.

Lorenz, K. (1966). *On aggression.* London: Methuen.

Matthews, P. (1993). *The Guinness book of records 1994.* London: Guinness.

McIntosh, P. C. (1963). *Sport in society.* London: C. A. Watts.

Meichenbaum, D. (1977). *Cognitive behavior modification.* New York: Plenum.

National Hockey League. (1993). *Official guide and record book: 1993–94.* Toronto: NHL Publishing.

Nideffer, R. M., & Sharpe, R. (1978). *ATC: Attentional control training.* New York: Wyder.

Poulton, E. C. (1957). On prediction in skilled movements. *Psychological Bulletin, 54*, 467–478.

Selye, H. (1981). Dealing with stress in a depressed economy. *Spectrum, 2*(2), 1–11.

Spirduso, W. W. (1980). Physical fitness, aging, and psychomotor speed. *Journal of Gerontology, 35*, 850–865.

Starkes, J. L. Motor experts: Opening thoughts. In J. L. Starkes & F. Allard (Eds.), *Cognitive issues in motor expertise* (pp. 317–358). Amsterdam: Elsevier Science.

Stones, M. J., & Kozma, A. (1984). Longitudinal trends in track and field performances. *Experimental Aging Research, 10*, 107–110.

Stones, M. J., & Kozma, A. (1986). Age trends in maximal physical performance: Comparison and evaluation of models. *Experimental Aging Research, 12*, 207–215.

Stones, M. J., & Kozma, A. (1988). Physical activity, age and cognitive/motor performance. In M. L. Howe, & C. J. Brainerd (Eds.), *Cognitive development in adulthood: Progress in cognitive development research* (pp. 273–312). New York: Springer-Verlag.

Suin, R. M. (1980). Body thinking: Psychology for Olympic champs. In R. M. Suin (Ed.), *Psychology in sports: Methods and applications* (pp. 306–315). Minneapolis: Burgess.

Veblen, T. (1953). *The theory of the leisure class.* New York: Mentor (original work published 1899).

Vipond, J. (1971). *Gordie Howe Number 9.* Toronto: McGraw-Hill.

Weekly Telegraph (1993). November 24–30.

Weekly Telegraph (1993). December 22–28.

Author Index

Staudinger, U. M., 36, 44, 47, 55,
60, 67, 71, 78, 79
Stavraky, G. W., 223, 224, 230
Steele-Rosomoff, R., 162, 167
Stein, D. G., 221, 222, 223, 224,
225, 226, 229
Stenevi, U., 222, 229
Sternberg, R. J., 54, 58, 60, 71, 79,
85, 105, 275, 284, 295
Sterns, H. L., 162, 168
Stevens, A. B., 61, 72
Steward, O., 223, 230
Stewart, K. J., 118, 123
Stine, E. A. L., 209, 217
Stine, E. L., 155, 168
Stock, B., 284, 295
Stock, W. A., 84, 105
Stoessl, A. J., 235, 246
Stone, G. O., 281, 295
Stone, R., 133, 144
Stones, M. J., 298, 309, 310, 311,
316
Stoudt, H. W., 152, 168
Strange, M., 279, 289, 295
Strater, L., 209, 212
Streib, G. F., 114, 125, 133, 144
Streiner, D. L., 140, 143
Stroebe, M. S., 113, 115, 119, 125
Stroebe, W., 113, 115, 119, 125
Strouse, T. B., 114, 123
Struyk, R., 154, 167
Studdert-Kennedy, M., 258, 259,
273
Suchman, E. A., 134, 144
Summerfield, Q., 258, 259, 263,
273
Sundaram, M., 235, 244
Sunderland, T., 197, 216, 234, 244
Suomi, S. J., 195, 215
Supa, M., 262, 273
Sutherland, R. J., 207, 216
Svagelski, J., 83, 105

Swan, G. E., 114, 115, 125
Swann, W. B., 95, 106
Sweet, M., 154, 166
Swenson, M. R., 233, 243
Syme, S. L., 111, 122

T

Tanenhaus, M. K., 283, 294
Tanke, E., 157, 158, 168
Targ, D. B., 140, 144
Tariot, P. N., 197, 216
Tarsey, D., 224, 230
Taylor, J. O., 231, 244
Taylor, R. J., 135, 140, 142, 144
Taylor, S. E., 94, 95, 106, 113, 118,
120, 125
Teasdale, J. D., 91, 106
Tenaglia, A., 114, 123
Tennen, H., 118, 121
Teri, L., 66, 79
Terry, R. D., 238, 246
Tesch-Römer, C., 49, 52, 58 , 68,
79, 109, 125
Teuber, H. -L., 202, 215
Thatcher, R. W., 254, 274
Thoits, P. A., 131, 144
Thomas, J. T., 309, 315
Thomas, K. T., 309, 315
Thomas, L., 235, 244
Thompson, L. W., 113, 123, 125,
157, 168
Thompson, M. A., 58, 73
Thompson, R. F., 193, 198, 202,
212, 216, 217
Thompson, W. E., 46, 54, 77, 114,
125
Thomson, R., 130, 143
Tomsak, R. L., 235, 246
Tooby, J., 53, 71
Toukko, H., 235, 246
Toulmin, S., 7, 19

Subject Index

A

Accommodation, 13-16, 22, 25, 26,
31, 33, 87-89, 92
  compensation and, 148-151
  flexibility, 94, 99, 100
  goals, 87, 92
  moderating conditions of, 91, 97-
100
  processes, 97
  shifts in, 88, 91, 100, 101
Activity theory, 129
Adaptive process, as proactive/
reactive, 36, 37
Adulthood, adaptation to, 108
  as process of differentiation, 107
Age-control relationship, 97, 98
Age-related changes, adjusting to,
85-87
Age stratification theory, 130
Aging, 148, 192, 193, 204, 208,
209
  accommodive/assimilative
modes, 87-89
  achieving congruence, 87
  adaptation, 84-88
  attention and, 158
  behavior modification, 151
  being old, 100, 101
  cognitive accuracy/speed and,
60
  compensation and, 50

control and, 97, 98, 101, 102
  decremental model, 128, 131
  depression and, 84
  developmental decline, 120
  emotional regulation, 57
  environmental demands and,
148-156, 164
  environmental modification, 153
  gains and losses, 84, 85, 88, 150
  goal flexibility, 87-89, 98, 99
  housing and, 139
  intelligence and, 58, 287
  long-term care, 56
  loss of plasticity, 35, 36, 38
  losses in, 127-136
  memory for context, 208-210
  memory repair and, 196-200
  mobility and, 154
  neuron loss, 192
  performance rate and, 32, 33
  print exposure and, 287
  protective biases in, 95, 96
  religion and, 134
  resilience and, 101, 102
  social compensation in, 136-141
  sociological theories of, 128, 129
  speeded tasks and, 30-33
  see also, Compensation, Environmental modification devices
Alcoholism, 113
Alzheimer's disease, 5, 61, 174,
192, 194, 197-200, 235